AF478431

Atlantic Studies on Society in Change
No. 42

Editor-in-Chief Béla K. Király

War and Society in East Central Europe
Vol. XXIII

INSTITUTE FOR BALKAN STUDIES
THESSALONIKI, GREECE

co-publisher

War and Society in East Central Europe
Vol. XXIII

Southeast European Maritime Commerce and Naval Policies
from the Mid-Eighteenth Century to 1914

Apostolos E. Vacalopoulos
Constantinos D. Svolopoulos
Béla K. Király
Editors

SOCIAL SCIENCES MONOGRAPHS, BOULDER, COLORADO
ATLANTIC RESEARCH AND PUBLICATIONS,
HIGHLAND LAKES, NEW JERSEY
DISTRIBUTED BY COLUMBIA UNIVERSITY PRESS

1988

East European Monographs No. CCLXVI

216—Institute for Balkan Studies—216
Thessaloniki

Table of Contents

V. Ports

VI. Maritime Law, Quarantine and Piracy

VII. Conclusions

Acknowledgements

This volume, dealing with South-East European maritime commerce and naval policies from the middle of the eighteenth century until 1914, considerably enriches the whole series on the various aspects of war and society in East Central Europe between the mid-eighteenth and the early twentieth century. Needless to say, the contribution of a number of eminent specialists from Europe and the United States has made this collective endeavour a particularly noteworthy achievement. Important primary sources have been employed and valuable, hitherto unknown, material has been brought to light. We have here a rich and multifarious treatment of the diverse aspects of political and economic maritime competition in the sensitive geographical area between the Danube and the Eastern Mediterranean.

The Institute for Balkan Studies is pleased to have had the opportunity to contribute to this important undertaking. The Seventeenth Symposium held under the aegis of Brooklyn College was an unqualified success in Thessaloniki and it helped renew and extend this Institute's close association with institutes and scholars of the United States, as well as with leading experts from all over Europe. The Board of the Institute and its associates retain the fondest memories of the close collaboration they enjoyed, in the course of the Thessaloniki Symposium and during the publication process of the present volume, with Professor Béla Király, who inspired and co-ordinated the whole programme.

Constantinos D. Svolopoulos
Professor at the University of Thessaloniki
Director of the Institute for Balkan Studies

Preface to the Series

The present volume is the twenty-third in a series that, when completed, will constitute a comprehensive survey of the many aspects of war and society in East Central Europe. The chapters of this and forthcoming volumes have been selected from papers presented at a series of international, interdisciplinary scholarly conferences conducted by the Brooklyn College Program on Society in Change in cooperation with other institutions of higher learning.

These volumes deal with the peoples whose homelands lie between the Germans to the west, the Russians to the east and north, and the Mediterranean and Adriatic Seas to the south. They constitute a particular civilization, one that is an integral part of Europe, yet substantially different from the West. The area is characterized by rich variety in language, religion, and government, and, not surprisingly, a similar variety can also be observed in concepts of national defense, in the nature of armed forces, and in ways of waging war. The study of this complex subject demands a multidisciplinary approach, and, accordingly, our contributors represent several academic disciplines. They have been drawn from universities and other scholarly institutions in the United States, Canada, and Western Europe as well as in the East Central European Socialist countries.

Our comparative investigation of military behavior and organization attempts to ascertain what is peculiar to particular nations and ethnic groups, what has been socially and culturally determined, and what has resulted from the exigencies of the moment. We try to define different patterns of military behavior, including decisionmaking processes, attitudes, and actions of diverse social classes, and the degree of restraint (or lack thereof) typically shown in war. We endeavor to present considerable material that can help us to understand how the process of social, economic, political, and technological change as well as changes in the sciences and in international relations influenced the development of doctrines of national defense and altered actual practice in such areas as military organization, command, strategy, and tactics. We also present data on the social origins and mobility of the officer corps and the rank and file, and on the differences between the officer corps of the various services, and above all, on civil-military relations and the origins of the East Central European brand of militarism. For a fuller understanding of the relationship among war, the armed forces, and society, the series also examines the economic and commercial aspects of life. The studies will, we hope, deepen our understanding of the societies, governments, and politics of East Central Europe.

Our methodology takes into account the changes in the study of war and national defense systems which have occurred in the last three decades. During that period, the study of war and national defense systems has moved away from a narrow focus on battles, campaigns, and leaders and now views a country's military history in the context of the evolution of an entire society. In fact, historians, political scientists, sociologists, philosophers, and other students of war and national defense have come to recognize the interdependence of changes in society and changes in warfare; they accept the proposition that military institutions closely reflect the character of the society of which they are a part. Recognition of this fact is a keystone of our approach to the subject.

Works in Western languages now provide adequate coverage of the diplomatic, political, intellectual, social, and economic histories of the peoples of East Central Europe. In contrast, few substantial studies of their national defense systems have yet appeared in Western languages. Similarly, although some comprehensive accounts of the nonmilitary aspects of the history of the entire region have been published in the West, there is as yet no comprehensive account of the area's national defense systems in any Western language. Nor is there any study of the mutual effects of the concepts and practices of national defense in East Central Europe. Thus, this comprehensive study of war and society in East Central Europe is a pioneering work.

This volume surveys the maritime and riverine experience, history, and policies of the peoples and nations of East Central Europe over two centuries, and their relationship to the development of the region and its relations with external powers.

As Editor-in-Chief, of course, I cheerfully take full responsibility for the comprehensiveness, cohesion, internal balance, and scholarly quality of the series I have launched. I intend this work to be neither a justification nor a condemnation of the policies, attitudes, and activities for any of the nations involved. At the same time, because the contributors represent so many different disciplines, languages, interpretations, schools of thought, our policy in this, as in past and future volumes, is to present their contributions without modification. In this sense, this volume is a sampling of the schools of thought and the standards of scholarship in the many countries to which our contributors belong.

Béla K. Király
Editor-in-Chief

Forword

The XVIIth to XXth Conferences on East Central European Society in Change extend from the accession of the Enlightened Maria Theresa, Frederick II, and Elizabeth Petrovna in 1740-41 to the wartime and revolutionary deposition of their successors in 1917-19. My opinions, it should be noted, are only loosely connected with my sketch of the growth, decline, revival, and apparent disappearance — except in international law — of an idea with as many ramifications as that of the sovereignty of the sea, to ensure the freedom and safety of the cheapest form of long-distance bulk transportation.

Western "mercantilist" ideas of the command of the sea are derived from the short-lived Athenian empire, as described by Thucydides. Medieval Western empires, except for those of Venice, Genoa, and the Hanseatic League, were primarily agrarian. Their ideas of empire were Spartan and Roman, as depicted by Xenophon and Polybius. Their soldiers were Spartan in their loyalty and training, Roman in their technological pragmatism, Athenian in their philosophy, rhetoric, and culture. This extended to the duties of the monarch himself, as recorded, in Greek, by Marcus Aurelius Antoninus. For the landlocked nations of East Central Europe, Roman ideas of monarchy, land warfare, and economics — in the Physiocrats' insistence on land and agricultural labor as the basis of state power — cut far deeper than ones of maritime sovereignty to ensure the exchange of men, goods, and ideas.

1. The events which structure our military-maritime discussions of continuity and change in this once landlocked agrarian civilization fall into 60-year time slices. Clustered around ideas about which social problems were most in need of solution, and the best ways to solve them, they punctuate the narrative of Western international relations under a balance-of-power system.

2. Traditional narratives of changing ideas, loyalties, and institutions rest on elitist and mythic, literary and biographical evidence. The traditional narratives are the dramatic, epic stories of great captains, companies, cities, empires, nations, traders, and innovators. Statistical and prosopographical evidence is scarce and scattered.

3. The opening of the ocean at the beginning of the Sixteenth Century gave the North Atlantic mercantile monarchs new power to direct the movement of people, goods, and ideas over that "common highway" described by Alfred Thayer Mahan in his study of the *Influence of Sea Power upon Western European History 1660-1783*.

4. Some of Mahan's "conditions affecting the sea power of nations" were anachronistic when his work was published in 1890. These were to be major problems for emerging nations trying to expand their maritime contacts on the basis of Mahan's "conditions."

5. During the 60-year time slices from 1740 to 1920 in which the Great Powers adjusted their balances, East and South Central Europe's nations were alternately victims and beneficiaries. Land warfare had been generally paramount as the Continental Powers pushed East over the North European plain, partly because their industries focused on land weapons and transport, and mobilization and production facilities for their new conscript people's armies, and partly because insular powers could withdraw from vulnerable allies or markets.

6. This failure was related to the failure of Continental, Napoleonic theories of the technical, economic, and political future of victory. In the twentieth century, Germany failed twice to win a two-front war. Sea power was again important in a war of attrition. Air power reached a bit beyond the client states of the Latin and Carolingian empires, before making superpower warfare suicidally dangerous. The resulting balance of mutually assured destruction did, however, increase the blackmailing power of some of their more distant non-European allies and proxies.

7. Athenian and Spartan maritime and agrarian ideas and institutions have persisted throughout a long history of international relations under a balance-of-power system. The best "explanations" for the shifts of loyalties from tribal and city state to imperial, their reversal, and revival in East and South Central Europe are geoeconomic or geopolitical. Which system could best exploit the divided

national resources of this ancient arena of combat in a particular time period? Air weapons and electronic communications could let some small nations escape from the tyranny of their geographical positions. The promise of fairer shares of the world's resources is the only weapon left for winning small nations' hearts and minds. Marcus Aurelius did tell the Romans, "My city and fatherland is, as Antoninus, Rome: as a man, the Universe." Utopian then, it may be less Utopian now. That his *Mediations* were written in Greek, in Carnuntum, near the Austrian-Czechoslovak-Hungarian Danubian junction, holds out hope for the internationalization of other waterways before that of the resources under them.

Theodore A. Ropp

I

Introduction

Stephen Fischer-Galati

Maritime Commerce and the Balkans
Before the French Revolution

The significance of trade in the Balkans and its impact on the political, social, economic, and cultural development of the Ottoman empire and its vassal states in Southeastern Europe before the French Revolution has failed to receive the attention it deserves from historians. Whatever the reasons — inadequacy of historical records, emphasis on political history, concern with nationality and territorial issues, arbitrary assumptions regarding Ottoman attitudes toward capitalism — we basically lack a conceptual and analytical framework for an economic interpretation of the history of the Balkans before the nineteenth century. In this overview of the significance of maritime commerce in the history of the Balkan peninsula, we shall attempt to provide a few ideas which may be helpful in examining or re-examining issues related to this conference on "Society in Change."

The oft-expressed view that the Moslem rulers of the Ottoman empire were disinterested in economic activities beyond those sanctioned by the Koran and that their "passivity" has been responsible for the economic and social retardation of the Balkans has been largely refuted, *inter alia*, by such distinguished historians as Halil Inalcik and Traian Stoianovich. True, social immobility was a fundamental feature of Ottoman society and rigid social structures and strictures impeded the development of an aggressive class of Moslem merchants engaged in maritime trade. However, the Ottoman sultans tolerated, and frequently even encouraged, maritime trading activities by non-Moslem members of the empire itself or its vassal states. The economic significance of Salonika, Dubrovnik, or the Greek islands in maritime trade affecting the Balkans is as well known as is, for that matter, the role of Greek, Jewish, and other non-Moslem merchants in the Levant trade as such. Whether Balkan merchants were engaged in maritime trade in Balkan products or whether they were transit agents for Ottoman and foreign goods derived from areas outside the Balkan peninsula, they were subject to regulations which aided rather than impeded economic activity and corollary social and political advancement. The various theses on the relation between religion and the development of capitalism have not yet been adequately explored with respect to Orthodoxy, or even to Islam as such, or in relation to non-Islamic religions within Islamic empires. Yet, it does seem fair to say that Orthodoxy was not incompatible with capitalism and that, at least in the Ottoman experience, neither was Islam. The favored position of Jews in the years before Sabbatai Zevi's apostasy and of the Greeks both before, and especially after the middle of the seventeenth century — not to mention other Balkan merchants — tends to indicate that the fates and fortunes of the merchants engaged in maritime trade were determined less by dogmatic and hostile actions of sultans, Ottoman officials, or Moslem merchants than by internecine conflicts among non-Moslem merchants and by competition between Balkan and foreign merchants, Venetian, French, British, Dutch, and others. In fact, the Greek merchants continuously enhanced their political, economic, and social status so that by the eighteenth century they had become indispensable economic and political agents of the Porte within the Christian Balkans.

But, we should not exaggerate the quality or magnitude of the achievements of the Greek establishment in the Ottoman empire before the French Revolution. The Phanariots, whether engaged in politics or economic activities, displayed a degree of servility toward the Porte which was extreme by West-European standards. The spirit of capitalism was also underdeveloped both in terms of attitudes toward commercial practices and awareness of the role of the merchant class in the shaping of political and socio-economic change. The frequently-advanced notion that Balkan merchants engaged in foreign trade in general, and Greek merchants engaged in maritime trade in particular, broadened their political horizons and sought to imitate their Western counterparts as a result of exposure to the ways and ideas of the West — particularly during the eighteenth century — is generally untenable. Although it is true that many a Balkan merchant could hold his own in competition with outsiders, it is also true that, with few exceptions, the mentality and attitudes of Balkan merchants, including Greek maritime entrepreneurs, remained largely a product of the Ottoman Balkans and of Eastern Orthodox conservatism. And this was particularly true of those whose economic, and even political, fortunes were intimately related with Russia. There had, of course, been exceptions over the centuries of maritime trade involving Dubrovnik, Salonika, the Aegean and Mediterranean islands, the Levant and Greek, Ragusan, and Jewish merchants engaged in that trade. But, even in the "Golden Years" of the Ottoman empire, merchants of Southeastern Europe and the Balkans were seldom able to compete successfully with their Western counterparts seeking either domination over the Mediterranean or, at least, a solid foothold in the Eastern trade.

Much of this has been blamed on the unscrupulous tactics of Western traders and on the Porte's own economic and political interests which facilitated the attainment, more often than not, of French, British, Dutch, and even Venetian commercial and political goals. There is much truth in this analysis but a few caveats also lie therein. The Turkish sultans' relations with West European governments and merchants were governed by the interests of the Porte which were both political and economic. The Capitulations, starting with those of the sixteenth century, were not necessarily instrumentalities for satisfying the economic interests of West European trading nations in return for their meeting the political and strategic interests of Ottoman rulers. Sultans, too, had definite economic interests, albeit subordinated to political ones, which could be assured by the Capitulations. And, Ottoman rulers were not alone in misunderstanding the evolution of Western capitalism in the sixteenth and seventeenth centuries and the impact which the new trade routes would have on the Mediterranean and Levant trade and on the general economic and political future of their empire.

Still, the disastrous inflation and military difficulties which affected the Ottoman empire in the seventeenth and eighteenth centuries, while increasing the Porte's economic and political dependency on France, and to a lesser degree England, did not entail loss of control over the empire's internal affairs. The innumerable sultans who succeeded one another in those centuries were not totally incompetent and their counselors and military commanders, even others than the Küprülis, displayed political resourcefulness and imagination which precluded subservience to outside interests. The power games and political manipulations in Constantinople were unparalleled in their deviousness and guile and involved competing foreigners, the Moslem establishment, the Phanar, and such seemingly auxiliary — but by no means insignificant — participants as pirates, highway robbers, and other "non-Western" contributors to chaotic stability.

This is to say, such unsavory practices as the system of "avanias," and other abuses generally characterized as "Levantine," or the activities of pirates at sea or their counterparts on land helped, rather than hindered, the achievement of the goals of the Porte and Balkan and Southeast European merchant interests competing with foreign traders representative of the national interests of European states seeking ties with the Ottoman empire. The empire was clearly not insolvent in the eighteenth century when revenues from maritime trade were sufficient to maintain more than a modicum of security for the Porte, not to mention the economic security of all engaged in trading activities with or within the empire.

Nonetheless, it would be difficult to deny the significance of the consequences for the Ottoman empire and the Balkan peoples resulting, directly or indirectly, from the intensification and expansion of maritime trade during the century of the French Revolution.

Most significant, both in the short and in the long run, were those connected with the rise of Russia and maritime trade in the Black Sea. The restrictions imposed on Russian maritime traffic after the ignominious defeat suffered by Peter the Great at Stănileşti, in 1710, did not lessen the Russians' interest in expanding their sphere of influence in Southeastern Europe and in turning the Black Sea into a Russian lake. In the interim, given the internal convulsions related to the succession to Peter the Great in Russia and to the apprehensions of the Porte with respect to the loyalties of the Romanian voevods, the fortunes — political and economic — of the Phanar and of Greek merchants, who monopolized Russia's maritime trade through the Black Sea, skyrocketed. As such, it had the effect of promoting Russian devices for undermining the Ottoman empire through the promotion and exploitation of Greek interests. The "Greek Plan," concocted by Catherine the Great, and Russia's military activities in the Morea during the Russo-Turkish War (1768-74), unsuccessful from both a Russian and Greek point of view, were nevertheless reflections of the significance of the Greek connection for Russia and of the Russian connection for Greek commercial interests in general.

Only secondary in importance was the relationship between the rise of Greek economic and political power in the Balkans and Southeastern Europe and Balkan and Southeast European nationalism. Hellenization of the Christian millet and of the Romanian principalities, apart from alienating the peasant masses, was regarded as hostile to the interests of the rising Balkan merchant class, not to mention landowners. That these property-owning groups were more astute politically than the masses is unquestionable, and it seems fair to assume that the roots of modern nationalism in the Balkans are related to antagonisms generated by Hellenization, and, also, that it was more anti-Greek than anti-Turkish in character. Granted that anti-Ottoman sentiment was pervasive within Balkan Christendom in the eighteenth century, antagonism was expressed in religious — anti-Moslem — rather than nationality terms. Anti-Greek sentiment, however, was nationalistic at least to the extent to which it differentiated between religion and ethnicity. Whereas the Christian Balkan merchants readily identified themselves as Orthodox, they were to add a "nationalist" hyphen to that identification, to wit, Greek-Orthodox, Serbian-Orthodox, Romanian-Orthodox, as Hellenization and commercial rivalries intensified in the years before the French Revolution. Moreover, anti-Semitism increased both in scope and character as commercial activity expanded in Southeastern Europe, as Jewish merchants of Salonika and elsewhere had to deal with the consequences of economic and political developments adverse to the interests of aliens by religion and nationality.

If other manifestations related to national consciousness and national antagonisms occured in the eighteenth century, partly as a consequence of the Austrian occupation of Serbia and Little Wallachia, or of Russian occupations of Moldavia and Wallachia, they were not, as a rulle, related to commercial rivalries. In any case, they were unrelated to maritime commerce since Austrian access to the Black Sea, as an extension of trading and free navigation rights on the Danube secured by the Treaty of Passarowitz, was obtained only in 1784. Moreover, Danubian trade assumed importance only in the nineteenth century, and even then did not generate crises and antagonisms comparable to those arising from competition in maritime and land commerce.

A few conclusions may be ventured on the basis of this essentially unenthusiastic appraisal of the impact of maritime trade on the Balkans and Southeastern Europe in terms of bringing that part of Europe into the mainstream of the history of capitalism and modernization.

If, in Western Europe, the eighteenth century was decisive in terms of the struggle of the propertied classes identified with rationalization of the economic order of *anciens régimes* or of regimes that still did not fully meet the requirements for modernization — political, economic, and social — of the bourgeoisie and the respectable middle-class, capitalist-oriented, landowning classes, this was not, generally, the case in the Balkans and Southeastern Europe. The reasons for the differences between the attitudes and aspirations of the Western bourgeoisie and the Eastern merchants and landowners can be ascribed only in part to limitations imposed upon capitalist development by the Ottoman Porte, or by Eastern Orthodoxy, or by Islam. Nor can they be ascribed, as they have been so often, to the rapid decline of the Eastern trade routes and Mediterranean commerce after the discovery of the New World and the ensuing shift of trade routes to the Atlantic. In fact, despite the imbalance between Eastern and Western sea routes, the Eastern trade regained much of its past significance in the eighteenth century — in both economic and political terms — in no small measure because of political conditions affecting the stability of the Ottoman empire in face of the rising power of Russia, and, at least temporarily, also, of that of the Habsburgs. If for no other reason than the survival of the Osmanli dynasty and its vast possessions, the rulers of the Ottoman empire of the seventeenth and eighteenth centuries encouraged and promoted economic activities — both by land and sea — which would at least cut the empire's losses and secure the *status quo* of, if not regain, the more glorious prestige it enjoyed in the first half of the sixteenth century. And the great beneficiaries of this policy, and, for that matter, of the decline of the Ottoman empire were the Greek merchants engaged both in maritime and land trade, their confrères in the Phanar, and, albeit to a lesser degree, other Balkan merchants whether Christian or Jew. Nevertheless, the spirit of capitalism and the opportunities for economic gain and potential political emancipation from what has been generally described as the Ottoman yoke were limited by a tradition of subservience and collaboration with the Porte, by a lack of exposure to, and comprehension of, the essence of Western-European capitalism and social and political thought. The Balkan mentality and attitudes, clearly reflections of isolation and preservation of traditional values within authoritarian, theocratic political and socio-cultural orders and structures, were reinforced through extensive trade and cultural relations with autocratic, theocratic, Russia and the Holy Roman Empire, and, perhaps paradoxically, through competition in the maritime trade with French, British, Dutch, and other Western merchants. Levantine attributes and tactics, sanctioned and protected by the Porte, were deemed to be advantageous in competitive situations and furthered the retention and evolution of a Balkan mentality that would secure the interests of the trading and propertied Christian, Jewish, and even Moslem merchants and landowners in the Balkans and Southeastern Europe. As a consequence, the "objective conditions" of that part of Europe were decisive in determining the economic, social, cultural, and political roles, evolution, and history of the merchant and propertied classes and go a long way toward explaining the essential problems which were to characterize the history of the Balkans and Southeastern Europe after the French Revolution.

Thus, there appear to be good reasons for why "Liberty, Equality, Fraternity" became the slogan of the revolutionary and post revolutionary Western bourgeoisie and respectable middle-class society, and why "Autocracy, Orthodoxy, Nationality" survived, as long as it did, in the East despite the economic significance of those engaged in maritime — and even in non-maritime-related — trade both before and after the French Revolution.

II

Maritime Commerce and Naval Policies of France and Great Britain

Simeon Damianov

French Commerce with the Bulgarian Territories
from the Eighteenth Century to 1914

France is one of Bulgaria's oldest and most traditional trading partners. For five centuries (almost until the end of the nineteenth century), when Bulgaria was under Ottoman domination, French trade relations with the Bulgarian lands for a long time proceeded within the framework of her Eastern commerce. The true flourishing of French economic penetration in the Levant occurred in the sixteenth century with the signing of the well-known Capitulation of 1535 between Suleiman the Magnificent and François I. Making use of the privileges granted them, French merchants quickly displaced their Ragusan, Genoese, and Venetian rivals and consolidated their position in the Turkish market.

If in the sixteenth and seventeenth centuries relations between the two states were still on an equal footing, in the eighteenth century, with the decline of the Ottoman empire, they became inequitable. In order to win France's military and diplomatic support against the Habsburg empire and Russia, the Sublime Porte frequently had to make new concessions to French merchants. On the basis of the commercial treaty of 1740 customs duties on the goods imported from France were lowered by up to 3 percent *ad valorem*. In this way the French already controlled almost the entire foreign trade of the Ottoman empire.[1] Capitulations secured for the French merchants immunity and inviolability, exempting them from practically all domestic taxes and charges, and this made them far more competitive in comparison with local merchants.[2]

Of the degree of French commercial penetration in Turkey, yearly statistics show that throughout the eighteenth century, about three-fourths of Turkey's trade, amounting to about 40 million livres, or nearly 30 million, was with France. It was precisely then that the French colonies in the Levant, directed by the Marseille Chamber of Commerce, originally set up under Colbert's direct care, turned into powerful centers of French economic expansion in Turkey.[3]

France's trade with Turkey reached its apogee on the eve of the French Revolution. According to approximate estimates, from the beginning of the eighteenth century to the Revolution in 1789, French imports from, and exports to, Turkey increased fourfold, and during 1783-92 reached an average annual level of 54 million livres, which consisted of about 33 million in French imports to Turkey and 21 million in Turkish exports to Marseille.[4] This huge trade was carried out with the help of an extensive network of commercial agents, recruited chiefly from among the Greek, Armenian, and Jewish commercial bourgeoisie living in the big city ports of Istanbul, Izmir, Salonika, Beirut, and Trabzon.

Rapid development of French manufacture in the eighteenth century rested on the basis of the progress of French trade with Turkey. Marseille's important export item was Languedoc broadcloth, in great demand on Turkish markets. From 1703 to 1791, its export to Turkey rose from 1100 to 4700 tons *per annum.* As information from that time testifies, "Jewish and Greek merchants in Turkey sell only French broadcloth."[5] Besides broadcloth, France imported into Turkey large quantities of silk fabrics, cotton textiles, coffee from the islands of Martinique and Bourbon, sugar (also from the colonies), the natural dyes indigo and cochineal brought from the islands of Jamaica and Santo Domingo, black pepper from Goa, metal articles, glassware, medicines, luxury articles of all kinds, and so forth.[6]

In exchange for all that, France received wool, raw hides, cotton, and raw silk. Cereals were also available despite an existing Turkish ban on their export abroad; by special permission of the Sublime Porte or smuggled, large quantities of foodstuffs were sent to meet France's needs particularly in years of poor harvests and hunger.[7]

This considerable trade was strongly hampered during the Napoleonic Wars. In 1802, by virtue of the Treaty of Amiens, Napoleon succeeded in restoring France's right to be treated by Turkey in accordance with the principle of most-favored nation, and French ships, for the first time, obtained official permission to sail freely in the Black Sea which until then had been closed to European navigation.[8] Trade between the two countries, however, was increasingly restricted owing to British naval operations during the Continental

Blockade. In 1807, this trade, as was claimed in a letter of the Marseille Chamber of Commerce to the Minister of Foreign Affairs in Paris, "no longer exists."[9]

France's difficulties were skilfully exploited by her enemies, especially in connection with Napoleon's Egyptian campaign; for, Britain and Austria obtained for themselves extremely low customs tariffs. From that moment on, British influence in Turkey became predominant. It was only in the years of the July Monarchy (1830-48), when industrial production in France increased, that the French commercial bourgeoisie went on an offensive to recover its lost positions. The conditions created after the conclusion of the commercial treaty of 1838 eased its task, and the volume of Franco-Turkish trade began to rise. If in 1825 it was below 30 million francs, a quarter century later (in the early 1850s), commercial deals more than trebled and reached 90 million francs.[10]

The Ottoman empire assumed ever greater importance for France not only as a market for industrial output, but also as a source of raw materials. This, to a large extent, explains why the French bourgeoisie, trying to win greater influence in the Ottoman empire, opposed any attempts at its dismemberment. After 1841, when she finally overcame illusions for complete hegemony in Turkey by placing her Egyptian protégé, Mehemet Ali, on the throne in Istanbul, France already strictly adhered to the principle of preserving Turkey's territorial integrity.

The Crimean War (1853-56) in which France, together with Britain, helped Turkey against Russia, was a turning point in the struggle for conquering the Turkish market. In 1855, trade between France and Turkey reached 203 million francs, and in 1856 exceeded 223 million francs;[11] this shows that it more than trebled in only a few years' time. The increase came chiefly from the considerable supplies of ammunition and foodstuffs to the Turkish army during the war. Much more was done on this basis after the war. The taste for European goods increased noticeably in Turkey. Serviced almost entirely by French vessels, Marseille's commerce engaged in enormous deals on the Turkish markets.[12]

In the 1860s, the industrial revolution in France was near completion. Then only Britain surpassed France in industrial might. Opportunities for export increased still more. It may be said, and without exaggeration, that in the 1860s and 1870s, French trade in Turkey reached its apex. The new commercial treaty of 1861 provided for much more favorable terms, especially for the export of Turkish raw materials to France. Although import customs duties in Turkey were raised from 5 to 8 percent in comparison with the 1838 treaty, export customs duties now were lowered from 12 to 8 percent with the proviso that they would drop each year by a percent to settle, in 1869, for good, at one percent *ad valorem*.[13]

The data in Table 1 give us a visual idea of the rapid growth of trade between France and Turkey after 1860.

T a b l e   1

*Trade Between France and Turkey
in 1860-77 (in francs)*[14]

Years	French imports to Turkey	Turkish exports to France	Total
1860	86,000,000	109,000,000	195,000,000
1864	129,293,000	166,905,000	296,198,000
1872	186,700,000	119,800,000	306,500,000
1873	233,800,000	173,900,000	407,700,000
1877	184,000,000	157,600,000	341,600,000

If we analyze the structure of French imports to Turkey, we will note that, after 1860, France supplied the Ottoman empire chiefly with silk fabrics (worth 7.5 million francs a year on the average), ordinary and special hides (6.5 million francs), woollen cloth (2.5 million francs), various kinds of woollen yarn and processed wool (20 million francs), linen and hemp textiles (1 million francs), sugar (some 10 million francs a year), etc.[15] If we compare the data for the average annual size of French imports to Turkey during 1859-75 with those of the average annual imports in 1825-34, we will see that in 30 years French imports increased nearly fifteen times (from 11 million to 150 million francs a year). Earlier France regularly exported from Turkey more than she imported; in the 1870s, the situation changed: French imports to Turkey already exceeded Turkish exports of agricultural produce to France.

Exports to France consisted mainly of cocoons (35 million francs on the average annually), raw reeled silk (4 million francs a year), unginned cotton (25 million francs), raw hides (1-2 million francs annually), so on and so forth. Of paramount importance for French industry was also Turkish wool worth about 20-30 million francs a year.[16] During the period from 1835 to 1875, that is, in some 40 years, Turkish exports to France increased from 15 million to 175 million francs in comparable prices, i.e., nearly twelve times.[17]

It should nevertheless be pointed out that, no matter to what extent trade relations between France and Turkey developed, up to World War I the Ottoman empire ranked but eighth on the list of French foreign trade. In 1866, for instance, the total volume of French imports and exports amounted to an impressive sum of 6 million francs, whereas France's trade with Turkey was some 265 million francs; this means that Turkey and her dependent regions made up a mere one twenty-third part of total French foreign trade.[18]

This fact could be explained chiefly by the low purchasing power of the empire's subjects, particularly of the peasantry which continued to adhere to the traditional principles of a closed, self-sufficient domestic economy. French goods were of high quality, beautiful, and durable but rather expensive in comparison with British and Austrian goods which competed with them and which were, as admitted by contemporaries, of lower quality but cheap and adapted to the "Oriental taste."

Set against this background of the development of Franco-Turkish commercial ties in the nineteenth century, we may best judge the relative place of the Bulgarian lands under Ottoman rule in the system of French commercial interests in the Orient. Many are the proofs of the constantly growing role of the Bulgarian lands in trade relations between **France and Turkey.**

The French commercial bourgeoisie evinced marked interest in the Bulgarian lands as early as the eighteenth century. This may be explained by the fact that it was namely then that the center of gravity of Ottoman economic power shifted from the Asian to the Balkan provinces of the empire. The growing economic role of the Bulgarian lands made it necessary for France already in the early eighteenth century, to open consular points not only on the Aegean coast but also in the interior of Thrace. It is also known that, in 1685, a French consulate was opened in Salonika as a center of penetration in Macedonia, and in 1700, another in Kavalla. In 1718, a representative of a French firm in Constantinople settled also in Adrianople.[19]

Nor were projects for expanding the French consular network in the more distant parts of the Bulgarian lands lacking. The study of Bulgaria's geography and economy convinced the French diplomatic representatives in Constantinople of the need of a swift penetration not only in Rumelia, i.e., in southern Bulgaria, but also in the areas along the Black Sea, not to mention in northern Bulgaria.[20] Already Louis de Villeneuve, French ambassador to Turkey in the 1730s, recommended to the court of Versailles the opening of a French commercial house in one of the big Bulgarian towns on the Danube: Ruse or Svishtov — where French fabrics were not known, but from where they could be distributed not only along the Danube but also in Wallachia and Moldavia. His successor, Castellane, suggested that a consulate should be set up in Plovdiv as well.[21] However, these projects were not realized during the eighteenth century.

The points of support of the French economic penetration in Thrace and Macedonia, and hence, in the interior of the Bulgarian lands, then were the ports on the Aegean coast and in particular Salonika, and Kavalla, and Enez. Salonika, where the French gained a predominant position, was of the greatest importance. Toward the end of the eighteenth century, in Salonika and Kavalla, there were eight French commercial houses which were very active. During the decade from 1783 to 1792, from Marseille to Salonika were imported annually goods worth some 3 million livres, and in turn, Salonika exported farm produce amounting to more than 6 million livres, which means that trade between the two towns amounted to about 9 million livres a year.[22]

Adrianopole connected to the port of Enez by the Maritza became an important center of commerce with the Bulgarian lands in the eighteenth century. Throughout that century, the French were the only foreign merchants there. And, on the eve of the 1789 Revolution, there were four French commercial establishments whose annual balance of trade amounted to some 2-3 million francs.[23]

Since the Black Sea remained closed to foreign vessels, French goods were brought first to Constantinople, and then from there, forwarded to the ports of Varna, Burgas, Balchik, and Sozopol. Although the role of these ports at that time should not be exaggerated, in no case should it be overlooked either. The general impression of the Western explorer of the Bulgarian lands was that "Bulgaria's import trade is enormous; there are no foreign commodities which would not be found in great variety here."[24]

Of greater importance for the French merchants were the productive possibilities, and consequently, the export potential of southern Bulgaria and Thrace which were regarded as some of the most developed provinces of the Ottoman empire; where during the traditional annual fairs in Uzundjovo and Sliven, huge deals were concluded. Charles de Peyssonnel reports that as early as the middle of the eighteenth century, Rumelia exported large amounts of cheap wax of excellent quality, that the production of high-grade silk was abundant, and that the export of wool, cattle hides, tallow, tobacco, and other items was also considerable. The real wealth of these lands was the production of cheap cereals which the Sublime Porte bought to feed the empire's population and army.[25]

Approximate calculations show that of the total Franco-Turkish trade, which on the eve of the Revolution amounted to 65 million livres, about one-third, i.e., some 20 million livres, came from the Bulgarian lands. From other data we see that during the five-year period from 1763 to 1767, French merchants through Constantinople alone exported Bulgarian agricultural produce worth nearly 9 million livres.[26]

Yet, on the whole, the volume of French trade with the Bulgarian lands in the eighteenth century was limited. Three facts can explain this: one, French commercial-industrial capital at that time was not that developed so as to cover also the peripheral provinces of the Ottoman empire; two, a developed network of roads was lacking in the Bulgarian lands, and this, too, impeded the penetration of French trade; and three, the Bulgarian bourgeoisie itself, economically weak and not consolidated, continued to prefer cooperation with Russian and to a certain extent Austrian, commercial firms, because of geographic proximity and a more reliable and regular commerce.[27]

The situation changed markedly half a century later, on the eve of the Crimean War. In the mid-nineteenth century, there occurred an upsurge in Bulgaria's economy, some capitalist forms of production appeared, roads were improved, the Black Sea became accessible to European commerce, and the export of cereals was allowed. Moreover, Marseille's commercial relations became more intensive not only with Salonika where France again came to the fore, but also with Kavalla, Enez, Adrianople, and Constantinople from where southern Bulgaria's output was exported.[28]

The increased role of the Bulgarian lands in French commerce saw the establishment of a French consulate in Varna in 1843.[29] Consequently, in the 1840s, large quantities of grain were sent from there to Marseille; for example, in 1847, a year of bad harvest in France, wheat and barley worth over 10 million francs came from Varna.[30] In fact, Varna itself became one of the top places in the Ottoman empire in terms of volume of business.[31]

Other Bulgarian Black Sea ports also developed rapidly during the same period. In 1845, French economist Hommaire de Hell, after having traveled all along the western coast of the Black Sea, was amazed by the "great agricultural revolution" that was taking place in the areas which were economically connected to it. He was surprised by the rapid progress of exports and the busy life in all Black Sea ports. "Indifferent villages," he wrote, "have gradually turned into commercial ports of great importance; in the shipping bulletins there began to appear in succession, along with Varna, the hitherto unknown names of Burgas, Balchik , Mesemvria and Anhialo." The French economist emphasized that, if in 1841 two Sardinian captains had the idea of carrying salt to Burgas, they had to wait more than three months to fill a cargo of wheat; four years later (i.e., in 1845) they could export from that very same post 350,000 Marseille measures of grain (as well as 650,000 from Varna and 220,000 from

Balchik). At the same time farming improved to such an extent that the best harvests of the past could hardly be compared with the most ordinary harvest of 1844-45. "On my arrival in Balchik," Hommaire de Hell wrote, "the traffic of transport vehicles was such that it took me more than an hour to reach the house of the mayor of the village; trains of carts, stretching in the plain as far as the eye could see, were visible in all directions."[32]

The growing importance of the Bulgarian lands for Western commerce was one of the causes for France and Britain to oppose dismemberment of the Ottoman empire during the Crimean War. The intensification of trade between Marseille and Bulgaria after the war was aimed at binding the latter with the French economy in a more lasting fashion. Now, commercial firms (the Evlogi and Hristo Georgiev brothers, the Tupchileshtov brothers, the Robev brothers of Bitolja, the Papazov brothers of Kazanluk, etc.) were involved in this trade. French commerce continued to be predominant chiefly in southern Bulgaria; north of the big mountain chain crossing Bulgaria, French goods were comparatively poorly-known owing to Austrian competition.

If we have to grade the importance of the ports on the Aegean coast for the development of French commercial expansion in the Bulgarian lands, we should indisputably give Salonika pride of place Through it the French controlled the whole of Macedonia and western Thrace. Traditionally France fully met the needs of this market for coffee (1-1.5 million francs annually) and sugar (some 1 million francs annually). The import of French textiles gave way to Austrian and British competition and was growing ever more insignificant.[33]

France based her leading position in Salonika not on imports but on the export of local production. In 1864, for instance, the total exports of Salonika came up to 27 million francs, France's share amounting to 20 million, and in 1865, of a total of 24.5 million francs, France accounted for 17.5 million. French merchants continued to export practically all the cotton grown in the hinterland of Salonika (worth more than 10 million francs *per annum*), almost all the output of raw silk (up to 3 million francs), the entire production of wool (up to 1 million francs), and about one-third of the grain earmarked for export (also worth about 1 million francs).[34] And, this was generally true also in the 1870s. France continued to be superior to her British and Austrian competitors in exports, but as far as imports were concerned, on the whole, she lagged behind them.[35]

A study of Salonika's commercial links with France is of key importance for us, because it gives us a chance to evaluate the scale of French commerce with the Bulgarian lands up to the Russo-Turkish War (1877-78) and Bulgaria's liberation from Turkish domination. Calculations show that, up to 1878, its annual trade with Europe amounted to about 60 million francs on the average, of which some 17 million francs were France's share (4 million of imports and 13 million of exports).[36] Practically all the imports were consumed in areas where the Bulgarian population was predominant. These areas also ensured the bulk of the farm produce which was exported from Salonika to France.

This should hardly surprise us. Statistical data show that, by the middle of the nineteenth century, northern and southern Bulgaria, Dobrudja, Aegean Thrace, and Macedonia, which were the most economically developed provinces of the Ottoman empire, paid 52 percent of all taxes on agricultural output in the empire. It was namely in these provinces that, in the eighteenth and nineteenth centuries, ethnic Bulgarians consolidated their influence.[37]

The port of Kavalla was closely linked with that of Salonika. If the important commercial centers of Seres and Bitolja gravitated toward Salonika, a large part of Aegean Thrace was closely connected with Kavalla. In the 1870s about half of Kavalla's trade was orientated to France. Thus, in 1873, for instance, French trade there amounted to 9 million francs, consisting of 2 million in imports of French goods and 7 million in exports of local products to Marseille.[38] The ships of the Marseille company "Messageries maritimes" called at the port of Kavalla once a week, and this port became the import and export point of a large area where the Bulgarian population was also predominant. France's commercial operations with Dedeagach,[39] as well as with Constantinople,[40] developed approximately at the same tempo.

Adrianople remained the principal entrepôt of French commerce in Thrace. Large quantities of imported goods converged here; from here was organized their distribution throughout Adrianople Thrace;

and so was the export of raw materials needed by French industry. In the 1860s, trade in wool, raw silk, oleaginous seeds, cereals, and other products most of which were exported from Adrianople through Enez, Rodosto, and Burgas to Marseille assumed the utmost importance.[41] France's influence in Adrianople was further strengthened by the numerous French colonies in Constantinople which in 1870 numbered approximately 7000 people.[42]

After the Crimean War, in the town of Plovdiv, situated in the heart of Thrace, a French consulate was opened (1857). This town and its big and rich area were quickly won for the French commercial cause. From 1858 almost the whole output of silk, and in the 1860s large amounts of wheat as well, were exported almost exclusively to France.[43] The great market possibilities of Provdiv and its area urgently posed the question of the importation of French industrial goods. At the insistence of Vice-Consul Champoiseau in Plovdiv, in 1858, a French company opened an office with the purpose of supplying Rumelia with all the commodities that France exported abroad.[44]

French merchants, however, failed to displace the cheaper Austrian goods on the Plovdiv market. In this connection the vice-consul concluded pessimistically: "It is regrettable to see an area like European Turkey, with a population of more than 8 million, does not even know the goods whose production which we are unsurpassed and which we may find a way to deliver here instead of sending them to South America with a thousand times higher risk of loss." Champoiseau feared that if French trade hesitated to take this road, "soon it will be too late, all places will be taken, all markets won" by competitors who were "if not smarter, surely at least bolder."[45]

In the 1860s and 1870s, France fully satisfied the Plovdiv market with sugar and coffee. She accounted for one-quarter of its total trade, importing goods worth 1.5 million francs a year, and her exports, where she occupied first place, exceeding imports by three-fold, reached 4.5 million francs. So, in this period the Plovdiv trade amounted to 20-25 million francs annually; France accounted for one-quarter of the total commercial balance of the town and its surrounding areas.

Intensifying her presence in Plovdiv, French mechants turned their attention to Kazanluk where the famous attar of roses was produced.

At the same time and even much later, the French firm "Bylain" established direct contact with the producers of attar of roses. About 500 kg were exported to Marseille, i.e., 30 percent of total output; 20 percent to Britain; 30 percent to Germany and Italy; 10 percent to the United States; and 10 percent consumed in Turkey and Arabia.[46] The towns of Sliven, Stara Zagora, and Burgas emerged as exporters of wool, cereals, and silk. And, within a short period of time, Burgas surpassed Varna as a Black Sea major port, because of its more convenient location and richer hinterland.[47]

Thus, having established their predominant influence in southern Bulgaria, French merchants directed their attention to northern Bulgaria, as well. In 1867, a French consulate was opened in Ruse, the principal town of the Danubian vilayet. Through the Black Sea ports (chiefly Varna) Marseille received cereals, wool, and silk collected even in Turnovo, Kilifarevo, Dryanovo, Gabrovo, Tryavna, and Elena.[48]

The approximate average annual volume of French commerce with the Bulgarian lands during the two decades after the Crimean War can be seen from Table 2.

Table 2

Average Annual Trade of France with the Bulgarian Lands from 1856 to 1876 (in francs)[49]

Points of Penetration	Total Volume of Trade with Europe	France's Share in Total Trade		
		Imports from France	Exports to France	Total
Salonika	60,000,000	4,000,000	13,000,000	17,000,000
Kavalla	20,000,000	2,000,000	7,000,000	9,000,000
Dedeagach	15,000,000	2,000,000	6,000,000	8,000,000
Enez	5,000,000	1,000,000	2,000,000	3,000,000
Constantinople	200,000,000	2,500,000	7,500,000	10,000,000
Adrianople	43,000,000	3,000,000	20,000,000	23,000,000
Plovdiv	25,000,000	1,500,000	4,500,000	6,000,000
Burgas	20,000,000	—	4,000,000	4,000,000
Varna	24,000,000	1,000,000	1,500,000	2,500,000
Dobrudja	10,000,000	—	5,000,000	5,000,000
TOTAL	422,000,000	17,000,000	70,500,000	87,500,000

It is seen from this data that France accounted for about one-fifth of the total volume of the trade of European states with the Bulgarian lands. In the total balance of French commerce with the Bulgarian lands, exports sharply exceeded imports; a ratio of 4:1 in favor of exports (70.5 million francs in exports as against 17 million in imports). Once again, this shows that the Bulgarian lands served chiefly as a raw material reserve for French industry.

In the total average annual trade of France with the Ottoman empire which came up to some 300 million francs, Bulgaria's participation was not less than one-quarter (87.5 million francs). Hence, the great importance of the Bulgarian lands for French commercial capital. The balance sheet also indicates that Britain and Austria together held about 70 percent of the imports of industrial goods into the Bulgarian lands, and France, about 20 percent on the average, and very seldom 25 percent. About 40 percent of Bulgarian exports, however, were absorbed by France. Thus, the European countries complemented one another in the economic use of the Bulgarian lands despite intensive competitive competition. French commercial influence consolidated chiefly in those Bulgarian lands which gravitated to the Mediterranean, i.e., in southern Bulgaria with Aegean Thrace and Macedonia.[50] As a whole, European trade with the Bulgarian lands contributed to the progressive development of farming and its adaptation to the needs of a capitalist economy.

After the Congress of Berlin (1878), commercial relations between the Principality of Bulgaria and the other states were regulated by the commercial treaty concluded between the Ottoman empire and the Great Powers in 1861. It was only after the signing of independent commercial treaties between Bulgaria and the Powers in 1896-97 that specific custom duties were established; equitably and mutually advantageous trade relations were instituted, however, only after the abolition of the capitulatory regime and the recognition of Bulgaria's independence in 1908.

The study of France's commerce with Bulgaria up to World War I is considerably facilitated by the existence of regular statistics, archival materials, and evaluations by competent persons. Here we shall, therefore, limit ourselves to the most general findings about the volume and structure of Franco-Bulgarian trade from Bulgaria's liberation

from Ottoman domination to her breaking off of diplomatic relations
with France in autumn 1915.[51]

The real significance of French imports from, and exports to, Bulgaria during the 37-year period from the Congress of Berlin to 1915
is best set against the background of Bulgaria's overall trade with the
other states.

Table 3

Bulgaria's Trade with Foreign States
from 1881 to 1915 (in gold leva)*

Five-Year Average	Imports	Exports	Total
1881-85	48,839,236	38,474,127	87,313,363
1886-90	70,557,992	62,396,479	132,954,471
1891-95	83,553,709	77,541,063	161,094,772
1896-1900	67,954,988	68,503,445	136,458,433
1901-1905	95,006,532	120,021,506	215,028,038
1906-10	140,214,490	118,602,188	258,816,678
1911-19	183,347,675	139,642,175	322,989,850

*The table has been drawn up on the basis of the annual publications of the
Statistical Bureau in Sofia "Statistika za tŭrgoviiata na Kniazhestvo Bŭlgariia
[1090: Tsarstvo Bŭlgariia]s chuzhdite dŭrzhavi." In operating with the values, it
should be borne in mind that up to World War I the Bulgarian gold lev was equal
to the French gold franc.

On the basis of the same sources, the share of French commerce
with Bulgaria in absolute figures and percentages may be seen from
Table 4.

Table 4

French Participation in Bulgaria's Trade with European States from 1881 to 1915 (in gold leva)

Five-Year Average	Imports	% of Total Imports	Exports	% of Total Exports	Total	% of Total Trade
1881-85	2,041,368	4.17	3,304,918	8.51	5,346,286	6.12
1886-90	3,744,784	5.31	13,569,837	21.74	17,314,621	13.09
1891-95	3,593,722	4.43	15,947,536	20.56	19,541,258	12.10
1896-1900	3,621,909	5.32	7,909,223	11.54	11,531,132	8.45
1901-1905	5,832,912	6.13	7,309,893	6.09	13,142,805	6.11
1906-10	9,101,136	6.48	7,252,480	6.11	16,353,616	6.32
1911-15	14,844,716	8.10	8,087,360	5.10	22,932,076	7.22

The analysis of the figures in Tables 3 and 4 permit us to draw an essential conclusion: after 1878 France continued to rank among the most important European states trading with Bulgaria. A number of French goods found a ready market in Bulgaria: processed hides and sole-leather, washing soap from Marseille, corduroy, the well-known "Paris goods" (fashionable ladies' and men's clothes, fine woollen and cotton textiles, yarn, hats, lace, and perfumes), medicines, jams, canned food, household articles, champagne, liqueurs, cement, Marseille tiles, vine stock, silkworm grain selected by the Pasteur method, etc. Starting with the modest figure of 2 million leva in the first years after Bulgaria's liberation, French imports rose to nearly 15 million leva at the beginning of World War I, i.e., an absolute growth of about 750 percent.

Structural changes in the development of French capitalism in the late nineteenth and early twentieth centuries, however, had an effect not only on the size, but also on the character of French imports into Bulgaria. Whereas Germany, which outstripped France in the rate of economic development, turned increasingly into a powerful supplier of heavy industrial goods, France continued to supply mainly articles for light industry. And, French financial monopolies were already engaged in usurious operations which brought them more reliable profits than industrial investments.

Yet, in light of Bulgaria's protectionist policy in those years, the conditions for marketing French industrial goods became relatively ever more unfavorable. The greater distances, the higher transportation costs involved, and the backward technical base of French industry made its products more expensive and non-competitive. France, therefore, as in the past, ranked fourth, and most often fifth, as importer (after Austria-Hungary, Britain, Germany, and Turkey). In general, she marketed 4-5 times less goods than Austria-Hungary, 3 times less than Britain, and 3.5 times less than Germany. Her relative share in Bulgarian imports throughout this period came up to a mere 6.1 percent.

The organizational shortcomings of French commerce, of which there was so much talk in the reports of the consular agents and which were regarded almost as the sole cause for its lag, were, in point of fact, of secondary importance. The question actually lay simply in the weaker interest in commerce of French financial capital since it was decisively oriented toward lending operations. French banks with branches in Bulgaria, did not assist importers, as did the Austro-German banks, by granting long-term credits and by discount operations for local middlemen. In this respect, Austro-German banks coordinated their activity better with Bulgarian commercial centers by granting them loans even for up to one year.

In this connection, one of the greatest authorities on the problems of French commerce in Bulgaria, the French vice-consul in Varna and secretary of the French Legation in Sofia of long standing, Alexandre Mercinier, wrote, in 1912, and not without justification: "Bank credit on the basis of commercial contracts concluded abroad is not practised in France... In this rests the cause for which our exports, particularly to the Orient, are compelled to restrict themselves, whereas this credit exists in Austria-Hungary and Germany... In point of fact it has ensured the great expansion of the German and Austro-Hungarian industry which now exercises its commanding influence on the foreign markets in general and in the Orient in particular.. It was necessary to imitate them so as to assert ourselves; our banks in the mother country had to agree to help our export trade by their credit; without their effective intervention it will not succeed in making considerable headway."[52]

If France was a second-rate importer of industrial goods to Bulgaria, she no doubt played a more significant role as exporter of Bulgarian farm produce. Bulgarian cereals and raw materials (hides, raw silk), as well as attar of roses, invariably found a ready market in France. Particularly intensive were French exports from Bulgaria during the decade after the Union of Eastern Rumelia with the Principality of Bulgaria (1886-95), when the average annual value of exports exceeded 14.7 million leva. As earlier, the activity of the French merchants was stronger in southern Bulgaria, thanks to the more convenient transport connections across the Mediterranean and the Aegean.

At the end of the nineteenth and the beginning of the twentieth centuries, France, however, was also pushed into the background as a buyer of Bulgarian products. Her importance in this field was on a level with that of Austria-Hungary and gave way not only to the biggest traditional exporters of Bulgarian goods, Turkey and Britain, but also to Germany and Belgium The comparison of figures shows that after 1900 France accounted for only 5-6 percent of total Bulgarian exports. Generally for the whole period under review, her share made up 10.53 percent of exports.

If we compare the figures of imports and exports, we find that Bulgaria's trade balance with France was, on the whole, active, i.e., exports to France exceeded by about one-third French imports to Bulgaria (with the exception of the last few prewar years when French armament firms supplied considerable quantities of artillery and ammunition to Bulgaria). The average annual ratio for the whole period was 6 million leva of imports as against 9 million leva of exports. This fact also expressed the specific feature of French economic development at that time: Bulgaria was regarded as an agricultural and raw material appendage of French industry, but this very industry was not in a state to satisfy the Bulgarian market with the industrial goods it needed.

In sum, data on imports and exports show that from 1878 to 1915 France participated in Bulgaria's trade with a round figure of 535 million leva. Her share in the country's trade balance came up to 7.97

percent, which meant that her trade constituted about one-twelfth of the trade of European states with Bulgaria. To the end of the nineteenth century, France, by her relative weight as Bulgaria's trading partner, occupied fourth place (next to Austria-Hungary., Britain, and Turkey), and, after Germany's emergence on the stage of Southeastern Europe, fifth.

Trade with Bulgaria admittedly represented an insignificant part of France's imports and exports. Leaving aside France's vast colonial empire, her average annual trade in the 1880-1910 period amounted to 9 billion francs, including 5 billion in imports and 4 billion in exports.[53] It follows from this that the goods imported into Bulgaria (some 6 million francs a year on the average) formed a mere 0.13 percent of total French exports in industrial goods, whereas products (worth some 9 million francs a year) exported from Bulgaria to France made up about 0.22 percent of total imports of the French Republic. If we combine imports and exports, we conclude that 15 million francs (=leva) a year on average, represented only a 0.17 percent share for Bulgaria in France's total foreign trade.

These at first glance insignificant figures should not deceive us. It should also be taken into account that at that time Bulgaria's population was 10 times less numerous than that of France. One should equally bear in mind that the degree of development of the economy, trade, and market in Bulgaria was very much lower than in France. In spite of that, in the 37-year period from 1878 to 1915, France exported industrial goods worth 215.3 million francs to Bulgaria and imported Bulgarian goods for nearly 320 million francs.

In conclusion we will point out that in the objective assessment of the results of French commerce with Bulgaria, we should proceed from the fact that in the course of a century and a half France by her commercial activity contributed to the integration of the Bulgarian economy into the system of European capitalism, and hence, to Bulgaria's entrance to the modern world economy. By this were prepared, consciously or not, the conditions for the speedy liberation of Bulgaria from Ottoman domination.

French trade with Bulgaria was realized by a series of firms connected with the Orient. The figures of the volume of this trade indicate that, although inferior in intensity and scope to that of Britain and the countries of the German-speaking states, the French commercial bourgeoisie, in many cases, was their most serious competitor in the struggle for winning the Bulgarian market.[54]

Notes

1. P. Masson, Histoire du commerce français dans le Levant au XVIII-e siècle (Paris, 1911), 270 *et passim*.

2. M. Brunswik, Etudes pratiques sur la Question d'Orient (Paris, 1868), 8 *et passim;* G. Pelissie du Rausas, Le régime des Capitulations dans l'Empire ottoman I (Paris, 1910), 28 *et passim*.

3. Ch. Roux, Les Echelles de Syrie et de Palestine au XVIII-e siècle (Paris, 1928), 17 *et passim*.

4. J. Juliani, "Du commerce de Marseille avec le Levant," in Archives du commerce et de l'industrie agricole et manufacturière, III-e année 11 et 12 (Paris, 1835); cf. H. Sée, La France économique et sociale au XVIII-e siècle (Paris, 1939), 124.

5. "Remarques sur plusieurs branches de commerce et de navigation," Journal de Commerce (Mars, 1759, Brussels), 137 *et passim*.

6. El. Abesci, Etat actuel de l'Empire ottoman (traduit de l'anglais) II (Paris), 242 *et passim*.

7. P. Masson, 352.

8. M. Antoine, Essai historique sur le commerce et la navigation de la Mer Noire (Paris, 1820), 257 *et passim*.

9. E. Salvador, Histoire commerciale, politique et diplomatique des échelles du Levant, d'Orient, Marseille et la Méditerranée (Paris, 1957), 339.

10. "Commerce de la France avec la Turquie de 1825 à 1845," Annales du commerce extérieur, No. 2 (Septembre et Octobre 1847), 96 *et passim*.

11. *Ibid.*, No. 11 (Décembre 1857), 26-29, "Commerce de la France avec la Turquie en 1855 et 1856."

12. *Ibid.*, No. 18 (Février 1864), 58 *et passim*, "Commerce de la France avec la Turquie. Examen de ses résultats depuis 1840."

13. Gabriel effendi Noradounghian, Recueil d'actes internationaux de l'Empire ottoman III (Paris, 1902), 120 *et passim*.

14. Annales..., No. 18 (Février 1864), 58 *et passim;* No. 21 (Octobre 1865), 65-68; No. 26 (Septembre 1868), 36 *et passim;* No. 32 (Novembre 1879), 246-48.

15. Atlas graphique et statistique du commerce de la France avec les pays étrangers pour les principales marchandises pendant les années 1859 à 1875, publié par ordre de M. Teisserenc de Bort, sénateur, ministre de l'agriculture et du commerce, sous la direction de M. Ozenne, conseiller d'Etat, secrétaire général,

par F. Bonnange, archiviste du Ministère, Paris, 1878 (cf. les tableaux: Etoffes pures, Peaux préparées, Tissus de laine, Laines en masse, Tissus de lin et de chanvre, Sucre).

16. *Ibid.*, cf. les tableaux: Soies en cocons, Soies bourrées, Coton non égrainé, Graines, Peaux brutes, Laines.

17. Annales..., No. 26 (Septembre 1868), 36 *et passim*, "Commerce de la France avec la Turquie et ses dépendances en 1864, 1865 et 1866."

18. E. Levasseur, Histoire de commerce de la France II (de 1789 à nos jours) (Paris, 1912), 801.

19. P. Masson, Histoire de commerce français dans le Levant au XVII-e siècle (Paris, 1896) 431-33.

20. Ch. Peyssonnel, Traité sur le commerce de la Mer Noire, 2 vol. (Paris, 1787); *ibid.*, Observations sur le commerce de la Mer Noire..., etc. (Amsterdam, 1798); G. A. Olivier, Voyage dans l'Empire ottoman, 2 vol. (Paris, 1798); F. de Beaujour, Le commerce de la Grèce, la Macédoine et la Thrace, 2 vol. (Paris, 1800); J. B. Lechevalier, Voyage de la Propontide et du Pont-Euxin (Paris, 1800).

21. P. Masson, Histoire du commerce français dans le Levant au XVIII-e siècle (Paris, 1911), 612-13.

22. J. Juliani, "Du commerce de Marseille avec le Levant," in Archives du commerce et de l'industrie agricole et manufacturière, III-e année, 11 et 12 (Paris, 1835). Cf. M. L. Lascaris, Salonique à la fin du XVIII-e siècle d'après les rapports consulaires français (Athènes, 1939); N. Svoronos, Le commerce de Salonique au XVIII-e siècle (Paris, 1956).

23. J. Juliani, 106.

24. Ch. Peyssonnel, Observations sur le commerce de la Mer Noire (Amsterdam, 1798), 243 *et passim*.

25. *Ibid.*, 244-45.

26. P. Masson, 617. Cf. Hr. Gandev, "Tŭrgovskata obmiana na Evropa s bŭlgarskite zemi prez XVIII i nachaloto na XIX vek," in Godishnik na Sofiiskiia universitet — Istoriko-filologicheski fakultet XL (Sofia, 1944), 32.

27. V. Paskaleva, "Za tŭrgovskite vrŭzki mezhdu Franciia i bŭlgarskite zemi ot nachaloto na XIX vek do Osvobozhdenieto," in Istorikcheski pregled (1960: 5), 56-57.

28. N. V. Michoff, Contribution à l'histoire du commerce de la Bulgarie. III. Rapports consulaires français. Documents officiels et autres documents (Svichtov, 1950), 207, 213 *et passim*.

29. A. Papadopoulo-Vretos, La Bulgarie ancienne et moderne sous le rapport géographique, archéologique, statistique et commercial (St. Petersburg, 1856), 217 *et passim*.

30. *Ibid.*

31. Aug. Viquesnel, Voyage dans la Turquie d'Europe (Paris, 1868), 326, 333.

32. H. de Hell, "Situation agricole et commerciale des côtes occidentales de la Mer Noire," in Courrier de Constantinople, 3-e année, No. 98 (23 January 1847). Cf. N. V. Michoff, 172-77.

33. Annales...., No. 26 (September 1868), 25-27, "Macédoine. Mouvement commercial en 1864-1865."

34. *Ibid.*

35. *Ibid.*, No. 32 (November 1879), 222-23, "Salonique. Commerce et navigation en 1877-1878."

36. *Ibid.*

37. Hr. Gandev, in Istoriia na Bŭlgariia I, (Sofia, 1961), 335.

38. Annales ..., No. 31 (July 1875), 163-64, "Kavala. Commerce et navigation en 1873."

39. *Ibid.*, No. 32 (November 1879), 209-10, "Enos et Dédéagh. Mouvement commercial en 1876."

40. N. V. Michoff, 602-03, 656 *et passim*, 710 *et passim*.

41. Annales...., No. 28 (May 1870), 72-76, "Production et commerce des laines dans la province d'Andrinople en 1867"; No. 30 (April 1872), 81-85, "Production et commerce de la soie en Roumélie"; No. 32 (November 1879), 199 *et passim*, "Adrinople. Mouvement commerciale en 1877."

42. A. Durand, France et Turquie au point de vue commercial et industriel (Paris, 1906), 55.

43. Annales..., No. 26 (September 1868), 21-24, "Commerce des principaux marchés de la Roumélie."

44. Archives du Ministére des Affaires étrangères de France. Correspondance consulaire, Philippopolis I (1857-91), f. 16, Champoiseau à Walewski (25 September 1858).

45. *Ibid.*, f. 20, Champoiseau à Walewski (1 February 1859).

46. Annales..., No. 28 (May 1870), 76-79, "Commerce et production de l'essence ou huile de rose (gulïaghi) dans les provinces d'Andrinople et Philippopolis."

47. *Ibid.*, 47-48, "Turquie. Mouvement général du commerce en 1859-1866."

48. G. Aubaret, "Province du Danube," in Bulletin de la Société de Géographie, IV-e série, 12 (July-December 1876), (Paris), 147-84; N. V. Michoff, Beiträge zur Handelsgeschichte Bulgariens (Officielle Dokumente und Konsularberichte). II. Österreichische Konsularberichte, Bd. II, (Sofia, 1945), 179, 302.

49. Cf. S. Damianov, Franciia i bŭlgarskata natsionalna revolutsiia (Sofia, BAN, 1968), 40.

50. *Ibid.*, 42. Cf. V. Paskaleva, 83.

51. S. Damianov, Frenskoto ikonomichesko pronikvane v Bŭlgariia ot Osvobozhdenieto do Pŭrvata svetovna voina 1878-1914 (Sofia, BAN, 1971), 108.

52. Archives du Ministère des Affaires étrangères de France. Bulgarie. Affaires commerciales 4 (1907-1917), f. 219 *et passim*, "Exposé du vice-consul de France à Varna Al. Mercinier sur l'exportation française en Bulgarie de 1906 à 1911."

53. E. Levasseur, Histoire du commerce de la France II, 618.

54. S. Damianov, Frenskoto ikonomichesko pronikvane v Bŭlgariia, 110.

D. J. Delivanis

Maritime War and Trade in Southeastern Europe, 1740-1920: The Case of France

Professor C. Svolopoulos has asked me to write a paper on the participation of France or Italy or Germany in maritime war and trade in Southeastern Europe, 1740-1920. As only France was a great power during all this period, it seemed logical to focus on France, inasmuch as the reports of the French consuls in Thessaloniki, Cavalla, etc., constitute a valuable source of information about developments in this part of the world.

As far as the choice of 1740 and of 1920 are concerned, let me stress that in 1740 the Ottomans were able to reconquer Belgrade, and thus, stop "the Austrian Drang nach den Osten" which permitted them for some decades to be less preoccupied with this question, whilst up to a certain degree peace prevailed in Southeastern Europe. In the same year France renewed her Capitulations on more favorable and permanent terms, thereby securing for French trade a preponderance in the eastern Mediterranean. Of course, Russia tried in 1770 to spur the inhabitants of Peloponnesos to revolution which met with complete failure and never abandoned the dream of southward expansion, nor that of coming in due order to replace the Ottoman empire. We see this in the treaties of Küchük Kainardji (1774), which opened the Black Sea to Russian vessels and to all ships, even if owned by Ottoman subjects, flying the Russian flag and secured to the latter Russian protection which benefited very much Greek shipowners; of Andrianople (1829); of San Stefano as the latter was revised in Berlin (1878); of London (1913); and of Sevres (1920, never ratified).

In order to judge maritime war and trade in Southeastern Europe in these years, it is necessary to stress:

— The latter was influenced substantially by the pirates who increased risks to shipowners, to owners of the freight and to both passengers end crew. It made imperative the arming of vessels and hiring extra seamen to deal with pirate attacks.

— Subjects of the Western powers, and so of France, were not tried by Ottoman courts, but by their own consular courts by virtue of the Capitulations; furthermore, they were practically exempt from Ottoman taxes.

— Normal relations between France and the Ottoman empire were interrupted more than once; war however was only first declared when Napoleon Bonaparte landed in Egypt in 1798, and after defeat of his fleet at Abcukir, when he tried without success to seize Syria and other Ottoman provinces; second, during World War I, in November 1914 after the attack of the Ottoman fleet against Russia in the Black Sea, and led to the dissolution of the Ottoman empire with the Treaty of Sevres (1920). The latter was replaced by the Treaty of Lausanne (1923), concluded, however, by the latter's successor — the Turkish Republic.

— Trade in Southeastern Europe, and particularly in the Ottoman empire, was unfavorably affected by pirateering and banditry making transport by both sea and land risky, and to a minor degree, by inflation in the form of continuous debasement of coins, and by continuous difficulties of the Ottoman agents in punctually meeting debt payments.

— Banks could not develop under these conditions outside Constantinople and Thessaloniki, as clearly shows the example of the Ottoman Bank (1840), with headquarters in London and main seat in Paris. It had a sprinkling of branches all over the empire, but local bankers ran their businesses outside the major cities at great risks.

It is under these conditions that we shall deal with French maritime war and trade in Southeastern Europe, and particularly with the following points:

1. volume of legitimate trade in both directions at stable and current prices;
2. volume of contraband in both directions as far as the latter could be ascertained with the means available;
3. composition of imports and exports;

 4. influence of wars;
 5. influence of pirate and bandit activity on both sea and land;
 6. nationality of those active in imports, in their channelling goods to the consumers, in exports, and in the concentration of the goods to be exported before being shipped;
 7. possibility of insurance against risks;
 8. taxation by authorities and by those who secured receipts illegally;
 9. profits of French suppliers;
10. profits of local suppliers;
11. profits of local intermediaries;
12. profits of French customers;
13. profits of local customers;
14. relation of the French trade with Southeastern Europe to the total French foreign trade in value and in volume;
15. relation of Ottoman trade with France to the whole foreign trade of the Ottoman empire.

After this, I will deal first with the wars affecting the Ottoman empire in this 180-year period, and then with maritime trade, and particularly with the above mentioned fifteen points.

Before dealing with these points it will be necessary to examine the wars between 1740 and 1920, to the extent that they affected the Ottoman empire's foreign trade. As already mentioned war broke out between France and the Ottoman empire in 1798-1802 and 1914-20. There were however, a number of wars involving the Ottoman empire which did affect trade with neutral France and neutral non-European countries, the latter with transhipment in Western Europe. Of course pirate activity was particularly intense before French occupation of Algiers and Tunis. Let me mention in this connection:

a.   the already noted Russo-Turkish War with the Orloff uprising in Peloponnesos in 1770, the defeat of the Ottoman fleet near Chios, and the loss by Turkey of the greatest part of the northern coast of the Black Sea: this war ended with the Küchük Kainartzi treaty of 1774;

b. the war between the Ottoman empire on the one side and Austria and Russia on the other (1787-90);

c. the wars of the French Revolution and Napoleon (1790-1815);

d. the Russo-Turkish War (1809-12);

e. the Greek Revolution (1821-30) which led to the Russo-Turkish War (1827-29), concluded by the Treaty of Andrianople in 1829, guaranteeing Greek independence from the Ottoman empire, and the Porte's compliance, as stipulated in this treaty, with whatever France, Russia and the United Kingdom would decide on the structure, the organization, and the frontiers of Greece;

f. the war waged against the Ottoman empire by its vassal Mehmet Ali (1832-39);

g. the Crimean War (1854-56);

h. the Russo-Turkish War (1877-78);

i. the war against Greece (1897);

j. the war against Italy (1911);

k. the two Balkan Wars (1912-13);

l. World War I (1914-20).

Naturally these wars except the last were carried out in a way which cannot be compared with the devastation of the two world wars, but they did not influence favorably the economy of the Ottoman empire, nor did they increase its foreign trade, and so of course, trade with France. Unfavorable repercussions of pirate activity have not to be omitted, but it may be said in this connection that through them the level of all economic aggregates was constantly lower than it would have been if the pirates could have been neutralized on a greater scale, or even completely. To a certain degree these effects diminished as pirates met with rather efficient defenses from their probable victims; as pirates refrained from periodically attacking Western European vessels, especially when warships of the nationality involved were in the area; as pirates preferred until 1830 to loot in those sea lanes which were relatively close to Algiers and Tunis; as Ottoman forces did their best, albeit not always efficiently, to protect Western European trade inasmuch as those in charge were afraid that the gradual decay of the Ottoman empire would induce foreign powers to claim damages, and thus lead to a deterioration of the relations of the

Western powers involved with the empire. This would have been even more probable if the Western powers had proof of Ottoman inefficiency to protect their own subjects, let alone those foreigners dealing with them. It has further to be stressed that the wars affecting the Ottoman empire were usually carried out on land and less on sea where the pirates held sway. For the latter obliged shipowners to increase investment in guns and men. They constituted accordingly a major problem until as already said, France's occupation of Algiers and of Tunis. Among the dozen wars mentioned before, some that had induced the French to undertake military action, with a view, one to protect their trade; two, to reaffirm their presence and strength in the Mediterranean as a whole, and particularly in those sea lanes through which their foreign trade was carried out; and three, to confirm their role as protector of all Catholics living in the Ottoman empire, are:

— the Russo-Turkish War (1770-74);
— the French Revolution and Napoleonic Wars, which led to the interruption of the diplomatic relations between France and the Ottoman empire (1798-1801), as well as of international trade by the British blockade;
— the war between the Ottoman empire and its vassal Khedive Mehmet Ali of Egypt;
— the war between Italy and the Ottoman empire;
— the Balkan Wars; and
— World War I.

Of course in those wars, but for the last, the respect of belligerent powers for private property, private claims, and agreements was complete and particularly as far as the subjects of Great Powers were concerned.

Thus six out of twelve wars had strong repercussions on the empire's foreign trade, and thus on the French importers and exporters. All of them were, however, weakened, first, by the continuous inflation raging in the Ottoman empire; second, by the very low taxation in force there inasmuch as the foreigners were not often obliged to bribe local employees as it rather frequently happened with the Ottoman subjects, mainly those living outside Constantinople; third, by the practical impossibility of the Ottoman authorities to proceed against foreigners protected by the Capitulations; fourth, by the latter's exemption from military service and from any obligation whatsoever connected with a foreign war or riot. The usual presence of Western, and particularly of French, warships in the Mediterranean constituted another important factor in favor of French foreign trade with the Ottoman empire, thereby permitting high profits without excessive risks.

Let me end by mentioning the two wars in which the Ottoman empire was not involved affecting French maritime trade with the latter: the American Civil War (1861-65) and the Franco-Prussian War (1870-71). The first deprived Western and Central Europe of cotton, indispensable for the textile industry, and so textile manufacturers were happy to get the Macedonian cotton produced on a grand scale in the province of Serres, and to a certain degree, in the province of Thessaloniki. Thus the exports westward increased substantially until the war ended in the United States, and American cotton exports to Europe resumed. The Franco-Prussian War reduced France's production and export inasmuch as its most industrialized areas, I mean Paris and the northeast of the country, had suffered much destruction and were occupied by the Germans who annexed by virtue of the Treaty of Francfort (May 1871) Alsace and Lorraine. This diminished industrial possibilities for France as far as manufactured goods were concerned until new investments to replace those lost were carried out in the Parisian area and in northeastern France. Of course this development had repercussions on both French imports from and exports to the Ottoman empire. Last but not least, large-scale slaughter of the Armenians both in 1885 and 1915, considering how numerous, how clever, how active, and how successful they were in the empire's economy and particularly in foreign trade, constituted another setback which of course affected unfavorably French trade with the Ottoman Empire.

1. In view of the continuous fluctuations of the various currencies, and even of gold and silver, it is not easy to present foreign trade tables for the eighteenth and nineteenth centuries and for the early nineteen hundreds. Values of commodities were calculated in local

monetary units, and they fluctuated so often and so much. It has to be added that the values declared at customs, particularly when foreign exchange controls are not applied, very often do not correspond to reality. It has also to be stressed that a fluctuating percentage of goods declared at customs was not paid for various reasons. It would have been preferable from this angle to consider the data of payments really carried out by the banks, but they have been destroyed after a certain period of time, and as a rule the banks are not ready to assign their staff to research this historical information, as they are needed for the banks' current operations. It has also to be considered that particularly in the years 1740-1920, private clearings were not forbidden and were rather often applied for various settlements. Under these conditions it is not worthwhile to include in this paper figures for currencies whose values remain unknown whenever settlements were carried out. It may simply be said that as the purchasing power of the subjects was not substantial in these years, imports were not very important whilst exports were unfavorably influenced by low productivity, by risk of robbery during transport to harbors, and by difficulty of transport owing to bad road conditions, to poor port facilities, and by inadequate transport to the few railways which started operating in the last decades of the last century.

2. Though it is not possible to evaluate more or less accurately the commodities cleared through customs, it is almost impossible to try to estimate the value of the commodities imported and exported illegally, inasmuch as Ottoman customs were no less notorious for being able to prevent the flow of contraband, owing to short staff, to the latter's tendency to avoid risks, and besides the Ottoman empire offered no overtime. It may thus be conjectured that contraband had been rather important inasmuch as it was considered an honorable job.

3. Imports from France included all manufactured goods, as Ottoman local industry before the end of the nineteenth century was practically non-existent, and as in 1900-1920 it was limited to the production of those consumer goods which did not require sophisticated machinery, skilled workers, and a satisfactory infrastructure. Colonial goods were transshipped via France, and then dispatched to the Ottoman empire. Thus they appeared at times as French exports to the Ottoman empire. Ottoman exports to France included, on a large

scale, cotton and tobacco, and on a lesser one, various agricultural products.

4. The influence of war on French foreign trade with the Ottoman empire has already been analyzed.

5. The repercussions of the pirate and bandit activity has also already been analyzed, as far as it touched on the Porte's foreign trade.

6. Those involved in French exports to the Ottoman empire were mainly French Levantines, Greeks, Jews, and Armenians established in the great ports, especially Constantinople, Thessaloniki, Smyrna, and Cavalla. Those who guided carried French goods from port of arrival to final consumers in towns and villages; were almost always Greeks, Jews, and Armenians; the contribution of Levantines was smaller, and that of the French themselves negligent. The same relation existed in the handling of Ottoman commodities exported to France, and the production of which was carried out to begin with by Turks, Greeks, Bulgarians, and Serbians.

7. Despite the development of insurance firms in Western and Central Europe their propensity to insure against risks in French trade with the Ottoman empire was not particularly great, as risks were substantial; as the possibilities to assess damages outside the great ports were not particularly developed; and as the volume of trade did not justify the elaborate and costly organization needed for rational operation.

8. Taxation of the French importers and exporters, as well as their collaborators enjoying the status of "Levantines," was very low thanks to the Capitulations. They permitted them to avoid largely the necessity of bribing local public officials, at least in comparison with bribes paid by those not protected by Capitulations.

9. The profits of French suppliers and of importers were substantial, provided of course the goods were not stolen by pirates or by bandits, nor destroyed by fire, neither lost on sea, except of course if the goods involved were insured against risks. It is practically impossible to assess the average profits as no data worth considering are available.

10. It is equally impossible to judge the importance of the profits of the local intermediaries, suppliers, and consumers who were exposed to substantial risks without the practical possibility of getting insu-

rance, and without the protection as a rule of the Capitulations, as they were Ottoman subjects.

11. We must not overestimate, both in absolute and in relative terms, the importance of French foreign trade with Southeastern Europe, which was until 1830 only the Ottoman empire; afterward the Balkan states were added.

12. The same applies to the Ottoman trade with France. After 1830 it was supplemented by Balkan states' trade with France.

It may be said, in conclusion, that the maritime wars in Southeastern Europe for 1740-1920, did not lead to great battles between France and the Ottoman empire except for the French fleet's destruction at Aboukir (1799) by the English fleet acting partly in behalf of the Ports, and the great Battle of Navarin (1827), where the Ottoman and the Egyptian fleets were destroyed by France, Russia, and England. Of course, trade in general, and so also French trade, came then to a standstill for some time; but otherwise repercussions of war were rather limited for the reasons we have explored.

Bibliography

Economic Structure of the Balkan Countries in the Eighteenth and the Nineteenth Centuries (Melissa, Athens, 1932) (in Greek).

Paparigopoulos C. and Karolidis P., *History of the Greek Nation* 6 (Athens, 1932) (in Greek).

Svoronos C., *Le commerce de Salonique au XVIIIe siècle.*

Vacalopoulos C., *Le commerce des ports de Salonique et de Cavala 1850-75 Balkan Studies* (1981), 22:1, pp. 85-108.

Barry Dennis Hunt

The Eastern Question in British Naval
Policy and Strategy, 1789-1913

...we are inclined to forget how impotent [sea power] is of itself to decide a war against great Continental states, how tedious is the pressure of naval action unless it be nicely coordinated with military and diplomatic pressure....

Julian S. Corbett (1911)

...we are attempting to maintain the largest Empire the world has ever seen with armaments and reserves that would be insufficient for a third-class military power.

General Brackenbury (1899)[1]

British governments have always faced dilemmas whenever they had to draw realistic connections between their many foreign interests and their limited military resources. In 1936, following the Abyssinian crisis, Admiral Sir Ernle Chatfield assessed the multiple vulnerabilities of Britain's scattered empire and concluded that it was "even open to debate whether it is really strategically defensible."[2] In this the First Sea Lord echoed frustrations that his nineteenth-century predecessors understood all too well. The clash between the illusions and realities of Britain's sea-based power was no less evident to those earlier statesmen, admirals, and generals who were charged with giving some substance to the image of *Pax Britannica*.

Britain's credentials as "mistress of the seas" rested, as the observations above suggest, not on any foundation of overwhelmingly superior and deployable military force, but on the peculiar system of making war she had developed throughout the eighteenth century and reapplied so successfully between 1789 and 1815, a system built on the foundations of very constricted military means; an army which was always tiny (and even more so by Napoleonic European standards) and a Royal Navy which, although numerically and qualitatively more than a match for its rivals, was also a surprisingly small force, its personnel even at its peak in 1810 reaching only 113,000 men. Sensibly and intelligently used, these resources were able to guarantee the security of the home islands and most overseas holdings. Offensively, however, they could produce only meager results unless, that is, they were also combined with Britain's immense commercial and financial resources to produce an instrument whose most powerful effects lay in its potential for creating and preserving the great Continental Coalitions needed to confront France on land. Her naval mastery so spectacularly won at Trafalgar in 1805 could not be directly exploited through Britain's military power alone. But placed in the service of an open-ended and opportunistic strategy of blockades, amphibious projections, monetary loans, grants, and arms transfers, that mastery was used to exploit cracks in the Napoleonic edifice and nurture those political circumstances that encouraged the rise of nations who ultimately did bring Napoleon to book. It was, therefore, as an instrument of alliance politics that Britain's maritime system exercised its most telling effects, and it would continue to do so throughout the period after 1815.

This ordering of instincts conditioned the British to view the Mediterranean as a means more than an end of their wartime policy. Until Napoleon's invasion of Egypt, their gaze was directed primarily toward its western end, between the Italian narrows and Gibraltar. Nelson's smashing of the French fleet at Aboukir Bay in 1798, Captain Sidney Smith's success at Acre, and General Abercrombie's destruction of the abandoned French army in Egypt did turn attention to its eastern reaches. And Malta, Corfu, and the Ionian islands were then occupied to forestall any further surprises. These islands' continuing value, however, lay mainly in their use as bases from which trade-defense operations were carried on. Not until after 1815, did the eastern Mediterranean begin to take on the appearance of something other than a secondary strategy cul-de-sac.

This is the place neither to advance general explanations of nineteenth-century British imperialism nor to account for the shifting nature of its main driving forces after the Napoleonic wars as *laissez-faire* political and economic ideas displaced those of the earlier mercantilists. Suffice it to emphasize that as much as Cobden, Bright, and the Manchester School hoped that the gospel of Free Trade, by binding nations together in a brotherhood of mutual interest, might help to eradicate some of the main causes of future wars, more practical British statesmen displayed remarkable consistency in their appreciation that some links would continue to exist between economic progress and the exercise of military power. Even before the 1860s and 1870s, when it became obvious that the ideal of a universal Great Commercial Republic was shared by few Europeans or others in Asia and Africa, the differences that divided individual British governments on defense matters turned essentially on the issue of how much the *Pax Britannica* did depend on military capabilities and of what kind. The global sprawl of British possessions, interests, and investments was vulnerable everywhere. However, its defense was justified; all governments agreed at least that it should be done as cheaply as possible. In this they had much in common with both their forebears and descendants. It was also generally acknowledged that the Royal Navy was the chief guarantor of imperial security, although even Lord Palmerston, who sensed better than most the potentials of sea power, too appreciated the limits of naval sufficiency:

> We do not want Egypt or wish it for ourselves, any more than any rational man with an estate in the north and a residence in the south would have wished to possess the inns on the north road. All he could want would have been that the inns should be well kept, always accessible, and furnishing him when he came with mutton chops and post-horses.[3]

Initially, Britain's global influence presumed that in overseas affairs she faced no serious competitors, and that in European matters, her policy makers continued to appreciate where her sea-based influence could and could not be brought to bear. When, after the 1870s, both her external monopoly and her industrial and naval supremacy were challenged directly, the illusion of defense on the cheap was revealed for what it was.

What is equally important to highlight about the post-Napoleonic British empire was its dramatically repositioned strategic center of gravity — away from the Atlantic towards India. It would likewise be misleading to overplay the timing, pace, and degree of what Professor Vincent Harlow called this "swing to the East."[4] Europe and the Americas would continue to top the list of British commercial priorities, although these, generally speaking, decreasingly required the props of overt military force. Since the late eighteenth century, this eastern thrust became the major facet of British economic, political, and military power. But Indian empire, and the regional sub-system by which other parts of Asia, the Indian Ocean, and the Pacific came under British influence were both at the same time strategic assets and liabilities. This reality transformed the Mediterranean from a strategic dea end into the nexus of Britain's whole strategic structure. The security of what Gerald Graham so aptly called this "Mediterranean Corridor" became fundamental to her foreign policy throughout the nineteenth century:

> Dominating all political discussions of Near East problems was the fear that Egypt and the Levant might fall into hostile hands and bar the land roads between London and Bombay. All the main foreign policy decisions that weie made in respect of the Ottoman Empire were influenced by, if not based on, the fact that these and adjoining provinces lay a-thwart the corridor that linked England with the East; and however meager the total of serviceable men-of-war in an era of parsimony and peace, lines of communication to India conditioned the normal distribution of British naval forces outside home waters.[5]

Early in the century, the Mediterranean squadron superceded the home or Channel forces as the foremost and indeed, throughout much of the century, Britain's only concentrated battle force. In 1816, the then Tory government decided to preserve its hold over the Mediterranean more firmly than ever before. In addition to Gibraltar, Malta, and the Ionian islands centered on the base at Corfu were retained (the latter until 1864) and garrisoned as Imperial fortresses. This departure was attacked at home by the Whig opposition on grounds of cost and as a threat to civil liberties. But Lord Castlereagh's policy suggested that defense arrangements predicated on accommodating the political aspirations of colonies and possessions heading toward self rule had to give way in these particular cases of preserving strategic bases from which British trade and interests had been previously threatened. "Our policy has been to secure the Empire against future attack. In order to do this we had acquired what in former days would have been thought romance — the keys of every great military position."[6] These Mediterranean bases, along with those covering the longer Cape of Good Hope route, were retained to sustain an already existing empire. Inevitably other Europeans viewed these defensive measures as preludes to more expansion, and the consequent rivalries they engendered only heightened the British sense of vulnerability. Of those rivalries, the most persistent and perplexing was that with Russia whose real ambitions concerning India and Turkey were never easily discernible to observers then or historians since. But, it was the coincidence of Russia's rise and Turkey's decline as empire that generated the essence of the "Eastern Question" which linked the Dardanelles and the Balkans to the central equation of power in Europe and Asia. The Eastern Question, in all its many guises, arose from the determination of all the Great Powers to deny Russia new gains from the decay of the Ottoman empire where, if the stake was the Balkans, Austrian concern was paramount; and if the Straits and Constantinople, those of Britain and France.

For the first several decades after 1815, the French continued to worry the British most. In part, this fixation represented ancient reflexes, reactivated in the 1830s by indications of renewed French meddling in the Iberian peninsula and occupation of Algiers. The publication in 1844 of Admiral Prince de Joinville's *Notes sur l'état des forces navales de la France* confirmed Britain's worst fears of a French naval revival, and for some years, up to the Crimean War, London directed its attention more to the threats of invasion or attacks on commerce in waters closer to home.[7] By 1869-70, France's activities in the Mediterranean were even more alarming. To the west, it appeared, Morocco and Tunisia were about to be incorporated with Algeria. In the east, French influence in Syria and Lebanon was growing, and in Egypt, de Lesseps' newly opened Suez Canal vividly symbolized the *de facto* control of France's bankers. Following the humiliation at the hands of Bismarck and Moltke in 1870, the French expanded their fleet, concentrating their most powerful units in Toulon, such that by 1888 their two-to-one superiority over the Royal Navy sparked another scare, resulting in the 1889 Naval Defense Act. It would take another ten years and a second naval act (the 1893 Spencer Program) before Britain's Two-Power Standard in battleships had been fully redressed, and she could, at the time of the Fashoda crisis, stare the French down in full confidence. By then, however,

Britain's calculations had to take into account the fact that, since the signing of the Franco-Russian Alliance in 1894, any warlike moves of alliance forces in unison would likely entail closure of the Suez Canal, a British naval withdrawal, and the extension of Russian power through the Dardanelles, Syria, and Asia Minor.

Russia, of course, was always better placed to menace the overland route to India, and access through the Dardanelles would give her Black Seas Fleet control over the entire Levantine coast. It was to deny this possibility that the British accepted the necessity of propping up Turkey as a protective buffer. The Ottoman empire, and more especially Constantinople, was, therefore, seen to be India's first line of defense against Russian interference. The possibility that Russia might outflank the Straits by moves down the Euphrates valley toward its confluence with the Tigris did not arouse British concerns until the 1840s. Even then, the Admiralty was not unduly alarmed, since there was, in that region, no potential base that could not easily be neutralized by some readjustments in the distribution of frigates and sloops on the East Indies station. Nor was it clear that, in this period at least, the Russians themselves had any consistent view of their own Eastern policy. No less than the British, they were concerned that no great power should have exclusive control of the Straits, and in 1870, they unilaterally dispensed with the restrictive Black Sea clauses of the post-Crimea Treaty of Paris, of which more presently. Russian imperial expansion after 1870 lacked any centrally divined basis beyond, perhaps, a willingness to use it as a lever to offset Britain's initiatives in the Balkans, Asia, or elsewhere, almost irrespective of the issues involved.

So long as the Turkish empire survived both external threats and internal challenges, the Dardanelles remained the key to British policy in the Levant. Efforts then to ameliorate Turkey's relations with her neighbors, and to encourage improvements in her internal management, inevitably led to conflicts between strategic imperatives that dictated support of the power that held the Straits; yet, humanitarian principles recoiled from Ottoman treatment of various minorities, Balkan and Armenian. The Balkans did not overly concern (or interest) British strategists, providing always that Austria, Italy, and Greece remained on friendly terms. The Italians in particular were seen as Britain's main conduit to the Triple Alliance powers, and the Italians, it was assumed, needed no reminders of the extent to which Royal Navy influence had forestalled outside interference in Italy's own unification in the 1860s, nor how much their colonial ambitions in North Africa and the Red Sea region were underwritten by the Anglo-Italian Mediterranean Agreement of 1887. During the Russian scare of 1878, a new factor did excite British strategic interests in this region. This was the so-called Big Bulgaria arrangement imposed by Russia on Turkey in the San Stefano Treaty of March 1878, through which Bulgaria's acquisition of an Aegean coastline would have helped her patron to bypass the issue of access to the Dardanelles. In the end, the Berlin Treaty (July 1878) restored the situation by denying Bulgaria its hoped-for southern coastline.

On Turkey's eastern marches, Anglo-Indian experts saw the Caucasus region as a place to preempt possible Russian incursions. During the Crimean War when British forces did advance to the Sea of Azov and occupied coastal sites, the Russians countered this threat by pinning down the Anglo-French army on the Crimean peninsula.[8] After the war, Russia did move in to the region and established a major base at Tiflis in Georgia. During the 1878 struggle, they also took over the Turkish provinces south of the Caucasus. British plans to counter these extensions militarily were — as will be seen — never fully developed. Fortunately, Disraeli's threats in 1878 to send the Indian Army into Turkestan, to despatch troops to Tiflis and to Malta, and to call up the fleet to Besika Bay were never transformed into action, but the possibilities revealed a good deal about British thinking and options. War was avoided in 1878, but Russian troops remained at Kars and Batum. Disraeli's acquisition of Cyprus as part of the Berlin settlement[9] was posited on the assumption that a base of operations designed to counter Russia's moves would contribute materially to Turkey's security. Cyprus's usefulness as a *place d'armes* that much closer than Malta, was suspect from the outset, however, and in any case, was completely overtaken by Britain's occupation of Egypt four years later.

These events served to point up the fact that neither military occupations of Turkey's peripheral areas nor bribery of local authorities could completely guarantee Turkey's imperial integrity. Local agitations could be handled or tolerated so long as they did not affect any European power's sphere of concern. But, when internal unrest or revolt threatened any portion of their interests, the strategic arguments for preserving the Ottoman status quo invariably overrode those that favored internal progress. This was the contradiction that every British prime minister and foreign secretary had to face. However much as individuals they abhorred Turkish incompetence or excesses, none of them until World War I deviated from the assumption that the Sultan was a more acceptable custodian of the roads eastward than any string of ambitious potentates. At no time in the first half of the century was this better illustrated than in the Syrian Crises of 1832-33 and 1839-40.

These crises were generated by the ambitions of Mehemet Ali, whose virtual independence as Egypt's Khedive emphasized Ottoman imperial weakness and invited interventions that could lead to a clash of European powers. In such a case, British forces could physically seize the Suez isthmus area, although not without making the situation worse. This determined the British to protect the route not from Cairo but from Constantinople through the use of Turkish armies backed by the sloops of the Mediterranean squadron. That hope collapsed in 1832 when Mehemet Ali's forces marched through Syria, defeated the Turks at Konieh, and threatened Constantinople itself. The Sultan's appeal for naval backing produced a squadron of Russia's Black Sea Fleet at the Golden Horn, but no immediate British response. More pressing crises in Portugal and Holland-Belgium, as well as worries in the West Indies and Ireland, meant that the Royal Navy's total of fourteen ships-of-the-line then in commission could not be safely or quickly reassigned. The reinforcement of Admiral Malcolm's forces in the Mediterranean with ships-of-the-line began finally in April 1833, and a counterdemonstration was begun at the end of May. By autumn, Malcolm had six battleships and by the following March (1834) a total of seven. These ships, backed up by a squadron still off Portugal, together with France's six, were more than a match for Russia's eleven or twelve.[10] But the response came too late to recover the situation. Eight months earlier, on July 8, 1833, Russia had signed with Turkey the Treaty of Unkiar Skelessi, providing for a mutual defensive alliance and containing a secret clause that closed the Dardanelles to all foreign warships. On paper, at least, Russia had gained very considerable security against the possibility of British access to the Black Sea where she could threaten Russian communications. Britain gained nothing beyond a reason to initiate the first serious official examination of her naval dispositions that in November 1838 indicated how the Royal Navy compared to others, including Russia, France, Egypt, Turkey, and the United States.[11]

In every other respect, this resolution of the 1832-33 crisis was incomplete. Mehemet Ali's threat to Constantinople was removed, but his control over Syria, which threatened both the Euphrates and Red Sea routes, was not. When in 1837 he precipitated the second phase of the crisis by his moves into central Arabia and the despatch of a column through Mesopotamia toward Baghdad and another along the Red Sea coast toward Aden, Palmerston moved without hesitation. A small expedition from Bombay captured Aden in January 1839, and in June, the East Indies Squadron under Sir Frederick Maitland stalled Kurshid Pasha's advance in the Persian Gulf by taking the island of Bahrein.[12] These preemptive grabs stalled the Khedive's Arabian ambitions with relative ease, and, incidentally, reinforced Britain's ability to control these areas and forestall future meddling in coastal tribal politics. Aden was held thereafter under lease from the Sultan of Lehej and proved to be an especially useful base and coaling station, reinforcing the notion that holding Indian Ocean and Persian Gulf by a combination of a small squadron and good harbors was in itself enough.[13]

But it was in the eastern Mediterranean that an overall resolution of the crisis had to be found. For there, despite steady reinforcement, the Royal Navy faced an overwhelming superiority of French and Egyptian forces. By the end of 1839, the British had available twelve ships-of-the-line (all third rate), seven frigates, and ten steamers. Three more line-of-battle ships stationed in the Tagus could be called in, although these were also assigned to cover home waters then left to the protection of a tiny force of eight brigs. That the Admiralty was prepared to run these risks says a good deal about the demands of the Navy's other stations in the East Indies, China, and the Americas which stretched her total of twenty-one ships-of-the-line then in commission.[14] This Mediterranean squadron faced a French force of more completely manned and larger ships, under the energetic leadership of Admiral Lalande, including seventeen of the line and twenty frigates of which eleven of the line were in the eastern Mediterranean. These were backed up by nineteen ships-of-the-line and twenty frigates of the Turkish Navy which had declared for Mehemet Ali and lay at Alexandria. That this distorted balance was never put to the test of battle owed everything to Palmerston's judgement that local Franco-Egyptian superiority was neutralized by his diplomatic triumph in creating the Four Power Convention of July 15, 1840 with Austria, Prussia, and Russia. It was this Continental coalition's guarantee of Turkey's integrity that covered Admiral Sir Robert Stopford's expertly executed joint operations in September along the Syrian-Lebanese coast, including the capture of Beirut, Tyre, Sidon, and finally, in October, the reduction of the St. Jean d'Acre fortress. There, as a result of excellent gunnery and not a little good fortune, and Sir Charles Napier's actions against the Egyptian army, resistance was finished.[15] Under the subsequent Alexandria conventions concluded by Napier, Mehemet Ali's wings were clipped. He was forced to give up conquests in Crete and Arabia, and was left with control of southern Syria and the hereditary succession of his family in Egypt.

For Britain the lessons were obvious. Success has come not because of any local military superiority but of a naval presence in league with a calculated diplomacy that understood how far the major powers were prepared to push for, or against, the Khedive's ambitions. This is not to underrate the risks had it come to a clash of French and Royal Navy units. In that case, Palmerston would have had to call in allied ships as indeed had happened in 1827-28 during the Greek independence crisis when British naval inferiority in the Aegean had required the assistance of a Russian squadron. As Lord Palmerston himself suggested — in words which modern students of deterrence theory might find congenial — his judgment here included the idea that any such deterioration of conditions locally always held the prospect of much more general consequences:

> We shall not be daunted by any superiority of naval force which she may choose or be able to send thither. We shall go to work quietly in our own way, in the presence of a superior force, if such there be, just as undisturbed as if it was laid up in ordinary at Toulon. France knows

full well that if that superior force should dare to meddle with ours, it
is war; and she would be made to pay dearly for war so brought on.[16]

This was the essence of what Canning earlier had called Britain's
"engine of menace."[17] What needs to be added, however, is that in
this crisis both Britain and France had strained their peacetime naval
establishments to the limits. Had the French government been able
to back its position with new war votes, Palmerston would have had
few options. The real basis of his "calculated gamble"[18] was his judgement that no such backing could be obtained in Paris. Nor should
it be assumed that Stopford and his captains had any illusions about
the risks they had run, or of the serious deficiencies in naval administration and reinforcement that the dash and skill of his subordinates
could not completely hide.

In general terms, the Syrian episode typified the way in which diplomacy and naval control worked in the service of Britain's standard
policy of preserving the Near East status quo through "concert"
action. And, it continued to work, as in 1854-55, when, with Turkish
agreement, Franco-British forces passed the Straits to attack Russia;
and at the 1856 Paris Treaty negotiations when Austria, Britain, and
France imposed a settlement that supposedly neutralized the Black Sea
and ended Russian threats to Constantinople. Again, in 1878, a British squadron was despatched to Constantinople, with Austrian
endorsement, to forestall renewed Russian penetration of the Balkans.
In other instances where concerted action was not possible, as in the
1863 Schleswig-Holstein question and the U.S. Civil War, independent British action was not taken. Nor, for example, was any military attempt made to stop French entry into Mexico or Indo-China
in the 1860s.

Nevertheless, the Crimean experience, did also suggest that the
practical military limits of that established policy had been stretched
severely or at least needed careful redefinition. What such a refined
strategy would continue to depend upon, in naval and military terms,
was not easily or quickly discerned. The mid-century Royal Navy,
for all that it remained a subject of domestic criticism and debate,
was nonetheless numerically and qualitatively superior to any of its
rivals. Its operational superiority was demonstrated — perhaps all
too clearly — when, in 1854, it achieved at a stroke what Nelson and

his "band of brothers" had taken endless years to win at Trafalgar — complete maritime supremacy and more, the virtual elimination of enemy shipping from the high seas. The fact was, between 1815 and 1854, the navy had survived four decades of government parsimony, and yet, preserved its traditional capabilities more or less intact. It had also preserved most of the administrative shortcomings in personnel, administration, and logistics that should have been addressed much earlier (or more completely); shortcomings that had attended the openings of most of Britain's previous wars in the eighteenth century. Like many of them, the Crimean War took the British by surprise. As a result, no serious preparations were made ahead of time. Many of these deficiencies would be tackled in the years that followed, most especially the perplexing issues of the new technologies of steam power and rifled naval artillery.[19] These questions would take years to sort out and would preoccupy naval minds to the end of the century and beyond. Yet, it is worth noting, by 1861 with her worldwide system of coaling bases, few of which were more than 4000 miles apart, Britain was better placed to protect her trade routes with steamships than any power was to attack them. The Crimean experience also revealed that a navy designed primarily to serve the needs of peacetime pressures and crises management, as an instrument of "meance," could not, under modern circumstances, be easily or rapidly enough transformed to war footing. Up to 1854, Britain had sought to to influence Russia, not to fight her. Few contemporary mid-century observers, however, could necessarily sense those changes in Britain's external circumstances that would now gradually end her preeminence in industrial, commercial, and naval terms.

It would be forcing the pace of historical reality to suggest that the Crimean War, followed in quick succession by the Indian Mutiny and the Second China War, spawned any genuine renaissance in British strategic thinking, most especially in terms of producing a comprehensive doctrine of empire defense or even some high-level interdepartmental machinery by which it might have been formulated. That would have to await the aftermath of the Boer War and the creation of the Committee of Imperial Defense in 1902. Yet, in comparison to what has been called a "remarkable.... poverty of constructive thought"[20] on such matters before the 1860s, that which followed is all the more noteworthy. Most often it would be advanced by "experts" outside of, or just on, the fringes of official government departments whose own "reform" efforts in this decade — epitomized by the Cardwell Army reforms — continued to be marred by excessive departmentalism and a preoccupation with spending reductions. The appearance of such new organs and institutions as the *Journal of the United Service Institution* (1857), *The United Service Magazine* (1859), the Royal Colonial Institute (1868), and the creation of the Army's Staff College (1859) at least provided the beginnings of new forums where defense matters could be examined in an increasingly open way.[21]

Of the more general causes for questioning the bases of Britain's maritime-imperial strategy in this period 1850-70, none was more pervasive or persistent than that of rapid technological changes associated with the "steam revolution." Its implications in terms of naval architecture have been mentioned. No less disturbing was the question of steam's applications to land communications. Throughout the rest of the century, the expanding network of railroads and telegraph cables conferred on Continental powers the potential for strategic flexibility that equalled, or even outdistanced, those previously monopolized by maritime powers,[22] and called into question the continued viability of amphibious strikes and blockades. However well successive British governments matched their competitors in battleship construction in the 1880s and after, there remained the question of whether in these changing geopolitical and technological circumstances, their power could be brought to bear. These doubts, as will be seen, go a long way in explaining much of the diffidence of Britain's Mediterranean policy and strategy in the final decades of the century.

A more immediate worry in terms of the Mediterranean and India was the dramatic redistribution of the balance of European military power that followed Germany's defeat of France in 1870. The resultant transfer of Britain's main invasion threat from home waters to the North-West Frontier contributed to what has been called the "Indianisation" of the entire framework of her strategic thinking until 1900.[23] Britain's reduced abilities to recruit allies from amongst European nations that were thereafter armed and ready to mobilize in response to their own immediate security needs further highlighted

India's importance as a source of manpower, and as a base of operations. No less significant was a growing feeling of India's vulnerability to threats of Russian invasion or of Russian-inspired insurrection, possibilities that loomed all the larger when, also in 1870, Russia took the occasion of France's humiliation to end the Crimean "System" by repudiating the Black Sea clauses.

There developed, at this point, a pronounced dichotomy in British strategic thinking between those who continued to back the established maritime strategy with its supporting Turkish (and Persian) alliances, and those who pressed for recognition that only in the North-West Frontier-Central Asia region could Britain confront Russia head on. Adjudicating between these competing perspectives was virtually impossible in the absence of any permament, high level, planning machinery in London. One cannot here account for the long delay in Britain's development of professional staffs — analagous to Germany's Great General Staff perhaps — that could balance competing Admiralty, War, Foreign, Colonial and India Offices, views and interests. In their absence, responsibility for such matters devolved to *ad hoc* committees, individuals, and various unofficial sources. This method of doing business accorded well with a characteristic disdain or mistrust of "expert advice" not only of most prime ministers and foreign secretaries but also of the services' heads, including most first sea lords and the Duke of Cambridge who as Commander-in-Chief of the army (1859-95) stifled most reforms. Intelligence branches were established by the War Office in 1873 and the Admiralty in 1883, but even these precursors of a modern staff structure continued to rely heavily on individual reports. Still they did provide highly detailed assessments, although their effect on policy was frequently negative in the sense that they served only to rule out certain options.

What did emerge from War Office studies in 1870 was a recognition that Britain should not become militarily involved in Europe where, since strategic calculations were now governed by forces in being (or near being) of several hundreds of thousands, Britain's power might well be ignored. Only on questions where her maritime power could be applied — as in the Mediterranean — did she still count militarily. It was this reaffirmation that gave impetus to London's (or Whitehall's, as distinct from Simla's) attempts to come to grips with perceived shifts in Russia's Turkish policy after 1870. Evidence that Russia had absorbed the lessons of Prussian-Clausewitzian methods, of major reforms in her army and navy, of new concentrations in Bessarabia and Transcaspia, and the construction of support fleets in the Black and Caspian Seas, all pointed to a disturbing new potential which allied to the forces of Pan-Slavism and Pan-Arabism directly threatened the Balkans and Suez areas. Much of what was discovered about these activities turned out to be of academic interest only. What they illustrate about British options as seen by some of her more perceptive experts is nonetheless important.[24]

Military intelligence assessments undertaken in 1870 concluded that, while Russia had made impressive improvements since the Crimean War, they were still incomplete and would limit her offensive potentials for the immediate future at least. Less reassuring however, was the conclusion that her improved conscription, logistics, and railroad systems had conferred new capacities of strategic mobility and flexibility that made her virtually invulnerable to invasion by any single power and no less impervious to amphibious probes on her peripheries. This latter point was reinforced by Lieutenant General Sir John L.A. Simmon's assessment[25] which emphasised the absence of any sensitive position that if taken would force Russia to terms quickly. Attempts to repeat an amphibious strategy of attrition, as at Sebastopol, were now simply closed off by Russia's abilities to counter coastal lodgements before they could be consolidated to produce a decision. Simmons argued, therefore, that the only way to counter Russia in the Balkans was to forestall moves likely to increase her influence in that area by supporting resistance movements in Armenia and the Caucasus. His reasoning presumed active Turkish cooperation and the existence of a Turkish army that could resist invasion from across the Danube, thereby securing Royal Navy communications into the Black Sea. Even so, without allied support, British forces could not be committed without first increasing the size of the Mediterranean squadron, defensive improvements to Malta, and additional war anchorages in the Aegean and possibly the Black Seas, to neutralize any inland Russian advances. Simmon's recommendations, thus, aimed at the exercise of naval superiority in the Black

Sea off the Danube, the despatch of British agents to direct the Turkish resistance movements, and expert assistance to the Turks to modernize the Quadrilaterial and Armenian fortresses and their linking land communications.

Had these recommendations been given effect, they might have helped to preserve Turkish integrity as an instrument of deterrence, but not as a militarily conclusive strategy. They assumed a worse-case situation — that is, Britain acting alone — and illustrated an attempt to square the circle as after 1870 British strategy remained focused on the issues of secure sea lanes and an adequate Turkish buffer. What they did show was that *without allied support*, Britain retained her traditional capabilities, but only to pursue an open-ended or indeterminate strategy. Her dilemna was partially alleviated by the 1878 Berlin Congress and the Cyprus Convention and her later occupation of Egypt and the Sudan (1882-85). Russia's collateral occupation of Merv and Penjdeh, her growing ascendancy over Persian affairs, and the appearance in India of a powerful and erudite military bureaucracy led by such eminences as Lords Roberts and Kitchener, would see more and more a tendency for Simla's view of India's defense to supercede Whitehall's. Interestingly, at the time of the 1885 Penjdeh crisis, the only way the War Office could contemplate India's defense was by means of an expedition to Batum. And until 1890, the concept of using Turkish armies to fight diversionary operations persisted despite the rift in Anglo-Turkish relations that began with the occupation of Egypt. By 1896, the steady widening of that rift had removed one of the major reasons for Britain's desire to preserve the Sultan's integrity. By then too, there had developed a tacit awareness that India could not be defended at all. In 1887, following receipt of an Indian Mobilisation Committee report that had urged stopping Russia in Afghanistan, General Henry Brackenbury, director of Military Intelligence in London, had pressed for a clear definition of a boundary line beyond which Russian expansion would not be tolerated and of what reinforcements and operational designs would be employed.[26] In his response, Salisbury made clear his doubts whether such a line was possible:

"making war with Russia all over the world" is an empty phrase unless we command the Turkish army; and I think it is as certain as any diplomatic forecast can be that we never shall have command of the Turkish army.[27]

What emerged then from studies carried out by London and Simla, between 1887 and 1892, was an awareness that without heavy reinforcements from the United Kingdom, Indian resources alone could not deal with Russia; that, if war did break out, operations in central Asia would have to be supported by simultaneous actions in the Baltic, the Black Sea, and the Far East aimed at exhausting Russia and forcing her toward a favorable peace; and that, therefore, all decisions regarding Russian policy, even with respect to India, would be taken by the Cabinet in London, and not by Simla.[28]

During these same years, the Admiralty was preoccupied with other issues, and not until 1892, did the Naval and the Military Intelligence departments undertake any joint approach to the Straits question. Until 1889, when its Two-Power Standard was formally reasserted, the Admiralty's main worry was to preserve whatever naval materiél it could from governments — Liberal and Conservative — that were bent on trimming estimates to pre-Crimean levels. Although, by the early 1870s the Naval Lords felt confident about the Navy's commitment to steam and iron technology, they still had to juggle the impacts of dockyard closures, personnel cuts, and after 1870, a sharp drop in new iron-clad construction. Moreover, reductions of some 40 to 50 *percent*[29] in ships assigned to overseas policing functions raised problems inasmuch as they were frequently expected to handle responsibilities left uncovered by the War Office's coincidental recall of its colonial garrisons. These reductions implied that more naval resources would be available in European waters, but they were motivated more by cost than strategic considerations. The cuts did not rest on a fully developed doctrine of Imperial Defense, but reflected rather the continuing piecemeal approach to policy making in which economy was assumed to be synonomous with efficiency. The Admiralty's efforts to prevent them from cutting too deeply concentrated, therefore, on the argument of secure sea lanes and the safety of the trade on which Britain depended for her survival. When years later, in 1901, Lord Selborne told his cabinet colleagues that "Its Credit and Its Navy seem to me to be the two main pillars on which the strength of this country rest, and each is essential to the other,"[30] he was mouthing a sentiment that no nineteenth-century cabinet disputed. It was this argument that the Admiralty marshaled to preserve naval spending at acceptable levels both before 1889 and also afterward when other powers openly challenged the Royal Navy with their new "shoot at sight" *guerre de course* forces.

This use of trade defense as a budget rationale did not mean, however, that the Admiralty had come to any clear consensus on operational doctrine regarding the merits of blockades by battle squadrons to contain enemy raiders, the use of overseas cruiser forces, or of escorted convoys. The first attempt at a systematic approach to these questions was carried out by the Carnarvon Commission of 1879 which revealed just how superficial and amateurish official thinking was. The testimony of the First Sea Lord, Sir Astley Cooper Key, offered little beyond vague generalities about preserving "command" and "covering the seas with our cruisers." His disingenuous admission that no studies of convoy methods under modern conditions had been contemplated, his unquestioning faith in the continued viability of battleship blockades, and his inability, if not unwillingness, to supply the commission with detailed technical information said too much about official naval thought.[31] Although the Royal Commission's findings were overtaken by the 1880 change in government, they did make clear at least the extent to which Britain then did depend on trade for survival, and established in detail Admiralty, War Office, and colonial responsibilities for cruisers and defended coaling stations. As to requirements in European waters, the commissioners worried that steam propulsion had undermined blockade, but given the Admiralty's hesitations and circumspection could do little more than call for an immediate increase in the fleet to put it on a war footing. Britain's ability to outbuild her rivals was an important long-term asset, but it would mean little in a modern war in which forces-in-being mattered more. Because its terms of reference precluded examination of the "Imperial Fortresses" of Gibraltar, Malta, Bermuda, and Halifax, the Carnarvon Commission devoted little direct attention to the Mediterranean. It was assumed that, in war, trade there would either be covered by the battlefleet or be diverted via the Cape, an assumption repeated in subsequent studies by the Admiralty's

Foreign Intelligence Committee set up in 1883 (renamed the Naval Intelligence Division in 1887) partially as a result of navalist agitation led by Captain J.C.R. Colomb, Admiral Charles Beresford, and others pushing for a larger navy and a planning organization to direct its use.[32]

This public agitation begun in 1883 with W.T. Stead's famous "Truth About the Navy" articles in the *Pall Mall Gazette*, substantiated by a report of Admirals Dowell, Vesey Hamilton, and Richards (the "Three Admirals Report") on the 1887-89 fleet exercises that revealed discrepancies about steam ships' abilities to evade blockades, and led to the 1889 Naval Defence Act.[33] This important milestone ended the transitional phase in Admiralty building policy by authorizing the *en bloc* construction of eight large *Royal Sovereign* battleships. Also, the approval for two smaller battleships, thirty-eight cruisers, four gunboats, and eighteen torpedo-gunboats finally gave substance to those war footing demands, in theory at least. But giving strategic direction to this massive increase in materiél was another matter, particularly as the act also set in train a building race with France and Russia that would not be fully redressed without another major building program in 1893.

Since 1888, the French had begun to redistribute and concentrate their newer units at Toulon, leaving comparatively weaker forces in the Reserve and Channel squadrons in the north (Cherbourg and Brest). In November 1889, the British responded by upgrading their Mediterranean squadron from eight to ten battleships and two armored cruisers. The next month, they restructured the Channel squadron of older ironclads into a strong unit of four battleships and two cruisers to be based on Gibraltar as an immediate Mediterranean reinforcement, should war with France threaten. Home defense was left to a reorganized force of four port-guard ships and nine coast-guard ironclads backed up by other reserves to be mobilized. Even by the early 1890s, however, new French building and the fortification of their controversial base at Bizerta had undermined official confidence in these moves to neutralize France in the west. Too, in the eastern Mediterranean, where the on-going deterioration of the Turkish navy since 1878 had reduced it, in British eyes, to operational irrelevance, the creation of Russia's modern Black Sea squadron of five new battleships posed new possibilities of amphibious operations anywhere along the coast from Varna to the mouth of the Bosphorus. Constantinople lay open to attacks that could outflank the land fortifications (between Tchekmedji on the Sea of Marmora and Derkos) that Simmon's engineers had worked on in 1876-77. The only response the Admiralty could devise against this threat of a Russian *coup de main* against Constantinople was to divide her own Mediterranean forces into two squadrons—one based at Gibraltar, the other at Malta. The latter, the Levant Squadron, was to be kept at five battleships, equal, or superior, to the Black Sea squadron, and was ordered to cruise east of Cape Matapan within 48 hours of Besika Bay. How it was to be brought into action by itself, probably without Turkish assent and with the French fleet still unaccounted for, would remain the crucial strategic question.[34] As an instrument of menace or deterrence — *à la Palmerston* in 1840 — this decision had some merit. Operationally, it had little credibility since in the case of Russia's acceptance of a challenge, or worse one supported by France, Britain's bluff could be too easily called. And once Russia took Constantinople and the powerful Dardanelles defenses, no combination of British military and naval forces could restore the situation. It was this obvious disparity between her interests and her capabilities that provoked the joint DNI-DMI studies in 1892.

In the end, these studies confirmed the worst.[35] They suggested that a force of 10,000 troops, given some improbably favorable circumstances and luck, could hold the Dardanelles shores. They could not, however, preempt a Russian move on Constantinople, and therefore, any notions of passing the Straits, as in 1807, 1854, and 1878, with a view to strikes along the Black Sea coast were impracticable. Consequently, there was no alternative to the policy of bluff. However, in 1892, Salisbury resisted this bleak assessment of Britain's deteriorating strategic position and continued to argue that considerations of "prestige" alone demanded that some solution be found. Nevertheless, even he had realized since the 1887 War Office — Indian Army mobilization studies that without the energetic backing of Turkey's armies, any Black Sea projections were ruled out.[36] Nor did the situation improve as evidence of continued French building (the Gervais Program of 1891) and increasingly intimate Franco-Russian relations (their alliance was signed in January 1894 and announced in June 1895) highlighted the degree to which the Mediterranean balance had turned against Britain. The result was the naval scare of 1893 and the passing of what amounted to a second Naval Defence Act of the Spencer Program of new *Majestic* class battleships, six cruisers, and thirty-six destroyers; although it was not until 1898 that their appearance on station reestablished the naval situation.

For the next few years after 1892, the cabinets of Rosebery and Salisbury (and their admirals and generals) faced a nightmare not so much because they equated Franco-Russian capabilities with any intentions of actually going to war, but rather in view of the Mediterranean strategic situation following from their alliance, and Turkey's inaction, that Britain herself could not now contemplate any forward foreign policy for fear of generating a crisis. This dilemma lay at the base of what became a running and largely unresolvable debate over naval dispositions. Where to concentrate the fleet — at Gibraltar, Malta, or Alexandria — to meet the French first, to cover the Atlantic and Channel, or the Levant, or all three? The question could not be answered easily, or prudently, without divining ahead of time the operative external circumstances. This may help to explain the absence of any comprehensive war plan or fleet orders for some time to come. In the interim, the only option open was to maintain the Levant or Eastern Squadron, in Lord Spencer's words, "as an act of bounce." As the first lord informed his commander-in-chief in the Mediterranean in May 1894, "It is a question of bluff, but it has so far succeeded..."[37] There were, of course, other factors and issues pressing in on British options in these years — the Sino-Japanese War (1895), the Venezuela Crisis with the United States, difficulties with France on the Niger and the Nile (1897-98), and of course, with Germany over the Kruger Telegram of 1896 and the Tirpitz Naval Law of 1897 — all of which suggested that a policy of holding the line and little more was prudent.

These dilemmas are, perhaps, best illustrated by Britain's response to the Armenian massacres of 1894, her efforts through 1895 to achieve Concert action for Turkish reforms, and the decision to back up these moves by ordering Admiral Seymour and the fleet to visit Beirut, Alexandretta, Marmoris, and Mitylene. The squadron arrived at Budrum in early July, and, throughout the summer, cruised the Greek Archipelago, and then, in late September, left Salonika for Lemnos. At that point, when Salisbury played with the idea of ordering it into the Straits, he ran headlong into the opposition of his cabinet, and above all, the Admiralty. Admiral Frederick Richards left no doubts about his grasp of the wider situation. The real danger in his view was:

> ...of opening up the Eastern question with Turkey as an enemy and Russia and France as very shaky and dangerous abettors. This is a political question, but one of a nature to which the Admiralty cannot be indifferent, as the passage of the Dardanelles would be the logical ending to the present policy of demonstrating with the Fleet in the face of Europe, while the other signatories to the note are doing nothing but urging us to put the fat in the fire.
>
> To attempt to force the Dardanelles under these conditions would in my judgment be an act of madness.[38]

British historians have made a good deal of Salisbury's "belligerence" in this instance, of his resentment of his colleagues' timidity, and his well-known mistrust of "expert" advice. Whatever his motives or assessments of his external adversaries, his "calculations" concerning his domestic backers were seriously flawed. His cabinet's decision did make it clear, however, that the strategy of defending India via Constantinople and the Straits was finished. Active diplomacy in Turkey was closed off, and military-naval offensives elsewhere had been ruled out. Salisbury's decision to focus thereafter on "our position in the Nile and withdraw as much as possible from all responsibilities at Constantinople"[39] did not represent a change in British policy objectives concerning the Near East, but was rather, one of means. What also became evident was that since Britain could neither provide, nor bring to bear, the kinds of military resources needed to handle possible "worst case" strategic situations, her policy and diplomacy must be aimed at preventing their occurence in those extreme forms.

In the 1898 Fashoda crisis, Salisbury confronted a divided and unsupported France and achieved a victory in bluff-calling no less impressive than Palmerston's. But his triumph offered only a brief respite before the outbreak of war in South Africa (1899-1902) brought home again Britain's vulnerabilities in too many other places. Even as the trauma of this Anglo-Boer struggle unfolded and set in motion long-needed reforms in higher defense organization that later included the creation of the Committee of Imperial Defence (CID) and a General Staff for the army, Salisbury committed Britain to an accommodation with the U.S. in the Caribbean and Western hemisphere, to the Anglo-Japanese Treaty (1902), and to the *Entente Cordiale* (1904) with France over African and other colonial questions. Russia's humiliation at Tsushima in 1905 would be followed up by the new Liberal government's pursuit of an "Asian" settlement in 1907. The latter, though intentionally imprecise about its Persian Gulf and Turkish Straits aspects, did defuse the Indian frontier problem bringing to an end, in Sir Edward Grey's words, "the old policy of drift, with its continual complaints, bickerings and dangerous frictions."[40] Since, however, no similar arrangement that might accommodate Germany's imperial and naval ambitions was possible, this diplomatic "revolution" also revolutionized Britain's strategic situation by forcing its center of gravity away from the Mediterranean to the North Sea. And, thereafter, strategic priorities everywhere would come to be determined by that northern perspective. This is not to suggest that Britain could, or did, ignore her overseas imperial interests in India, the Near East, or anywhere else, but rather that, through its confrontation with the German High Seas Fleet, the Royal Navy covered empire communications everywhere else until 1918. By 1912, the failure of the Haldane mission to Berlin made it clear that Britain's efforts to improve relations with Germany (and to circumscribe her *de facto* commitments to the *Entente* powers) had failed. When, also in 1912, Germany's supplementary naval estimates — the *Novelle* — pushed the naval arms race to break point, the British were left with no options but to reorder their strategic priorities to face the greatest threat. Winston Churchill's attempts to withdraw the Royal Navy altogether from the Mediterranean produced some painful soul searching at home, but, in the end, it became clear that his reasons were unanswerable. With her naval and military resources committed beyond their limits, there was no alternative to viewing the Mediterranean as a secondary theater where only resources sufficient to hold Malta and Egypt, and to cement her commitments to France and Russia, would be kept.

The full impact of this shifting northward focus was not immediately apparent in terms of British naval and military dispositions. The Mediterranean Fleet continued until 1905 to be the Royal Navy's primary one, its strength maintained at ten battleships, actually rising to fourteen in 1902.[41] This was due, in part, to the influence of Admiral Sir John Fisher who took over as Mediterranean commander-in-chief (1899-1902) just before the outbreak of the Boer War. His worry that his forces were still numerically inferior to the combined French and Russian squadrons, of fourteen and five respectively, formed the basis of his bitter harangues of the Admiralty, pointing out that his station was still "The vital point of a Naval war." As he informed the First Lord in December 1900:

> you can no more change this than you can change the position of Mount Vesuvius, because geographical conditions, Sebastopol and Toulon, and the Eastern question, will compel the Battle of Armageddon to be fought in the Mediterranean.[42]

In 1904, however, by which time Fisher had returned to London to initiate the controversial personnel, scrapping, manning, and redistribution reforms associated with his name, the thrust of all his schemes was to meet the German threat which Admiral Reginald Custance as DNI (1899-1902) had been warning about since 1900.[43] These policies showed their impact on the Mediterranean Fleet as it was cut first to eight battleships, then after 1907 to six, to provide men and resources for his new Channel and Atlantic Fleets to which the newest ships were assigned. Such war planning as was carried out under Fisher's guidance in 1907-08, and again under Admiral Wilson in 1910-11, when it did deal with the Mediterranean, was plagued by the same ambiguity and amateurishness that characterized all naval planning before 1914, and was echoed in the unstructured, hesitant, and secretive way the Admiralty dealt with their French counterparts after 1904.[44] Generally, from 1905 to 1912, official naval thinking assumed that, at the outbreak of war, all but a few cruiser forces would be recalled to home waters. Nor did the Italian and Austrian navies occasion much alarm, their potential being more than offset by the French and Russians; that is, until 1910, when it became known that both these powers had committed themselves to the construction of *Dreadnought* battleships.[45]

In War Office thinking, there was for some time a similar residual carryover of earlier assumptions, especially concerning India's defense. The pessimism that characterized London's and Simla's planning, particularly since the admission of the navy's inability to force the Dardanelles, left no acceptable alternatives, hinged mainly on Lord Kitchener's and the Indian Army's demands for massive troop reinforcements (by 1904, some 158,000). As late as 1906, several months before Grey became foreign secretary, Kitchener continued to draw up schemes for India's direct defense as an alternative to a Russian *entente*. By then (as early as May 1904) the War Office at home had already begun within the CID to challenge India's primacy in defense planning and to assert its own claim for the British army to be something more than a source of reinforcements for Kitchener, a process which was given its most important push by the start of secret Anglo-French staff talks in December 1905.[46]

Perhaps two of the more interesting assessments completed in this period were those initiated in July 1906 by the CID's request for an Admiralty and War Office reexamination of the problems of forcing the Dardanelles to take Constantinople.[47] The Admiralty's response, prepared by the DNI, Captain C.L. Ottley, and submitted in August, concluded that in light of modern naval defensive matériel — especially mines — a ships-alone operation was "almost out of the question." A transit of the Straits might be possible only after a secret and well-prepared combined operation had seized, or destroyed, the Dardanelles defense. Risks of failure, especially to Britain's broader imperial interests, he warned, would have to be very carefully weighed. In this reaffirmation of the earlier 1892 studies, it might be noted, worry about the French fleet was no longer a factor. The Army's assessment, prepared by Colonel Charles E. Callwell of the DMO's Strategic Section — an acknowledged expert and advocate of inter-service cooperation — similarly rejected the idea of independent naval action. He went further, however, to argue that the difficulties of opposed landings were now such as to make them "virtually impracticable" and that he could not recommend an attempt at the Dardanelles, or anywhere in Turkey. This pessimistic judgment was accepted by the CID in February 1907[48] who then also took the highly unusual step of ordering the destruction of all copies of the Callwell Memorandum, lest its contents become known and remove the value of even the threat of such an action in the future. Unfortunately, seven years later when Callwell was called upon to recount its contents and conclusions, these gueries were brushed aside by a Winston Churchill then committed to a Dardanelles offensive that the few who knew about it could stop.[49]

The culmination of the policy of concentrating strength closer to home waters came in 1912 when the Admiralty tried to withdraw all the remaining battleships in the Mediterranean. Germany's addition, under the 1912 *Novelle*, of a permanent third battle squadron of the High Seas Fleet pushed the building race to its crisis. The Royal Navy's twenty-two battleships in home waters (including six in the Atlantic Fleet at Gibraltar) were now faced with a standing force not of seventeen battleships and four battle-cruisers but one of twenty-five and twelve respectively. Despite Foreign Office alarm about the loss of British influence and prestige, and War Office demands for additional troop allocations from India and the United Kingdom to hold Egypt and Malta, the cold reality was that the Royal Navy simply had neither the resources in *Dreadnoughts* nor trained crews to meet the more immediate threat of German superior numbers in the North Sea. As Churchill summed up the situation in May 1912:

> ...It wd be vy foolish to lose England in safeguarding Egypt. Of course if the Cabinet and the House of Commons like to build another fleet of Dreadnoughts for the Meditern. the attitude of the Adm'l will be that of a cat to a nice fresh dish of cream. But I do not look upon this as practical politics. ... But if we win the big battle in the decisive theatre, we can put everything else straight afterwards. If we lose it, there will not be any afterwards. London is the key of Egypt. Don't lose that.[50]

Several weeks later, he reiterated the navy's predicament with a warning about the dangers of maintaining a battle fleet in the Mediterranean for "appearances" sake only:

> It would be a bluff which would deceive nobody. The influence and authority of the Mediterranean Fleet is going to cease, not because of the withdrawal of the Malta battleships, but because of the completion of the Austrian and the Italian Dreadnoughts. It will cease certainly and soon whether the Malta battleships are withdrawn or not,...

The power will have passed automatically to others, and only the empty but expensive symbols will remain. The Malta battleships left in the Mediterranean will in time of peace be only a pretence of strength which everyone will see through; and in time of war, a loss serious in themselves - still more serious by their subtraction from the decisive theatre.[51]

No less important, the personnel of Britain's four *Duncans* and two *Swiftsures*, soon to be outclassed by the ten new *Dreadnoughts* of the Italian and Austrian fleets, were needed to man newer more powerful ships then building at home. Here was the tacit admission that since Britain had neither the time, resources, nor political commitment to build another squadron for the Mediterranean, the outer limits of the Anglo-German contest had been reached. Beyond providing a defensive capability in the Mediterranean based on a cruiser squadron, and destroyers and submarines operating from Malta and Alexandria, there was little more the Royal Navy could do on its own. Eventually the "Malta Compromise," worked out in May-June 1912, to meet Foreign Office and War Office complaints, boiled down to the provision of at least sufficient naval units there to give the French an edge on any Italian-Austrian combination. This resulted in a promise to keep a force of two to three, eventually four, *Invincible* class battle-cruisers to watch and track the enemy fleet. But even this modest commitment proved difficult to meet. *Inflexible* arrived on station in November 1912, but was not reinforced by *Indomitable* and *Invincible* until August 1913. By the outbreak of war, only three were assigned to Admiral Berkeley Milne's Mediterranean command. During the 1912-13 Balkan Wars crisis when a great international flotilla assembled at Salonika and Constantinople, Milne was reinforced temporarily by the eight *King Edward* pre-*Dreadnoughts* of the Third Battle Squadron to forestall any major move by Austria and to demonstrate Britain's continuing stake in Mediterranean events.

It was against this backdrop that the final details of Anglo-French cooperation were worked out. These plans, if such they can be called, to meet an Italian-Austrian challenge in war left a great many questions unanswered. Not the least of these was an obvious contradiction between Admiralty efforts through its attached naval missions to discourage the ambitions of the Greek and Turkish navies and the Foreign Office's search for new *Dreadnought* building contracts for their small but potentially important fleets. Whereas Germany and Britain did manage to settle differences over railroad construction in Turkey by early summer 1914, competition for naval contracts threatened an already precarious Mediterranean naval equilibrium more.[52] Most of those dilemmas, if not resolved, were at least reduced to manageable proportions by Italy's decision in 1914 to remain neutral. It was that decision that rendered the Mediterranean a secondary war theater for Britain. And the tragic failure of Churchill's Dardanelles-Gallopoli initiative the following year insured that it remained secondary to the wearing logic of the distant blockade in the North Sea and the awful logic of attrition on the Western Front.

Notes

1. Julian S. Corbett, *Some Principles of Maritime Strategy* (1911). General Sir Henry Brackenbury, Cmd. 1789, Report of the Royal Commission on the War in South Africa, Appendix E, minute dated 15 Dec 1899.

2. As quoted in L. R. Pratt, *East of Malta, West of Suez: Britain's Mediterranean Crisis, 1936-1939* (1975), p. 3.

3. Lord Cromer, *Modern Egypt* (1908), Vol. I, p. 92.

4. V. T. Harlow, *The Founding of the Second British Empire, 1762-1793* (1952), Vol. I, pp. 62-145.

5. Gerald S. Graham, *The Politics of Naval Supremacy; Studies in British Maritime Ascendancy* (1965), p. 65; also his, *Tides of Empire: Discursions on the Expansion of Britain Overseas* (1972).

6. *Hansard*, 1st Series, XXXII, p. 1104.

7. C. J. Bartlett, *Great Britain and Sea Power, 1815-1853* (1963), pp. 155-64, *et passim.*

8. Karl C. Revells, "An Eye on Sevastopol: British Naval Policy and Operations During the Russian War, 1853-1856." (Ph. D. diss., Queen's University, Kingston), chapters 8 and 12.

9. Robert A. Spencer, "Great Britain and Turkey, 1878-85." (Ph. D. diss., St. John's College, Oxford, 1950), pp. 66-78.

10. Bartlett, *Great Britain and Sea Power*, pp. 88-95.

11. Adm. 3/264, Political Secretary, Charles Wood, memorandum (Nov. 1838) and Adm. 1/3488, Admiralty memo., 18 Feb. 1839.

12. *Ibid.*, 1/219; 2/1695, folios 270-71.

13. Gerald S. Graham, *Great Britain and the Indian Ocean; A Study in Maritime Enterprise, 1810-1850* (1967), pp. 274-80, 282-305.

14. Bartlett, *Great Britain and Sea Power*, pp. 136-38.

15. see: W. B. Rowbotham, "Naval Operations on the Coast of Syria," *Journal of the Royal United Services Institution* (Nov. 1952), pp. 566-78.

16. Sir H. L. Bulwer, *Life of Viscount Palmerston* (*1870-76*) II, pp. 308-309.

17. H. V. Temperley, *The Victorian Age in Politics, War and Diplomacy* (1928), pp. 49-50.

18. Kenneth Bourne, *Palmerston: The Early Years, 1784-1841* (1982), p. 617.

19. See: N.A.M. Rodger, "British Naval Thought and Naval Policy, 1820-1890: Strategic Thought in an Era of Technological Change," in C. L. Symonds, ed., *New Aspects of Naval History* (1981), pp. 140-52.

20. W. C. B. Tunstall, "Imperial Defense, 1815-1870," in *Cambridge History of the British Empire* (1961), Vol. II, p. 824.

21. See: Jay Luvaas, *The Education of an Army: British Military Thought, 1815-1940* (1964); and D. M. Schurman, *The Education of a Navy: The Development of British Naval Strategic Thought, 1867-1914* (1965).

22. This was the central argument of Sir Halford Mackinder's 1904 lecture, "The Geographical Pivot of History." See: Paul M. Kennedy, *The Rise and Fall of British Naval Mastery* (1976) Chapter VII; also P. M. Kennedy, "Imperial Cable Communications and Strategy, 1870-1914," in his, *The War Plans of the Great Powers, 1880-1914* (1979), pp. 75-98.

23. A. W. Preston, "The Eastern Question in British Strategic Policy During the Franco-Prussian War," Canadian Historial Association, *Historical Papers 1972,* pp. 55-88.

24. *Ibid.*, 65-67, note especially the Reports of the Consul-General at Belgrade Colonel W. R. Mansfield, F. O. 78/2138-40. See also: W. E. Mosse, *The Downfall of the Crimean System* (1965); F. J. Cox, "Khedive Ismail and Panslavism," *Slavonic and East European Review*, XXX, (Dec. 1951), pp. 185-206.

25. Simmons Papers, F. O. 519/1, Memordum, 15 Dec. 1870.

26. F. O. 65/1321, War Office to Foreign Office (SECRET) 16 Aug. 1887; including Memorandum by Brackenbury, 7 Aug. 1887.

27. *Ibid.*, Minute dated 19 Aug. 1887.

28. W. O. 106/48, E3/2, Summary of the Report of the Indian Mobilisation Committee 1887. The Military Resources of Russia, and Probable Method of Their Employment Between Russia and England (SECRET) 1902. Also W. O. 32/218, No. 40116, Report of the Conference on Question of Indian Reinforcements (SECRET), 19 Dec. 1892.

29. C. J. Bartlett, "The Mid-Victorian Reappraisal of Naval Policy," in K. Bourne and D. C. Watt (eds.), *Studies in International History* (1967), pp. 200-201, 208.

30. CAB, 37/59/118, Selbourne Memorandum, 16 Nov. 1901.

31. Brian Ranft, ed., *Technical Change and British Naval Policy, 1860-1939* (1977), in particular his chapter, "The Protection of British Seaborne Trade and

the Development of Systematic Planning For War, 1860-1906," pp. 1-22.

32. *Reports of the Royal Commission Appointed to Inquire into the Defence of British Possessions and Commerce Abroad: First Report and Evidence, 1881; Second Report with ASppendix 1882; Third and Final Report, 1882.* Copies in the National Maritime Museum (Milne Papers, 141/1), and P.R.O. (Carnarvon Papers, 30/6). The genesis of the Carnarvon Commission can be traced to Captain J.C.R. Colomb's 1867 pamphlet *The Protection of Our Commerce and the Distribution of Our War Forces Considered;* see Schurman, *Education of a Navy,* pp. 16-35. Also important was the 1875 Report by Colonel Sir William Jervois of the Inspectorate-General of Fortifications; and the efforts of Admiral Sir Alexander Milne (1st Sea Lord 1866-8 and 1872-6) who with General J.L.A. Simmons played key roles in the 1878 Colonial Defence Committee. Simmon reports to the Cabinet on the state of Constantinople's defenses were an important contributing factor to the creation of Lord Carnarvon's Commission on which Milne and Simmons represented the Admiralty and War Office. See also, D. M. Schurman, "Imperial Defence, 1868-1887," unpub. Ph. D. Thesis, Cambridge (1955), pp. 98 et *passim,* 171-72; and cmd. 50-91-1, 1887, LVI, pp. 314-15.

33. Parl. Papers 1889, L. (735), *Report of the Committee on Naval Manoeuvres, 1888.* Also, Arthur J. Marder, *The Anatomy of British Seapower: A History of British Naval Policy in the Pre-Dreadnought Era, 1880-1903* (1940), Chapter VIII.

34. Marder, *Anatomy,* pp. 155-56.

35. *Ibid.,* 158-60.

36. Cab. 37/30, no. 39, Cabinet print, Nov. 1891.

37. Spencer Papers, First Lord to Foreign Secretary, 17 Apr. 1894; First Lord to C-in-C Mediterranean, 1 May 1894; quoted in Marder, *Anatomy,* pp. 222, 223.

38. *Ibid.,* p. 242.

39. J. A. S. Grenville, *Lord Salisbury and Foreign Policy: The Close of the Nineteenth Century* (1964), p. 94.

40. Beryl Williams, "Great Britain and Russia, 1905 to the 1907 Convention," in F. H. Hinsley, ed., *British Foreign Policy Under Sir Edward Grey* (1977), p. 137.

41. Cab. 17/3, C. I. D., Table Showing the Naval and Military Provision of Great Britain in the Mediterranean, 1886-1912.

42. A. J. Marder, ed., *Fear God and Dread Nought: The Correspondence of Admiral of the Fleet Lord Fisher of Kilverstone,* (1952), vol. I, pp. 167-68.

43. See: Ruddock F. MacKay, *Fisher of Kilverstone* (1973), pp. 326-37.

44. See: Naval Records Society, *The Papers of Admiral Sir John Fisher* (ed. P. K. Kemp) 2 vols., 1960 and 1964; *Policy and Operations in the Mediterranean 1912-14* (ed. E. W. B. Lumby), 1970. Also, Paul Haggie, "The Royal Navy and War Planning in the Fisher Era," *Journal of Contemporary History* (1971); B. D. Hunt, *Sailor-Scholar: Admiral Sir Herbert Richmond* (1982), pp. 12-14; S. R. Williamson, *The Politics of Grand Strategy: Britain and France Prepare for War 1904-1914* (1969); D. M. Schurman, "Historians and Britain's Imperial Strategic

Stance in 1914," in J. E. Flint and G. Williams (eds.), *Perspectives of Empire* (1973), pp. 172-88.

45. Paul G. Halpern, *The Mediterranean Naval Situation, 1908-1914* (1971), pp. 11-12, 30-31, and Chapters VI and VII; A. J. Marder, *From The Dreadnought to Scapa Flow* (1961), Vol. 1, pp. 287-310.

46. Williams, "Great Britain and Russia," pp. 135-36; J. McDermott, "The Revolution in British Military Thinking from the Boer War to the Moroccan Crisis," *The Canadian Journal of History*, vol. IX, no. 2 (1974); Nicholas J D'Ombrain, *War Machinery and High Politics: Defence Administration and Peacetime Britain, 1902-1914* (1973).

47. Cab. 2/2, C. I. D. Minutes, 92nd meeting 26 July 1906; Adm 1/8884, "War with Turkey: The Forcing of the Dardanelles, 1906"; W. O. 106/42, File C3/21b, "Minutes of General Staff leading to meeting of C. I. D.," 1907.

48. Cab. 2/2, C. I. D. Minutes 96th meeting, 28 Feb. 1907.

49. Cab. 38/12/60, Secretary's Note, 24 Feb. 1915. See also, Hunt, *Sailor-Scholar*, pp. 12-14.

50. Halpern, *Mediterranean Situation*, p. 23.

51. *Ibid.*, p. 31.

52. *Ibid.*, pp. 314-54. For an interesting personal glimpse into the workings of the British prewar naval missions to Greece (and Turkey), see, Mark Kerr, *Land, Sea and Air* (1927).

III

Danubian Navigation

Richard Charles Frucht

War, Peace, and Internationality:
The Danube, 1789-1916

The assassination of Archduke Franz Ferdinand lit a fuse under the European tinderbox that resulted in a catastrophe the likes of which contemporary Europeans had heretofore not experienced. Order and stability, the essence of an age often associated with the reign of Victoria, disappeared. Europeans, who were so appalled by the carnage of the American Civil War, now entered into a fratricidal struggle that seemed to destroy all chance for rational behavior, for the rule of international law.

If there was a bright spot in the otherwise bleak scenario that commenced in summer/autumn 1914, it was the matter of the international status of the Danube. Despite the belligerency of four of the riparian states, international law, at least along the lower Danube, prevailed and remained not only an ideal, but an almost sacrosanct one, until 1916. The implementation, development, and ultimate success of the rule of international law at the mouth of the Danube was thus a remarkable, even though relatively overlooked, chapter in European diplomatic history.

Among the ideas brought forth during the French Revolution was the concept of internationalizing the continent's waterways. Incorporating the ideas of such varied sources as Roman law and the writings of the seventeenth-century Dutch legal theorist Hugo Grotius, Europe's statesmen began to remove national restrictions and privileges from rivers considered to be international in character; their ultimate goal became one of ensuring free and open commerce for all vessels, reducing competition that might widen into larger confrontations, and preserving the neutrality of the rivers during times of armed conflict. The ideals were noble, but the ledger was mixed, for balancing the delicate question of riparian rights with the often vague concept of internationality proved to be no small matter. This was especially true in the case of the Danube.

The Danube, which Napoleon once called "the King of Rivers,"[1] is no ordinary waterway. Not only is it Europe's longest river, but, more importantly, no other artery flows through, or forms the borders of, so many disparate nations. Moreover, during much of the nineteenth century, half of the river, including its most important sector, the delta, flowed through a region plagued by instability, conflicting great power interests and aspirations, and wars of both liberation and expansion. As such, the Danube became an integral part of the larger Eastern Question. Its commerce was vital not only for the economies of the riverine states (which included, at times, as many as four great powers), but, by the mid-nineteenth century, it was also perceived to be of great importance to the industrializing nations of Western Europe, particularly Great Britain.[2] Therefore, any notion of internationality had to deal with not only the delicate question of national sovereignty, but also the interests and demands of the great powers as well. Europe's statesmen thus confronted a complex environment of turbulence and unsettlement, of riparian concerns, and the realities of great power politics. Bringing even a semblance of order and stability to the waterway would be no small task.

As a highway for both commerce and migrations, the Danube had always experienced military engagements, from the operations of the Romans to the wanderings of the barbarians, from the wars of petty princes to the expansion of the powerful Ottoman sultans, from the sieges of Vienna to the resurgence of Habsburg power. The nineteenth century differed from these earlier epochs not because wars were avoided or less frequent; rather, the wars brought the foundations of internationality which, despite the often chaotic conditions, remained a noble, yet elusive, objective.

In the narrative to follow, principal attention will be placed on the period commencing with the Crimean War, and will center on the region south of the Iron Gates. This is not to imply that the matter of war and peace, as it affected the Danube during the nineteenth century, was confined solely to the post-1854 era. Certainly Napoleon's 1809 Danube campaign, as but one example, belies that notion. Nor does it infer that north of the Iron Gates, that is, Austrian and German territory, the questions of war, peace, and internationality were considered less important. Rather, it was not until the time of Crimean War that geo-political considerations were such that the Danube could be internationalized. However, owing to the nature of great power politics, as well as the seemingly impenetrable quagmire known as the *Eastern Question*, this could only occur south of Habsburg lands, that is, nongreat power territory.

In times of peace, the Great Powers sought to dominate the agencies devised to guarantee freedom of navigation on the river; in times of war, they often looked to extend that influence even further. War and peace thus shaped the manner in which internationality was applied. The former created the opportunity to internationalize the river, but it also dictated the ways in which internationality would be implemented; peace gave it time to work.

An international river may be defined as any body of water that flows through or along the territory of two or more states. Since only a river that is navigable solely within one country may be subjected to exclusive jurisdiction, the declaration and guarantee of a river's internationality is essential as a protection against economic hindrances imposed by a riparian state upon the commerce of another.[3] Internationality implies that freedom of navigation will exist for all vessels as long as a riparian state suffers no direct harm. Therefore, rivers, in the view of international law, should serve as conduits for economic activity, with as much cooperation, and as few impediments, as possible.

Ideally, consensus among the riverine states is essential in promoting free trade and access to the waterway. The mere fact that a river flows through a state's sovereign territory does not mean that that artery can be considered exclusive property.[4] Instead, common interests must be taken into account. As such, for each river, some fundamental statements of internationality must be devised, either through bilateral agreements among the riparian countries themselves, or, preferably, through a treaty drawn up by an international conference.[5]

However, two major stumbling blocks stand in the path of devising such agreements. First, every solution must balance the ideal of internationality with the reality of sovereignty. No state "will allow itself to be stripped of an elementary right of protection of its welfare and integrity."[6] To ensure that no one state (or interest) grabs an unequal advantage, a commission, composed of the riparian countries, must be created to oversee all operations. That agency, however, must never place the interests of the collective body or one state above the sovereign prerogatives of an individual riverine country. When that occurs, especially when non-riparian powers play a central role in the determination of the agency's functions, the commission may be viewed as "infringing on sovereignty."[7]

The second problem in formulating a successful treaty lies in the fact that the mere definition of internationality itself is a subjective one, and is thus open to the vagaries of national priorities. As such, the question of an international river's position is ultimately a diplomatic concern. During the past two centuries, the resolution of the Danube Question involved issues far more complex than the simple guarantee of freedom of navigation; much more was at stake. In a world which seemed to subscribe to the Clauswitzian notion that war and politics were intertwined, the matter of war, peace, and Danubian internationality became muddled, a matter for Europe's statesmen to unravel and resolve, but only in a manner amenable to their own best interests. Support for the concept of the river's "internationality" was thus often little more than a facade behind which self-serving national concerns operated.

Before 1812, Danubian issues were confined primarily to the struggle between the Ottoman empire and its regional Great Power rivals, Austria and Russia. Although the first formal statements regarding the use of the Danube were incorporated into the Treaties of Passarowitz and Karlowitz,[8] the provisions were neither pressed nor enforced. The presence of the Turks at the mouth of the Danube lessened the importance of such guarantees. The Treaty of Bucharest, which ended the Russo-Turkish conflict (1806-12), altered the balance of power, however, since it brought the southwestern border of Tsarist Russia to the Danube. Moreover, it stipulated that Russian shipping could freely use the river.[9] In so doing, Russian interests, for the first time, came into direct contact with those of Austria, a regional rivalry of riparian great powers that by the 1850s necessitated the establishment of formal Danube decrees.

For now, confrontation and controversy were limited since maritime commercial activity on the Danube was still in its infancy. In fact, when the peacemakers met in Vienna in 1814-15 to end the Napoleonic Wars, discussions centered on the Rhine rather than the Danube; without representation from the Porte, the delegates could not take up the matter of the Danube at all. Nevertheless, the provisions of the Congress of the Vienna would have far-reaching consequences for the Danube since it provided the basis for all future river regimes.

The Vienna accords stipulated that navigation "of the rivers [Main, Meuse, Mosel, Neckar, Rhine, and Scheldt], along their whole course, ...shall be entirely free and shall not, in respect to Commerce, be prohibited to any one; it being understood that the Regulations established with regard to the police of this navigation shall be respected, as they will be framed alike for all, and as favorable as possible to the commerce of all nations."[10] Each state should be responsible for the upkeep of the river in its territory "in order that no obstacle may be experienced to navigation."[11] Any change in the basic terms of the agreements would require the "consent of all the Riverine States."[12]

The articles contained in the *Actes du Congrès* of Vienna were to become the framework for all subsequent treaties governing international rivers. Since 1815, the riverine commissions, operating not only on the rivers specified in the original treaty, but on the other international waterways added to the system later, generally resolved disputes in an atmosphere of relative harmony. Effective power remained in the hands of the riparian states themselves. Only on the 1700 mile-long Danube would diplomacy fail to provide the necessary balance between natioanl aspirations and the ideals of internationality.

The Treaty of Bucharest (as well as the subsequent Treaty of Akermann), by being a unilateral agreement between St. Petersburg and Constantinople, dealt solely with rules governing Russian and Turkish shipping. Since the delta, the outlet to the Black Sea, was under the control of Russia and the Porte, natural friction was bound to develop with others seeking to use the river, most notably Great Britain and the other great riverine state, Austria. For the latter, the delta was the key to the development of maritime commerce. For Britain, the Danube represented an important avenue for future trade; moreover, the lands of Southeastern Europe could serve as a source of foodstuffs and primary products essential for industrial development. As such, the Danube became an important facet in the increasingly explosive Eastern Question. Not only was the region a center of great power rivalry, owing to the uncertainty of Turkish control and the resulting power vacuum, but the powers perceived the Danube to be economically and geo-politically vital. Any gain by one state seemed to threaten all interests.

In 1829 Russian influence over Danubian affairs reached its zenith. Nicholas' army broke through the Turkish river defenses fourteen months after the outbreak of war with the Porte in April 1828. And, even though Russia's forces could not realistically seize Constantinople without disturbing the balance of power, and the city on the Bosporus would forever elude their grasp, the Russians, through the Treaty of Adrianople, gained a virtual monopoly over the river's maritime commerce.

Although Adrianople technically opened the lower Danube to all international trade, by ending Ottoman control over the delta (especially its principal maritime ports of Galați and Brăila), Russia, by its physical presence at the mouth of the Danube, now was in a commanding position to dictate the nature of future commerce, to its own advantage. The Turks were prohibited from building forts along the southern banks of the St. George channel, the new northern boundary of the once-mighly Ottoman empire, a restriction that did not apply to the Russian side of the Kilia channel. In addition, Russia received the complete authority to quarantine all vessels at the mouth of the river.[13] In a treaty remarkable, in a way, for its lack of territorial aggrandizement in Europe, Adrianople put an end to the exclusive Turkish grain trade on the Danube. Yet, in so doing, the river suddenly became a European concern since Russia, with little interest in the Danube as an economic entity, now held effective control over it.

The Danube basin was a commercial competitor to Russian grains exported through the port of Odessa; it thus became commercially expedient for St. Petersburg to practice a policy of arbitrarily quarantining ships at the island entrances to the delta,[14] and allowing the

treacherous arms of the river, the Kilia, Sulina, and St. George channels, to fall into such a state of disrepair that by the 1850s the depth
of the Sulina, the principal delta artery, had fallen to an average of
between six and ten feet.[15] This meant that during the harvest season
only ships with less than a 10-13 foot draft could reach port with relative safety,[16] thereby forcing additional, costly transshipments.
Such obstructionism naturally increased the price of wheat exported
from Galaţi compared to grains shipped from Odessa; in some cases,
the price varied as much as 50 percent.[17] Russia's policy of neglect
and obstructionism thus could not help but collide with growing Austrian and British interests favoring free and open commerce along
the Danube.

Already by the 1830s Russia's *de facto* ownership of the delta was
readily apparent to the British. In 1839, Lord Palmerston questioned
whether the great powers should extend the Vienna provisions to the
Danube by placing them before the Sultan,[18] an interesting , if not
fanciful notion. The volume of British trade dramatically increased in
the 1840s;[19] even with such impediments, British importation of
maize, barley, and wheat from Moldavia and Wallachia rose 255
percent during the decade.[20] In 1847, nearly five percent of all British
grain purchases came from the Danubian Principalities.[21] At the same
time, Austrian commerce was growing, in part due to the development of such state-supported enterprises as the *Donau Dampfschif-
fahrts Gesellschaft* [Danube Steam Navigation Company] which had
been granted a monopoly over Austria's Danube trade in 1846.
Without any agency to regulate commerce and supervise the complex
task of clearing the mouth of the river, friction between Russia and
the other trading nations began to mount.

Even though St. Petersburg signed an agreement in 1840 guaranteeing freedom of navigation in the delta for a period of ten years,[22]
Russia's policy remained one of benign neglect; all British and Austrian protests based upon the Vienna principles fell upon deaf ears.
Although Russia never deliberately opposed access to the river, its
policies effectively closed the waterway. Thus, while the matter of the
Danube was not the cause for the outbreak of the Crimean War in
1854, the river was nonetheless uppermost in the minds of Europe's
statesmen, diplomats, and military planners.

Considering the fact that Russia's military occupation of the Principalities in 1853 was, in many respects, the first action of the Crimean conflict (since, by entering what was technically Ottoman territory, it was a virtual declaration of war), actual fighting along the Danube was surprisingly minimal. If Britain and France feared that Russia's move into Wallachia was a prelude to formal annexation,[23] their entrance into the hostilities made the Danube front inconsequential in determining the war's final outcome. In fact, Austria's later occupation of the Principalities proved to be of greater consequence in bringing about a satisfactory conclusion to the war than the relatively brief fighting along the river frontier in 1854. France, Britain, and Austria may have paid lip-service to the idea of a Danube campaign,[24] but there was little ardor for such an undertaking. Even the commander of the Tsar's Danube armies urged Nicholas to abandon the front early, and the moves against the Turkish garrison at Silistria were broken off in June. Although obstacles were placed at the mouth of the river to obstruct troop movements and commerce, Russian troops pulled back behind the Pruth. With that strategic withdrawal, and the resulting Allied blockade of the river's entrance,[25] for the remainder of the conflict more shots would be fired at the bargaining table than on the Danube front; for the Danube, the Crimean War became as much a war of diplomacy as one of bullets and bayonets.

On August 8, 1854, the governments of Austria, Great Britain, and France declared that any settlement of the conflict must include provisions aimed at internationalizing the Danube. During the preliminary discussions held in Vienna, the Danube Question had a prominent place, and when the Treaty of Paris was written, the signators included five articles devoted specifically to the waterway. Article XV stated that the Danube "henceforth forms a part of the Public Law of Europe" and that the "Contracting" parties would "take it under their Guarantee."[26] No obstacle could be placed in the path of free navigation. To ensure compliance, a River-State Commission, composed of Austrian, French, British, Prussian, Russian, Sardinian, and Turkish representatives, would be responsible for keeping the river clear, establishing duties, and treating "the Flags of all nations... on the footing of perfect equality."[27] At the same time, the conferees created a special agency to clear the debris from the delta; this European Commission of the Danube was charged with completing its task in two years, after which it would turn over all delta operations to the River-State Commission. The latter would then have sole jurisdiction over the entire course of the artery, thereby reconfirming the goal of the Vienna accords that "the administration of an international river, as far as joint administration in necessary, should be left in the hands of the riparian states."[28]

Internationalization of the river and jurisdiction by the riverine states were clearly the goals of the Paris signators. However, with the Danube, agreements were easy to reach on paper; implementing them was entirely another matter. Austria saw the River-State Commission as an ideal vehicle for its interests, a fact clearly evident in the organization's charter, the Act of Navigation of November 7, 1857. The act, though, was never ratified by the governments represented at Paris since it granted exclusive power to the fleets of the revirine states to service the upper Danube, an action which Britain, the nation most directly affected, contended would violate the spirit of the Vienna accords.[29] Thus, the individual riparian states devised their own sets of rules for the portion of the waterway that flowed through their territories, and the European Commission of the Danube, instead of dissolving after two years, became the only functioning agency on the waterway.

Owing to the controversy surrounding the other agency, the European Commission of the Danube did not actually begin operations until its original mandate had expired. Its task, however, was a major one, as its members grappled with ways to deal with the serious state of disrepair in the river's three channels. During the war, not only had obstacles been placed at the entrances to the Black Sea, but the swiftly moving current had created (or enlarged) sandbars, thereby further narrowing the shipping lanes. Now in April 1858, with the paralysis of the River-State Commission readily apparent, the technical committee initiated a program of repairs aimed at narrowing the Sulina, the principal channel, in order that the passage "might be deepened by the concentrated action of the river."[30] By 1860, the Sulina's depth had regained prewar levels. The agency had therefore fulfilled its charge, but without an organization for the entire river, the commission's *raison d'être* had already changed; by default, it had become the sole guarantor of the Danube's internationality.

First, its members extended its life and drafted rules regulating navigation along the lower Danube. Then, after the Porte failed to deliver the funds necessary to maintain operations, the commission enacted a series of tolls, and floated loans through European banks, thereby generating capital needed to maintain operations. By 1865, the previous temporary arrangements had been codified and, through the Public Act of that year, its members designated the European Commission of the Danube to be an administrative, engineering, judicial, and planning agency "under the guaranty of international law."[31] It had the power to regulate, fine, inspect, and appoint, in other words, act as a self-perpetuating organization under the guarantee of the great powers. Only a change in the policies of its members could alter the situation.

In 1871, Russia renounced the provisions of the Treaty of Paris which neutralized the Black Sea, a move which necessitated both a re-examination as well as a reaffirmation of the European Commission's international status.[32] In response to St. Petersburg's pronouncement, the London Conference of 1871 internationalized all works, establishments, and even employees of the agency, an act which moved the idea of internationality beyond mere geography to one in which the representatives and facilities of the organization fell under the international umbrella. In the event of future war, which appeared more likely in light of Russia's actions, the plenipotentiaries agreed that the European Commission would be neutral,[33] a declaration called into question only a few short years later.

In July 1875, an uprising in Hercegovina ended the relative quiet that had existed in Southeastern Europe since the Crimean conflict. While Austria-Hungary and Russia, linked by the fragile Three Emperors League, talked about gains to be made if the Balkan states succeeded in throwing off Ottoman rule, the course of events instead drew Russia into the hostilities in April 1877.

By agreement with Romania, Tsarist troops moved toward the Danube. Russia's plans dictated that its advance troops, numbering approximately 190,000 men, were to sweep across the river and destroy Ottoman rule in the Balkans forever,[34] an ambitious plan aided by the fact that Turkish border defenses, although sound on paper, were poorly utilized.[35] By the end of June, Russian troops were across the Danube in strength.[36] However, the spirited defense of Ottoman forces at Plevna, and the failures of the Russian High Command, soon stalled the drive. Although the ease with which the Russians crossed the river may have frightened the British,[37] the disaster at Plevna imperiled Russia's entire Balkan campaign and threatened the need for Russia to withdraw behind the Danube. Only the timely intervention of Romanian troops in August tipped the scales; in December, the Plevna garrison surrendered. The Danube front was secure. But, while the focus of the war became Bulgaria and British concerns for the Straits, the question of the Danube's internationality was suddenly a matter of European concern again; this time however, the plenipotentiaries also had to contend with a new participant and the demands of nationalism.

Romania's intervention in the Russo-Turkish War had not only added a new combatant, it also made essential the inclusion of the Bucharest government in all future Danube discussions. Romania believed that her participation in the conflict would result in the enlargement of her territory, through the annexation of the Dobrudja as well as land along the right bank of the Danube.[38] Although Romania did indeed receive compensation in the south, it, like the Western powers, was shocked by the terms of the Treaty of San Stefano. The loss of southern Bessarabia to Russia, which restored the latter's riparian status, caused Romania, like the others, to await anxiously the deliberations in Berlin.

The conclusion of the Russo-Turkish War of 1877-78 marked the end of armed conflict (until 1916) along that portion of the Danube operating under international guarantees. The Berlin accords would pledge the European governments to the sanctity of internationalization of the river, but, as with its predecessor in 1856, the great conference could not balance the delicate forces of nationalism, internationality, and great power politics; in so doing, they failed, in the end to fulfill the goals established at Vienna and Paris.

In the recognition that general European interests and demands were at stake in the delta, and that the Habsburg government would oppose any attempt to form an agency with jurisdiction in its territory, the conferees avoided all discussions of incorporating the European Commission into a larger entity aimed at regulating the entire river. Although the treaty called for the creation of a modified version of the ill-fated River-State Commission, through a "European Commission, assisted by the Delegates of the Riverian States, and placed in harmony with those which have been or may be issued for the portion of the river below Galatz,"[39] the actual project put forward in 1879 by a subcommittee composed of Austria-Hungary, Germany, and Italy, dealt primarily with the middle Danube, that is, the portion of the river between Galati and the Iron Gates.[40] By making the Austrian representative to the so-called Mixed Commission the permanent president with the casting vote, the plan, on paper, would have enabled Vienna to dominate Danubian trade. Moreover, Austria could hope that the newly independent nations in the basin would become dependent on the Viennese monarchy for practical reasons of trade. It is not surprising, therefore, that the other members of the European Commission, the body responsible for approving the project, viewed the plan with disfavor. Britain, for example, whose shipping accounted for approximately 49 percent of all the commercial traffic in the delta,[41] disliked the exclusion of all non-riparian states from the new agency. By the same token, Romania, the newest member of the organization, having been made a full partner after gaining independence at the Congress of Berlin, opposed any plan designed to regulate only the waters south of the Iron Gates. For four years the delegates fruitlessly sought a compromise, a middle-ground between Great Power suspicions and nationalist sentiments.

In 1883, the powers called the final major prewar diplomatic conference devoted to the Danube. In addition to the principal objective of the gathering, that is, prolonging the life of the European Commission, the London conferees adopted a French counterproposal to the original Austrian project of 1879 that would have removed many of Vienna's powers of control over the middle Danube (while still limiting the extension of internationality to waters within the borders of the smaller riparian states, Romania, Serbia, and Bulgaria). Only through the use of a technicality denying Romania full voting rights, on the basis that only the original Paris signators could renew the prerogatives of the European Commission of the Danube, had the delgates been able to break the stalemate over the middle Danube. It proved to be a futile maneuver; the animosity of the Bucharest government, exacerbated by the snub at London, would not only prevent the Austrians from gaining hegemony over the middle Danube, it also thwarted any chance to establish an agency in the region.[42]

Whereas the "solution" reached in London may not have been entirely satisfactory to all the members of the European Commission, it was viewed by the Romanians as standing "against the complete liberty of navigation of the Danube."[43] King Carol agreed that the concept of strict "regulations... designed to assure the liberty of all ships" on the middle Danube was amenable to his government but that the rules had to "be applied by Romanian authorities."[44] Without the cooperation and support of the smaller riverine states, whose waters were to be regulated by the new agency, the Mixed Commission for the middle Danube could never begin operations. Without Romania's approval, or the use of force, the great powers could never compel the Bucharest government to comply with the London protocols.[45] Romania, for the first time, had successfully played upon the often conflicting special interests of the powers and used the discord to its own best advantage.

With the inability of the London conferees to expand the territory under international control beyond the delta, the unity sought by the Vienna and Paris conventions became an unrealizable ideal. The Crimean War had brought the idea of internationalization of the Danube to the conference table; the outcome of the Russo-Turkish War had merely reconfirmed the principle without providing the mechanisms for bringing the concept to fruition. Yet the stalemate of 1878-83 should not necessarily be interpreted as a failure. The two wars brought discussion of the need to internationalize the waterway to the forefront; the inability actually to implement the ideas did not mean that internationality had failed. On one small portion of the river, where Great Power interests demanded accommodation, the agency not only functioned with great efficiency but its members operated in an atmosphere of cordiality and harmony. As such, the internationalization of the delta was not only a success, but a remarkable one considering the unsettled, and often volatile, nature of affairs in Southeastern Europe.

The very definition of internationality demands that a consensus be reached among the riverine countries while, at the same time, addressing the matter of sovereignty. Considering the conditions in the Danube basin in the nineteenth century, it is not surprising that this could not be obtained. The quarrel between Romania and its Great Power partners on the European Commission, for example, symbolized the Dr. Jekyll/Mr. Hyde nature of Danubian internationality. As a small nation dependent on the export of primary products, any penetration and domination of its economic lifeline would have denied Romania the opportunity to construct a protective customs policy similar to the ones "applied against" [it] by incomparably stronger European powers and by [its] neighbors."[46] Romania, therefore, consistently proposed that all river agencies be strictly supervisory in nature, rather than regulatory, as the powers desired. Whereas Vienna viewed the Danube as a vehicle for economic expansion, Bucharest considered organizations like the European Commission, that by statute existed "in complete independence of territorial authorities,"[47] to be a threat to the very nature of the nation's independence. Peter Carp, a leader of the Conservative party, reflected the prevailing view when he noted that the "Liberty of the Danube has for us a politically grave importance [and] attaches itself to the existence of our state."[48] Moreover, the Commission's prerogatives, including free access to telegraph facilities and the use of a separate flag, became more than mere irritants; they were an effront to national pride.

Yet, at the same time, the European Commission represented a convenient protection against possible Russian or Austrian expansionism. In 1856, the threat to Danubian shipping posed by the Crimean War, and the fears that either St. Petersburg or Vienna might seek to dominate the river prompted the great powers to make the Danube a central issue at the Paris conference. In 1877-78, despite pledges to the contrary, Russia seized southern Bessarabia, Romanian territory since 1856. In 1883, Austria appeared ready to extend its influence to the middle Danube, an area outside its own boundaries. The presence of non-riparian Great Powers, therefore, provided a potential buffer against such machinations arising in the future. Romania might lose port revenues to the agency's treasury, but the benefit of outlets to the sea, free of both silt and the hungry glances of its neighbors, offset the liabilities and perceived loss of sovereignty. Romania could vocally attack the regulatory nature of the European Commission but its opposition to the supervisory function was curiously muted. Instead of dismissing the agency entirely, some government leaders asserted that only under the European Commission, "one of the greatest institutions created by the civilization of the nineteenth century,"[49] could the nation "be assured that the Danube will be truly free."[50] Carol, in 1894, praised the "great service performed by the Commission for the work of commerce and navigation in the Danubian delta," adding that his nation received all "the advantages."[51]

Instead of being a contradictory policy, Romania's response to the European Commission was a pragmatic one that reflected both the nature of Great Power politics and the vulnerability of a small state, the latter a situation all too evident in 1878 with the loss of Bessarabia. Bucharest consistently supported the concept of internationality, but only if its application did not violate Romanian sovereignty and instead protected the country's interests and territoriality. Thus, the long-range goal may have been one that emphasized the eventual dissolution of the European Commission, and its replacement by a river-wide organization that reflected the views of all its members, but, until that occured, the Commission was a necessary evil, (but one only in the sense that it violated the independence of action Romania might have expected to exert in the delta under normal circumstances).

For the Great Powers, too, the European Commission was not perfect. Yet, it represented a means of safeguarding all commercial interests while, at the same time, ensuring that no single nation gained a stranglehold over the vital outlet to the sea. Even though the upper Danube was governed by a multitude of national agencies, trade continued to flow smoothly. When disputes among the powers did arise, the European Commission provided a forum for discussion. Even during the Balkan Wars of 1912-13, the river remained open and the commission had little trouble fulfilling its obligations despite other difficulties brought on by the belligerency of the Balkan states.[52] As long as the conflicts could be localized, and the European powers remained observers rather than combatants, the status quo prevailed.

In the three decades before the outbreak of World War I, therefore, the internationalization of the Danube perhaps may not have reached the expectations envisioned at Paris, but the relative calm permitted the idea not only to gain acceptance in the area to which it was applied, but to flourish as well. When Europe went to war in 1914, the European Commission, made up of representatives from belligerent states (with the exception of Romania), continued to operate without acrimony and without interruption. The opening meeting of the October 1914 session set the tone, as the delegates praised Romanian King Ferdinand for the host country's neutral stance[53] and the members were exhorted to observe "their traditional courtesy and cooperation."[54] It was as if the notion of internationality had come to supersede the interests of the respective member states, as if the idea of internationality was indeed almost sacred. Although this élan would dissipate by 1915, and the entrance of Romania into the conflict the following year would extend the war's battle lines south of the Iron Gates, for two years cordiality reigned.

Unfortunately, events were not as kind to the Danube and its operations as were its representatives on the European Commission. With the closing of the Straits, naval operations in the Black Sea, and the fighting between Serbia and Austria-Hungary, commerce slowed to a virtual standstill. Nevertheless, despite the fact that the agency became isolated and its mission was reduced from one of aiding the flow of traffic to one of merely keeping the Sulina's lanes dredged, as long as Romania stayed neutral so too did the lower (and even middle) Danube.[55] In an era marked by the savagery of the Somme and Verdun, this was no small achievement.

Thus, although on the surface Danubian internationality failed, the solution reached for the lower Danube was at least a partial success. Considering the nature of the Eastern Question, that in itself is worthy of praise. Rules for the Rhine may have operated with relative smoothness until 1914, but only because there was calm in the region. International guarantees for the Danube could never be implemented with the same degree of success; conditions were radically different as were the motives of the various participants. Only in the delta was so much at stake that the powers had to reach an agreement. Wars created the need first to implement, and later, to refine the concept of internationality to reflect the Danube's unique situation. As long as further conflicts could be avoided, internationality could succeed. But just as war changed conditions in Southeastern Europe on countless occasions, so too, would the extension of the struggle south of the Iron Gates in 1916 once more alter the situation in the basin and force Europe to examine once again the peculiar nature of the Danube's internationality.

Notes

1. Henry Hajnal, *The Danube: Its Historical, Political and Economic Importance* (The Hague: Martinus Nijhoff, 1920), p. 118.

2. The impact of the importation of grains upon the West European economies is often overstated, but the perception dictated policy. See: John R. Lampe and Marvin R. Jackson, *Balkan Economic History 1550-1950* (Bloomington, Indiana University Press, 1982).

3. Georges Kaeckenbeeck, *International Rivers: A Monograph Based on Diplomatic Documents* (London: Sweet and Maxwell, Limited, 1918), p. 1.

4. *Ibid.*, p. 14.

5. *Ibid.*, p. 19.

6. *Ibid.*, p. 16.

7. *Ibid.*, p. 15.

8. Paul Gogeanu, *Dunărea in relaţiile internaţionale* [The Danube in International Affairs] (Bucharest: Editura politică, 1970), pp. 25-26.

9. *Ibid.*, pp. 26-30.

10. Hajnal, p. 46.

11. *Ibid.*, p. 47.

12. D. Sturdza, *Recueil de Documents relatifs à la Liberté de Navigation du Danube* [Collection of Documents concerning the Liberty of Navigation on the Danube] (Berlin: Puttkammer and Mulbrecht, 1904), p. 4.

13. Joseph P. Chamberlain, *The Regime of the International Rivers: Danube and Rhine* (New York: Columbia University Press, 1923), pp. 30-31.

14. Commission Européenne du Danube, *La Commission Européenne du Danube et son œuvre de 1856 à 1931* [The European Commission of the Danube and its work from 1856 until 1931] (Paris: Imprimerie Nationale, 1931), p. 5.

15. Chamberlain, pp. 34-36. The Turks had traditionally kept the depth at sixteen feet.

16. Lampe and Jackson, p. 100.

17. Chamberlain, p. 36.

18. Hajnal, pp. 66-67.

19. See: statistics cited in Lampe and Jackson, *Balkan Economic History...*, pp. 102-103.

20. Paul Cernovodeanu, "An unpublished British source concerning the international trade through Galatz and Brăila between 1837 and 1848," *Revue Roumain d'Histoire*, XVI, (1977), p. 517.

21. Paul Cernovodeanu, "Anglo-American Trade Relations during the Second Half of the Nineteenth Century," (Unpublished paper delivered at the Anglo-Romanian History Colloquium, London, May, 1978), p. 3.

22. Sturdza, pp. 7-11.

23. Paul W. Schroeder, *Austria, Great Britain and the Crimean War* (Ithaca: Cornell University Press, 1972), p. 139.

24. *Ibid.*, pp. 148-50.

25. Chamberlain, p. 41.

26. Hajnal, p. 78.

27. *Ibid.*

28. Chamberlain, p. 51.

29. Sturdza, p. 63; Kaeckenbeeck, pp. 107-109.

30. Lt.-Col. Sir Henry Trotter, *Operations of the European Commission of the Danube During the Years 1894-1906* (London: Harrison and Sons, St. Martin's Press, 1906), p. 3.

31. Chamberlain, p. 57.

32. See: Barbara Jelavich, *The Ottoman Empire, the Great Powers, and the Straits Question 1870-1887* (Bloomington: Indiana University Press, 1973) and *Die Grosse Politik der Europäischen Kabinette 1871-1914* [The Major Policies of the European Cabinets 1871-1914] (Berlin, 1922), II.

33. Sturdza, pp. 108-109. In addition, the Austrian demand to allow additional warships to be stationed at the mouth was rejected. Jelavich, pp. 44-45.

34. B. H. Sumner, *Russia and the Balkans 1870-1880* (Oxford: The Clarendon Press, 1937), p. 302.

35. The British were reporting a sizeable build up of Turkish forces as early as 1875-76. Sir A. Buchanan to the Earl of Derby (5 February, 1876), *British Documents on Foreign Affairs: Reports and Papers from the Foreign Office Confidential Print*, eds. Kenneth Bourne and D. Cameron Witt, Series B: The Near and Middle East 1856-1914, 2 ("The Ottoman Empire: Revolt in the Balkans 1875-1876," ed. David Gillard), p. 165. Estimates of Turkish army strength was 158,000; the forces were basically defensive in nature but armed with modern weapons. N. Ciachir, *Războiul pentru independența României în contextul european* [The War for Romanian Independence in the European Context] (Bucharest, Editura Stiinţifică şi Enciclopedică, 1977), pp. 176-77.

36. The main crossing came at Zimnitsa on the night of June 26-27. Sumner, p. 317.

37. *Ibid.*, pp. 317-18.

38. Charles and Barbara Jelavich, *The Establishment of the Balkan National States, 1804-1920* ("A History of East Central Europe," eds. Peter F. Sugar and

Donald W. Treadgold, vol. VIII, [Seattle, 1977]), p. 151. This was reported as early as 1876 when the British learned that Romania was prepared to mobilize in order to secure the delta. C. St. John to the Earl of Derby (23 July, 1876), *British Documents*, p. 310.

39. Hajnal, p. 99.

40. The plan also provided for the eventual incorporation of the European Commission into the Mixed Commission.

41. Cernovodeanu, p. 8.

42. See: Gh. N. Căzan, "La Question du Danube et les relations roumano-austro-hongoises dans les années 1878-1883" [The Danube Question and Romanian-Austro-Hungarian Relations: 1878-1883], *Revue Roumain d'Histoire*, 1979, XVIII, 1, pp. 43-61.

43. M. Kogălniceanu, *Chestia Dunării* [The Danube Question] (Bucharest: Tipografia Academiei Române, 1882), p. 6.

44. Vintilă C. Brătianu, *Chestia Dunării: expunere facuta în Adunarea Deputăţilor* [The Danube Question: Speech to the Gathering of the Deputies] (Bucharest: Imprimeria Statului, 1920), p. 27.

45. Moreover, the ratification of the secret alliance between Vienna and Bucharest lessened the former's interest in pressing the issue. Căzan, pp. 60-61.

46. Ivan T. Berend and György Ranki, *Economic Development in East Central Europe in the 19th and 20th Centuries* (New York- Columbia University Press, 1974), p. 88.

47. Sturdza, p. 123.

48. Dinu C. Arion, *Chestia Dunării* [The Danube Question] (Bucharest: Tipografia "Cooperativa," 1916), p. 20.

49. Voyslav M. Radovanovitch, *Le Danube Maritime et le règlement du différend relatif aux compétences de la Commission européenne sur le secteur Galatz-Braila* [The Maritime Danube and the dispute concerning the authority of the European Commission in the Galaţi-Brăila sector] (Geneva: Georg et Cic, S. A., 1932), p. 19.

50. Cernovodeanu, p. 13.

51. Radovanovitch, p. 19.

52. For the Balkan Wars, two excellent sources are: Andrew Rossos, *Russia and the Balkans: Inter-Balkan rivalries and Russian foreign policy 1908-1914* (Toronto: University of Toronto Press, 1981); Ernst C. Helmreich, *The Diplomacy of the Balkan Wars 1912-1913* (Cambridge: Harvard University Press, 1938).

53. Arhivele Statului Galaţi: Fond Comisia Europeană a Dunării (ASG/CED) [State Archives at Galaţi: European Commission of the Danube Collection], Nr. 50, file 238.

54. ASG/CED, Nr. 51, file 1919/51, Session extraordinaire, October 15-17, 1919, protocol 1.

55. For the history of the Danube during World War I and the subsequent peace conferences, see: Richard Frucht, *Dunărea Noastră:* [Our Danube] *Romania, the Great Powers and the Danube Question 1914-1921* (Boulder: East European Monographs, 1982).

Emil Palotás

The Problems of International Navigation on the Danube in Austro-Hungarian Politics during the Second Half of the Nineteenth Century

In the nineteenth century three important congresses played a significant role in the formation of international relations. All contributed to regulating navigation on the large international rivers in Europe and to establishing international legal norms of navigation. The Congress of Vienna (1815) declared the general principle of free and unhindered navigation as well as the necessity of uniform regulation of international waterways, and according to indentical principles. The Congress of Paris (1856) extended the principle of free navigation to the Danube, but failed to apply consistently the Vienna formulae, for, by the specific legal regulation on the mouth of the river, it actually divided the river itself into two parts. This international legal separation was further deepened by the Congress of Berlin (1878). Habsburg diplomacy played an active role in all three congresses: it had a hand in all negotiations, and to that extent, contributed to the development of navigation on the Danube; but, it also played a role in elaborating the rights contained in these treaties that could not be implemented.[1]

In the final stages of the Crimean War, when preparing for the congress terminating the crisis, heated internal debates arose in Vienna over the Austrian objectives. The Danube question played a part of the monarchy's general Balkan strategy. In these internal debates the military supported a direct territorial expansion, but it quickly came to light that this was unrealistic. The Foreign Office was less realistic, since it was still obsessed with maximalist ideas—it expected a significant increase in the Habsburg's political and economic influence at the meeting of the Great Powers then under way. At *Ballhausplatz* it was hoped that the Balkans, where the Russians having suffered a defeat, would be occupied by Austrian monarchy.[2] But the Western powers, too, had an eye on the Balkans. Resolutions made in 1856 were much more in harmony with the desires of the latter than the expectations of the former. That holds true for the articles concerning the Danube as well. The Paris treaty stipulated, on the one hand, full freedom of navigation on the Danube for everyone along the river's full length, making the riparian states the elaborators of statutory law on this theoretical basis. It further called for the formation of a committee of the riparian states for that purpose. However, it made an exception to the general rule on one stretch of the river; the treaty laid down a specific procedure concerning an area at the mouth of the Danube and, with the express aim of facilitating traffic of large vessels coming from the sea, it established the *European Danube Commission* [Commission Européenne du Danube, CED] for organizing and managing the technological and other activities which had become necessary in the mouth of the river. CED membership was restricted to representatives of the Great Powers only, and so, mostly to the non-riparian states.

Leading Austrian circles were in no way satisfied with the results of the Paris congress. Few Habsburg aims were realized, and treaty provisions concerning the Danube did not meet the earlier hopes. They considered as unequivocally negative the fact that the treaty declared the Danube a fully conventional river to which the Congress of Vienna's navigational principles applied. Stipulations also failed to clarify the exact relationship between the two Danube commissions. Although the treaty stipulated that the CED could remain in being only for two years, that its authority was circumscribed territorially, and that following its dissolution the Riparian Commission would take over its functions, in other issues, the very same treaty indirectly created a legal basis for a possible conservation of CED authority and likewise stipulated that CED's dissolution and extension of the Riparian Commission's authority were to be decided upon by a new European conference, that is, the treaty made change desired by the Viennese government dependent upon the approval of the other Great Powers.[3]

Although events of the two decades following the Congress of Paris are fairly diversified, the essence of Austria's Danube policy in this period can be summarized briefly as follows: to defend itself against the Western Great Powers considered to be the main enemy. Only under duress would Vienna accept the fact that external powers gained the formal right to participate in making decisions which were then to be applied on the stretches of the Danube belonging to the Habsburg monarchy. In the period following 1856, the Western Great Powers made several attempts at securing for themselves some kind of general supervision over the whole Danube, and to that end, they interpreted strictly the relevant Congress of Vienna's principles. And, Austria defended itself desperately against these attempts.

Austria received an important role in the practical implementation of the Paris treaty. Since, at that time, it tried to limit Western powers' influence on the settlement of the Danube question, it gave priority to the Commission of Riparian States where it could, as member, exert its full authority on other riparian states. Austria hoped that its leading role would be secured by the favorable composition of this commission — Bavaria, Württenberg, and Turkey. Consequently, at its initiative at the end of 1856, the commission met in order to elaborate norms of international navigation, and to include them in a uniform framework.[4] The commission quickly finished its work and the document prepared was initialed on November 7, 1857. The "Navigation Acts" [*Acte de navigation du Danube*], born in this way, was the first, and only, attempt until post-World War I at regulating on an international legal basis navigation and traffic on the Danube, which treated the river as a uniform whole and contained stipulations concerning its full navigable length. An important feature mentioned that the acts were confined only to general stipulations and made the practical implementation of rules the responsibility of riparian states.[5]

Thus, the Navigation Acts of 1857 established an important legal precedent which was to be frequently referred to in times to come, but which exerted very limited influence on the practice of the Danube navigation in the nineteenth century, for simply it never became operative in the sense of the international law. Following its elaboration, Austria faced two conflicts right away. On the one hand, it was attacked by the Great Powers on account of meaningful issues of content; on the other, however, the form the acts took, thwarted aims of the three Danube principalities: Serbia, Wallachia, and

Moldavia, and thus put Austria in a conflict with them as well.

The Great Powers raised objections, in the spirit of the moderate protectionism in vogue at the time, that the Navigation Acts discriminated against non-riparian states, excluding them from opportunities of internal navigation [*cabotage*]. That solely the egotism of the Western countries initiated this objection is justified by the fact that in those days unlimited navigation freedom was not ensured for everyone on the international rivers in Western Europe either.[6] Beyond that, they wished to secure for themselves the right to alter later any provisions of the acts which Vienna, for its part, refused to accept. The question of revision of the Navigation Acts of 1857, in other words, the cause of the Commission of Riparian States, was permanently on the agenda up to 1871. The Western claims were anew discussed whenever the Great Powers met at a conference tackling timely issues of crisis in Southeastern Europe. At these meetings, Vienna's main objective was to preserve its unlimited rights of disposal of its own waters. By skilful tactics, it finally reached this goal: the Austrian stretch was left out of every actual international regulation. But, Austria paid a price, for it had to give up the idea of the Commission of Riparian States' usefulness; in brief, the only way to fend off the claims of interference put forward by the Great Powers. Thus, the Austrian approach changed from the 1860s onward, as the idea of obstructing the Commission of Riparian States' work came into the foreground.

As already mentioned, the Navigation Acts also gave rise to a different kind of conflict. At the time, the Danube principalities were little interested in the economic, technological, and administrative legal impacts of international navigation. They paid more attention to political considerations. Regulation of the Danube offered them excellent opportunity to give special emphasis to their independence through an act of international law, as the equal creators of a multilateral international treaty. For, the Paris treaty did include Serbia and the two Romanian principalities in the work of the Commission of Riparian States to set up the rules, but it failed to clarify unequivocally their precise status in the commission. Representatives of the three principalities did participate in the elaboration of the Navigation Acts of 1857, but following its signing, Austria and Turkey refused to grant them the right of ratification.[7] For that reason, the small countries refrained from any further collaboration, and thus, the acts' practical implementation also became impossible. And that is why it only remained a precedent in international law, and was the first occasion when Austria indulged in open conflict with neighboring, small southern states, on acount of its Danube policy.

Roughly simultaneously with the Commission of Riparian States, the European Danube Commission, consisting of the representatives of the Great Powers, was established. Its activities resulted in rapid qualitative changes in the process of the formation of the international legal norms of navigation on the Danube. This commission got down to work with great élan the task set by the Congress of Paris: the regulation of the mouth of the river in the technological and physical sense. However, it was not satisfied with its initial, modest competence, but soon included, too, among its attributes, ship traffic creating separate rules of navigation and river police, at first only of a temporary character. In the first years, implementation and supervision was the task of the local Turkish authorities, i.e., the sovreign power. Decisive change began in 1861, when the Great Powers drew up a specific system which created a completely original legal state of affairs for the mouth of the river.[8] Accordingly, the European Danube Commission itself stipulated and proclaimed regulations of an obligatory character and applied a separate set of tariffs. The commission took care of its execution, and set up a separate mechanism to that end. Not only did CED secure the power of law making and execution for itself, but it also exercised judicial powers insofar as it passed final judgment in cases of infringements of regulations. Quite understandably, the Turkish government refused to recognize, for a long time to come, this new system which anticipated CED's complete extraterritoriality. The Porte's approval was extracted by collective European pressure. This new system received the name, "Public Act Relative to the Navigation of the Mouth of the Danube" [*Acte Public*] and was approved in November 1856.[9] Its coming into force infused, as such, a new quality to the legal regulation of the Danube. Not only did the lowest stretch of the river become radically divorced from the rest of the Danube, but its legal status and practice were completely different from those of any other European river. Thus, while the Commission of Riparian States, destined to perform the international legal regulation of the whole river, terminated its activities before actually coming into existence, the mouth began to live a specific life of its own. Following ratification of the *Acte Public,* only one problem remained on the table: the tenure of CED. Western states advocated making it eternal; Austria and Russia, albeit for different reasons, opposed it.

The Treaty of Berlin regulated the Danube question with exhausting meticulousness. It again declared navigation on the Danube of general European interest and breathed further life into CED, until 1883. It confirmed CED's earlier functions, rights, and privileges, extended its authority up to Galați, and at the same time, accepted Romania among its members. Article 55 stated that CED was to work out in detail navigation, river police, and supervision regulations for the stretch of the river extending from the Iron Gates up to Galați, with the collaboration of the riparian states, and harmonize these regulations with the regulations valid along the Danube below Galați or the ones serving the same purpose to be issued in the future. Thus, regulations without any provisions for execution or supervision. Along the stretches above the Iron Gates, self-determination of riparian powers was not limited by anything; along the stretch running from the mouth of the river up to Galați, the will of the CED representing the great powers was manifest and, as to the stretch between Galați and the Iron Gates, norms of navigation were to be stipulated again as well as implemented, but again only on the basis of a European mandate.[10]

When, in autumn 1878, in connection with carrying out congress resolutions, Austro-Hungarian policy concerning the Danube question still was to be determined, Austrian Minister of Commerce Chlumecky put forward a surprising idea. He transposed the Dual Monarchy's center of interest to the lower Danube, on the stretch starting at its border and extending up to Galați. [This part of the Danube was christened the *middle stretch* in order to stress its separate character in comparison to both the mouth and the stretch above the Iron Gates. In the following we shall speak about this "middle" stretch in that sense, too.] Using the Treaty of Berlin's failure to provide for the regulation's execution, Chlumecky wished to secure a specific influence for Austro-Hungary. But, he did not wish to leave implementation of the regulations exclusively to the riparian states concerned — Romania, Serbia, and Bulgaria — and therefore, he wanted to make the stretch between the Iron Gates and Galaţi international in scope [to some extent following the pattern of the mouth of the river] and wished to entrust certain functions to an international institution created for this purpose [*Donau-Inspektorat*] instead of the powers in the immediate area. This body was to be entrusted with supervising adherence to regulations, holding the offenders responsible, or even punishing them. According to Chlumecky's idea, two South German middle states, Württemberg and Bavaria, as well as, obviously, the Habsburg monarchy, were to participate in the *Inspektorat*, not to mention the states territorially competent, and Vienna's representative was to hold permanently the position of president, too. Nonetheless, this proposition failed to win the favor of the Foreign Office. It gave rise to a severe internal debate in which the Hungarian minister of commerce supported Chlumecky, and moreover, at one point, he even went a step further — he proposed that in the supervisory commission, in case of a tie, the president should cast the deciding vote.[11]

In the debate, Foreign Minister Andrássy repeatedly emphasized that the Great Powers would not accept Austro-Hungary's exclusive claim nor would the small countries agree to the Dual Monarchy's curtailment of their rights. He acknowledged that as to a settlement of the legal questions of navigation on the lower Danube not sufficiently clarified, attempts must need be made at improving existing conditions to the monarchy's benefit, but, for that purpose, he did not consider it necessary to establish new and unusual institutions. His stance was that implementing regulations was the task of the powers in the region only; their adherence, however, could be supervised by the CED through a special commissary. He believed, too, that Austro-Hungarian interests could most appropriately be represented through this European commission.[12] All the participants in the debate agreed that the interest of the Habsburg monarchy demanded preservation of its positions on the lower Danube, the dominant position of navigation under Austro-Hungarian banners. However, as to the ways of reaching this goal, the opinions of the Austrian and the Hungarian ministries and the Dual Monarchy's common Foreign Office strongly differed from one another. The latter's approach was determined not only by its representing a different view in relation to the means of implementation but by its independent position of the importance attached to the whole Danube question as well. The syllogism of Chlumecky and his Hungarian colleague betrayed an extreme simplicity: the lower Danube was dominated by Austrian navigation, hence Austria was entitled to supervising all ship traffic there and all the rest of the further consequences were of no interest; Andrássy was spurred on by these very same possible consequences, in a word, to a completely different conclusion. Where Chlumecky attached too great significance to the particular interests, Andrássy laid greater stress on general considerations. For him, the Danube question must not alienate the small countries from the Habsburg monarchy, nor should it not offer Russia an opportunity to use the Balkan states' dissatisfaction to win them over to its side. In formulating this position, the Foreign Office took into account two things. One, it tried to satisfly formally the condition of the Berlin treaty and remain more or less faithful to its spirit. This meant adhering to the principle of freedom of navigation without strings attached, and thus, was why *Ballhausplatz* wished to act in unison with the other Great Powers on the "Berlin settlement." Two, it favored a procedure whereby "Europe" would thwart the Balkan states' attempts of emancipation from foreign rule, thereby challenging Austria-Hungary's hegemony. Perhaps, in response to old habits, Chlumecky did not give the small states their due and considered the Habsburg monarchy capable of attaining a privileged position all by itself.[13]

This internal conflict lasted for exactly one year, and only then did the Foreign Office give up reason to hope that the Austrian and Hungarian governments would listen to reason and abandon propositions which were unrealistic and definitely harmful. In autumn 1879, it was finally forced to implement a plan it considered harmful in its consequences.

In that autumn, the Austro-Hungarian diplomacy submitted Vienna's plan made for regulating the Iron Gates-Galați stretch to the

CED. That marked the beginning of the second chapter of debates about the new international legal order of the "middle stretch." The lengthy fight that took place in the international arena is somewhat better known to historical literature than the process of previous internal bickerings.[14] It is necessary here, however, it seems, to add a few remarks in order to form a more complete picture of subsequent events. First, it must be stressed that three equally significant factors, following the logic of self-interest, played important roles in the debates. So, the Habsburg monarchy became involved in conflicts not only with the small Danubian states but repeatedly with other Great Powers, too; it tried to utilize the debates to its benefit just like it did with the conflicts among the Balkan states. Second, following the Congress of Berlin, the Danube question, just like the matter of a trans-Balkan railway, became a source of contention with national-political overtones. Economic policy conflicts have frequently been overestimated on account of home policy considerations. When discussing the Danube question, the contemporary Balkan view frequently referred to the Austrian "claims to power," which is partly understandable; it is, however, more difficult to comprehend why this slogan intended for internal usage is at times conjured up in recent professional literature as a real danger. Beyond that, it would be edifying to analyze more thoroughly differences in approach of the individual small countries, to compare different reactions to the same problem in Romania, Bulgaria, and Serbia. On that basis, the Danube question and the railway problem might serve as excellent case studies for investigating the specific interjection of economic policy and *other* considerations in the period under examination.[15]

As a first step, the CED appointed an *ad hoc* commission which prepared a preliminary plan about the regulation of the Iron Gates-Galaţi stretch. Besides Austria, Germany and Italy were members of the commission. The avant project was completed by spring 1880; it contained the substance of well-known Viennese ideas; its authors turned the *Inspektorat* into a mixed commission; and, within the CED this avant project was discussed at several sessions. Austria had little reason to hope for success from the very beginning, for in the circle of Great Powers, England remained the Dual Monarchy's principal adversary until the very end; among the small countries,

Romania, now a CED member, most actively opposed Vienna's plans for the "middle stretch," and in most cases, won Bulgaria's support in this matter.

Just like before, England took up the mantle of freedom of navigation if the issues under debate were matters of principles; in practice, however, it showed a greater flexibility; and in actual fact, it made efforts to extend the prerogatives of "Europe," that is, the CED. In the avant project debates, it resisted the creation of an international body but not the idea of corporate supervision, which it clearly perceived as a vehicle solely for Austrian interests. England countered with modifications, the thrust of which was to bring the mixed commission under CED, that is, Great Power, control. At the beginning Romania held a similar view and was inclined to accept freedom of navigation between the Iron Gates and Galați, under "Europe's" sponsorship, but nevertheless insisted that the practical aspects of implementation be carried out exclusively by the riparian states.[16] Just like in the wake of the Congress of Paris when Austria strove to find a way to maintain sovereignty along its own stretch of the river, now, Romania and the other two Balkan countries were doing the same; naturally, since they were smaller states, and for reasons of national pride, they gave much greater importance to the question.

But, Bulgaria and Serbia remained outside the CED; only their temporary representatives were present at the debates of the avant project by the European commission. As long as Serbia was in sharp conflict with its northern neighbor over a general commercial treaty, it strongly opposed Vienna's plans. But, beginning in autumn 1881, after the conclusion of the treaty, it tacitly supported the Dual Monarchy. Bulgaria remained adamant until the very end, although it was the least reckoned with and in the most complicated international legal position. Its internal relations underwent several changes; liberal governments suceeded conservative ones without leaving but few traces on its approach to the Danube question, for be they pro-Russian or pro-Austrian, cabinets did everything within their reach to emphasize Bulgaria's autonomy.[17]

Vienna's hopes were dashed in autumn 1881 by the attempt at mediation by CED's French representative of the CED in order to bring about a compromise between Austria and Western Great Powers.

During negotiations, Vienna tested Britain's flexibility on questions of the "middle stretch" by stating: should London resolutely adhere to its refusal on the idea of a mixed commission, then Austria would oppose the prolongation of the existence of the CED, and call for its dissolution when the matter came up for discussion in 1883. Nevertheless, a preliminary compromise was worked out between the Western powers and Vienna, to the effect that, in future, Austria's influence could be manifest along the stretch between the Iron Gates and Galaţi, and that of "Europe" to the south of it.[18]

Simultaneously, as the Great Powers inched their way toward compromise, Romania's position hardened, and henceforth, it objected consistently to all forms of internationalization. Now it aimed clearly at the elimination of Great Power influence in the "middle stretch." Even in the tiniest details, it insisted on unlimited sovereignty.[19]

The last Great Power's conference on the Danube question was convened in London in February 1883. Although lengthy, careful diplomatic preparations preceded it, the participants, however, failed to reach a general agreement. Romania's presence constituted the first obstancle. In 1882, Foreign Minister Kálnoky had proposed the inclusion of Romania in the CED negotiations, since it was a member of this commission since 1878; thus it was only fair that Bucharest participate in the debates. The English memorandum initiating the conference accepted the Austrian argument.[20] Another problem was Romania's stubborn resistance to the draft regulation concerning the "middle stretch," which favored the interests of the Habsburg monarchy. Since 1880 secret negotiations had been qoing on between Vienna and Bucharest on a mutually satisfactory solution, and they were still under way on the eve of the conference, but without any results.[21]

The conference's meaningful work started on February 10. At first, a decision had to be made on the possible inclusion of the three small riparian states. The German representative put forward the argument that the meeting, as to its character, was the direct continuation of the previous European conferences, and therefore, it was desirable to preserve as far as possible its Great Power character. Although the English and the Austro-Hungarian representatives were inclined to accept Romania's participation with full rights, they, too, bowed to the logic of Berlin's argument, and so the decision was made that Romania and Serbia could participate, but with the right of negotiating only. Bulgaria was not allowed even that; it could express its desires only through the mediation of Turkey. None of the three countries accepted this solution and their representatives boycotted the work of the conference.

The conference quickly disposed of the first point on the agenda: at Britain's initiative, it accepted the territorial extension of the CED from Galați up to Braila. The next point was the most important one for Vienna: final acceptance of the regulations elaborated for the "middle stretch" and approved by the majority of the CED in the previous year. Here, too, a quick and unanimous positive decision was had. At the conference itself, the only problem which aroused concern was that of the prolongation of CED's expired mandate. Already, before the conference, Russia had expressed its desire for full freedom of navigation on the Kilia branch forming the northern part of the Danube delta [and, at the same time, the Russian-Romanian border]. Russian Foreign Minister Giers stated that this in no way prejudiced the work of the European Commission of the Danube (i.e., the Sulina branch), but that St. Petersburg was willing to approve the extension of CED's mandate only if the London conference recognized all its rights on the Kilia branch, since, after all, Russia was a riparian power, and only if the legal jurisdiction of the European commission was eliminated on this stretch of the river.[22]

At the outset, England did not show any inclination to capitulate before the Russian ultimatum; therefore, for the time being, negotiations reached a crisis pitch. Austro-Hungarian diplomacy tried to mediate in order to reach a compromise. Kálnoky was happy to see that his English colleague Granville was inclined to do so.[23] The latter was convinced by his own advisors that Russia's claim threatened freedom of navigation only in principle, and solely in that branch of the river where there was no international traffic. They argued that accession to the Russian demand did not result in financial drawbacks, but refusal, however, would risk CED's very existence. Statistical data prove that even in the 1880s England was the main beneficiary of the trade conducted through the mouth of the Danube for which the financial-technological conditions were created by the

CED.[24] The compromise formula approved the claim of the Russians; it prolonged the mandata of the CED for 21 years; at the same time, it made automatic prolongation possible in the case where none of the parties to the treaty initiated a modification of the regulation one year before the date of expiration.

Most of the Great Powers were satisfied with the Treaty of London of 1883.[25] Russia was the big winner, though; it righted a grievance it nursed since 1878. The treaty was highly appreciated in London, too, for prolongation for 21 years and the automatic renewal of the European Danube Commission had practically become permanent. The London treaty gave, more or less, final form to the rights of the river mouth and the CED which remained unchanged until the end of World War I. But, the situation was different in the case of Austria-Hungary. After signing the treaty, Vienna enjoyed a brief feeling of euphoria; the resistance of the small countries thwarted effectively Vienna's desire for regulating the "middle stretch." Since Romania had been excluded from full participation at the conference, it refused to recognize its results as binding on itself. It taciturnly agreed to certain treaty issues, including the extension of the competence of the CED up to Braila. Together with Serbia and Bulgaria, it also applied the technical norms of the treaty. But an international system of supervision was never introduced along the stretch below the Iron Gates.

Thus, Vienna's intention of increasing its own influence through a special supervisory body could not be realized. Naturally, the respect commanded by the Habsburg monarchy was not enhanced by the failure it sustained. But events confirmed the Viennese Foreign Office fears, and following the Congress of Berlin, the small countries in the Balkans became active agents molding international relations they were concerned by.

Notes

1. On the basis of the documents preserved in the diplomacy and trade policy sectors of the State Archive in Vienna, a detailed depiction of the Danube policy

of the Habsburg monarchy is rendered by Emil Palotás, *A nemzetközi Duna-hajózás a Habsburg-monarchia diplomáciájában 1856-1883* [International navigation on the Danube in the diplomacy of the Habsburg monarchy] (Budapest, 1984).

2. Bernhard Unckel, *Österreich und der Krimkrieg: Studien zur Politik der Donaumonarchie in den Jahren 1852-1856* (Lübeck-Hamburg, 1969), 156, 203, 244-45.

3. Palotás, *A nemzetközi Duna-hajózás*, 22-23.

4. *Ibid.*, 24-26.

5. For the text of the regulations, see, Leopold Neumann et Adolphe Plason, *Recueil des Traités et Conventions conclus par l'Autriche avec les puissances étrangères* I *(Nouvelle suite)* (Vienna, 1878), 392-97.

6. Palotás, *A nemzetközi Duna-hajózás*, 29; also, see, Henri Hajnal, *Le droit du Danube international* (The Hague, 1929), 55.

7. Palotás, *A nemzetközi Duna-hajózás*, 28-29.

8. Hajnal, *Le droit*, 71-72.

9. For the complete text, see, D. Sturdza, *Recueil de documents relatifs à la liberté de navigation du Danube* (Berlin, 1904), 80-98.

10. For the text of the Berlin treaty, see, Imanuel Geiss, ed., *Der Berliner Kongress 1878: Protokolle und Materialien* (Boppard am Rheim, 1978).

11. Emil Palotás, *Ziele und geschichtliche Realität: Wirtschaftsbestrebungen Österreich-Ungarns auf dem Balkan zur Zeit des Berliner Kongresses im Jahre 1878* ("Studia Historica Academiae scientarium hungaricae" (Budapest, 1980), 157.

12. *Ibid.*, 34.

13. E. Palotás, *Die Donaufrage in der internationalen Politik vom Berliner Kongress bis zur Londoner Konferenz 1878-1883* ("Etudes historiques hongroises 1985" Vol. II [Budapest, 1985]), 163.

14. The best summary of the earlier professional literature is Hajnal, *Le droit*, chap. XIII-XVI. The traditional Romanian concept is reflected in the works published most recently in Bucharest too: Şerban Rădulescu-Zoner, *Donărea, Marea Neagră şi Puterile Centrale 1878-1898* (Cluj-Năpoca, 1982); Gheorghe Cazan-Şerban Rădulescu-Zoner, *Rumänien und der Dreibund 1878-1914* (Bucharest, 1983). Although having access to the rich material of the Vienna Archive, the Austro-Hungarian policy is reflected in a simplified manner with several factual mistakes by Uta Bindreiter, *Die diplomatischen und wirtschaftlichen Beziehungen zwischen Österreich-Ungarn und Rumänien 1875-88* (Vienna, 1976).

15. A starting point for such a comparative analysis could be, e.g., the depiction of the events on the one hand in the books by Gheorghe Cazan-Şerban Rădulescu-Zoner, *Rumänien und der Dreibund* and Elena Statelova, *Diplomatijata na Knjazhestvo Bulgarija 1879-1886* (Sofia, 1979), and in the volume by Palotás, *Ziele und geschichtliche Realität*, on the other hand.

16. Palotás, *Die Donaufrage*, 165-72.

17. Statelova, *Diplomatijata*, 25-27.

18. Palotás, *Die Donaufrage*, 173.

19. *Ibid.*, 174.

20. *Ibid.*, 177.

21. Palotás, *A nemzetközi Duna-hajózás*, 103-107, 129, 134-35.

22. Palotás, *Die Donaufrage*, 178.

23. *Ibid.*, 180.

24. L. A. Maher, "Great Britain and the International Control of the Danube, 1856-1883" (PhO diss., University of Oxford, 1968), 153-154, 162-64.

25. For the text of the treaty, see, D. Sturdza, *Recueil*, 472-77. The same work also contains the final and complete text of the navigation, river police, and supervision regulations elaborated for the Iron Gates-Braila stretch and approved by the conference, 478-507.

Spiridon G. Focas

The Greeks and Navigation on the Lower Danube, 1789-1913

Tempora mutantur, nos et mutarum in illis!*

The Lower Danube is that sector of the river between the Cataracts the Iron Gates, and the Black Sea, from which flow the three principal branches and mouths of the Danube. Of this sector the portion between the port of Brăila and the mouth of the Sulina is known as the *Maritime Danube*, accessible to sea-going vessels.

The principal territories adjacent to the river, and included in this subject, are those which eventually formed the two Romanian Principalities: Moldavia and Wallachia, later to be named "România." Geographically situated along the left bank of the Lower Danube, in these territories was concentrated in antiquity the activity of the Greeks as well as that of their successors.

According to archaeological and historical evidence the ancient Greeks were the first people to have established navigation of commercial value along the Lower Danube, thus tying in their Black Sea colonies with the Mediterranean regions. Gradually adapting themselves to local conditions, they made of the Lower Danube, in the words of the great Romanian archaeologist, Vasile Pârvan "a Greek water of communication as far as the Siret tributary."[1]

Following Graeco-Roman collaboration in commerce and navigation on the Black Sea and the Lower Danube, and after other successive political developments, came the Graeco-Byzantine era which lasted even through the early period after the establishment of the Romanian Principalities preceding Ottoman domination. During this period, Greek activity had the advantage of the protection of the Romanian Princes, who were under the spiritual influence of the Greek Patriarchate at Constantinople.

The presence of the Greeks in Danubian navigation and commerce

* The times are changed, and we are changed with them.

was so predominant during the period preceding Ottoman domination that it even left traces in Romanian folk songs, in which complimentary as well as derogatory references to Greek behavior are encountered.[2] Strangely enough, the peasant authors of these songs lived nowhere near the banks of the Danube.

After 1789, the starting point for this present study, Greeks within the territory of the Romanian Principalities, as well as those involved in navigation, continued to work within the framework of the Ottoman empire. Those in navigation were employed on Turkish vessels, were private owners of caiques, or were sailing riverine and maritime vessels under the Ottoman flag. Along with the freedom of action they enjoyed under the Turks, Greeks in navigation also benefitted from the establishment of the Phanariot regime in the Romanian Principalities in 1711. Also to their advantage was the privilege of substituting the Russian flag for the Turkish one, this on the basis of a secret clause in the 1774 Peace Treaty of Kütschük-Kaïnardji, this privilege giving the Greeks in navigation the possibility of carrying out activities in support of movements of liberation from the Sultan's yoke. Subversive Greek literature printed in Vienna was distributed throughout Greek regions of the empire by vessels flying Russian and Turkish flags.

The 1789-1913 period may be subdivided into three specific and distinct, eras, namely 1789-1829, 1829-56, and 1856-1913. In this 124-year span, the contribution of Greeks in navigation to the evolution of change in East Central European Society was not a determinant factor. Their activity and their contribution unfolded concomitantly with the evolution of the social, economic, political, and technical circumstances in East Central Europe and in Southeast Europe.

Between 1789 and 1829, Graeco-Turkish activity in Lower Danube navigation continued normally in local transportation as well as in that toward the empire, especially toward Constantinople. Competition came only after conclusion of the Treaties of Passarowitz (1718) and Belgrade (1739), when, at the same time as the gradual economic expansion of Vienna into the Ottoman empire, vessels under the Austrian flag were granted the right to limited navigation downstream on the Lower Danube. Parallel with this, Vienna also undertook research on site in support of this expansion, such as that carried out by the engineer, Sulzer, who reported on the prevalence of the Greek language on the Lower Danube and the important position held by Greeks in the navigational commerce.[3]

Besides the Salonika - Semlin - Belgrade - Budapest - Vienna route of economic ties between the Ottoman empire and Central Europe after 1718, there was also a route which started from the port of Brăila. Goods imported from Constantinople by sailing ships were taken over by Greek merchants and reshipped to Hungary and Austria via Braşov. This route was named "the Brăila - Braşov Road."

Between 1829 and 1856, when Russia, on the basis of the 1829 Treaty of Adrianople, annexed the Danube delta, a new and important change favorable to navigation was expected. With Russia's success in abolishing the Ottoman monopoly in the two Romanian Principalities and in the Serbian one, Danubian navigation and economy began to be included in the European circuit. The dynamics of this change was somewhat diminished due to the natural obstacles at the mouth of the Sulina, the most important being the low depth of the water. Added to this disadvantage was the quarantine regime, imposed by Russia in order to control the spread of the great epidemics of cholera and plague existing in the entire Lower Danube valley and bordering regions.

The countries most interested in free and unrestricted navigation were England, for the import of cereals, and Austria, for the development of her incipient steam navigation. Although neither of these two countries, nor Russia, had at that time the technical and sanitation knowledge and possibilities to overcome these two obstancles, still a diplomatic conflict arose between England and Russia. The former pressed for normalization of the navigation at the mouth of the Sulina, by then become even more difficult because of the practices being employed. In order to make work, gangs from the Sulina underworld took advantage of the navigational difficulties and deliberately sank or grounded vessels, thus creating possibilities for salvage operations, transshipment, and prospects for thievery.[4]

Referring to these practices, Charles Cunningham, British vice-consul in the port of Galaţi, characterized Sulina as "a little California where fortunes were to be made."[5] Although this statement was largely accurate, still a comparative and objective evaluation arises,

It should be taken into consideration that Sulina's reduced population was part of corrupt society within the framework of the Ottoman empire. Admittedly, those practices were to the detriment of a navigation that was becoming rather international, although the principles of internationality as drawn up in the 1815 Act of the Congress of Vienna, did not apply also to the Danube at that time.

Aside from the two previously mentioned obstacles, there also existed the problem of piloting, as practiced by improvised pilots — usually Greeks — whose Greek, Turkish, or Russian vocabulary was unintelligible to captains and crews of foreign vessels.

That same vice-consul, as well as other Sulina critics, did not point out any similar navigation problems existing at that time in other regions considered much more "civilized." The "pirates" of Sulina, referred to by the critics, were far less obnoxious than those of London's underworld,[6] than those who practiced the infamous procedure of "shanghai-ing," or than those of San Francisco's "Barbary Coast."[7] Acts opposed to the free expansion of navigation and commerce, between 1829 and 1856, were practiced in the ports of Galați as well. From an incident reported by the Sardinian consul at Galați, one can deduce the preponderence of Greeks in the navigation and commerce of this port. Greeks considered other foreigners as competitors. Although the Greeks were in the majority, they were up against the competition of Sardinians and Austrians, the rivalry at times taking on the character of "une espèce de combat naval," the Sardinians "voulant mitrailler les Grecs provenants la plupart des îles Ioniennes," as some critics reported.[8] Such rivalries existed also between Greeks and Slovenes, the latter being instigated by the Austrian consul, under whose jurisdiction they were.

During the Crimean War, these practices at Sulina, and at Galați were somewhat eliminated by the Austrian Army of Occupation in the Romanian Principalities by means of military measures, including martial law and even "la Bastonnade."[9]

A diplomatic conflict between England and Russia because of the navigational obstacles arose after 1836, in effect becoming one of the causes of the Crimean War. In this conflict, the Greeks were politically on Russia's side, but comercially on England's.

After 1840, when the Greeks and Turks involved in riverine navigation on the Lower Danube, came up against the beginning of an effective Austrian and Hungarian competition, the confrontation became unequal. Whereas the fleets of the former ones had become out-of-date, those of the opponents were modern. Although Greek and Turkish ownership was still on a private individual basis, the Austrians and Hungarians were organized in joint-stock companies, subsidized and politically supported by the State. Crews of the Austrian fleet had been trained in theory and practice in state naval schools; those on the Greek and Turkish fleets were illiterate. However, the crews of the latter had lengthy practical experience and, even more important, were familiar with the hydrographic details of the river. The Austrians and Hungarians carried out scientific research on the Lower Danube, but the Greek and Turkish navigators performed by instinct. Among the well-known Hungarian researchers was Count Stephen Széchenni who initiated the work at removing the physical obstancles at the Iron Gates.[10]

The Greeks managed to counterbalance the competition by the efficiency of their small crafts, their hard work, and low operating expenses, including even on food. One Sardinian consul reported that the latter item as having been reduced to bread and olives.[11]

On the competitive market of transportation of exports and imports through the ports of Galați and Brăila, in 1838, the Greek and Ionian flags together represented 30 percent of a total of 790 vessels, 202 and 38, respectively. The Turkish flag came next with 24 percent, fellowed by the Sardinian 18 percent, the Austrian 12 percent, and the Russian 9 percent.[12] Despite the numerical superiority of the Greek and Turkish maritime flags in 1838, they were still at a disadvantage because of the high maritime insurance premiums. The Sardinian consul in Brăila attributed that to the "frequency of fraud" in the Greek operations and the "multiple wrecks caused by insufficient knowledge of nautical science on the part of Turkish navigators."[13] Gradually, toward the end of the nineteenth century, the rhythm of the general navigation traffic rose, and due to the increase in steamship traffic, that of the Greek maritime fleet decreased.[14]

After 1856, on the Lower Danube as well as on the entire navigable course of the river, a great change took place in the form of a slow and progressive "revolution," with positive effects on all branches of activity along the entire Danube valley, effects which benefitted also the Greek society in Lower Danube navigation.

Components of this change were of a political order, international law; technological order; modernization of navigation; and of a social order. In this change, the small riparian states of the Lower Danube (Bulgaria, România, and Serbia) gradually imposed their rights in the navigation of their respective riverine sectors. From the political and international aspect, the problem of complete freedom of navigation was resolved through the 1856 Peace Treaty of Paris. On the basis of this treaty, local disputes among Austria, Russia, and Turkey were transferred to the European level, in which navigation was considered internationalized and included in European Public Law. By internationalization of navigation, based on the principles of the 1815 Act of Vienna, peace in navigation was maintained up to World War I. Greek riverine and maritime activity in the Lower Danube developed markedly under the regime of internationalized navigation. The introduction and development of steamships by Austria and Hungary influenced the modernization of transports along the Lower Danube, modernization in which the Greek fleet gradually took part.

Under the social aspect, the European Commission of the Danube, established by the same treaty (Paris 1856) for improvement of navigation at the mouth of the Sulina, gradually absorbed a considerable number of foreigners in its operations, Greeks among them. It created also a pilot corps and in 1900 out of a total of 154 pilots for Sulina and for the river, 88 were Greeks, while the rest were Turks, Romanians, Italians, Bulgarians, and Serbs.[15]

Shortly after two situations occured which could have diminished the effects of the new change. When Austria proposed, in the 1857 Act of Navigation,[16] that the Navigation Regulations be introduced in the Lower Danube the Greeks and the Turks were in opposition, apprehensive of competition from the Central European fleets. Another reduction could have been brought about by the provisions, in that same act, denying to non-riparian vessels the right of cabotage between ports of riparian countries. In such cases, the activity of vessels flying the Greek flag would have suffered. In the end, the

1857 act was rejected by England and France at the 1858 Conference of Paris.[17]

The rapid and extraordinary increase of exports through the mouth of the Sulina, especially that of cereals from all the Danubian countries, brought about great changes, both in the exercise and administration of navigation and in the social environment. Exports (cereal, lumber, etc.) rose from 2,718,509 tons between 1868 and 1870 to 13,434,673 tons between 1906 and 1910.[18] During this period, cereals went out through the Sulina and gold flowed in. Profits arising from this increase in commercial and navigational traffic, after the introduction of the international regime, were realized also by steamship agencies and insurance agencies, especially those in the ports of the Maritime Danube sector, most of them in Greek hands. There existed at Sulina, up to the time immediately following World War I, huge yards of Cardiff coal belonging to the Greeks Kyriakidis, Embiricos, and Theodoridis, and to the English firms of Watson and Youell and Rin & Marck of London.

An important aspect of this traffic after 1856 was the decrease in the traffic of sailing vessels and the numerical increase of steamships, which rose from 5.80 percent between 1856 and 1860 to 90.11 percent between 1906 and 1910.[19] This new element was temporarily detrimental to the traffic of the Greek-flag vessels.

Four principal causes and aspects concurred in bringing about Greek predominance in the navigation and commerce of the Lower Danube, up to the end of World War I. The first was the structure of ownership of vessels. Almost up to 1870, the majority of Greek riverine craft were under private individual ownership, or were owned by two or three persons, usually related. Generally, the owner of a small-tonnage vessel also fulfilled the function of captain. In order to counteract the competition, the owner had to reduce operational expenses to a minimum. For example, the crew of a small barge was composed of one individual and his family, his guard dog, and a few hens in a coop. After 1870, and especially after 1878, some of the private, or associated, owners became individual owners on a capitalist basis, and in step with the modernization of navigation, began gradually to replace the wooden vessels with the iron ones from the naval shipyards in Budapest and Vienna.

Some Greek capitalist owners of river fleets were also owners of large estates or of flour and pasta mills situated in the ports, the technical equipment being imported from Austria - Hungary and Germany. At the end of the nineteenth century there existed a select generation of cereal exporters and ship owners of different nationalities, including Greeks.[20] Some of the Greek capitalists residing in the ports of Brăila and Galați also had eighteen maritime vessels, acquired through the fruitful exploitation of riverine vessels and other commercial activity in Romania.[21]

Another category of Greek small-business owners sprang from the commercial world of café owners, bakers, and restauranteurs, who invested their profits in partnership with others in riverine and maritime vessels. They were beneficiaries of certain practices in navigation resulting from the freezing up of the river. Before the freezes, barges loaded with cereals destined for export were towed up to the port of Sulina, where the river portion was maintained navigable. By means of elevators, the cereals from the barges were transshipped on the maritime vessels brought into port. The large number of crewmen — consumers gathered there nourished the investments of the category of small-business owners mentioned above.

A second aspect was of patriotic order. For transporting cereals from the collection points along the river to the ports of export (Brăila and Galați) or to the flour mills located also in the ports, Greek landowners preferred the barges and tugs of their compatriots. Greek brokers preferred to lease Greek vessels to foreign cereal exporters and for repairs, small Greek shipyards were preferred. From a couple of cases reported by the Austro-Hungarian consul at Bucharest, it seems that Greeks in navigation were more ardently patriotic than their compatriots inland. Greeks in Brăila had sent important sums of money to co-national insurgents on Crete,[22] and, in 1880, 183 of them left Brăila for Greece to volunteer in the war against Turkey.[23] A third aspect was the interdependence between the Greek brokers for leasing riverine or maritime ships, and the foreign ship chandlers or companies. Ultimately, social and club relationships among the capitalists of Greek vessels and the other commercial or navigation capitalists also played a large role.

Because of the huge volume of transportation of goods resulting from the internationalized regime of navigation, the potential of Greek navigational activity did not diminish, despite the competition of the fleets of Austrian and Hungarian companies[24] and of the new Romanian companies established after 1890.[25] Furthermore, with the increased volume of exports through the Sulina and the modernization of transports, it became necessary to increase the number of tugs for towing the cereal-laden barges from the collection points to the ports of Brăila, Galați and Sulina, where transit or transshipment operations took place. Of a total of 88 tugboats registered at the end of the nineteenth century, 49 were under Greek registry.[26] Also, floating elevators were introduced to replace the manual operations emplyed at Brăila or Galați, for the transit of cereals being exported by riparians other than Romanians.

River craft of small tonnage, flying the Greek flag, also sailed the Pruth, which was internationalized because of its geographic location between two different states, Romania and Russia.

Before 1913 and immediately after, the storing-up of cereal supplies by the belligerents-to-be in World War I influenced the numerical increase of river fleets on the Lower Danube, including those of the Greeks, the latter by 1916 representing 44 percent of the total number. In the maritime traffic through the mouth of the Sulina, during that same period, the preponderence alternated between the Greek and the British flags.

To this brief summary of the successive facts and circumstances concerning the evolution of Greek activity in the Lower Danube up to 1913, will be added certain aspects of a social and economic order specific to the period following the year 1856.

Attracted by the many possibilities for employment and profit following the internationalization of navigation in 1856, immigrants from the Balkans, especially Greeks, began coming to the ports on the Lower Danube. The Romanian Principalities were dubbed the "America of the Balkans." Sulina was transformed into a mosaic of nationalities, in which the Greeks predominated. Sulina being a port and a cosmopolitan city under the Ottoman empire up to 1878 and after, its population lived in an oriental and international environment, under the protection of a variety of passports: Romanian, Turkish, Greek, Russian, English, and Austrian. This plurality of nationalities was suggestively described by a former Romanian, port captain at Sulina, by dubbing Sulina a "Europolis."[27]

Within the frame of Sulina's social mosaic, a compact and homogeneous Greek society developed, which in time extended to the other Danubian ports. The influence of this social order was so strong that the Greek language became standard in commercial and navigational fields as well as in social circles. Even much later, in 1938, the author of this present study met elderly people in Sulina who still knew only Greek and the mayor of the city, a Romanian, spoke fluent Greek.

In general, Greek newcomers settled in certain districts of the Danube ports inhabited by their compatriots. There, until they learned the local language, they could find some occupation in navigation or trade, thus making their immigration easier. In Brăila, for example, where this author grew up, there was a sector along the river with the Turkish name of "Karakioi" where most of the Greek population was dependent on navigation activity. In this area began the careers of those who in time, and due to their assiduous labor and aided by favorable economic circumstances, became important ship chandlers and ship owners in fluvial navigation. Together with the big Greek merchants they made up the upper class of Greek society along the Lower Danube, residing in the central cities of the ports. A point of interest is the fact that Panait Istrate, humanist and writer famous in Romanian literature, whose father was a Greek named Valsamis, was born and lived during his youth in the Comorofca and Karakioi sectors of Brăila.[28]

About 80 percent of the crews of river vessels flying the Greek or other foreign flags came from those sectors. Because of the great number of Greeks involved in navigation the special title of "Captan" [sic] was created and accorded, at times humorously, to barge steerers and to ships' captains alike. This nickname was adopted in that same humorous vein by the Romanian population throughout the small and the larger cities of the Lower Danube. Most of the Greeks in navigation were originally from Cephalonia, the next largest number from Ithaca.

Backed by the freedoms accorded by the international regime of navigation, some of the larger Greek shipowners reacted on two occasions against certain measures passed by Romanian authorities. During a legitimate campaign started by the Romanian government after 1859, to abolish donations from Romanian monasteries to Orthodox ones abroad, Brăila authorities banned religious services in Romanian churches in the Greek language.[29] A compromise arranged by Prince Alexandru Ion Cuza (whose mother was Greek) was unsatisfactory, so the Greeks simply arranged to have services officiated on a barge flying the Greek flag, and hence, benefitted from the extraterritorial rights due it by virtue of the international system of navigation.

In 1878, the Romanian government banned the right of cabotage between Romanian ports to vessels of non-riparian countries. Faced with this measure, the ship owners, whose barges plied the Danube under the Greek flag by virtue of that same International regime, removed their vessels to Reni and Ismail, which at the time were under Russian occupation.[30] The move, which numerically represented 47 percent of the barges and 52 percent of the tugboats of the total Lower Danube fleet, had negative results on the cereal exports and caused the Romanian government to reconsider its initial measure. Because of the tolerance displayed by the Romanians, the position of the Greek citizens in no way deteriorated as a result of the two incidents.

Among the specific characteristics of the Greeks in navigation is that of the absence of any process of assimilation. Contrary to the many compatriots in the interior of the land — who in time became assimilated politically and socially with the majority population, even adopting Romanian citizenship — those in navigation had retained their Greek citizenship and ethnicity.

Aside from the idea of a deliberate resistance against integrating with the majority population, retaining their nationality of origin of most Greeks in navigation resulted mainly from the freedom of navigation under the Greek flag, in accordance with the international regime of navigation; freedom of commerce; the hospitality and friendly relationship with the Romanian people; the free functioning permitted to churches, schools, clubs, and national and cultural associations; and, the status of economic independence.

A change occurred, too, in the matter of education of the wealthy Greek upper class. The children of this class went to schools and colleges abroad or to the foreign schools and cultural institutions — French, Italian, German, English — in the ports. Western influence was thus propagated in the ports, as well as in the larger Romanian cities. The results were not exactly those expected by the parents. The students returning from abroad, with more advanced ideas, and accustomed to other social environments, did not continue the activities initiated by their parents, considering them not corresponding to the higher education they had received. They found themselves detached from the social life of their place of birth and emphasized their westernization by substituting foreign expressions of speech for their Greek and Romanian expressions. Not having had the commercial or navigational experience, they did not succeed in keeping up the commercial enterprises of their parents in the periods of economic crisis such as that following World War I.

Several examples can be revealing of the numerical decrease, after World War I, of the barge fleets of some of the large shipowners:[31]

Number of barges in 1902		*Number of barges in 1920*
M. Caravia, Brăila	7	1
Chrisoveloni, M. Z.	12	—
Statatos Brothers	24	10

Unlike some of their compatriots of Romanian citizenship living in the interior, Greeks in navigation did not get involved in local politics. One could say they were practically "mercenaries," active in trade and navigation.

Greeks did not form an island apart in the midst of the majority population. The Romanian historian, C. G. Giurescu, stated: "The minority element in Brăila had a loyal attitude towards their fellow citizens in the majority and towards the Romanian State."[32]

The activity of the Greeks in the navigation and commerce of the Lower Danube, as well as that of those inland, was an integral part of Romanian political and social interests as well as of the national economy.

After 1875, with the occasion of the "customs war" between Vienna and Bucharest, Romania took measures to escape from one of the situations that had detrimental effects upon its national economy and its balance of trade. Because of the lack of mechanized mills, Romania was importing from Hungary flour and pasta products made from the grain Romania had exported to Hungary. When Romania, after 1878, initiated her own policy of industrialization, certain of the more prominent Greek shipowners constructed mechanized flour and pasta mills in the interior of the country as well as in some of the Lower Danube ports. The largest of these were in Brăila, the properties of the Greeks Valerianos, Panait Violatos, Apostolos Melissaratos, Gheorghiadis, and Serafidis.

Some of the large ship owners and cereal exporters supported financial, social, and urbanistic activities in the ports. In Brăila, for example, there existed in the center of town, a group of large buildings, including theater and cinema halls and a library, on the roof of which was the sign "Ralli Donation" until World War II. The buildings had been a donation from the cereal exporter Rallis. In 1843, Greek and Italian merchants and chandlers contributed to the beautification of the city and port of Galați. In 1857, too, merchants and shippers, 60 percent of whom were Greeks, thanked the mayor of Galați for the urban improvements made for the benefit of the city — improvements to which they also had contributed.[33]

Among the Romanian-ized Greeks, descendants of the former Phanariot Gospodars, was the economist Alexandru D. Moruzi (1815-1878), who after holding various positions in the government of the Principality of Moldavia, was named Mayor of the port city of Galați (1871-73). In that capacity, he took measures for developing trade and navigation, initiating the construction of quays in the port, of public buildings, and proposed the establishment of warehouses in the port. He also upheld maintaining a free port status (*porto franco*).[34]

In Brăila, Greek print shops printed newspapers with both Romanian and Greek text, and in addition to the Greek community school, there also functioned a professional school for girls. The latter had been established by the Greek Archimandrate, Hrisant Penetis, who donated to the school his entire fortune "in appreciation of the manner in which he had been received by the Romanians."[35]

This summary presentation reflects the activity of Greeks in navigation and commerce along the Lower Danube during the period 1789 to 1913. As a general conclusion, the following can be noted: the ancient Greeks had established commercial navigation on the Lower Danube, their descendants working together with the riparians had continued the process, and the Austrians and Hungarians participated in its modernization up to World War I.

What became of the Greek presence after 1913? The answer to that question implies going briefly beyond the period indicated in our subject. It began to decrease immediately after World War I and ceased after World War II, due to political and social circumstances. Only a very reduced traffic of the Greek maritime flag plies the Maritime Danube between the port of Brăila and the Black Sea. As could be expected in the evolving process of the change, locals replaced the foreigners. The dream of many Greeks involved in the field of navigation, before World War I, was to return to their native land, Greece, but it could not be fulfilled. Acclimatization with the hospitable local society and mixed marriages became the factors for indefinite postponement of their repatriation. After World War II, some chose the path of refuge toward Greece and other lands. What is now left of the Greek presence of the Lower Danube are the gravestones, bearing inscriptions in Greek — among them those of the author's grandparents and parents — in the cemetaries of the Lower Danube ports. And perhaps, here and there, a memorial candle burning.

We feel that the Greeks should appear on the first page of any histories of the Black Sea and the Lower Danube, as those who had staked out the Alpha of commercial navigation there.

Notes

1. Vasile Pârvan, *La pénétration héllénique et héllénistique dans la vallée du Danube* (Bucharest, 1931), 42.

2. Ion Chelcea, *Crecii în colindele noastre* [The Greeks in our carols] (Cluj, 1931).

3. Nicolae Docan, *Memorii despre lucrările cartografice privitoare la răsboiul*

dintre 1787-1791 [Memorandum on Cartographic Studies Concerning the War of 1787-1791] (Burcharest, Academia Română, 1911), Memorii, Secția Ist., Seria II Tom. XXXIV, pp. 16-17.

4. John Stokes, in Dispach by Lieutenent Trotter, "Reporting upon the Operations of the European Commission of the Danube during the years 1894-1906," presented to both Houses of Parliament, August 1907, with the reference to "Commercial," No. 9 (1907), printed for his Majesty's Stationary Office (London, 1907); also see, Ed. Engelhardt, *Etudes sur les embouchures du Danube*," (Galatz, 1862), 53, and *La Commission Européenne du Danube et son œuvre de 1856 à 1930* (Paris, 1931), 9-10.

5. Lloyd to Col. Neale, March 30, 1850, Foreign Office 78/977, by Prof. Radu R. Florescu in Acta Historica, Tomus II, *The Struggle Against Russia in the Romanian Principalities, 1821-1854* (Monachi, 1962), p. 271, note 70.

6. London's Underworld, ed. by Quennel Peter, selections from "Those that will not work," the fourth volume of *London Labour and the London Poor*, by H. Myhew (London, n.d.), 18, 25, 65, 291.

7. Herbert Asbury, *The Barbary Coast. An Informal History of the San Francisco Underworld* (New York, 1933), 3-38, 110, 148.

8. From the report of the Sardinian Consul at Galatz, 24 May, 1838, in D. Bodin, *Documente privitoare la legăturile economice dintre Principatele Române și Regatul Sardiniei* [Documents Concerning the economic Ties between the Romanian Principalities and the Kingdom of Sardinia], Uniunea Fundațiilor Culturale (Bucharest, 1941), 39.

9. Ed. Engelhardt, 56.

10. George Barany, *Stephen Széchenni and the Awakening of Hungarian Nationalism, 1791-1841* (Princeton, Princeton University Press, 1968), 244, 253.

11. From the report of the Sardinian Consul at Brăila, 5 February 1852, in Bodin, 244.

12. From the report of the Sardinian Consul at Galatz 29 March, 1839, in Bodin, 50.

13. From the Report of the Sardinian Consul at Brăila, 5 Feb. 1852, in Bodin, 238.

14. From the report of the Sardinian Consul at Galatz, 17 March, 1852, in Bodin, 267 statistics.

15. B. N. Youghaperian, *"L'Annuaire du Danube,"* (Brăila, 1902-1903) 199-200.

16. Acte de navigation du Danube, signé à Vienne le 7 Novembre 1857 élaboré par la Commission Riveraine de Danube, in D. Sturdza, *"Recueil de documents relatifs à la liberté de navigation du Danube* (Berlin, 1904), 37, 51.

17. *Confèrences de Paris 1858 relatives à l'organization des Principautés roumaines,* in D. Sturdza, 67.

18. *"La Commission Européenne et son...,"* 377, 514.

19. *Ibid.,* 573.

20. Among them, Greeks: Valianos, Theophilatos, Apostolos Melissaratos,

Chrisovelonis, Frații Stathatos, Marcopoulos, etc; Jews: Frații Mendl, M. Roth, Daniel, Joseph Loebl, etc; Italians: Ed Fanciotti, Peirano, Pedemonte, Gattorno.

21. Youghaperian, see, nominal statistics.

22. Haus-, Hof- und Staatsarchiv, Wien, Politische Archive, Konsulate, XXXIII, 200, Ibraila, Jahr 1873, f. 5 v-6, cited by C. C. Giurescu, *Istoricul orașului Brăila* (Bucharest, 1968), 214.

23. *Ibid.*, Konsulate, XXXIII, 232, Ibraila, 5 October 1880, cited by C. C. Giurescu, 243.

24. Première Société I. R. P. Autrichienne de Navigation à vapeur sur le Danube entre Ratisbonne et Soulina (DDSG), Société Anonyme Hongroise de Navigation Fluviale et Maritime (MFTR).

25. *Navigațiunea Fluvială Română* (NFR), Romenia's State, 1890; *Societatea Română Danubiană* (SRD), private co. 1914; *Societatea Danubiană*, private co., 1910.

26. Youghaperian, *L'Annuaire du Danube, 1894-1895* (Brăila, 1900), 17-21.

27. Eugen Botez (pen name Jean Bart), *Europolis* (Bucharest, 1939).

28. Giurescu, *Istoricul orașului Brăila*, 208.

29. *Ibid.*, 195.

30. C. Băicoianu, *Le Danube aperçu historique économique et politique* (Paris, 1917).

31. C. Tonegaru, *Semaforul Dunării și al Mării Negre* (Brăila, 1920), nominal statistics.

32. Giurescu, 241.

33. Victor Slăvescu, *Viața și opera economistului Alexandru D. Moruzi, 1815-1878* [Life and Works of the Economist Alexandru D. Moruzi] (Bucharest, Academia Română Studii și Cercetări, 1941), 20-21.

34. V. Slăvescu, 35-41.

35. Giurescu, 244-245.

Virginia Paskaleva

Shipping and Trade on the Lower Danube
in the Eighteenth and Nineteenth Centuries

The present article sets forth the results of the author's research over the course of two decades on Central Europe's trade relations with the lands along the lower Danube in the eighteenth and nineteenth centuries. She has relied on a considerable number of works and documents in various languages, scattered in different libraries in Central Europe, and especially on the documentary wealth of the First Austrian Royal Shipping Company in Vienna. Two main problems arise out of the very complex history of the economic bonds of the peoples of the Lower Danubian basin with Central Europe: One, the study of the mechanism and the realization of the commercial ties and relations among the Balkan and the Central European peoples — the scope and structure of trade and the activity of middlemen between the Lower Danubian region as the main center and the individual Central European regions from tùe eighteenth century until the declaration of the Russo-Turkish War (1877-78); two, the contribution of the "small peoples" (the Balkan peoples) toward the restoration of economic life in Central European regions, left by the Ottoman troops in the eighteenth century, and toward the gradual transformation of these peoples into an object of trade penetration by an economically stronger Central Europe as a result of the growing industrial backwardness of the lands along the Lower Danube during the third quarter of the nineteenth century.

The main conclusions from this long research work are as follows:

At the same time when the industrial revolution started in Britain, gradually spreading to the European continent,[1] the manufacturing mode of production asserted itself in Central Europe, but the transition to superior forms of commodity production, the logical outcome of its historical evolution, did not take place in the Ottoman empire, nor in its lands in the lower Danubian basin. Yet, a number of studies prove that, during the period from the 1740s until the 1780s, industry in the Balkan provinces showed certain tendencies and possibilities for transformation into an industry of a superior type.[2] Still, numerous negative internal and external factors curtailed the initiative even of the boldest undertaker. One of the main, and perhaps the most important, brake on this process was the Sultanate itself — autocratic and despotic in character and feudal and theocratic in substance. Unlike the Central European aristocracy, the Ottoman nobility was not striving to establish a certain degree of industrial protectionism. By and large its social status in Ottoman society differed from that of aristocracy in Central Europe. In the last decades of the eighteenth century the Ottoman state was torn by internecine wars, by bloody clashes between local rulers.

Trade between Central Europe and the lands of the lower Danubian basin was in the hands of Balkan middlemen. Occasionally the difficult conditions under which they worked and the results they obtained are underrated in literature. At first Ottoman subjects were regarded with favor throughout Central Europe, but when profits began to flow into their coffers the hostility toward them grew and reached its climax in making them swear allegiance to the Austrian crown, with the express purpose of putting an end to their further settlement on Hapsburg territory.[3]

In practice, however, their presence was of need during the following decades of the nineteenth until the extension of the modern transport communications made it possible to establish direct contacts between businessmen and trading firms of both countries.[4] This is why the results of the activity of the Balkan inhabitants(Greeks, Wallachians, Serbians, Bulgarians, Aromanians [Tsintsars], and others) is assessed as positive. These above results are all bilateral:

a. In the economic situation which existed in Central Europe during different periods, the "Greeks" linked one customs region with another, one town with another, one village with another. The belated emergence of local merchants, for example in Hungary, enabled Ottoman subjects, favored by contractual relations, and thanks to their qualities, to develop activities linking individual economic structures,[5] especially during the first half of the eighteenth century when they contributed to the development of material production and to the formation of a broader domestic market in vast Central European regions (a list of the commodities traded will be found in the Appendix). We, therefore, assess as positive the contribution of the representatives of the lesser East European peoples among the varied mosaic of Central European ethnic groups.

b. Their activities also had another aspect. Attempts of some of them in the manufacture of textiles, which encountered the firm resistance of craft guilds. Thus, in 1771, we see the dyers' of cotton yarn guild in Brașov complaining that in 1768 a few "Greek" merchants had found a "red" factory which dyed large quantities of cotton yarn, which put guild members out of work.[6] The craftsmen petitioned the local court, but the court decided that since the "Greeks" alone knew the secret of dyeing, they were highly valued by the Austrian emperor.

In the 1770s in Schwechat near Vienna, some 60,000 workers were engaged in the production of cotton, semi-silk, and silk stuff for the "Orient," and a large part of this production was directed by "Greeks."[7] But, generally speaking, the Ottoman subjects reluctantly invested capital for industrial purposes. Still, they were foreigners in Central Europe, and there was no legal order in the Ottoman empire.

c. The Balkan inhabitants were equally active in the lands of their birth. The network of assistants, purchasers, and carters which they established stirred into action and different regions, towns, and villages. Suffice it to recall, the organization of the growing trade with cotton and cotton yarn, or the trade in coarse woollen cloth and ready-to-wear clothes, made use of it. Trade capital stimulated, expanded local production, promoted exports, and at the same time, enriched the local market, connecting it with more distant markets. The growth and scope of commodity-capital relations during the precapitalist period arc of great importance, provided that the respective state creates suitable conditions to this effect.

From the very beginning, settlers on Austrian territory did not have equal social status. Some of them carried larger sums of money with them, managed to find their bearings more quickly than the others, and became more active. They managed to adapt themselves more successfully to the new social environment, and it was easier for them to have a run of luck in a foreign land, although with difficulty they managed to work their way to the upper strata of an alien society. We shall adduce only two examples. During 1710-40, the Bulgarian family Bibič was one of the richest in Transylvania. In 1737, Jacob Bibič received the title of Imperial Counsellor.[8] Michail Jon Cumbru, who was born in Macedonia, settled in Braşov in 1782, became an Austrian subject and engaged in broad trading activities.[9] Within two decades, he established a vast network of collaborators, commission agents, correspondents, and so forth, in all the larger Balkan, Hungarian, and Romanian towns, as well as in Vienna and Leipzig. Some 1884 archival documents astound us with the scope of his trade, import, export, and transit, not only in commodities, but also in coins, bills of exchange, and other valuables.

Such activity of merchants like Cumbru contributed to the decay of old feudal relations, linked backward regions with the vast international market, and paved the way for the development of bourgeois society.

Another process got underway during the third quarter of the seventeenth century. Under the influence of German mercantilism, the formation of trading companies began in Vienna for the penetration of the Orient via the Danube. Already in 1667, the Vienna Oriental Trading Company tried for the first time to sail down the middle Danube with nine ships, loaded with German merchandise, for Rusé.[10] The expedition was led by Lelio de Luca, who settled for a while in Rusé and then traveled to Adrianople, carrying with him samples and specimens of his commodities. At the beginning of 1668, he was in Constantinople, where he attempted to set up a branch in the Turkish capital. Good trade results gave the Vienna mercantilists reasons to believe that, in future, the trade of Central Europe with Southeastern Europe and Constantinople would develop under very favorable conditions. However, the plague and hostilities gradually curtailed its activities.

Austria's commercial treaty with the Porte (August 16, 1718), attached to the Požarevac Peace Treaty after the defeat of Ottoman forces in Central Europe, was very encouraging from an economic point of view. Emperor Charles VI was particularly active in his efforts to conquer positions all along the Danube, a natural commercial route for the empire's economy. The new "Imperial Privileged

Oriental Company," founded in 1719, was granted the right to trade by land and water with all the provinces of the Ottoman empire. In 1720, the company's capital amounted to 217,000 florins.[11] It was also granted the right to build ships for trade in the Adriatic, to establish factories for textiles, sugar, etc., as well as the privilege to mine copper ore. Things went smoothly until 1729, but afterward for various reasons the company began to lose money and Maria Theresa dissolved it in 1741. The failure of this company notwithstanding, trading companies became a steady tendency in Central European trade, and in the next few decades, became a tradition. The Danube was the real "trade route," and its adjoining areas down to the river's estuary were the "natural" outlet for the manufactured goods of Central Europe, as well as a region from which raw materials could be received.

Russia's victory in the Russo-Turkish War of 1768-74, which ended with the Kutchuk-Kainarji Peace Treaty, marked a turning point in the Hoffburg's oriental policy. Under this treaty, Russia received an outlet on the Black Sea and the Danube delta. Thus, after 1774, Vienna's attention was permanently focused on the valley and the delta of the Danube and on the Balkans in general.

The idea of better-organized trade along the whole course of the Danube rapidly made headway among the business circles in the Austrian capital. One of its proponents was the wealthy Viennese merchant and banker, Johann Freiherr von Fries,[12] and a newly founded company for trade with the Orient bore his name. In 1777, the new joint-trade association was also formed by four Balkan merchants, two of whom were Greeks. In two years, Fries' company sent three ships with Central European goods to Rusé where a warehouse was set up to receive its goods.

The Fries Company attained its goal — step by step the two banks of the Danube got to know each other and became familiar with the opportunities for trade in the basin. For various reasons, the company did not operate a long time, in 1782, it wound up its last deals in Seres and Salonika. In the final analysis, through this company, the economic potential of the Balkans became clearer to the Central European governing circles.

When in the 1780s, there was a considerable increase in manufacturing output in Bohemia, Moravia, and Austria, Viennese business circles began to consider possible markets for their goods. Emperor Joseph II was particularly interested in the trading company, founded in 1781, by Anton Willeshoven.[13] On June 11, 1782, "Patriot," the first ship of the Willeshoven Company, started from Vienna toward the lower Danube. It had a cargo of 1000 hundredweight or centners (c. 45,500 kgs), consisting of different commodities, such as broadcloth, cotton and silk stuff, chinaware, mirrors, brassware, buttons, knives, cords, lace, paper, dyes, clocks, iron, lead, and chocolate. The expedition was successful, but, in 1784, the company went bankrupt for various reasons.

During the Russo-Turkish War (1787-91), in which Austria also took part, many Central European merchants reached the lower Danube via Transylvania and distributed their merchandise in the Romanian principalities and Bulgarian ports of Silistra, Rusé, and Svištov.[14] So, in the last decades of the eighteenth century, Central European industry and trade acquired specific positions in the lands along the lower reaches of the Danube.

At the beginning of the next century, Austro-Turkish, respectively Austro-Balkan, trade was restricted owing to the hostilities.[15] No official statistics are available for that period, and for this reason, it is impossible to determine its volume. With no other country did Austria maintain such favorable contractual trade relations as with the Ottoman empire until the 1840s, but the whole trade was still in the hands of "Turkish" subjects overland via Transylvania and by sea via Trieste, and to a certain extent, it remained a "liability" in the Austrian trade balance. Almost until the Crimean War, trade remained in the hands of Balkan inhabitants, some of whom were Austrian subjects and others who had taken provisional residence in the Austrian provinces. Vienna was well aware of this, and consequently, protected their activities, and through them, its own economic interests and positions in the Balkans.

With the inauguration of Austrian steamship navigation on the lower Danube in the 1840s, a new stage began in the development of socio-economic ties between Central Europe and the lands along the lower Danube. The rich archives of the First Privileged Steamship Company in Vienna provides us with reliable statistical data about the development of steamship navigation in the course of one decade (1843-53) in lower Danubian basin. If we consider three main indicators: the number of passengers, the transported goods in centners (1 centner = 100 pounds = c. 45.5 kgs), and the monies transported in florins, we find the following:

Year	Passengers	Goods in centners	Florins
1843	3738	36,426	1,247,732
1853	12,015	378,997	2,693,260

Within a decade, the number of the passengers tripled, the weight of the cargo increased over ten times, and the amount of transported money doubled because of the lack of credit and banking institutions. This was an unprecedented upsurge, and generally speaking, the results were positive.

In order to promote the extension of steamship communications on the lower Danube, the company's management carried out vast organizational work within that period. As a very detailed review of the "business deals along the Lower Danube" shows us, by the end of 1842, Austrian steamship navigation already had representatives, new buildings for its employees and passengers, coal yards and warehouses, horse stables and repair shops, fire extinguishing machines, hydraulic presses, and decimal balances in the following Lower Danubian ports and with the following value:[16]

Ports	Value in florins
Drenkowa	295,244
Orșova	1,116,230
Gladostniza	108,331
Kladova (Kladovo)	12,835
Vidin	10,130
Svištov	under organization
Rusé	34,828
Giurgiu	355,957
Brăila	53,039
Galați	50,450
Tulcea	4000

We ought to bear in mind that steamship administration developed agencies on the Bulgarian banks more slowly, kept less inventory there, and in general, organized more cautiously its infrastructure there, owing to lack of security and to obstacles on the part of Turkish authorities. The almost free regime on the Romanian banks was more favorable for the establishment of a comparatively extensive technical base. Even in Giurgiu, a smaller port than Rusé, more manipulations were made, warehouses were bigger, etc. Along the Bulgarian banks, there were long quarantines due to the sudden outbreak of the plague brought to the Bulgarian lands from Asia Minor, as the Austrian informers incessantly complained.

The balance sheets for 1843-47 show the upward development of steamship navigation along the Romanian and Bulgarian banks. Thus, the following percentages are given for 1845 for the increase of the circulation of passengers and goods on the middle and lower Danube:

Ports	*Value in florins*	*Year*	*Passengers*	*Goods in centners*	*Florins*

Ports	*Percentage increase*	
	Passengers	*Goods*
Vienna - Linz	35	6
Vienna - Pest	22	36
Pest - Zemun - Orşova	90	100
Orşova - Galaţi	32	16

Comparatively speaking, the number of passengers along the Orşova-Galaţi stretch (the runs included both the Bulgarian and Romanian banks) was almost the same as along the Vienna-Linz stretch. Undoubtedly, traffic of passengers on the lower Danube was considerable and so was the traffic of goods.

Austrian ships carried the whole mail — letters, parcels, and monies from Europe to the Balkan countries and Turkey, and vice versa. The rendezvous of the ships of the Danubian Steamship Company and of the Austrian Lloyd at Galaţi, — initially four times monthly and after 1848, six times monthly — secured the steady transportation of mail, money, and commodities from Vienna to Constantinople, on the one hand, and from Trieste to Constantinople, on the other. The ships already covered the distance from Vienna to Orşova in four days and nights and went on to Černa Voda. In order to avoid difficulties at Sulina, because of the sandbanks, passengers and goods were transferred to carts and horses at Černa Voda and carried to Constanta eight miles on a good road. Special shelters for men, horses, carts, and goods were established at Černa Voda and Constanta.

In the 1840s Vienna became the center of the newlybuilt railway lines in Central Europe, thereby facilitating communications with Southeastern Europe, and in general, Europe with the Balkans. Moreover, the company reached an agreement with the Romanian Government to intensify links between the ports on the Romanian and Bulgarian banks, called in the documents "Turkish" banks.[17] Barges, boats, and steamers with passengers and cargo circulated from the Bulgarian to the Romanian ports and back. This peculiar activity was very beneficial to the economic life on both banks of the river and their hinterland. But the British flag began to appear increasingly often in the same waters on which Central European shipping was endeavoring to impose its domination.

The quiet Danubian banks, as they were described by Ami Boué and J. P. Fallmayrer, came to life, old ports grew active, and small, insignifcant settlements began to play an economic role. Thus, for example, Orşova was originally a very insignificant settlement, but within a few years its importance increased. The Bulgarian port of Lom owes its upsurge to a certain extent to Austrian shipping and to Central European trade during that period.

With the extension of steamship navigation, especially after the removal of some natural obstacles at the Iron Gates, the small riverside settlements became centers of a brisk trade with the hinterland and even with more distant areas, which until then, had remained outside active trade. Direct links were established among the Romanian, Bulgarian, and Serbian ports in which put Austrian steamers on different runs.

The statistical material also reveals changes in the volume and structure of trade. Import lists show a much broader range of manufactured goods which is easy to explain in view of the progress of industrial production in Central Europe.

Rusé gradually became the largest center of trade with Austria and a transit point for the Austrian goods, sent via the Danube. This town became "the most important juncture... for Austrian [i.e., Central European] trade," reads a report sent to the newspaper, *Austrian Lloyd*.[18] Rusé is situated halfway between the Iron Gates and the river's estuary; it is connected with Varna via Šumen and with Kazanlâk via Târnovo through the Balkan range, and from Kazanlâk to southern Bulgaria. We should not forget the proximity of Rusé to Giurgiu, where many commodities arrived from Transylvania and the Romanian lands. Import increased further when special consignments were unloaded from Vienna and Pest for the various annual fairs. Usually a quarter of the imported articles were absorbed by the Rusé market, and most went to the interior of the country.

If we attempt to use the available data to draw up comparative statistics for the Austrian import and export trade to and from Rusé for 1842-52, we shall get the following pattern for Austrian trade:

T a b l e I

Imports from Austria into Rusé (1842-52)[19]

Year	Method	Goods (in centners)	Value in florins
1842	steamers	3179	718,142
1843	steamers and overland	7059	813,709
1844	steamers and boats	9590	1,656,180
1845	quarantine due to plague	—	—
1846	steamers	7336	872,000
1847	steamers, boats, and overland	10,534	1,359,500
1848	steamers	3673	704,320
1849	steamers	2269	—
1850	steamers, boats, and overland	—	1,318,000
1851	steamers, boats, and overland	14,887	998,408
1852	steamers	4157	—

The above figures have been obtained by adding different data for commodities, sent by the Austro-Czech complex by steamers and brigs, as well as overland via Wallachia from Transylvania. For 1845, only partial data are available; so, it is not possible to make a precise assessment of imports and exports in that year. But the data do show that it is much larger than the following year, when large consignments of British goods coming from Constantinople were unloaded in Varna and were distributed in Rusé. Owing to the 1848-49 revolutions Austrian imports in Central Europe fell by nearly half. In 1849, a strict quarantine was declared on the Bulgarian banks because of an outbreak of the plague.

Exports from Rusé were made under the same conditions.[20]

Table II

Year	Goods (in centners)	Value in florins
1842	414	75,927
1843	1375	71,873
1844	738	80,650
1845	—	—
1846	1191	101,200
1847	847	53,000
1848	125	10,400
1849	—	—
1850	2545	137,000
1851	1873	165,800
1852	3089	—

The above commodities were exported mainly on Austrian steamers. There is no positive information about goods transported overland. The tables are primarily based on consular reports which contain the greatest amount of information on imports and exports on steamers. Although approximate, the tables show that imports were considerably greater than exports. On the other hand, we must bear in mind that Bulgarian wheat and other agricultural produce were exported via Galaţi and Varna on the big seagoing steamers of the Austrian

Lloyd for Trieste, from which they were occasionally re-exported to other ports. Hence, a much greater amount of farm produce were exported via Rusé to Galați and Varna, and thereafter transported by Austrian vessels and steamers not only for Hapsburg provinces. Austrian consular reports and information from the Bulgarian land, which became more frequent during the 1840s, point out on more than one occasion that Trieste with its steamers and vessels (the old sailers continued to operate side by side with modern steamers) was one of the major channels of Austrian economic influence in the regions from the Danube to the Aegean Sea, including Salonika and the whole Black Sea coast to the east. Prices of Bulgarian farm produce were not high, but for specific periods after 1840, exporters were compelled to pay a twelve-percent duty on specific quantities of grain under the Balta Liman treaty — over which Austrian diplomats and consuls in Turkey persistently fought.

Next to Rusé came Vidin as an important marketing center of Austrian goods. By 1850, the average annual imports from the Habsburg empire into Vidin amounted to 320,000 florins and the exports from Vidin to 270,000 florins.[21] Vidin also supplied Austrian goods to many towns in the interior: Niș, Sofia, Vraca, Loveč, Pleven, from which it collected farm produce for export.

Svištov was yet another port with a brisk trade. On the eve of the Crimean War, Austrian imports via Svištov doubled. In 1858, total imports through another Bulgarian port, Lom, amounted to 180,000 florins, Austria's share accounting for 100,000.[21]

In Galați, Austrian trade kept its leading place ahead of Britain, France, and other European states, thanks to the goods sent there from three directions: overland from and through Transylvania, on the Danube from Vienna, and across the Black Sea from Trieste. According to French statistics, in 1840 Austrian ships alone, coming from Vienna, unloaded at Galați goods to the value of 750,000 lei, and in 1839, Trieste sent there coffee, colonial goods, fabrics, and paper to the amount of 1,833,000 lei.[21]

Two major factors began to bar the road to Central European economic influence in the lower Danubian basin around the middle of the nineteenth century. They were the growing import of manufactured commodities from Britain, France, Belgium, and other countries and the rapidly expanding export of wheat and other farm produce for the large European markets from the Danubian ports. Thus, in 1847, wheat to the value of over 1,000,000 florins was exported for Europe from the lower Danubian basin via the Black Sea. Usually 30 percent of the exported grain went to Britain, 25 percent to Constantinople, some 12 percent to Trieste, 28 percent to Marseille, Genoa, and Livorno (Leghorn), and approximately 10 percent to the ports on the upper reaches of the Danube, i.e., to Austria.[24]

No doubt the competition of Western Europe, and especially of Britain, with regard to Central European import and export trade in the lower Danubian region was menacing. Nevertheless, thanks to geographical proximity, the well-organized steamship navigation, different paths of penetration, the ability of the business circles to adapt themselves to the new situation, on the eve of the Crimean War, Austria's economic positions in the lower Danubian region were consolidated and extended.

During the third quarter of the century, the volume of the import and export trade in the lower Danubian basin considerably increased, notwithstanding certain fluctuations, ebbs and flows. The latter were due to a number of factors and circumstances; this volume depended above all on the state of the annual grain crops, on the yields of the industrial crops (cotton, tobacco, and in Rumania, the export of salt, etc.), on sheep breeding and stock raising, on the costly internal transport (See, Appendices). Depending on these factors, the population's purchasing power and the use of imported goods increased or decreased. All available economic information points to this inevitable ratio: increased or decreased export of farm produceincreased or decreased import of foreign-made light industrial products. A certain role was also played by the two big economic crises of 1857 and 1873, the plague in the lower Danubian lands, political developments, wars and insurrections which adversely affected both domestic and foreign trade.

One of the most important factors for the growth of trade at lower Danubian ports was the growth of market farming in the adjoining areas, a progressive factor in the belated capitalist development of the Balkans. Different data show that Central Europe absorbed part of the agricultural production of the lower Danubian basin, in our view approximately 30 to 40 percent (farm produce sent to Trieste via the Black Sea and to Vienna on the Danube), depending on the crops in Central Europe and on a number of other factors.

Undoubtedly, the import of Central-European goods was larger in volume, which meant an unfavorable trade balance for Turkish, as well as for Balkan, trade. The chronic adverse trade balance of the Ottoman empire is well known. But, in this particular case, market agriculture, helped by cheaper Austrian river transportation and by its more rapid inclusion in world trade, reduced the liabilities in the trade balance. In certain years the liabilities and assets were balanced, but it is diffult to prove this, owing to the lack of consistent and reliable data.

In the 1860s and 1870s, Central Europe was in a hurry to catch up with Britain and France in railway construction and in navigation on the big rivers. Within a ten-year period (1863-73), the railway network in the Danubian monarchy was extended threefold. Measures were taken to increase river navigation as well. Transport communications were rapidly established in the whole lower Danubian area. Its main communication line remained the lower Danubian navigation in which Austrian shipping played a predominant role, although the influence of Britain and other European countries steadily increased, especially in the Brăila-Sulina section. The internationalization of the Danube after 1856 also led to changes in the volume and structure of the import and export trade in the lower Danubian lands. Generally speaking, however, linkage with the whole Central European communications network, due to geographic proximity, should be positively assessed, inasmuch as it helped to put an end to the economic backwardness of the regions along the lower Danube, in spite of the less rapid capitalist development of adjoining lands; their agrarian structure did not change quickly. But, in the final analysis, during the intense establishment of communications among the individual European countries and peoples, the incorporation of these lands in the ever-more rapid capitalist development of Central Europe, and for that matter, of Europe as a whole, was an imperative necessity.

A p p e n d i c e s

I

L i s t

*of the Type of Commodities, Subject to Austrian-Balkan
Trade during the Eighteenth Century*

The drawing up of this list proved a difficult task. In existing sources (Austrian, Czech, Hungarian, and registers of the Romanian customs), as well as in certain scientific studies, the commodities are listed in different ways. The foreign documents list commodities exported from the Ottoman empire as "Turkish goods," or goods from Rumelia, Macedonia, and so forth, on the basis of very confused geographical notions. On the other hand, certain types of stuff are called by their European names, e.g., muslins, without explaining whether they were produced in the Ottoman empire, or were being re-exported as fine woollen fabrics from other countries, held in the warehouses of Balkan merchants. In many respects, there is no precision as to the types of goods exported from Central Europe to the middle and lower Danube. May of these are listed under numbers (Nos. 1, 2, 3...) of a given article, but these figures mean nothing today. Occasionally, they denote the quality of the merchandise, and in other cases, color scheme.

The range of goods exported from Central Europe was very broad, and it was considerably diversified during the last quarter of the eighteenth century. "Turkish" goods had a traditional character; most had already been exported by the Ottoman empire during the sixteenth and seventeenth centuries. But, in the eighteenth century, the volume of "Turkish" articles increased due to the growing need of raw materials for Central European industry. Quantities of the imported Central European goods were still limited, because the needs of the still patriarchal society in the southeastern regions of Europe did not grow rapidly and the tastes of the population had not yet become "modern," according to the European standards. And, during the first half of the nineteenth century, the inhabitants of the towns along the lower Danube became more ardent consumers of European goods.

I. Imports

Types of commodities imported overland into the Ottoman empire from Central Europe:

1. *Woollen fabrics — cloth*: From Moravia and Bohemia, 14 types of woollen plush with various color schemes, soft woollen cloth (molleton), differing from the coarse woollen cloth in various shades (camelot), mixed with cotton yarn, mulins, calamanco, ratine.

2. *Cotton fabrics*: 11 types of Silesian cotton cloth and stuff, cotton fabrics from Linz, Brno, white, printed, or plain, cheesecloth, flanelette, piqué, various types of cotton sateen, cloth for linen, batiste, taffeta.

3. *Silk stuff*: Imported more rarely, because various types of beautiful silk stuff (veils, taffeta, satin) were produced in the Ottoman empire and distributed in Europe. The foulard from Linz and tiffany were among the most famous imports to the Balkan lands.

4. *Glassware*: From Czechoslovakia, mirrors, porcelain; various sets were imported for the Romanian boyars and the wealthy Turks, as well as some items of luxury furniture. Coaches (carriages) were also imported for the high clergy, boyars, and pashas.

5. *Furs*: Fine, and well processed, such as, sable (Mustela zibelina) from Vienna.

6. *Ready-to-wear clothes*: dresses and blouses, socks and stockings, hats, cloth caps, gloves, shawls, various types of towels, kerchiefs, handkerchiefs, fezes.

7. *Haberdashery*: galloons, tassels, pompons, buttons, toilet articles, cosmetics, thread, jewelry.

8. *Hardware*: rifles, gun powder, swords and sabers, needles, brassware, ironware, knives, sickles, scythes (from Styria), tin, saws, locks and safety locks, files, iron hoops for casks, horse trappings.

9. *Chemicals and drugs*: vitriol, dyes in various colors.

10. *Spirits*: Fine wines, brandies, liqueurs, rum.

11. *Publications*: Books, newspapers, and magazines (in different languages).

Some of the goods were imported from Vienna, but they came from the Austrian exports via Trieste and Fiume and their origin could not be established.

II. Exports

Commodities exported overland from the Ottoman empire to Central Europe:

1. *Wool*: several qualities under different numbers.
2. *Hides*: calf and sheep, processed or semi-processed, called in the specifications "Cordouan," Morocco leather (reddish), white, yellowish.
3. *Cotton and cotton yarn*: white and red (the latter was particularly valued).
4. *Tobacco*: in leaves and crushed small.
5. *Silk*: raw and wound, silk stuff (satin).
6. *Homespun*: various types of thickness and ready-to-wear outer garments made from it.
7. *Cotton cloth*: coarser and fine; the former was called "Bocassi"; also, horse cloth and lace.
8. *Incense.*
9. *Silver trimmings* (filigree).
10. *Wax.*
11. *Spices.*
12. *Olive oil.*
13. *Dyes*: the very expensive plant saffron (Crocus sativum), a bulbous plant with yellow flowers from which yellow (orange-colored) dye was obtained.
14. *Sumach*: (Rhus Cotinus) for the tanning industry.
15. *Livestock*: From the Bulgarian and Romanian lands, whole herds of horses, buffaloes, and sheep were exported through Transylvania.
16. *Salt fish.*

Customhouses

*through which Balkan Merchants Passed
on Their Way to Central Europe*

1. Zemun (now Zemlin)
2. Mehadia
3. Calafat
4. Turnu-Roşu (Hungary) Vereštoron (Sibiu)
5. Braşov
6. Sopron (the Hungarian frontier customhouse on the way to Vienna)
7. Mezon (a Hungarian custonmhouse for dealers in cattle and grain)
8. Bratislava, a customhouse for owners of boats and small ships entering Austrian waters
9. Petervaradin
10. Certain documents also speak of the "Timišoara" sanitary point in Transylvania, which we were unable to identify. It is not known whether it was a customhouse or only a quarantine station. For the 1730s, we also came across the "Barakino" frontier customhouse in Serbia, through which the Macedonian merchants came, but we could not establish its exact location.

Data about customhouses are taken from various Austrian documents and from inquiries made by Austrian authorities, in which it was recorded through which frontier point and through which customhouses Balkan merchants had entered Austrian territory for the first time.

Statistical material which we have drawn from various company reports reveals the very sinuous line of the development of Austrian steamship navigation on the lower Danube during the third quarter of the nineteenth century.[25] The following table contains only a few indicators of the ebb and flow in steamship navigation on the lower Danube.

Circulation of Passengers, Goods and Monies on the Lower Danube (1857-75)

Year	Passengers	Goods (in centners)	Florins
1857	65,690	1,473,314	—
1858	47,465	1,167,609	2,509,105
1859	50,502	2,315,036	4,912,277
1860	62,488	2,893,149	5,501,956
1861	57,459	2,575,966	5,048,458
1862	53,254	3,757,571	5,215,448
1863	53,668	4,513,618	6,532,784
1864	102,303	5,556,389	5,464,787
1865	106,699	2,813,485	6,579,830
1866 +	—	—	—
1867	110,340	4,025,940	6,514,515
1868	147,004	3,942,302	10,310,230
1869	166,659	5,389,723	8,679,047
1870	165,695	3,225,057	8,545,421
1871 ++	—	—	—
1872	279,745	1,577,534	13,765,954
1873	210,909	8,209,987	11,120,428
1874	208,862	11,901,179	8,110,339
1875	291,574	7,199,300	5,446,393
TOTAL:	2,180,316	72,537,159	114,256,972

+ No data are available for 1866, for ships were transporting more troops during the Austro-Prussian War.

++ No data are available for 1871; ships were carrying troops and ammunition during the Franco-Prussian War.

Foreign competition, mainly British, had a considerable impact on the predominance of the Austrian merchant fleet in the lower Danubian basin from tùe 1850s until the 1870s. Two statistical sources attest to the rapid internationalization of steamship navigation on the lower Danube. One, the minutely collected data of the European Danubian Commission, the other, those of the adviser of the lower Austrian Chamber of Trade and Industry, Joseph Wolfbauer, who has used figures from the archives of the then-director of the Austrian Steamship Company M. Kassian, aided by Professor E. Süz, an expert on these matters.[26]

Vessels Leaving the Danube via Sulina (1851-70)

Country of Origin	1851 - 60		1861 - 70	
	number	tonnage	number	tonnage
Austria-Hungary	2269	628,179	2415	718,664
Britain	2124	426,309	2998	1,027,692
France	428	78,489	570	157,558
North German Confederation	593	101,428	479	100,737
Russia	383	60,666	1204	163,474
Italy	1222	206,938	3158	892,284
Greece	11,208	1,991,640	10,450	1,411,440
Turkey	3268	446,340	5068	439,635
Romania	1027	128,461	650	70,535

Notes

1. *Purş, J.* Prumislová revoluce. Vyvoj pojmu a concepce (Prage, 1973), cart. IV, p. 365.

2. *Sarc, Ö. C.* Tanzimat ve sanayimiz. Tanzimat Cilt I (Istanbul, 1940), p. 423.

3. *Otruba, G.* Die Wirtschaftspolitik Maria Theresias (Vienna, 1963).

4. *Peez, A.* Österreich und der Orient. Eine handelspolitische Studie (Vienna, 1875).

5. *Bur-Markovska, M.* Balkanite i ungarskiat pazar prez XVIII vek. (Sofia, 1977).

6. Archiva Biserica Neagra-Braschov. Fondul compania greceasca (24 Mai 1771).

7. *Peez, A.* p. 9.

8. *Trocsanyi, Zs.* "Das Schicksal der geadelten bulgarischen Familien in Siebenbürgen im 18.-19. Jahrh.," *Bulgarian Historical Review* (1981), Nr. 1-2.

9. Catalogul documentelor grecesti din Archivele Statului de la oraşul Stalin v. 1 (Bucharest, 1958).

10. Copey zweier Schreiben von Herrn Lelio de Luca... an die Herren Direktoren der orientalischen Compagnie. Gedruckt zu Wien (1668).

11. *Dullinger, J.* "Die Handelskompagnien Oesterreichs nach dem Oriente und nach Ostindien in der ersten Hälfte des 18. Jahrh," *Zeitschrift für Sozial-und Wirtschaftsgeschichte*, Siebenter Band (Berlin, 1900), p. 47.

12. Staatsarchiv Wien, Abt. I. Turcica, Fasc. 14, 6. Abt., Bl. 56.

13. *Halm, H.* Habsburgischer Osthandel im 18. Jahrhundert. Österreich und Neurußland II (Munich, 1954), S. 10, 23.

14. *Eudoxin de Hurmuzaki.* Documente privitorare la istoria Românilor, vol. XIX/1, pp. 187-88.

15. *Beer, A.* Die österreichische Handelspolitik im neuzehnten Jahrhundert (Vienna, 1891), S. 396.

16. Archiv der DDSG-Wien. Übersicht der Inventare auf den Stationen für das Jahr 1842. Übersicht der Geschäftsgebarung der unteren Donaulinie zwischen Orşova und Galaz (1842).

17. *Ibid.* Geschäftsbericht der Betriebs-Direction der ersten k. k. priv. DDSG über das Verwaltungsjahr 1847 (12 April 1848), p. 30

18. "Schiffahrt und Handel der Bonauhäfen Galaz und Braila im Jahre 1842," *Journal des Österreichischen Lloyd*, VIII Jahrg, Nos. 11, 12, 13 (Trieste, 1843), pp. 1-2, 1-2, 1-2.

19. *Michoff, Dr. N.* Beiträge zur Handelsgeschichte Bulgariens II, Österreichische Konsularberichte. Erster Band (Sofia, 1943), pp. 43, 76, 77, 87, 98, 99, 182-84, 199-200, 208, 299, 409, 360.

20. *Ibid.*

21. *Ibid.* p. 254.

22.-24. *Ibid.*, p. 259, 347, 353.

25. Archiv der DDSG, Geschäftberichte der Betriebsdirekion (1857-1875).

26. *Wolfbauer, J.* Die Donau und ihre volkswirtschaftliche Bedeutung (Vienna, 1880), pp. 160-61.

Manfred Rauchensteiner

Austro-Hungarian Warships on the Danube: From the Beginning of the Nineteenth Century to World War I

Going up or down the Danube nowadays involves numerous passport and customs controls. The river passes by seven countries without really passing through them, as was the case before World War I.[1] Today, to a greater extent than in former days, the Danube is a borderline. In addition, it has lost some of its importance as a commercial artery, not so much because it cannot compete with rail and road, but because it has become less important for Central and Eastern Europe. Today, too, the Danube divides rather than unites.[1]

Furthermore, I hold to the opinion that the Danube has lost much of its naval importance; and, there are many reasons for this. One main reason is certainly the fact that hydroelectric power plants and commercial traffic have led to the construction of dams and locks at shorter intervals, thereby creating even more slow-flowing waters and an increasing number of obstacles for warships and military vessels in general.

When dealing with military traffic on the Danube and with the largest and strongest navy on this river, the flotilla of the Habsburg empire in the nineteenth century, we have to depart from other presumptions.[2] For the Habsburg monarchy in the first half of the nineteenth century, the Danube was still primarily an obstacle, and where the river was the border to the Ottoman empire and where it passed the "military border," it was a sanitary borderline. But, in the second half of the nineteenth century, this changed fundamentally, and the Danube became important as a central waterway; the protection of commercial ships against pirates became the Danube flotilla's foremost task. Toward the end of the century, however, the importance of the river flotilla increased even more. Finally, the new Austro-Hungarian Danube flotilla became a part of the Imperial and Royal Navy, and this, thus, once again, changed its importance.

After the Napoleonic wars the river returned to its usual role.[3] The river flotilla restricted its activities mainly to the Danube below Budapest, and it was manned by the so-called *Tschaikisten-korps*. The Tschaikists, as a special organization almost 100 years old, gradually received larger ships which could carry heavier and newer weaponry. At the same time, its end could be foreseen with the appearance of sreamboats on the Danube, in contrast to the end of the "military border" which became obsolete from the military, economic, and political point of view. In 1829 the first Danubian Steamship Company (*DDSG*) was founded, and one year later, in 1830, the first steamboat traveled down the Danube from Vienna to Budapest. The Tschaikists, however, could still boast of new achievements, such as new rockets, and the rocket boats were surely the most spectacular, if not always the most effective thing introduced in the era of *Vormaerz*. Thus, the Tschaikists disposed of arms which could enable them to shell fortifications close to the riverside. But the aiming of the rockets was so inaccurate that effective fighting against smaller targets, especially against hostile riverboats, was out of the question. So, improvements in the protection of the Austrian monarchy by means of armed river vessels was considered. The most important suggestion for a reform of the Tschaikist Corps was made by Colonel Birago, commander of the Pioneer Corps.[4] He suggested the replacement of the old Tschaiks with their insufficient and inefficient arms by four gunboats armed with 18 cm guns, and another with a 12 cm gun, as well as the construction of 16 rocket ships and 26 rocket boats. All these units would be lightweight in structure, so that, if necessary, the ships could be disassembled by their crews and transported to any other river. But, Birago also suggested iron as primary material for construction and steam power. He, however, did not want to equip the gunboats and the rocket boats with steam engines, because then the required maneuverability would be lost. He wanted to use tug boats, the so-called *remorqueurs* instead.

Nevertheless, right before the outbreak of revolution in 1848, experiments were made with a steam-driven cannon boat, but no further details are known about this.[5]

The year 1848 saw no events of major importance on the Danube.

Since the Hungarian revolutionaries could not get hold of the Danube flotilla, and only a minor fraction of the boat crews were Magyars, they had to do without a flotilla in the war of 1848-49. Instead, the Tschaikists were at the disposal of the Banus of Croatia, *Feldmarschalleutnant* Jellačić, who finally withdrew them from their boats. He exclusively used their artillery skills and made them simple gunners. The *DDSG* offered its services to *Feldmarchalleutnant* Windischgraetz who used their boats as a ferry near Vienna. The respect *DDSG* gained from these services was to have future repercussions. But even more important were the experiences made by *Feldmarschall* Radetzky far away from the Danube on the battlefields in northern Italy. Radetzky had a small flotilla organized, manned by engineers / pioneers, which was at his disposal on the lakes of northern Italy, especially on Lake Garda and Lago Maggiore. And as this flotilla, formed out of a pioneer troop, proved to be so efficient that Radetzky wanted to continue to use it after this war; this corps became the successor to the Tschaikists. As mentioned above, they had not been used adequately. *DDSG* and the pioneers able to fulfill several tasks, established themselves an outstanding reputation also in the eyes of those who were to influence military policy and operational thinking in the years to come. Therefore, nobody spoke in favor of the Tschaikists, when, for several reasons, the military border was dissolved. They were transformed into a mere infantry regiment and were called *Titler Frontier-Infantry Regiment* after their former headquarters Titl.[6]

After 1848, the whole Imperial-and-Royal Army was subject to reorganization and experimentation. This also applied to the Danube Flotilla. Within the gunboat corps initiated by Radetzky, three flotillas were formed, one in Venice's lagoon, another on Lake Garda and Lago Maggiore in northern Italy, and finally still another on the Danube, consisting of the imperial yacht *Adler* (Eagle), three steam-powered gun ships, six gunboats, twelve patrol boats and six tow ships. The headquarters of the Danube Flotilla was at Pest.

The flotilla members wore a dark blue tunic with light blue facings and yellow buttons, a waxed linen hat, and bore the special corps rifle with a flogging bayonet. The gun crews carried a sailor's cutlass. The armed vessels were equipped with additional pistols and grappling irons. Thus, the sailors of the Danube Flotilla looked a little bit like pirates; but appearance does not tell anything about leadership and discipline. The commander of the corps, Colonel Mollinary, and the individual flotilla commanders, were outstanding officers. The whole officers corps was considered to be typically bourgeois, being more demanding than the infantry, but less snobbish than the cavalry, and the sailors were easier to handle than the often trouble-making sailors of the navy. In the flotillas, the engineer spirit dominated, resulting in high combat readiness and in constant eagerness to improve technical skills and to implement new techniques.

The Danube Flotilla, however, was more and more considered as a means of transportation. Therefore, and because *DDSG* had developed a high transportation capacity, a "militarization" of *DDSG* was considered as well. In 1853, a contract was signed with it, engaging this company to move material and troops in case of war for refund of costs.[8] The company could sign such an agreement easily, as in case of war, the naval traffic could be affected and many of the ships of the company would have been requisitioned by the army anyway. Being paid was therefore the better choice.

This treaty was applied for the first time in 1854, when, at the beginning of the Crimean War, the Austrian "Observation Corps" was moved down the Danube in twelve steamships and a large number of tow boats. For two years, the flotilla traveled all the way up and down the Danube to its mouth at the Black Sea.

It earned its stripes, especially by initiating improvements in river navigation and in the tactical possibilities ofered by many river regulations mainly at the Iron Gates, a narrow and dangerous passage below Belgrade. But the task of the flotilla on the lower part of the Danube was to observe rather than to intervene. On the other hand, tactical experiences in warface gained on the Danube below the Iron Gates were not of much use farther upstream. Mainly one task seemed to bear fruition: the principal task of the flotilla was to build bridges in times of war and to cover rivercrossings, and thus, flotilla training consisted mainly in bridging the Danube and transporting troops from one shore to the other in the following years. So, the Danube Flotilla, which had sprung from an engineer/pioneer corps, had come back to its parent arm of service. Therefore, we have to state that the Tschaikists ended up as infantry, but the Danube Flotilla of the Gunboat Corps as pioneers. Around 1859, basically only one high-ranking officer realized with enormous foresight the significance of the Danube Flotilla as an independent troop unit with very special tasks and wanted to end the entanglement and the one-sided orientation toward pioneering.[9] This was *Feldmarschalleutnant* Nagy von Alsó-Szopor, this unorthodox thinker, who had taught strategy at the *Kriegsschule* for years and who had developed a different idea of how to wage war against Prussia. But, in both cases, he lacked the possibility to have his ideas respected. Nagy wanted to use the Danube Flotilla as a floating means for offensive and defensive purposes.

After the war of 1859, the period of the pioneer Danube Flotilla came to an end. Since the Lagoon Flotilla and that on the lakes of northern Italy soon became part of the navy, small wonder why, in 1861, the Danube Flotilla was taken over by the navy, too. Gunboat Corps Headquarters was transferred to the Naval District Command at Venice. Crewmen were transferred to the navy, and a company of sailors was stationed in Pest.

Four years later, in 1865, the Danube Flotilla ceased to exist, and all usable ships were handed over to *DDSG*.[10] Consequently, it was *DDSG* which, when the Prussian armies were approaching Vienna, during the war of 1866, had to help establish the Danube defense line, provide transport, and prevent the Prussians from crossing the river by means of armed steamboats, where *DDSG* volunteers and pioneers served. What a really insidious situation. This improvised Flotilla was not engaged for just before the Prussians would have reached the Danube a cease-fire was agreed on and peace was established.[11]

So a new beginning had to be made for the Danube Flotilla. But for this new beginning, none of the experiences which Austria had made herself in the war of 1866 were used. The new beginning was practically exclusively determined by the experiences of the American Civil War. In the following years, the tactical and operational analysis of the monitor warfare on the Mississippi and its tributaries formed the basis of Austrian landlocked naval strategy. A second influence was the Danube Flotilla's inclusion in the naval command; with this decision it became clear that no longer would infantry or engineering ideas determine the scope of the river flotilla and its operational doctrines, but ideas of maritime warfare modified for landlocked waters.

In 1869, the Imperial Minister of War, Baron Kuhn, proposed the construction of two monitors for the river Danube.[12] The word "monitor" indicated a specific type of vessel similar to those used in the American Civil War. Naturally, these two ships could not establish a new flotilla. The two monitors, which cost about *fl.* 20,000 each, were supposed to form the nucleus of a flotilla whose largest part should still be taken from *DDSG*. The crews were supposed to come from the navy exclusively. One thing that should be avoided was reliance on the rather inefficient mixture of volunteers and pioneers.

Construction of the two monitors took place in 1870-71. These ships were 50 meters long, 8 meters wide, and had a draught of only 1.1 meter, and therefore, very flat, with a displacement of 318 tons; the steam engines generated 200 horsepowers; armament consisted of two 15 cm guns M61 and two rapid-firing guns, all in turrets; the armor of up to 50mm steel plating, offered considerable defensive strength.[13] Experiments were still going on, when the Danube Flotilla was deliberately put into action to test its mettle.[14] Monitor *Maros* was under fire for the first time when, together with two field artillerie batteries, she attacked the Turkish post of Samac and other positions held by insurgent forces on September 14, 1878, enabling the IV Corps to cross the Save. The second monitor, *Leitha*, shelled enemy positions on the river bank next to Novo-Brcka. This operation also showed the value of the very mobile and independently operating monitors.

But, despite the excellent results in the occupation campaign of 1878, the Danube Flotilla was not expanded rapidly, because at that time its tie to the navy proved a hindrance. In the course of the navy's expansion all attention was directed toward the maritime fleet, but what was even more important, all the money spent on it went into the maritime fleet, the battleships, and finally the dreadnoughts. Also, all the private support, including the Vienna Boys Choir which at that time started wearing their now traditional sailor-like uniforms was meant to stimulate enthusiasm for Habsburg maritime naval policy, not so much for the doubtlessly less attractive Danube Flotilla.

So the time passed before things started moving again, in 1888. The immediate reason for a renewed interest in the Austrian Danube Flotilla seems to have been the existence of such a flotillia in Romania. In order to tackle the problems at their roots the War Ministry's Naval Section offered a prize for an answer to the question: "What are the functions of an Austrian Danube Flotilla in war on our own territory, and what functions would there be on foreign territory?" The winner of this competition was *Linienschiffsleutnant* [Lieutnant-Commander] Constantin Pott.[15] He examined several questions in detail, thereby the basic framework for the construction and role of the Danube Flotilla in the decades up to World War I. In his studies, he pointed out that the Danube Flotilla, with its monitors, was in fact incapable of bridging the river, which was a purely pioneer task. At that time, the engineers were already equipped with the new floating Herbert bridging equipment, probably the most modern equipment in the world in those days. Flotilla ships would be good for guard duties and surveillance.

Steam power of warships should be made use of to ferry pontons, steam-powered longboats would be needed to be able to form trains of barges, and above all, more monitors should be built, for a river flotilla on the Danube had two main tasks: one, the protection of the riverine borderline in the southeast of the empire, and two, the defense of the central basin of Budapest-Vienna-Tulln.

On April 14, 1889, the Commander of the Naval Section of the Ministry of War submitted finally a "most humble" report which reviewed all these important facts.[16] The fact-finding of the Naval Section described the situation of the Imperial-and-Royal Danube Flotilla, which still consisted only of the two monitors, which had proved efficient in 1878. Furthermore, it said that the Russian and Turkish Danube Flotillas had played an important part in the Russian-Turkish War of 1877-78, probably because they had performed as what the British later called a "Fleet in Being": The presence of the Turkish Danube Flotilla alone required the Russians in the first phase of the war to move very cautiously, and prepare extremely carefully their rivercrossing operation, something usually not required in that type of warfare. With the extension of railway and road construction, the value of the Danube would increase rather than decrease. Crossings of roads and railway lines with the river had created points of major strategic importance. In the same report, the Naval Section also presented a summary of the riverine forces of other states on the Danube. Bulgaria possessed four steamships, nine smaller steam boats and two torpedo boats; Russia had two armored gunboats, six cruisers, three steam brigs, nine steam boats, one torpedo cruiser, one mine ship, and twelve torpedo boats; Romania's forces included 29 vessels of various types. The specification of the strength of the Russian Flotilla appeared to be problematic in more than one respects. For example, the report included ships on the Black Sea and on several other Russian rivers. Only a few of the cruisers and steam brigs could operate on the lower reaches of the Danube, and certainly not above the Iron Gates. If we consider, however, the date of the report, April 1889, the sense of this survey becomes evident: In the case of war with Russia, which was feared that year, the Austrian Danube Flotilla would still have been extremely weak. The 1890 budget included another monitor for the flotilla; but the Navy Section pointed out that this new type of monitor should not be followed by a group of mere monitors. The Danube Flotilla would also need patrol boats, spar-torpedo boats, and supply ships, and only the latter could be furnished by *DDSG*. The tasks of the Danube Flotilla were described as covering river crossings for the army, protecting bridgeheads and river bank positions, preventing enemy forces from crossing the river, disrupting enemy lines of communication, and fighting hostile ships operating on the river. This description of functions indicates quite clearly a switch toward offensive and naval tasks. From this time until the outbreak of World War I, there was a constant discussion about which riverine warfare doctrine should be adopted by the Austro-Hungarian Danube Flotilla.

After discussions and a basic decision taken by the Supreme Commander, and the emperor, the money for a fourth monitor was made available, but the type of ship and its equipment were still to be decided upon in 1889. Above all, one further wish should be fulfilled. The monitors should not only carry cannons, but also heavy mortars, which appear to have proved efficient in the American Civil War.[17]

These examples demonstrate very well how intensively the developments in other countries were studied and — above all — taken into account, especially in navy affairs, whereas this was not the case in other fields, such as the value of automatic weapons and the decline of the cavalry, factors which contributed to the heavy defeats the Austro-Hungarian armed forces had to suffer in the World War I.

In 1891-92, the two new monitors were constructed, *Szamos* and *Körös*.[18] Both were of all-steel constructions, 54 meters long, 9 meters wide, with a draught of 1.2 meters and a displacement of 448 tons, armed with two 12cm rapid-firing guns, two 7cm rapid-firing guns, and two 8mm machine guns; armor thickness was up to 75mm. Going downstream, the ships could reach a speed of 24 kilometers per hour. Gradually the construction of patrol boats was also undertaken, since each fighting unit was to be composed of a monitor plus two patrol boats and a supply ship.

In 1893, the flotilla slowly started to grow, an "Instruction for the Commanders of River Monitors" was published, describing the tasks and the command of the monitors.[19] Article 1 said that, in the case of war, the monitors had the task of operating on the Danube and its navigable tributaries according to the orders from the commander of the army unit to which they were attached. They had to support these units in their movements, during attack and defense, when crossing rivers, or by preventing enemy crossings. In peacetime, the flotilla was to be used for maneuvers and for special military tasks, and in addition to that, for shipping and river police matters. The regulations also prescribed the military, administrative, and logistic status of the Flotilla. The army corps under the command of the Imperial-and-Royal Harbor Command of Pola, required the utmost cooperation with the IV Army Corps, based in Budapest.

In the beginning, when the flotilla was still rather small, only one monitor per year was to operate, the other three would be mothballed. The active ship would perform exercises on the whole navigable Danube river system. For this purpose, 800 hours of full steam-power running were permitted by the commanding authorities; mothballed monitors were to be kept ready so that they could be activated within 24 hours. The men needed for the maintenance of the mothballed monitors formed the Naval Detachment, based in Budapest-Altofen, and commanded by the highest ranking naval officer available, who was also responsible for "military and maritime" safety. The logistic administration was handled by the naval depot in Pola. This also applied to any kind of ammunition not provided by the artillery depot of the army against receipt. Material supplements had, in any case, to be ordered from the Harbor Command at Pola; as far as the ammunition was concerned, coordination had to be sought with the Naval Section in the War Ministry. Purely riverine equipment and steamship supply were to be secured from *DDSG*. According to an agreement with *DDSG*, the latter established coal depots at exactly determined sites and with specific capacities at Linz, Pöchlarn, Vienna, Preßburg, Gönyö, Altofen, Mohács, Semlin, and O. Becse. While the stocks up as far as Preßburg were rather small — 15 to 20 metric tons only — at Gönyö there were 150 tons of coal available, at Altofen 100 tons, at Mohács 50 tons, and at Semlin 100 tons.

The commodities of the Danube Flotilla were standardized to such a degree that even the mothballed monitors were given strict orders on the amount of emery paper and soap to be used. Twice a year — on April 1 and on October 1 — a commissional report on the condition of the hulls had to be delivered.[20]

Apart from these general instructions for the monitors, special instructions and sailing programs were given to the monitors in service. Thus, in 1890, an instruction for *Leitha* stated that after the training runs the crews and especially the gunners, should practice the handling of their weapons.

When going upstream, which was to be done for short distances only, maneuvering and mooring the boat were to be practiced. Water conditions permitting, the upstream journey should go as far as St. Nicola, and the downstream run as far as Drenkova. When cruising on the Upper Danube, officers should be granted the possibility to study the installations of the engineer corps at Preßburg and Klosterneuburg. When going downstream, the Serbian tributaries of the Danube should be sailed, if navigable, as well. In Drenkova, the ship should stay for several days to enable the commander and the officers to travel all the way down to the Iron Gates on *DDSG* ships. The six-monthly sharpshooting exercises should be carried out on the Theiss, appropriately on the Titler Ried. The exercises were to be finished early enough in order to enable the boats to reach Budapest before the first of October. During the whole journey the river-bank descriptions and maps were to be consulted and corrected, if necessary.[21]

In 1894, two old monitors, *Maros* and *Leitha*, were completely overhauled and equipped with new engines. In the docks at Linz, new, stronger armor and new guns were applied. The construction of these ships made it impossible to install an additional gun on the stern,. however, because this would have increased their draught thus further reducing their speed.[22]

As has been shown, the impulse to build monitors had come from abroad. Similarily, the push to build patrol boats came from developments in other countries. Franz Zehden, a *DDSG* skipper, reported to the War Ministry, in April 1890, that the Russians were building some 350 boats on the lower stretches of the Danube for fast and secure river crossings.[23] Zehden even forwarded plans of these boats, which he called "armoured ramboats," and recommended that Austria should build boats like these, too. They could withstand rifle fire and shell fragments. Surely we can ask why a *DDSG* captain submitted such a suggestion. On the one hand, *DDSG* skippers naturally made observation of interest to the Navy Section when going down the Danube as far as its mouth. On the other hand, *DDSG* itself was certainly interested in a powerful Austrian riverine force to protect, among other things, commercial shipping on the Danube. And Zehdens reports met plans already made in the Naval Section. Objections were made that Zehden's boat had too great a draught. On the Danube and its tributaries upstream to the Iron Gates, a draught of only 70-80 centimeters would be possible. But, basically, the introduction of such boats was strongly promoted. It took until 1894, however, for the first new patrol boat to sail the Danube.[24]

This boat's hull had been built at Elbing Docks in Germany. It was then dismantled and transported to Linz, where it was reassembled. The armament consisted of one 8mm machine gun and two retractable torpedo launchers. A draught of 80cm permitted operations on most major rivers joining the Danube. Also, another so-called torpedo boat was transferred to the Danube. It had originally been built for the Adriatic Sea, but — despite its name — was never fitted with any torpedos.

As new ships were gradually added to the flotilla, the discussions about the value of the river force were renewed. This had many reasons. In 1894, riots in Budapest broke out and the commander of the IV Corps, *Feldmarschalleutnant* Rudolf Prince von Lobkowitz asked for the use of monitors.[25] As he received no answer immediately, he called upon His Majesty's General-Adjutant, *Feldmarchalleutnant* Bolfras, who ordered the monitors into action in the name of the emperor himself. This resulted in complete confusion, because the Minister of War, General von Krieghammer, did not know about this action and asked the Navy Section who had granted Lobkowitz command over those ships. The whole affair seemed to be even more unreasonable, since *Szamos* was undergoing gun repairs and was combat ready only within eight weeks. Obviously nobody had ever thought about the tasks of a monitor in calming civil unrest. Such a ship would not only have been inappropriate, but of little effective value and would have appreared as a provocation, in the fight against insurgents.

But other questions, too, have led to discussions about the applicability of monitors. It had been demanded for years, to arm the monitors with howitzers, and in 1898, the Administrative Section of the War Ministry had this problem examined again.[26] In the resulting document, the basic tasks of the monitors were defined once again: one, attack on hostile troops; two, attack on hostile strongholds and fortifications; three, destruction of bridges; four, destruction of villages; and five, fighting hostile boats. Each task was delineated in detail. It was concluded that the flat-trajectory guns of the monitors were of use only when fighting hostile ships; for all other targets, these guns were definitely less suitable than howitzers. It was recommended to arm all monitors with howitzers as main weapons instead of the 12cm guns of the type G. L. 34/C/87. The 7cm guns should at least be modified to fire in the high angle gradient, too. A further question was whether the existing monitors could be equipped with these weapons, or if howitzers should be installed on new ships only.

In profesional military magazines, the discussion was also started and was certainly influenced by the fact that the construction plans for riverine navy ships was considerably delayed.[27] In 1898, only the four monitors, one patrol boat and one torpedo boat (without torpedoes) were available. But as long as the tasks of the river flotilla were not clearly defined, continuation of the construction program could not be decided on. Extensive discussion obviously showed that the Austro-Hungarian army had no clear concepts of what to do with the river flotilla which belonged to the navy. And vice versa.

In an article in one of the leading Austrian military magazines, *Österreichische Militärische Zeitschrift*, in 1899, it was thereby stated that "we have practically no experience in combined operations of ground forces and the river flotilla." Much was thus expected from the maneuvers the IV Corps conducted in 1898, where the crossing of a large force with the help of the Danube Flotilla was to be exercised. In 1899, in the course of further maneuvers, the Danube Flotilla had to support ground operations of the II Corps, and especially operations of the flotilla against enemy strongpoints on the river bank were to be tested.

Three important experiences were derived from these exercises: Flat-trajectory guns should remain the main armament of the ships, yet howitzers should be considered as additional weapons. The constant change of the water level required an additional reduction of the draught. As a final point, more smaller units should be built, because they were more maneuverable and could be used in low water levels, too.[28] And another thing gradually became clear: The monitors had a problem concerning coal. Although they had access to *DDSG* coal depots, they required high quality pit coal to reach top results. A monitor like *Maros* could store 46 tons of coal on board, an amount sufficient for only four days. So it was necessary to guarantee the coal supply by either coal supply ships or by rail.[29]

One point concerning the discussion ought to be stressed: it was carried out mainly by infantry officers or at least members of the army; naval officers did not participate at all, although they were concerned. This lack of participation naturally reduced the value of all that had been said and written about combined operations. Evidently the navy paid little attention to the firmly expressed wishes of the army. The articles covered topics like the protection of the empire's border on the river, reconnaissance operations, attacking hostile fortifications and troops, river crossing operations, the defense of friendly bases,and the protection of ships transporting goods.Blockade of the river was considered as an essential task of the Danube flotilla, too. It was a naval officer who admitted that fighting hostile ships would be the exeption rather than the rule for the Danube Flotilla. Even in these rare cases, this would be a simple gun fight or a ram attack in the worst case, certainly almost no maneuvering at all. This author, *Linienschiffsleutnant* Paul Edler von Mecsenseffy, was an officer of the maritime navy and the officers of the riverine flotilla disagreed with him. In their eyes, only one type of operation was in keeping with the dignity of a real navy: a fight against another riverine flotilla. Since this doctrine ruled flotilla strategy certainly until 1914, *Vizeadmiral* Wulffen, author of a history of the Danube Flotilla in World War I, had reason to conclude that invalid conceptions about the capabilities of the flotilla had developed during peacetime and that most maneuvers included only mock combats between two monitor groups.[30]

In 1904, the last two heavy vessels built before World War I were put into service. The new monitors, *Temes* and *Bodrog*, were built in the Danubius Yard in Budapest. They had even more displacement than *Szamos* and *Körös* and were 56 meters long and 9.5 meters wide. They had the same armor, but larger engines so that they could reach a speed of 26km per hour downstream. Their armament consisted of two 12cm howitzers, two 12cm rapid firing guns, two 7cm rapid firing guns, and two 8mm machine guns.[31]

Further development of the Danube Flotilla was initiated by the interest in naval warfare shown by Archduke Franz Ferdinand. Until then, all military interest had focused on the army. But when, in 1906, Franz Ferdinand demanded that the navy should develop an offensive capacity, a large fleet construction program was conceived.[32] This also helped the Danube Flotilla. Surprisingly, even delegations and nations usually not in favor of arms development, such as the Czechs and the Polish, approved of the increased expenses. This led to a fast expansion of the navy. Within this navy development program the construction of patrol boats already proposed was started anew. In 1908 and 1909 boats C, D, F, G, and H were launched. C and D, like boat B, which had been built in 1906, were 28 meters long and 4.4 meters wide, with a draft of 70 cm and a displacement of 29 tons. Boats F, G, and H, however, were considerably smaller, with a displacement of only 15 tons.[33]

In 1910, the Naval Commander, Count Montecuccoli, finally proposed a navy development program including the construction of additional monitors and patrol boats.[34] Two monitors and six patrol boats were to be built. One monitor would cost 2.4 million crowns. As the current budget did not include the funds for these ships, special loans were used. The monitor *Enns* was thus financed and launched after one year of construction in September 1914; a second monitor was ready in 1915.[35] These monitors, torpedo boats, and other units were built in the Linz branch of the Trieste shipyard Stabilmento Tecnico, in the Danubius Yard in Budapest, and in other companies in Linz and Budapest.

In addition to this, the plans for the flotilla included supply ships, notably hospital ships and armored steamers. Barges for ammunition, coal, and other supply like food or clothing were built as well as new mine ships and boats housing the commanders and the staff.[36]

The crew of the ships was standardized. Each monitor had three officers and 70 ratings.[37] The patrol boats were manned by one officer and ten men. Including *DDSG* ships, train vessels, and hospital ships, and the Navy Detachment and Command in Budapest, the Danube Flotilla comprised approximately 1000 men.

Crews of the Danube Flotilla came — like the rest of the navy manpower — from the Naval Recruiting Districts of Trieste, Sebenico, and Fiume. The distribution of manpower by nationality was 31.3 percent Croats, 20.4 percent Hungarians, 16.3 percent German-speaking Austrians, 14.4 percent Italians, 10.6 percent Czechs, 2.8 percent Slowenians, 1.8 percent Polish, 1.2 percent Romanians, 0.8 percent Ukrainians, and 0.4 percent Slovaks.[38] As language they used the typical "Army-German" together with their mother tongues. Possibly some of them complained that they had to serve only on a river instead of the high seas, but as everybody knows, in the army you have to serve where you are ordered to.

In the years before the outbreak of the war in 1914, active service on the Danube would start with the end of the snow melting period, when at first a team of officers traveled along the Danube from Budapest upstream and downstream on a *DDSG* steamer, investigating the river, checking for changes in the river banks and profiles of the river bed. All data were marked on maps. At the same time the monitors which had been laid up in Ujpest, went to the docks where they had their hulls cleaned, were painted, and had other necessary repairs made. The patrol boats were simply pulled out of the water. All the equipment was taken out of the various depots, where it had been storaged over the winter. The Naval Depot in Pola sent the training ammunition. The war stocks of ammunition, however, were stored in the depots at Gubács and Örkény. Then the ships were brought down to the water again, and received their coal, food, and ammunition, and the crews went on board, first the sailors, followed by the officers. The training, which usually lasted until autumn with few interruptions, could be started.[39]

On July 21, 1914, the Naval Section of the Ministry of War forwarded a "Top Secret" order, alerting the complete flotilla, including the supply and hospital ships, for 23 July. Monitor groups were to avoid any spectacular moves and leave Budapest quietly, steaming to Vienna to receive further orders.[40] Then the ships went down the Danube again and moved south of Budapest. Finally the largest part assembled in the area of Zemun: Four monitors — *Temes* (under *Linienschiffsleutnant* Johann Vok-Collins), *Bodrog* (under *Linienschiffsleutnant* Paul Ekl), *Szamos* (under *Linienschiffsleutnant* Eduard Krankovsky), and *Körös* (under *Linienschiffsleutnant* Josef Meusburger) — three patrol boats, and three supply ships. At Brod, on the river Save, the two oldest monitors *Maros* (under *Linienschiffsleutnant* Karl Rodinis) and *Leitha* (under *Linienschiffsleutnant* Karl Topin), plus one patrol boat and two supply ships were gathered. Finally a small group, consisting of two patrol boats, assembled at Pancsova on the Danube.[41] On July 29, 1914, they opened fire. In all the years before, the Danube Flotilla had been considered purely as an instrument for experiments, but now the time had come to justify its existence.

Notes

1. This article is based on a paper which was presented in Kassandra on June 8, 1985. For the possibility of participating in the "XVII Brooklyn College Conference on Society in Change" I want to express my gratitude to Prof. Bèla K. Kiràly and to the Institute for Balkan Studies in Salonika, as well as to the Österreichische Forschungsgemeinschaft in Vienna, which made the travel funds available. For preparing the records in the Kriegsarchiv I have to express my thanks to Mr. Peter Jung. Erwin Steinböck allowed me to look through an unpublished manuscript dealing with the Danube as a battleground, My friend and colleague Erwin Schmidl was kind enough to read and criticize the paper for the presentation as well as this article.

2. The literature dealing with the Austro-Hungarian warships on the Danube can be divided into three distinct parts. The older literature, published in the second half of the nineteenth century, dealt with the origins and the development of this naval force up to that time. Then there was a breakthrough to the period after World War I, that in which the role of the Danube flotilla has been described. Modern Austrian historical research picked up the theme of the warships on the Danube about the middle of the seventies. Since then a greater number of publications appeared there. Unfortunately, in these recent publications the technical aspects are mainly discussed and not the operational and tactical aspects.

3. This period is briefly described in Wladimir Aichelburg, "Kriegsschiffe auf der Donau," *Militärhistorische Schriftenreihe* 37 (Vienna, 1978), p. 24. More detailed is A. Gjukić, *Ein Rückblick auf die Geschichte der österreichischen-ungarischen Donauflottille* (Vienna, 1889), p. 47. In particular, see also, Kurt v. Schmedes, "Zur Geschichte der Donauflottille," *Mitteilungen aus dem Gebiete des Seewesens* (Pola, 1914), pp. 1177-1212.

4. Schmedes, p. 1194.

5. *Ibid.*, p. 1197.

6. *Ibid.*, pp. 1198-1200. On this question, and on the fate of the Austrian flotillas on the Danube, there exists an unpublished manuscript from Erwin Steinböck of Vienna, which I have used courtesy of the author.

7. Schmedes, p. 1202.

8. *Ibid.*, p. 1203. An excellent publication dealing with the commercial shipment on the Danube, and particularly with the DDSG is the article of Virginia Paskaleva, "Die Schiffahrt im Unterlauf der Donau im dritten Viertel des 19. Jahrhunderts," *Bulgarian Historical Review*, No. 3 (Sofia, 1984), p. 46-71.

9. Kriegsarchiv Wien (hereafter KA), Memoires, Fasz. 15, No. 58: Memoire by FML Ladislaus Nagy von Alsó-Szopor.

10. Schmedes, p. 1209-1210.

11. This period is described in the Steinböck manuscript.

12. KA, Reichskriegsministerium, Marinesektion, 1868. A. H. Entschließung vom 2.12.1868. On the technical data *cf.*

13. Hans Hugo Sokol, *Österreich-Ungarns Seekrieg 1914-18* (Zurich-Leipzig-Vienna, 1933), enclosure "Schiffslisten".

14. Anon., "Fluss-Flottillen in Cooperation mit Landtruppen," *Streffleurs Österreichische Militärische Zeitschrift*, No. 3 (Vienna, 1899), pp. 97-98.

15. Gjukić, p. 3.

16. KA, Marinesektion, P. K. Varia 1889.

17. *Ibid.*

18. A detailed description of this new monitor-type is given by Paul Edlei von Mecenseffy, "Die Aufgabe der Donauflottille," *Organ der militär-wissenschaftlichen Vereine*" (Vienna, 1902), pp. 9-11.

19. KA, Reichskriegsministerium, Marinesektion, P.K.I-2/8, Res. No. 7, 20.1.1893.

20. *Ibid.*

21. *Ibid.*, P.K. No. 797, 12.5.1890.

22. *Ibid.*

23. *Ibid.*, P.K. 2012, 2 May 1890.

24. Mecenseffy, p. 11.

25. KA, Reichskriegsministerium, Marinesektion, P. K. 1-2/6, different pieces from April.

26. *Ibid.*, P.K. 1-2/9 (16 November 1898).

27. Compare the aforementioned articles and Anon., "Fluß-Flottillen in Cooperation;" Anon., "Fluß-Flottillen," *Streffleurs Österreichische Militärische Zeitschrift*, No. 1 (Vienna, 1900), pp. 113-29; Mecenseffy, "Aufgaben;" Anon., "Über Flußkriegsschiffe," *Streffleurs Österreichische Militärische Zeitschrift*, No. 1 (Vienna, 1907), pp. 799-810.

28. Mecenseffy, pp. 14-15.

29. *Ibid.*

30. Olaf Richard Wulff, *Die österreichisch-ungarische Donauflottille im Weltkriege 1914-1918* (Vienna-Leipzig, 1934), p. 13.

31. Cf. Franz Bilzer, "Schiffstypenblatt Nr. 7, S. M. Monitor *Temes*," *Marine-Gestern, Heute*, No. 1 (Vienna, 1977), p. 24.

32. Hans Hugo Sokol, p. 19.

33. *Almanach für die k.u.k. Kriegsmarine* (Vienna, 1914), p. 387.

34. Sokol, p. 20.

35. This monitor was called *Inn*. Cf. Herbert Winkler, "S. M. Monitoren *Enns* und *Inn*," *Marine - Gestern, Heute*, No. 2 (Vienna, 1982), p. 60-64.

36. Wulff, p. 12.

37. A typical crew was similar to that in Körös in 1898: There were three officers, 3 petty officers, 20 ratings, 3 artillery instructors, 14 masters (artillery), 8 gunners, 1 torpedo instructor and 2 torpedo men, plus 2 ratings on the bridge, 1 petty officer (weapons), 1 bugler, 7 petty officers for the machinery, 3 master firemen and 6 firemen, 1 cook and 1 medical corps man, for a total of 73 petty officers and ratings.

IV

Southeast European Maritime Commerce

Constantinos Papathanassopoulos

The State and the Greek Commercial Fleet During the Nineteenth Century

The recovering and gradual development of the Greek merchant marine seems to have coincided, in terms of time, with two particular historical events: the *de jure* recognition of the newly formed Greek state by the Sultan on the one hand, and the imposition of a monarchy on Greece on the other. Indeed, already, on the very eve of those events, Greek merchant-marine activities started little by little to show signs of their traditional vitality.

Following the formation of the modern Greek state, commerce, and especially maritime commerce, develops at a really impressive rate. This development should be studied within the general framework of state policies during the reign of King Otto (1832-62). Interest in strengthening the merchant marine and in facilitating the maritime commerce can be already seen during the short-lived rule of Capodistrias (1827-31). In a similar way, the aim of the Ottonian policies concerning both maritime commerce and a merchant marine was to provide the proper infrastructure for exploiting advantageously a conjuncture marked by the economic penetration of the West into the Balkans and the Near East on the one hand, and by the consequent expansion of the trade within the eastern Mediterranean on the other.[1]

Expansion of the trade relations between East and West in the east Mediterranean, economic development of southern Russia, monopolization of the grain trade in the Black Sea by the Greek merchant marine, the often-cited inventiveness and the experience of Greeks in maritime and commercial activities have been, so far, considered as the sole factors for the takeoff of the Greek maritime commerce in the years following Greece's War of Independence. Apart from the aforementioned developments, one should not ignore the crucial role played by a state policy of a protectionist character. As a matter of fact, the significance of such a policy cannot be underestimated, in so far as it existed in the attempts of the newly formed Greek state to reconstruct and reorient maritime commerce.

The role of the State in developing not only domestic but also foreign trade can be depicted, among other things, in the intoduction and adoption of the French Code of Commercial Law; in the establishment of commercial courts; in the intoduction of an altogether new monetary and metric system; in the attempts of providing a modern transportation network; and, finally, in the attempts to improve tariff laws.[2]

The state also played an equally significant role in the development of the merchant marine; here, the implementation of a protective policy succeeded in combining not only the growth but also the structural improvement of the Greek merchant fleet.[3]

These policies resulted in a spectacular development of both trade and maritime activities. It is worth mentioning that the growth rate of the Greek trade for the period 1833-40 was 194 percent. More specifically, for imports and exports, the rate was 63 percent; for through land transportation, 594 percent; and for coastal trade, was 178 percent.[4,5] Unfortunately, there are not relevant data for 1840-50. However, all the studies and sources of the period without exception, admit that this development continued uninterrupted in the next decade, as well. As an example, one may cite the impressive rate of growth of the merchant marine. Its capacity increased from 88,502 tons in 1838 to 266,201 in 1850, since the greatest part of both foreign and the domestic trade took place along sea routes.[6,7]

In Table I, one may observe the growth of the Greek merchant fleet during 1834-56.

At this point, however, there lurks a question which is crucial for the explanation of the growth and development of the Greek merchant fleet; namely whether or not and — if yes — to what extent the state had created conditions favorable for the financing of these activities either through the public sector itself, or through the private sector. It should be taken into account that for the period studied, there had not been any direct public financing. Besides, and as far as the organization of a corresponding financial infrastructure is concerned, it is certain that until 1860, when S. Yiannoussis

established the Greek Maritime Bank in Patras, there had not existed
any bank specializing exclusively in financing merchant-marine
activities. In the case of this sector of the economy, as in the cases of

*Table I**

The Growth of Greek merchant fleet from 1834 to 1856

Year	Ships			Tonnage			Crew
	1st Category	*2nd Category*	*Total*	*1st Category*	*2nd Category*	*Total*	
1834	2183	708	2891	—	—	75,000	—
1835	2410	760	3170	—	—	—	—
1838	—	—	3269	—	—	88,502	13,679
1839	—	—	3345	—	—	89,642	—
1840	—	—	3184	—	—	110,690	18,958
1841	—	—	3200	—	—	100,000	—
1843	2220	949	3169	15,180	122,378	137,558	19,005
1844	2400	1014	3414	15,880	130,823	146,703	—
1845	2470	1114	3584	17,280	143,823	161,103	—
1848	2527	1456	3983	17,309	237,914	255,233	15,000
1850	2534	1482	4016	18,070	248,131	266,201	—
1851	2890	1437	4327	—	—	256,193	27,566
1852	2825	1375	4200	19,696	228,055	247,751	27,372
1853	—	—	4153	—	—	247,995	26,302
1855	3538	1525	5063	32,396	264,405	296,801	30,000
1856	1500	2900	4400	—	—	260,000	30,000

* According to Article 10 of the Royal Act of November 14 1836, the Greek
merchant fleet was to be classified into two categories, the First to consist of
ships with a capacity up to 30 tons and the Second of ships with a capacity greater
than 30 tons.

Source: Constantinos Papathanasopoulos, *The Greek Commercial Navy (1833-
1856): Development and Restructuring,* Greek edition, (Athens, 1983), ch. 3, p. 88.

raisin agriculture and in public works, development was motivated
by domestic capital, whose role has been so far underestimated, if not
ignored. It is my belief that basic research into the Historical Archive

of the National Bank of Greece will help the modern historian to determine exactly the National Bank's financing of shipbuilding activities in the shipyards of the kingdom, and especially in those of Syros.[8]

The crisis of 1848 posed for the first time in an explicit way the problem of restructuring the Greek merchant marine through the introduction of steam engines and the building of steamships. In this case the crisis of 1848 affected directly not only its character but also the direction of its growth. In this sense, the problematic character of the Greek economy, the novelty in the behavior of capital, and the competition in the international naval transportation, necessitated the adjustment of the Greek navy to the new conditions of steamships.

The Greek Steamshipping Company was founded in January 1857. During 1849-55, attempts on the part of private capital for founding a domestic steamship company had been intensified. Two of these are worth mentioning. The first, a joint effort by the National Bank and Michael Tositsas, takes place in Athens, while the second, by a committee of landowners and merchants headed by Stephanos Pappas, occurs in Patras. Still another, successful this time, by the National Bank in 1855, is realized through the investment at Syros' maritime and commercial center. Until that time, any attempt at rationalizing the economic intervention of the state and at forming an adequate protective policy was hindered by the foreign dependency of the Greek state and by the foreign-policy expediencies. In this sense, one may speak of a retreat of the rational development of a Greek merchant marine before the expediency and "priorities" of foreign policy.[9,10]

Nevertheless, it should be taken under consideration that the newly formed Greek state was aware of the adverse conditions under which it had to intervene in order to facilitate the rational organization of the economy. Thus, an adequate criterion for evaluating and measuring state activities should be correlated with a combination of various other factors.

This is, also, true for 1849-55, when at a first glance, the state attitude toward rationalizing and restructuring the Greek merchant marine seems ambiguous, and to say so, hostile. This attitude was not due, however, to a supposed shortsightedness and irrationality inherent in state policies themselves. On the contrary, and if these attitudes are placed within the context of the aforementioned disadvantageous circumstances, one will come to the conclusion that the activities of the state had been, in fact, characterized not only by a historical rationality, but also by a systematic conception of what their long-term interests demanded. In the case of restructuring of the merchant marine, this prima-facie irrationality of state policies can be explained on the basis of reactions against such a restructuring on the part of Austria and the Greek National Bank. As long as the National Bank demanded the privilege of monopolizing the financing of the merchant marine and as long as Austria reacted against such a move, the Greek state had no other choice but playing a role which neither disrupted its relations with the Great Powers, nor, at the same time, permitted the creation of a transportation infrastructure.

Therefore, state policies had been in fact determined by a complex of causes and effects. For, as far as restructuring was concerned, Austria's opposition to the National Bank's plans determined the ultimate policy of Greece, thereby undermining the idea of a Greek steamship company. Failure of initial moves in this direction, however, was not viewed by the state as complete defeat, but rather as a postponement of an idea until more favorable circumstances came about.

It is not, then, accidental that the first Greek steamship company at Syros in January 1857 came in the wake of intervention of France and Great Britain in 1854, an intervention which resulted in a foreign policy of neutrality toward the Ottoman empire. Austria, for its part, supported such a policy.

The new company's original capital amounted to 3,000,000 drachmas divided in 6000 shares of 500 drachmas each. In fact, however, the company began its operations with an actual capital of 1,094,500 drachmas divided in 2189 shares distributed as following: 800 shares owned by the state, 400 by the National Bank, 188 by merchants from Syros, 300 by merchants of Greek origin living in Manchester, Marseille, Liverpool, London, and Amsterdam, 118 by Greeks living in Constantinople, Bucharest, Alexandria, and Odessa, 131 by Greeks from Corfu and Cephalonia, and 20 by Greeks from Arta and Lesbos. The rest were distributed among merchants from Athens,

*Table II**

The Growth of Greek merchant fleet from 1858 to 1901

| Year | Sailing Vessels | | | | | | Steamships | | Total | | Crew |
| | 1st Category | | 2nd Category | | Total | | Number | Capacity (tons) | Number | Capacity (tons) | |
	Number	Capacity (tons)	Number	Capacity (tons)	Number	Capacity (tons)					
1858	—	—	—	—	—	—	—	—	3920	268,600	—
1860	2857	29,193	1212	233,732	4069	262,925	1	150	4070	263,075	23,842
1862	3181	34,556	1153	222,612	4334	257,168	1	150	4335	257,318	23,849
1864	3297	37,356	1230	224,836	4527	280,192	1	150	4528	280,342	24,949
1966	4146	47,150	1355	276,425	5501	323,575	11	5240	5512	328,815	30,700
1868	3961	46,880	1450	282,781	5411	329,661	11	5240	5422	334,901	31,299
1870	4138	50,856	1733	347,847	5871	398,703	12	5360	5883	404,063	38,080
1872	3659	59,563	1093	194,391	4752	253,954	15	5993	4767	259,947	24,676
1874	4097	42,877	1085	199,367	5182	242,244	20	7833	5202	250,077	25,838
1875	4403	43,712	1107	210,079	5410	253,791	27	8241	5437	262,032	26,760
1882	—	—	—	—	5162	232,629	50	24,378	5212	257,007	—
1885	—	—	—	—	3141	259,183	72	36,272	3213	262,396	—
1890	—	—	—	—	—	—	92	83,839	—	—	—
1892	—	—	—	—	1739	206,537	—	—	—	—	—
1895	—	—	—	—	1009	246,196	107	144,975	1116	391,171	—
1900	—	—	—	—	—	—	139	178,137	—	—	—
1901	—	—	—	—	925	145,361	—	—	—	—	—

* According to the Act of March 10 1858, the first category includes ships with a capacity up to 60 tons, and the second, ships with a capacity greater than 60 tons. The data of the period after the year 1885 refers to sailing vessels with a capacity over 30 tons and to steamships with a capacity over 100 tons, as well.

Sources: A. N. Vernardakis, *Of Greek Commerce*, Greek edition, (Athens, 1885), pp. 230-31;
A. Andreades,"La marine marchande Greque et la Guerre," in *Les effets économiques et sociaux de la guerre en Grèce*, (Paris, 1928), pp. 6, 19;
Eleftheroudakis' Encyclopaedeia, ("Commercial Navy," Vol. V [Athens, n. d.]), Greek edition, p. 449.

Piraeus, Pyrgos, Gastouni, and Calamata. In 1859, its capital increased to 5,000,000 drachmas, while the number of the shares owned by the State amounted in 2000. Besides, the state granted the company the privilege of monopolizing sea transportation for 12 years, and at the same time, it bought the company three steamships for 24,000 pounds.

Still, the road to steam navigation for the Greek merchant marine was not a short one since the country's economy not did dispose of huge amounts of capital investment required for such a restructuring. In 1879, there were only 27 steamships; their number increased only at the turn of the century. To this rapid growth contributed Greek bankers, Greek merchants from abroad, and merchants from Eptanisa; indeed, in the first years of the twentieth century, shipowning capital is marked both by a high degree of centralization and by a modern structure.

In Table II, one may observe the development of the Greek merchant fleet from 1858 to 1901.

The foundation of the Greek steamship company had both positive and negative effects. Among the former one should cite development of domestic and foreign trade, expansion of an infrastructure, its supportive role to the goverment during the events of October 1862, its role during the revolt of Crete (1866-69), foundation of a foundry, construction of a dockyard; besides, in 1861, it employed 600 persons, and until 1869, educated 17 engineers. All these activities constitute a considerable contribution to the process of modernization. On the other hand, among the negative factors, one should mention the fact that, until 1869, the company's liabilities amounted to 5,000,000 drachmas, an amount that in 1892 grew to 32,000,000 drachmas.[11,12]

It seems, therefore, quite reasonable for one to pose the question whether that performance constitutes a "normal" budget deficit through which a rational economic intervention is being financed, an intervention aiming at the development of the Greek economy as a whole; or whether it is the price the state had to pay for purposes of a political survival and self-preservation, rather than for purposes inherent in the implementation of a rational policy of economic intervention,

The question is crucial to interpret the conditions under which the policies of the state and the private sector are interrelated; besides, it guides research toward the state and the private investors, one of which is the National Bank of Greece.

As to the bank's interest, an interest realized in investment, and the strategy that directs this interest, one may observe the following:

Since 1849, the National Bank had explicitly expressed its interest in creating, or participating in the creation of the first domestic steamship company, which, within the context of that strategy, was to undertake, too, the task of forming the proper infrastructure for both commerce and the merchant marine.

The Company of Greek Commercial Steamships and of the Digging of the Channel of Evripos constituted the first example of such an initiative by the National Bank. That, however, was not successful.[13] Nonetheless, it foreshadowed the bank's economic strategy concerning the merchant marine.

Thus, although the amount invested did not indicate the National Bank's aims at complete control of the transportation sector, this company's character and object was to establish concessions from the state which would enhance its role in a very important sector of the Greek economy in the nineteenth century. And this took place under the initiative of a committee of landowners and merchants from Patras, which may serve to clarity certain characteristics of its strategy.

The Steamship Company of Patras was established in order to serve the raisin trade and the exports of its shareholders, but, in fact, it never succeded, notwithstanding the assurances of G. Stavrou in attracting the investment of the National Bank.

One can discern two important reasons for that: reservations of the state and reactions of the entrepreneurs from Syros. The latter became evident first, in the absence of the entrepreneurs from Syros as shareholders of the company; additionally, the shareholders from Constantinople posed as a condition of participation the extension of the company's activities to Syros, an indispensable station for their transportation activities. State reservation came as a consequence mainly of the aforementioned reluctance of the most important sectors of domestic capital and of the National Bank to participate in the foundation of a company whose orientation was complete-ly different from its own.[14]

But the circumstances were different in 1857, when the new company was founded in Syros with the participation of the state, the National Bank, entrepreneurs and financiers from Syros, and Greek merchants from Constantinople. In this case, the National Bank held 400 shares. Two years later, in 1859, the National Bank lent the company a million drachmas in an open account, and in 1861, the state guaranteed a new loan of 320,000 drachmas.

In this sense, one sees in play the same reasons that prohibited the participation of the National Bank in the foundation of a company of Syros. Although the economic center of Syros was a pole of attraction for bank investment in the decade before 1857, the National Bank had not succeded in getting a foothold in this venture. Thus, whereas the bank set up an agency in 1847, it was only in 1857, when the Greek Steamshipping Company was founded, that this agency was transformed into a branch of the National Bank. This is underlined by the fact that the participation of the entrepreneurs from Syros in the company's original capital was limited to the entrepreneurs directly related with the National Bank. After all, the company's board of directors were elected from among them.

One can distinguish two groups that participated in the original capital of the company. The first, the National Bank and the Greek merchants from Bucharest, Odessa, Alexandria, and Constantinople; the second, Greek merchants from Corfu, Cephalonia, Marseille, Amsterdam, Liverpool, Manchester, and London. The latter were willing not only to invest and to concentrate capital for the company, but also to intervene in rationally organizing company policies toward the development of a merchant marine.

Indeed, if one isolates cases of Greek entrepreneurs from abroad who have shown an interest in the restructuring of the Greek commercial navy since 1849, one may discern the ways in which these interests were connected with the investing behavior in this sector. One may, then, distinguish a group which had an explicit economic strategy, and a group which limited itself to the formulation of fragmented policies. In both cases, however, these groups, if compared with the entrepeneurs from Syros, constituted a different class section with a completely different economic ideology.

Thus, while in the case of the company in Patras, one may differentiate between the capital owners/entrepreneurs from the West and those from the East, in the case of the company in Syros, one may differentiate further between subgroups within these two major groups. In the latter case, for example, the Greek entrepreneurs from London did not exhibit the same behavior as the Greek entrepreneurs from Manchester, Liverpool, Marseille, or from Eptanisa.

The attitude of the state toward the company's policy on the one hand, and the attitude of the company toward the policies of the state on the other, provides the ground for formulating a research hypothesis: namely, that the economic and class interests of the dominant classes direct the strategy and behaviour not only of these classes, but also of the company and the state. Thus, when, in 1855, the development of the Greek merchant marine entered a recession, this was no longer due to foreign policy expedients, but was mainly due to the the state which was unwilling to affect negatively certain organized interests.

It should be mentioned, however, that the state was a complex and multidimensional phenomenon. Under conditions of underdevelopment, of lack of a proper institutional framework, and of very low rates of capital formation in the private sector, the state had to play a determinant role. It should provide the proper infrastructure and organize the "public space." At the same time, it was involved in party politics and actively participated in the economic life of the country. It utilized, and was being utilized by various social forces. It either formed alliances with them, or took part in their conflicts. In this sense, the interconnection between state policy and policies of the private sectors and bank capital, constituted a framework of analysis wherein political factors played the dominant role.

Consequently, one cannot argue that the particular class interest of dominant groups held sway over the plans and policies of the state. They simply intermingled, and sometimes confused the will to invest, which was determined at large by considerations of the general interest, rather than by some ideally "rational" policy of intervention.

This last hypothesis may prove the safest method of approaching the question, since it does not isolate the state from its political and social context; nor, from the context within which the state manifests its social character.

Notes

1. Constantinos Papathanasopoulos, *The Greek Commercial Navy (1833-1856). Development and Restructuring,* Greek edition, (Athens, 1983), chap. 3, pp. 44-85.

2. *Ibid.,* pp. 50-68.

3. *Ibid.,* pp. 71-85.

4. *Ibid.,* pp. 45, 68-70.

5. *Idem,* "European Steamshipping and the commercial activities of Syros (1833-1853)," Greek edition, *Historica,* No 3, (1985), pp. 127-28.

6. *Idem, The Greek Commercial Navy (1833-1856). Development and Restructuring,* Greek edition, (Athens, 1983), chap. 3, pp. 85-93.

7. *Idem,* "European Steamshipping and the commercial activities of Syros (1833-1853)," Greek edition, *Historica,* No 3, (1985), p. 129.

8. *Idem,* "The commercial navy: from sail to steam" in *Facets of 19th century Greek society,* Greek edition, (Athens, 1984), p. 88.

9. *Idem, The Greek Commercial Navy (1833-1856). Development and Restructuring,* Greek edition, (Athens, 1983), chap. 6-7, pp. 126-227.

10. *Idem,* "Contribution to the history of Greek Steamshipping (1849-1857). Shareholders and distribution of the original capital-shares," Greek edition, *Mnemon,* X, (1984), pp. 140-52.

11. *Idem,* "The Greek Steamshipping Company (1857-1869). Hypothesis and problématique," Greek edition, *Mnemon,* IX, (1983), pp. 194-210.

12. *Idem,* "Contibution to the history of Greek Steamshipping (1849-1857). Shareholders and distribution of the original capital-shares," Greek edition, *Mnemon,* X, (1984), pp. 152-58.

13. *Idem, The Greek Commercial Navy (1833-1856). Development and Restructuring,* (Athens, 1983), chap. 6, pp. 126-69.

14. *Ibid.,* chap. 7, pp. 182-227.

Nikos G. Moschonas

Navigation and Trade in the Ionian and Lower Adriatic Seas in the Eighteenth Century

From the end of the fourteenth century. Levant transit trade was exclusively in the hands of Venetians. The Republic of Venice was the great naval power which dominated the eastern basin of the Mediterranean. Istria, Dalmatia, Albania, the Ionian Islands, some of the most important ports of the Peloponnesus, Negropont (Euboea), the Sporades and Cyclades, Crete, and Cyprus fell within its domain. Also, the Venetians retained significant commercial colonies in the great trade centers of the Levant, such as Constantinople, Trebizond, Tana, Theologo (New Ephesus), Palatia (Miletus), and Alexandria. Venetian naval domination was contested by its archrival, Genoa; the ensuing struggle was marked by a series of armed conflicts which culminated in the Peace of Turin (1381), following the War of Chioggia. The Genoese acknowledged by this treaty Venice's exclusive jurisdiction in the Adriatic and its superiority in the Levant commerce.[1] Long-range shipping lanes began and ended at Venice, connecting that city of lagoons with Adriatic ports, ports of the Ionian, Aegean, and Black Seas, as well as those of Crete, Cyprus, and the Near East.[2] In the Adriatic, the main ports were Ancona, Manfredonia, and Barletta on the Italian coast; Ragusa, Dulcigno, and Valona, of the Dalmatian and Albanian coasts.

In the Ionian Sea, Corfu and Modon were the main supply stations of Venetian commercial activity. The native population did not, it seems, engage in any particular merchant-marine activity at this time; in very light crafts they met local needs of the neighboring islands and the adjacent mainland, or carried goods by sea on a particular island. In sum, they had traditional ferry lines which even today continue to serve immediate needs.

Venetian superiority was again challenged with the rise — chiefly in the sixteenth century — of Ancona and Ragusa as important shipping centers in the Adriatic.[3] Ancona's center of import and export trade attracted a large number of Greek commercial firms.

Ragusa, which enjoyed a significant commercial presence in the Greek Levant from the end of the thirteenth century onward,[4] gradually developed into a shipping center which competed with Venice in transit commerce. This competition continued in the succeeding centuries, although new powers appeared on the scene, such as the Dutch, French, English, and Austrians. The later development of, say, Trieste in the Adriatic and Livorno (Leghorn) in the Tyrrhenean Sea, created the basis for an important transformation of the commercial status quo.

On the other hand, in the course of the eighteenth century, Franco-English shipping rivalry, with its broader aims and consequences,[5] appeared and dominated the central Mediterranean basin. Toward the end of that century, Russia appeared on the European scene as a new naval power. The competition between the French and the English in monopolizing the Levant transit trade, and especially that of the withering Ottoman empire, is a phenomenon parallel to the Venetian-Genoese competition during the last centuries of the Byzantine empire. From the Treaty of Karlowitz (1699), Ottoman import and export passed virtually into other hands, European merchant colonies in the main Turkish ports became regulators of the empire's economy, and Greeks, Armenians, and Jews expanded their financial activities. It is evident that, until Treaty of Passarowitz (1718), the main role in transit trade, especially in the Ionian and Adriatic Seas, was continually played by Venice. But, from the beginning of the eighteenth century, the French appeared an the scene and were particularly favored by international circumstances. French colonies sprang up, under the full protection privileges deriving of the Capitulations. The consulate in Arta, seconded by a network of sub-consulates in other cities of western Greece and Albania, such as Valona, Sayada, Preveza, Santa Maura (Leucas), Messolonghi, and Lepanto (Naupactus), became the official sponsor and coordinator of French economic interests in the Ionian Sea,[6] where the Venetians still monopolized transit trade. At the same time, local Greek elements began to operate, first in cooperation with the Venetians and later on with the French, who offered better terms and better prices.[7] At the end of the third decade of the century, new competitors appeared — the Neapolitans[8] and the English in collaboration with

Ragusans, Genoese and other Italians, Catalans, Majorcans, and Maltese, all protected by the British flag.[9] The English not only offered the best terms to Greek merchants, but also endeavored to attract local Greek elements. They favored Greek capital investment in English vessels as well as purchase of English vessels by Greek merchants, who linked their own interests with those of the English in the Levant (e.g., the case of the Ioannina merchant Theodosios Panou, consul of England).[10] The main object of this trade was high profits that in some cases even reached a 500-percent return on investments.[11] It was natural that the accumulation of capital would lead Greek merchants to expand their activities, by investing in the creation of a local merchant marine. Similarly, Venetians, by measures they took to confront their rivals, especially the transformation of Corfu into a center of transit trade and the favorable custom terms for Greek merchants, favored the development of the Greek commercial and shipping activity in the Ionian Sea.[12] Precisely in this area, open to the sea routes toward the great ports of Europe, emerged and developed the Greek merchant marine during the eighteenth century.

From about the middle of the eighteenth century, Greek vessels of medium tonnage enjoying the protection of Malta as Christian vessels, started to ply the chief lanes of the Mediterranean. The first vessels that appeared on these routes were those of Messolonghi, and they very soon became serious competitors for the Western Europeans, and especially for the French.[13] Also, the Messolonghi vessels, with lower freight charges, monopolized transit trade along the Ambracian Gulf - Malta - Messina - Naples and Ambracian Gulf - Ancona route. The active presence of Greeks in commercial navigation was correlated with the growth of Greek overland trade and with the international relations that the Greek merchants cultivated. The French, in their effort to limit Greek independent shipping activity and the penetration of other Europeans in the Ionian Sea, offered favorable terms of joint-ownership to Greek merchants on French vessels.[14] Primarily economic reasons led these merchants to prefer Greek-owned vessels, which sailed under the protection of Malta or Minorca — both English protectorates — or even under the flag of England. In addition, Greeks were very often appointed consuls or vice-consuls of European countries, such as England, the Kingdom of Two Sicilies, Ragusa, Holland, or Austria, in the Greek cities. They retained close connections with their fellow Greek merchants already installed in the large commercial centers of Italy, and thus abetted the trade interests of these countries at the expense of French navigation.[16] France attacked this problem by diplomatic means at the Sublime Port, arguing that these Greek consuls were subjects of the Sultan, and strove to effect their dismissal. The activity of these Greeks fostered the development of Greek navigation. France sought to maintain its positions in the Ambracian Gulf, but soon realized that this place was already surpassed by other ports, such as Venetian Preveza, at the entrance to the Gulf, Sayada further north opposite Corfu, as well as Messolonghi and Natoliko to the south. These ports operated almost exclusively with vessels of Greek ownership, or those of France's rival. Even worse, in 1755, the French consul at Arta disclosed that French captains themselves prefered Corfu for the discharge of goods carried from Italian ports and destined for Ioannina, instead of using the port at the Ambracian Gulf, where they would have to pay consular fees.[17] The growth of Corfu and Preveza as commercial transit centers from Western Europe to the Ottoman empire and vice-versa, was the substantive factor in the development of local Greek navigation. The commerce of Epirus and that of the Ionian Islands contributed decisively to the development of Messolonghi in navigation, since the powerful merchants from Ioannina and from the Ionian Islands invested in Messolonghi vessels.[18] The activity of Messolonghi in the Ionian Sea joined that of the Albanians of Dulcigno; however, soon emerged Galaxidi as a new shipping center in the Corinthian Gulf, thanks to the investments of the merchants of Zante and Patras.[19] It is also important to note that, at the same time, shipbuilding ventures commenced in the region. Small as well as more substantial vessels such as *polaccas*, frigates, and pinks were built in Messolonghi, Natoliko, Preveza, Kounoupelli, and elsewhere, in addition to those built in shipyards abroad (Leghorn, Trieste, Fiume, North Africa).[20] International circumstances, the competition of foreign powers, and the Seven Years War, were serious blows to French navigation and favored the evolution of Greek shipping. And, the French Revolution created new conditions that favored Greek transit trade even more.

Venetian sources testify that the Ionian Islands did not enjoy any serious navigation activity before the mid-seventeenth century. However, from the latter half of that century and throughout the next, the transportation of goods among the islands as well as to the ports of Epirus and those of foreign countries intensified. Although the Venetians made Corfu the center of transit trade in the Ionian Sea, in the other islands navigation was of limited range. Vessels of small or medium tonnage and of local ownership served local needs (transportation of products in the Peloponnesian and Epirus markets and the importation of foreign articles in the islands). However, it appears that there was significant capital accumulation in the islands of the Central Ionian Sea (Leucas, Ithaca, Cephalonia, Zante), which was invested in shipping.[21] When the French occupied the islands after the fall of the Venetian Republic, under the terms of the Treaty of Campo Formio (1797), they paid particular attention to the organization of local navigation and to the coordination of private shipping activities. The Ionians (as well as other Greeks) received the same treatment as French citizens in French ports.[22] In the case of the Ionian Greeks, this was natural as their vessels legally flew the flag of the French Republic. By the turn of the century, these islanders had invested considerable capital in vessels of large capacity sailing under the French flag. One may note that since the middle of the eighteenth century, some of the ports on these islands developed into important commercial centers that were able to serve the local needs as well as to assume the export trade in currants (Cephalonia and Zante). The transfer of the administrative seat of Cephalonia to Argostoli in 1757 is indicative of the importance attributed to it as the port for the Fortress of St. George, which until that time was the capital of the island. One must not overlook the activity of the islanders in contraband and piracy, factors important for the accumulation of local capital.[23] Cephalonians were renowned as being among the most skilful pirates of the Mediterranean. By the end of the eighteenth century, shipping in Cephalonia was undergoing great expansion. For example, the Sicilian traveler Scrofani mentions more than 200 large vessels and 5000 small craft.[24] The Cephalonian vessels sailed along all the routes of the Mediterranean and the Black

Sea, as well as of the Atlantic. This dynamic presence offered a glimpse of the important role that Cephalonian navigation would later on play in the economy of the Mediterranean.

The commerce and navigation of the Ionian Islands pose a problem that as yet has not been adequately explored. Nevertheless, local as well as foreign (particularly Venetians, French, and British) archives attest to the survival of rich documentary material. Of particular importance are the official registers kept by the local health offices. These books record sailing licenses, as well as permission granted to vessels to enter and leave a particular port; the latter documents also contain detailed data (port of origin, destination, type of vessel, captain and crew, purpose of trip, cargo, passengers, etc.) on each ship. To date, the author has located and catalogued in the Historical Archives of Cephalonia, three such registers of the end of the seventeenth century and 81 of the eighteenth century, with a total number of 6298 folios; also, nine bundles with a total of 727 documents, material issued by the health offices operating in the ports of Argostoli and Assos.[25] Relevent material has also been found in the archives of the other islands. Very important, too, are the passports of vessels and persons, surviving in large numbers, and the registers of the custom authorities. It is evident that the study of this material and its quantitative analysis will offer new dimensions to the subject of navigation and trade in this area.

In conclusion: During the eighteenth century transit trade in the Ionian and the lower Adriatic Seas was carried on by the merchant ships of Western Europe. The main role in this activity was played by the French with the English as their principal rival. The center of interest for foreigners was the Ambracian Gulf, where the Epirus export commerce was concentrated. In the course of the century, new areas of transit trade developed contributing to the restriction of the French activity, while, with the emergence of Greek shipping, the position of the French in the Ionian Sea was further shaken and shrunk. At the same time, owing chiefly to the currant trade, the ports of Ithaca, Argostoli, Patras, and Zante witnessed significant development. The main lanes of navigation were that of the western Mediterranean connecting the ports of France, Italy, Sicily, and Malta with the ports of the Ionian Islands and with the commercial anchorages along the coast of Epirus, and the Adriatic Lane connecting Venice, Trieste, Ancona, and Ragusa with the ports of Albania, Corfu, Preveza, and the Ambracian Gulf. To these lanes corresponded those of the Aegean and Black Seas extending to Crimea, as well as the lane of the eastern Mediterranean, connecting the Ionian Sea with the commercial zones of the Near East. The emergence and prevalence of the Greek merchant marine is a phenomenon of foremost importance.

Notes

1. Roberto Cessi, *Storia della Repubblica di Venezia* I (Milan - Messina, 1968), 330-31.

2. Freddy Thiriet, *La Romanie vénitienne au Moyen Age: Le développement et l'exploitation du domaine colonial vénitien (XIIe-XVe siècles)* (Paris, 1959), 355-57, 419-28.

3. Alberto Caracciolo, *Le port franc d'Ancône: Croissance et impasse d'un milieu marchand au XVIIIe siècle* (Paris, 1965), 31-41, 42-43 (Document I).

4. On the subject see, B. Krekić, *Dubrovnik (Raguse) et le Levant au Moyen Age* (Paris - The Hague, 1961), 151-58; cf. Alain Ducellier, "Aux frontières de la Romanie: Arta et Saint-Maure à la fin du Moyenâge," *Travaux et Mémoires*, VIII (1981), 113-24, especially 117-18.

5. See, Alfred C. Wood, *A History of the Levant Company* (London, 1964).

6. See, the broader study of Georgios A. Siorokas, *Tὸ γαλλικὸ προξενείο τῆς Ἄρτας (1702-1789)* [The French Consulate in Arta (1702-1789)] (Ioannina, 1981).

7. Serafeim Maximos, *Tὸ ἑλληνικὸ ἐμπορικὸ ναυτικὸ κατὰ τὸν XVIII αἰώνα* [The Greek Merchant Marine during the XVIIIth Century] (2nd ed.; Athens, 1976), 28-29. With respect to the economic rivalry between the Venetians and France in this area see Siorokas, *Tὸ γαλλικὸ προξενείο...*, 177-93.

8. Siorokas, *Tὸ γαλλικὸ προξενείο...*, 284-86.

9. Maximos, *Tὸ ἑλληνικὸ ἐμπορικὸ ναυτικὸ...*, pp. 31, 33; see also, Siorokas, *Tὸ γαλλικὸ προξενείο...*, 373-75. Not infrequently the Genoese, according to circumstances, used flags other than their own, such as those of the Kingdom of Naples, of France or of Jerusalem; see, *ibid.*, 286-87.

10. Maximos, *Tὸ ἑλληνικὸ ἐμπορικὸ ναυτικὸ...*, p. 34 ff.; Siorokas, *Tὸ γαλλικὸ προξενείο...*, 290-92.

11. George B. Leon, "The Greek Merchant Marine (1453-1850)," in Stelios A. Papadopoulos, ed., *The Greek Merchant Marine 1453-1850* (National Bank of Greece, Athens, 1972), 13-44, especially 28.

12. Maximos, *Tὸ ἑλληνικὸ ἐμπορικὸ ναυτικὸ...*, 31-33.

13. *Ibid.*, pp. 47-54; see also, Basilis Kremmydas, *Τὸ ἐμπόριο τῆς Πελοποννήσου στὸ 18ο αἰώνα (1715-1792)* [The Trade in Peloponnesus in the 18th Century (1715-1792)] (Athens, 1972), pp. 301-303.

14. Siorokas, *Τὸ γαλλικὸ προξενεῖο...*, p. 371.

15. The contribution of the Greek colony established in Port Mahon was significant; see, N. G. Svoronos, «Ἡ ἑλληνικὴ παροικία τῆς Μινόρκας: Συμβολὴ στὴν ἱστορία τοῦ ἑλληνικοῦ ἐμπορικοῦ ναυτικοῦ τὸν 18ον αἰώνα» [The Greek Colony in Minorca: A Contribution to the History of the Greek Merchant Marine in the 18th Century], in *Mélanges Octave et Melpo Mérlier* II (Athens, 1956), 323-43.

16. Siorokas, *Τὸ γαλλικὸ προξενεῖο...*, pp. 165-73.

17. See, the letter of the French consul (19 December 1755) published in Greek translation by Maximos, *Τὸ ἑλληνικὸ ἐμπορικὸ ναυτικό...*, 78.

18. See, Konstantinos Sathas, *Εἰδήσεις τινὲς περὶ ἐμπορίου καὶ φορολογίας ἐν Ἑλλάδι ἐπὶ τουρκοκρατίας* [Some Notices about Trade and Taxation in Greece under the Turkish Domination] (anastatic edition, Athens, 1977), 39-40; cf. Leon, "The Greek Merchant Marine...," 28.

19. Sathas, *Εἰδήσεις τινὲς...*, 48-49; cf. Leon, "The Greek merchant marine...," 28.

20. Sathas, *Εἰδήσεις τινὲς...*, 43-48; cf. Leon, "The Greek merchant marine...," 29.

21. The Cephalonians and the Zakynthians in particular demonstrated an early maritime activity; see, Kremmydas, *Τὸ ἐμπόριο τῆς Πελοποννήσου...*, 315; also, Apostolos E. Vakalopoulos, *Ἱστορία τοῦ Νέου Ἑλληνισμοῦ* [History of Modern Hellenism], IV (Salonika, 1973), 168-69; Georgios Ploumidis, "Ναυτιλία καὶ ἐμπόριο στὴ Λευκάδα (1783, 1818)" [Merchant Marine and Trade in Leucas (1783, 1818)], *Δωδώνη* [Dodone], XIII (1984), 399-418.

22. This is moreover declared explicitly in the letter of the General A. Gentili, commander of the Levant Division, dated Corfu, 28 Fructidor of the V year [14 September 1797] sent to the municipality of Assos, in Cephalonia, with a circular of the French consul in Ancona, in which it is solemnly announced, that the Greeks enjoy full rights both in religious and trade freedom in that town and harbour; *Historical Archives of Cephalonia*, Republican Governement, Provisory Municipality of Assos, file 2, documents 15 and 15a.

23. Regarding the piratic activities of the Ionian islanders see Siorokas, *Τὸ γαλλικὸ προξενεῖο...*, 383-87.

24. Saverio Scrofani, *Viaggio in Crecia, fatto nell'anno 1794, 1795* I (London, 1799), 40.

25. All this material has already been microfilmed by the Centre of Byzantines Research of the Hellenic National Research Foundation; the author intends to begin its study in the near future.

Paul Jonás

Lajos Kossuth's Maritime Policies

In 1947 Bibo Istvan, then director of the East European Research Institute in Budapest, assigned this writer the following research topic: "The History of the Hungarian Commercial Society: The First Stock Corporation of Budapest."

The research was begun reluctantly at the Hungarian Archives. Slowly, however, it became interesting. The atmosphere in the old part of the city where the archives were located was pleasant, the camaraderie which developed among the older researchers and the newcomer was conducive to the good of the project. Looking at original documents, the story unfolded, and one was able to understand why people became addicted to historical research. This involvement is similar, it seems, to police work; one should find the documents, analyze them, and present the evidence to the judges. The final *parvum opus* was published in 1948, among other papers of the institute's centennial anniversary volume on the revolution of 1848 and Kossuth. Time has passed, and after 40 years, it is now rewritten and presented to this audience.

The data and facts, based on the original research, have not changed. Interpretations and evaluations, however, have. In the first version, Kossuth shone as a superhuman national hero; 40 years later, this view is more tempered.

For this audience, the information contained in some paragraphs is well known. They are not stricken from the text because the paper presented in this conference aims for a general readership.

The author would like to express his sincere thanks to his old-time friend, Professor Béla K. Király, director, Brooklyn College Conference on Society in Change, and Professor Constantine Svopopoulos, director, Institute for Balkan Studies, Salonika, for giving him an opportunity to renew his old interest in economic history.

Kossuth Lajos: A Biographical Summary

(a) Kossuth: Highlights

The doctrines of autarky, protectionism, export promotion, and free trade influenced Kossuth Lajos' (1802-1894) commercial and maritime policies.

Kossuth's fame, as is well known, was not based on his own economic ideas, but as is the general rule of thumb of politicians, were borrowed from economists, and often in a half-digested form. His international reputation was that of a Hungarian revolutionary hero responsible mainly for dissolving the union of the Austrian and Hungarian crown in 1849. Kossuth, a lawyer by training, entered national politics at an early age and soon won a large following. He was arrested in 1837, but popular pressure forced the Metternich regime to release him in 1840. At different times of his career, he articulated both nationalist policies and liberal doctrines. He was, in turn, protectionist, mercantilist, and free trader. As a fiery orator, an articulate writer, a dynamic politician, he became the leader of the revolution of 1848, which, as it has been argued by today's historians, was constitutional in its nature.

When, in April 1848, Hungary was granted a separate government, Kossuth became finance minister. He continued and intensified his anti-Austrian stand. Minorities in Hungary, however, felt that Kossuth's Hungarian nationalism was opposed to the fulfillment of their own national aspirations, and he was particularly resented in Croatia.

When the Austrian government, supported by the ban (governor) of Croatia, Count Jellachich de Buzim, prepared to move against Hungary, Kossuth became the head of the Hungarian government of national defense. His government withdrew to Debrecen before the advance of the Austrians under Alfred Windischgratz.

In April 1849, the Hungarian parliament declared Hungary an independent republic, and Kossuth became its president. He won several battles, but in 1849, Russian troops intervened in favor of Austria, and Kossuth was obliged to turn the government over to General Gorgey. The Hungarian surrender at Vilagos marked the end of the republic.

Kossuth fled to Turkey, then he was invited to tour England and the United States. Since he learned English in prison, he was able to communicate well in these countries and received accolades as a champion of liberty. Kossuth lived in exile in England, and then in Italy. The Hungarians under the leadership of Deak Ferenc established a *modus vivendi* with the Austrians, but Kossuth was dissatisfied with the *Ausgleich* (compromise) of 1887, by which the Austro-Hungarian monarchy was created. He remained consistent with his past and his ideas, and refused an amnesty in 1890. After his death in Turin, Italy, his body was returned to Budapest and buried in state.

(b) Myths and Heros

One should add a general note to this short biographical resume.

Our preception of a national hero is based on the simplified role that the person projects. Kossuth presents a clear and sharply defined image, and many people, historians and non-historians alike, are convinced that they are intimately acquainted with his personality. Hence, we tend to favor those historical works which, rather than breasting the current to reveal something new to us, allow ourselves to be sucked into the maelstrom of the ready-made, the already-known. In this process, images are so often repeated that they become clichés that block our vision of reality, and they end up becoming inflexible myths.

The historian, who bases his work on such myths, will be rewarded by seeing his work appreciated almost as soon as it appears. The writer who puts facts in a different framework, somtimes clashing with preconceived views, is taking risks since he will receive his rewards only with the passage of time.

But, the basic historical facts remain; the evaluation of the instantly identifiable stereotypical image which Kossuth radiates, must change constantly. Fortunately, it does. In our times, re-evaluations concerning Kossuth are abundant. We should applaud them. Time alone will tell us what views should be accepted or rejected.

An Outline of
Kossuth's Economic, Commercial and Maritime Policies

(a) Four Projects for Economic Development

The issues presented in this paper, focus on Kossuth's economic and maritime policies. They are not dead chapters of economic history. For, many of today's politico-economic decisions are made on the same problems Kossuth faced: import substitution or export promotion; self-reliance or integration; protective tariffs or free trade; nationalism or liberalism.

These options have a familiar ring in the ears of every student of economic development.

Kossuth's economic, commercial and maritime policies can be summarized in four headings:

1. *The Hungarian Commercial Society (Magyar Kereskedelmi Tarsasag);*
2. *Association for Economic Protection (Vedegylet);*
3. *The Hungarian Maritime Company (Magyar Tengerhajozasi Tarsasag);*
4. *The Plan for the Vukovar-Fiume Railroad and the Establishment of the Railroad Company*

(b) Less Developed Nations and Economic History

It is often stated that we can learn from history despite the fact that this specialization is defined as an art and not a predictive social science. One of the goals of this paper is to demonstrate that some nations, which are now in the same development stage as Hungary was over a hundred years ago, can benefit from the story of other nations and from the struggles of leading national politicians.

Kossuth's economic and commercial policies can be regarded as a "case study" revealing what actions to take in order to engineer the "take off" in a process of economic development. It also shows, for decision makers, what are the decisions which should not be repeated.

"Take off" in Hungary was not achieved by Kossuth but by one of his cool-headed successors, Deak Ferenc.

(c) Economic History vs. Economic Models

We suggest that some chapters of economic history may be more instructive for practitioners than the examination of some famous mathematical development models.

We are not proposing a stand against development theory. It is not among our aims to prove the trivial proposition that history repeats itself. We only argue here that even in a different technological and international milieu, it is not a waste of time for decision makers to examine previous problems of economic history.

Kossuth's economic and commercial projects show us the thinking and actions of a nationalist, but, at the same time, a pragmatic politician who was not carried away by ideological prescriptions, and a man who had the courage to change his precepts and concepts for the well-being of his nation. The roads to the stage of takeoff for a less-developed country are many, the strategies and the mixes can be almost infinite since different combinations of "development menus" are available. Therefore, confusion and conflict, in the process of engineering a development process are not the exception but rather the rule.

(d) The Political Problems of Development

In the process of creating the preconditions for a strategy to achieve the stage of takeoff, Kossuth's struggles reveal the difficulties of every policymaker of yesterday, today, and tomorrow. To succeed in any economic project, we should take into consideration, in addition to the internal consistency of the proposals, the availability of the resources to implement a desideratum, and also, the confusing kaleidescope of a fragmented, constantly changing political framework, a regrouping of broken coalitions, newly minted alliances, and the possible actions of internal and international pressure groups.

Economic projects also need personnel. Politicians must have trusted lieutenants who implement ideas.

Who is the decision maker who has not been hurt by misplaced trust? Who did not make mistakes in the process of executing popular desiderata? Kossuth's maritime policies and how his ideas were put into practice tell the eternal story of political leaders' victories and failures. The selection of Szabo Pal Jr., for the President of the Hungarian Commercial Society, will be the example that illustrates this point.

(e) Protectionism of Free Trade?

National leaders seeking the independence of their nations often vacillate between protectionism and free trade. We would like to argue that these two positions, in different times, when conditions are changing, should not be evaluated as contradictory.

Less-developed nations often implement autarchic policies to avoid heavy dependence on foreign supplies flowing into their countries on unfavorable terms. The bulk of these goods and services are coming mainly from a dominant nation and, at the same time, the colonies, or dependent, nations, such as Hungary in the first half of the nineteenth century, are normally facing a strong tariff wall against their own products. In this case, a country does not have any other choice than to act in self-defense. It should insulate itself from the "begger-thy-neighbor commercial policy" of the dominant nation, in order to reduce exploitation. In this case, too, the dependent nation should protect growing infant industries from the vagaries of the world market and unfair competition of already developed, efficient, low-cost foreign industries.

The Association for Economic Protection, which Kossuth founded on October 6, 1844, was established as a defense against the Austrian tariff policy, and its aim was to boycott foreign, especially Austrian, goods in order to give incentives to local manufacturers and traders to start national production and commerce.

Let us examine just one issue: Hungarian wine going to Austria was taxed by 2 forints, Austrian wine coming to Hungary had to pay for the same amount, 2 krajcar. (The ratio between forint and krajcar is the same as between drachma and lepton).

Many Austrians were also shocked by this flagrant bias.[1]

(f) Import Substitution or Export Promotion?

The legacy of the sixteenth to the early nineteenth - century East

Europe was imports taking the place of industrialization. Import substitution can be implemented throughout by the use of high and increasing import duties, and at times, with quantitative restrictions, multiple exchange rates, and other devices. In Hungary, however, just as in colonial countries, tariffs were set by the foreign authorities; therefore, policymakers were severdy curtailed in their actions, and nothing else remained but to issue emotional appeals to the population and to urge them to buy goods produced in the country.

Nationalistic feelings work up to a point, and this approach can be especially successful if the economic exploitation of a country is obvious, and this fact is known and resented by the majority of the population. In mid-nineteenth century Hungary, Kossuth's appeals worked, and locally produced output increased. Nevertheless, it became obvious that the country, as anywhere else in the world, slowly encountered major difficulties with import substitution based on nationalistic and moralistic arguments.

Home industry had been established in a sheltered environment — prices were high, incentives for efficient production were negligible. In short, import substitution never represents a consistent application of a well thoughout strategy. It is basically emotional, and it could be described as the haphazard establishment of various industries under the pressure of recurrent balance-of-payment crises.

It became obvious that instead of an import substitution policy, it was necessary to shift to export promotion.

(g) Mercantilism: Export Promotion

Mercantilism became the economic system of major nations based on the premise that national wealth and power were best served by increasing exports and collecting precious metals in return. This economic doctrine and practice superseded the medieval feudal organization in Western Europe, especially in Holland, France, and England. The period 1500-1800 was one of religious and commercial wars, and large revenues were needed to maintain armies and pay the growing costs of government. Precious metals, especially gold, were in universal demand as the ready means of obtaining other commodities.

To acquire bullion, foreign trade was favored above domestic trade;

moreover, manufacturing, processing, and agricultural activities were regarded as efforts which providing goods for foreign trade. Naturally, in this framework, exports were not considered as an end in themselves, but as a means to finance necessary imports. Under mercantilist policies, a nation sought to sell more than it bought so as to accumulate bullion, i.e., the universally acceptable buying power for goods and services.

The role of the state in this system was to help individuals motivated by the profit motive, to form trading companies and corporations with the object of providing commodities for exports at high price, and securing goods of high quality at low cost. The implementation of this policy was the prerequisite for the industrial revolution, a term usually applied to the social and economic changes that mark the transition from a stable agricultural and commercial society to a modern industrial society. True, this new stage is characterized by a chain of disequilibria, a constantly spinning cyclical cobweb; however, this is an unavoidable cost in achieving the benefit of speedy economic development.

The powerful European industrialized nations realized that import substitution made growth on output more, rather than less, sensitive to the availability of foreign exchange, since the foreign exchange costs of import substitution are heavy and the savings were slow in coming.

Owing to this, more and more, developed nations began to rediscover and to use the concept of the Ricardian comparative advantage. Suddenly an interesting mixture of mercantilist and *laissez-faire* policies was in the vogue. Governments slowly reduced regulations and introduced "natural laws" for economic decision making.

(h) Plans for a Hungarian Commercial and Maritime Policy

Among Kossuth's projects, mercantilist and partly laissez-faire ideas were manifested in the establishment of the Hungarian Commercial Society and the the Hungarian Maritime Company.

The Hungarian Commercial Society was established on December 3, 1843, to develop commerce as well as maritime relationships. Its most important aim was to eliminate the middleman in the process of shipping goods abroad and to help agricultural commodities. On January 22, 1846 the society founded the Hungarian Maritime Company to emphasize the importance of seafaring and to exploit the opportunities offered by the port of Fiume.

Maritime Policies and the Establishment
of the Hungarian Maritime Company

(a) The Prerequisites of a Maritime Policy

The purpose of an economic plan is to attain ends that are considered socially desirable. Rational economic plans, however, need prerequisites for their execution. For example, before a nation is able to draw up plans for direct maritime commerce, it must have an access to the sea, it must have at least one maritime port, transportation to the port(s) should be established, and the country ought to have ships, and also, a developed legal system capable of regulating maritime commerce.

Goverments, especially in the nineteenth century, did not engage themselves in new developmental activities whose output had to be marketed. They were aware that such ventures might prosper for a while, but experience suggested that in the long run governmental involvement could cause embarassing losses. Governments in price-directed systems are not at all anxious to submit their performance to the test of the market.

These were the reasons why in Hungary the state government ruled out starting a maritime company with the money of taxpayers. As it turned out this was a wise decision.

(b) The Role of the Government: Infrastructure

Governments normally concentrate on building their infrastructure, such as highway, railroad, and port projects, then on dealing with complex industrial and managerial problems. Highways, ports, railroads can certainly fail too, but one can explain the reasons for the misfortune, and they can be built over and over again. Therefore, infrastructure turns out to be an ideal outlet for governmental funds, involving almost no risk and a minimum effort of maintenance.

This is one of the reasons why Hungarian governmental circles were overwhelmed, when on August 9, 1776, Maria Theresa — queen of Bohemia and Hungary and consort of the Holy Roman Emperor Francis, dowager empress after the accession of her son Joseph II — incorporated the port of Fiume as *separatum adnexum corpus* in Hungarian territory.

The development and maintenance of this port gave low-risk opportunities to bureaucrats. In addition, it created a position with a desirable title for the ruling nobility: "Governor of Fiume."[2]

(c) Fiume: Backward Linkages

The effect of this infrastructure was exactly what a Hirschmanian theory predicts: backward and forward linkages. It proves that modern theory of development works also in hindsight.[3]

The effect of the *backward linkage* was that, from 1790, Fiume provided an outlet to foreign markets for tobacco, grain, and meat producers, who, in turn, increased production and input in these branches of the economy. In addition, the port generated demands for other infrastructure, such as plans for railroad building. One of the most important parts of this project was the link between Vukovar and Fiume.

The transportation of merchandise from industrial or agricultural centers to Fiume was slow, difficult, or even impossible. Goods first had to be transported to the Duna or Tisza, then loaded on ships which navigated the auxiliary Szava, until Sziszek. There the merchandise, owing to navigational difficulties, had to be reloaded to smaller ships. The port of arrival was Karolyvaros. Here goods had to be transferred to horse-drawn carriages to complete the additional distance of 134 km. to Fiume. Simplification of this route could be solved only by building railroads, for part of this hazardous travel at least.

The project for the railroad to Fiume was incorporated in Public Law 1836:XXV.tc. The option was left open whether rails should run Pest-Fiume or Sziszek-Fiume. It was suggested, at this stage, that private capital should undertake its construction. Kossuth took the position that first a railroad should connect the cities Vukovar-Karolyvaros-Fiume, and then the ultimate goal should be tackled, the establishment of a transportation facility for merchandise and personnel from Pest to Fiume.

Kossuth and another leading Hungarian politician of the time, Count Szechenyi Istvan, often clashed, not necessarily in final goals, but in strategies. Szechenyi proposed a Pest-Fiume line, but Kossuth felt that this was irrational for the time being, owing to lack of necessary capital. The discussion, in which all the political leaders as well as the public took part, was vivid.

Three railroad companies were founded. The first under the auspices of the Hungarian Commercial Society in Pest, the second in the county of Szerem, sponsored by local landowners, and the third in Fiume. After long discussions, the companies of Pest and Szerem unified. Then, Kossuth traveled to Fiume, and with the backing of the Governor Kiss Pal, he was able to achieve the unification of all three railroad companies. Kossuth in his article published in the newspaper, *Pesti Hirlap*, stated on October 1, 1843, that: "As to the question of the railroad connecting Fiume with the nation, this is a vital project. The other steps for economic development rank below that."

The Commercial Committee of the Hungarian parliament in its 1843-44 session concluded, "We must start with the railroad connecting Fiume with the nation ... this railroad is the key for our commerce... the welfare of the nation depands on its execution," thereby echoing Kossuth's words. The two legislature houses accepted the railroad project between Vukovar and Karolyvaros.

In January 1847, the accumulated capital for the Vukovar-Fiume railroad was 8.5 million forint which represented the highest investment in Hungary. The project was also supported by 47 countries.

In 1848, among the laws passed was 1848:XXX.tc., which was signed by the sovereign (on April 11). This law dealt with the projects related to railroads. Among them was the section linking Fiume with Pest, but the idea of private capital was rejected and the state budget was named to provide capital for building this vital infrastructure.[4]

(c) Fiume: Forward Linkages

The *forward linkage* is manifested by the fact that from 1823 the shacks in Fiume disappeared and a city with streets developed rapidly. Moreover, the Fiumara, flowing to the sea at Fiume received the attention of engineers and became more tame. And, the port became the eighteenth most important international maritime port in 1910, and until World War I, it was used as the main weapon to implement Hungarian mercantilist strategies.

(d) Fiume: New Ideas

For an economic historian interested in changing thoughts, probably the most important effect of Fiume was that its existence complemented rigid Hungarian regionalism, parochialism. It became a gateway for new views, especially for creeping *laissez-faire* ideas. Fiume was a free port (*puto-franco*), i.e., merchants were free to store their merchandise in its territory without paying tariffs. This was a decision which had to be made since other major ports were administered under similar rules.

(e) Merchant Ships

According to a list of 1830 the Hungarian merchant marine consisted of 24 boats propelled by sails and used basically for coastal navigation.[5]

In the next five years, registers include 45 boats over 350 tonnes with three, four, and five sails. Investment in human capital was also starting, and in the Maritime Academy of Fiume, beginning in 1830, young men were able to receive training in the craft of sailing, i.e., navigation and other skills necessary for officers or captains.

At this time, the destinations of the Hungarian boats were Odessa, Constantinople, Alexanrdria, Smirna, Messina, Marseille, and even London.

(f) Law and Maritime Commerce

For a succesful maritime commerce, a system of law, concerning navigation and international commerce, was necessary. Because ships sail from nation to nation over seas that no nation owns, countries need to seek agreements over customs related to shipping. Maritime law, in origin, was based on customs only, but it shows the influence of the Roman civil law. In the later Middle Ages, when traders were more and more venturous in crossing waters, the rules of the sea were compiled in widely recognized collections, such as *Consolato del mare* (Consulate of the Sea), *The Rolls of Oleron*, and the *English Black Book of the Admiralty*. In England special courts were set up to administer the law under the high court of the Admiralty. Such jurisdiction must also cover all maritime contracts, torts, injuries, and offenses, and collisions at sea.[6]

In Hungary, Kossuth was instrumental in the legislation of commercial laws based on liberal principles, and these included also references to maritime commerce. Basically, the international regulations were codified in Hungarian civil law. These laws were especially important since they served to determine in advance what legal demands would arise and what steps ought to be made for meeting them. Kossuth attached great importance to working out, in systematic detail, and great consistency, that commercial contracts express the will of the parties involved.[7]

(c) Promotion of Maritime Commerce

Kossuth did not rest in the promotion of maritime commerce, and the title of one of his articles in the weekly *Hetilap* (January 27, 1846) became a slogan for the nation: "To the Sea Hungarian!" He continued in his dynamic rhetoric: "Every Hungarian should consider the sea as an involvement... if we look in the mirror of the sea it is impossible not to recognize its importance and it is impossible that we should not receive impetus for action...".

Kossuth had the portfolio of finances in the first independent government established in March 1848, and he continued pushing the development of Fiume, including the railroad to that port. The letter of Susani Jozsef, who represented Fiume in the legislature, proves, in accordance with the budget of 1849, that development of the port was ranked high.[8]

In the beginning of spring 1848 were the steps for the Pest-Fiume railroad started. The first step was to link Buda with Szekesfehervar.

But, the revolution starting on the Ides of March, 1948, put economic projects on a low burner for a long time.

Notes

1. See for the tariff: Hung. Archives *Canc. Acta Generalia* 2708/1842. For the views of Austrian historians: Adolf Beer, *The osterreichische Handelspolitik im XIX Jahrhundert*, (Vienna, 1898). On p. 45: "There is no question that the Austrian tariff duty was lethal for Hungary's economy." One questions, however, the wisdom of Austrian policymakers establishing this heavy discrimination against Hungarian wines and for subsidizing inferior quality Austrian wines. Who would drink Austrian wines in Hungary? Examining the goals and practices of the Association for Economic Protection, who would not think about the stand of Mohandas Karamchand Gandhi, the Indian political and spiritual leader, who in protest against the English government's salt tax, roughly one hundred years later in 1980, led the famous 200 m (320 km.) march to extract salt from the sea. Raul Presbish, the famous Argentinian economist, also suggested for Latin America an import substitution policy to protect the Hispanic nations from the cheap industrial products coming from North America.

2. Two governors became notable: Urmenyi Ferenc (1823-1837) and Nemeskeri Kiss Pal (1837-1848).

3. *Vide* Albert O. Hirschman, *The Strategy of Economic Development* (New Haven: Yale University Press 1967), pp. 100-17; 134-35.

4. For the complexities surrounding the plans for the railroad to Fiume see: Horvath Mihaly, *From Hungarian History, 1823-1848* (Magyarorszag Tortelmebol, 1823-1848) (Rath Mor: Budapest) 1886, pp. 365-67; 451-53.

5. See the names and other characteristics of these boats in Appendix I.

6. See: D. W. Bowett, *The Law of the Sea* (Princeton: Princeton University Press, 1967); C. J. Colombos, *The International Law of the Sea* (3rd ed) (Cambridge, Mass.: Harvard University Press 1967).

7. Among the so-called reform laws reflecting Kossuth's ideas we can mention the law governing bonds and credits: 1940:XV.tc; the regulations for business transactions, seafaring and setting commercial law became a separate subject matter with special courts. Kossuth was also careful to argue that Hungarian legislation should not contradict the codes of trading partners in order to facilitate the flow of trade: 1840:XVI.tc; Among these reform laws one of the most important was the 1840:XVII.tc. which stated the concept of "free entry" *i.e.*,

everybody was free to start any business any place and any time, subject only to zoning regulations.

8. Letter of representative Susani Jozsef to Kossuth, 24 August 1848, in commenting on the Budget of 1949 includes the following passage: "We would like to assure you, Mr. Finance Minister, that Fiume noted with pleasure that you were careful enough to conserve funds in the next budget for Fiume's development. The same times we took note that Count Szechenyi in his budget proposal did not think that an allocation was important for this purpose."Then as a practical politician he ends his letter: "Mr. Finance Minister, in all my life I have stood up for the general idea of uniform taxation. I still believe that no specific tax rates should be given regionally. However, in the case of Fiume we call your attention to specific conditions which would, I am sure, convince you that in some selected areas, such as ... we need tax reductions. Naturally this temporary relief will return to the nation more than proportionately in a short time period. Please allow us to list our arguments for your consideration:..................." *See, Budget* 1849, in *Congressional Papers* (Orszaggyulesi Naplo, 1848).

Despoina Tsourka-Papastathis

The Decline of the Greek "Companies" in Transylvania: An Aspect of Habsburg Economic Policies in the Black Sea and the Mediterranean

On February 24, 1784, the Sublime Porte issued an Act (Sened) which, among other things permitted Austrian subjects and vessels free transport of goods to and from Ottoman provinces, by river and sea.[1] This initiated an important change: the beginning of the decline of continental trade between the two empires, as well as that of the privileged Greek merchant guilds of Transylvania.

During the second half of the sixteenth and all of the seventeenth centuries Transylvania, then a principality subject to the Porte, had been an important crossroad for the exchange of goods between the Austrian and the Ottoman empires. Transylvania itself, and more particularly the reigning princes and local nobility, made considerable profits from duties on imported, exported, and transited goods through the complicated customs system established of old in the country.[2]

Greek and other traders from the European provinces of the Ottoman empire, as well as from Wallachia and Moldavia, were active in wholesale overland trade of oriental goods in the fairs of Transylvania, Hungary, and later, Leipzig.[3] The predominance of Greek merchants was very soon established, so as to induce, in 1636, Prince George Rakoczy I to grant a "Privilege" to the *Universitas Quaestorum Graecorum* of Transylvania; thus, Greek merchants were allowed to carry on wholesale trade in Transylvanian fairs and form self-governed "Companies," i.e., merchant guilds.[4]

The first Greek "company" was founded in Sibiu (Hermannstadt), in 1639,[5] followed by another in Brașov (Cronstadt), in 1678.[6] There may have been others, too, in other Transylvanian towns, but no archival, nor relevant source, materials have been as yet discovered to confirm this hypothesis. As for "companies" of other ethnic groups in Transylvania, there is very scarce, but positive, information in the archives of the Greek "company" of Sibiu, about a merchant guild of Armenians in Gherla (1672), of Jews in Alba-Julia (1684?), Bulgarians in Deva, and Serbs in the neighboring Banat — in Timișoara (Temesvar) —, probably from early eighteenth century onward.[7]

Two years after the Peace Treaty of Karlowitz, Emperor Leopold I renewed, in 1701, the Privilege of the *Societates Graecorum* of Transylvania, granting their members his personal protection and large immunities, in fact, the largest ever.[8] In 1777, Emperess Maria-Theresa also renewed the Privilege of Leopold for the *Societates* of the Greek merchants of Sibiu and Brașov, but she reduced their jurisdiction and the number of various tax exemptions previously enjoyed by their members.[9] The aim of this Privilege was obviously to induce many of these merchants to become subjects of the Austrian crown; it granted, however, enough immunities to motivate oriental goods merchants to establish their trade permanently in Transylvania.

It is not, of course, to be assumed that the whole oriental trade of the Austrian empire was conducted by land. Since the Peace Treaty of Vienna (1616), Austria endeavored to secure a place in maritime trade. Thus, this treaty, the Treaty of Commerce of Passarowitz (1718), and that of Belgrade (1739) contained articles by which the Sublime Porte and the Austrian empire undertook the obligation to secure and facilitate commerce for each other's subjects, be it by land o r sea. It should be noted, too, that, whereas land trade in the provinces of each party was merely mentioned, maritime commerce was treated in detail. The Treaty of Commerce of Passarowitz[10] did not allow Austrian ships to enter the Black Sea through the Danube; from the Danubian ports (Vidin, Ruse, etc.) or the Romanian ports on the Black Sea (Brăila, Kilia, etc.), goods could only be carted further inland or shipped by non-Austrian vessels to Constantinople, Trebizond, Sinope, and other ports on the Black Sea. Obviously, this method of transport cost less to Ottoman than to Austrian subjects, from whom were exacted various extraordinary taxes and duties by Ottoman officials, which the various treaties prohibited.[11] Thus, Ottoman merchants in overland trade maintained their predominant position, while maritime commerce was effectively obstructed. Sanctions against corsair and private activity in the Mediterranean and Adriatic were also provided in all the treaties, but they obviously had little force, as they were invariably violated.

The Sened of 1784 was issued by the Porte at the request of Austria, in order to enforce the application of the Treaty of Belgrade, more precisely Article 11. Furthermore, it modified the provisions of the Treaty of Commerce of Passarowitz concerning maritime trade:[12] Austrian ships were allowed to navigate freely through the Danube into, and from, the Black Sea, and through the Dardanelles as well. Thus, Austria finally reached one of its eastern economic policy goals, after more than a century and a half of military and diplomatic efforts.

The impact of the Sened was also felt, almost immediately, in the international trade carried by the two Greek "companies" of Sibiu and Brașov.[13] The limitation of tax exemptions and of various other immunities of the "companies" members contained in Maria Theresa's Privilege, brought about considerable change in their structure: wealthier members associated and formed several import-export trading firms, with branches and agencies in Vienna and elsewhere;[14] gradually, less prosperous members moved to other Austrian provinces or back to where they came from, while some engaged exclusively in retail trade.[15] Thus, the "companies" became chiefly ethno-religious communities with no marked economic profile,[16] possibly rallying non-member Greek residents of these two cities.

On the other hand, this was about the time when shipping and trade based in the Danubian and the Black Sea ports of the Romanian principalities began to expand.[17] Fluvial commerce was quicker, safer, and less expensive than overland transport, and naturally supplanted it, especially the transit trade between the two empires, a kind of trade in which many members of the two "companies" had been active. Transylvanian fairs were not as important anymore in international trade; firms trading in oriental products had replaced them almost completely by the end of the eighteenth century. This is clearly reflected in the number of members of the two "companies," which in early nineteenth century fell to approximately one-third of what it was a few decades before.[18] By the middle of the century, there were only 20 members left in the Sibiu "company," and almost no Greek community at large; the "company's" church, built in 1794, passed over to the jurisdiction of the Romanian Orthodox bishopric in 1856.[19] In Brașov the Greek "company" dissolved probably in 1850,[20] whereas a modest community existed, with its church and Greek priest, until the end of World War II.[21] The geographical position of Brașov was more advantageous for trade with the Danubian principalities and the Ottoman provinces south of the Danube. Greek merchants were still attracted to it, but, in the nineteenth century, they rather mingled with the Romanian traders in the *Cronstadter Griechische- Wallachische Handlungs-Sozietät,*[22] because they did not meet the strict requirements for membership in the "company" established by Maria Theresa's Privilege.[23] Thus, one of the many facets of the long Greek merchants' activity became definitely extinct. Nevertheless, their mobility as well as their adaptability to social, economic, and political change made them still prosper in East Central and Southern Europe up to World War I.

Notes

1. I. Baron Testa, *Recueil des Traités de la Porte Ottomane avec les puissances étrangères,* Paris 1893, Vol. IX, [Austria], 137-41.

2. Lidia A. Demény, "Regimul tricesimelor și punctele vamale din Transilvania în perioada Principatului autonom" [The *Tricessimae* and Customs of Transylvania during the Period of the Autonomous Principality], *Studii și Materiale de Istorie Medie,* VII (1974), 208-21.

3. Tr. Stoianovich, "The Conquering Balkan Orthodox Merchant," *Journal of Economic History,* XX (1960), 260-62; Olga Cicanci, *Companiile Grecești din Transilvania și comerțul european în anii 1636-1746* [The Greek Companies of Transylvania and European Commerce in the years 1636-1746], (Bucharest, 1981), 122-24.

4. T. Bodogae, "Le privilège commercial accordé en 1636 par G. Rákóczi aux marchands grecs de Sibiu," *Revue Roumaine d'Histoire,* XI, n⁰ 4, (1972), 647-53, who publishes the Latin text of the Privilege; Olga Cicanci, p. 24, considers it a privilege granted to the Greek merchants of Sibiu, while N. Iorga, *Scrisori și inscripții ardelene și maramureșene; I. Scrisori din arhiva Protopopiei neunite a Făgărașului și din alte locuri,* (Bucharest, 1906) [forming vol. XII of his series intitulated *Studii și documente cu privire la Istoria Romînilor*], p. V, considers it as a general privilege given for *all* the Greek merchants of Transylvania. See also, the brief review article of Despina Tsourka-Papastathi, "A propos des Compa-

gnies grecques de Transylvanie à Sibiu et Braşov," *Balkan Studies*, XXIII (1982) 423. On the legal status of foreign and Greek merchants in Transylvania before the Treaty of Karlowitz, see, Lidia A. Demény, "Le régime des douanes et des commerçants grecs en Transylvanie au cours de la période de la Principauté autonome, 1541-1691," *Makedonika*, XV (1975), 62-112; N. Camariano, "L'organisation et l'activité culturelle de la Compagnie des marchands grecs de Sibiu," *Balcania*, VI (1943), 201-208; Z. Trocsány, "Gesetzgebung der fürstlichen Epoche Siebenbürgens und die Rechtstellung der Balkangriechen in Siebenbürgen", *Etudes Balkaniques*, VII, n⁰ 1, (1971), 94-104.

5. The original text of the Privilege of 1636, published by T. Bodogae, 651-53, does not agree with the contents of the Privilege as described in the archive of the Greek Company of Sibiu (Biblioteca Academiei României Chereafter BAR, Mss. Gr. 976, ff. 26^{r-v}-27^r, 74^{r-v}), by N. Iorga, V-VI, N. Camariano, 210, Lidia A. Demény, 97, Olga Cicanci, 24. On the other hand, a request addressed by the Company of Sibiu to empress Maria-Theresa (BAR, Mss. Lat. 11, f. 1^v), informs us that the original Privilege granted by G. Rákóczi was lost "... per fatale incendium küküllovariense...." This was not obviously the Privilege of 1636, whose original has been found by T. Bodogae. This special Privilege to the Company of Sibiu must have been granted in 1637 or 1638; see, further discussion by Despina Tsourka-Papastathi, *He Hellenike Kompania tou Sibiu; Organose ke leitourgia* [The Greek Company of Sibiu; Organization and Function] (Salonika, under print), Chapter III.

6. The respective Privilege was granted by Prince Michael Apaffi, in 1678, published by N. Iorga, *Acte româneşti şi cîteva greceşti din archivele Companiei de comerţ oriental din Braşov* (Vălenii-de-Munte, 1932), 2-3.

7. BAR, Mss. Gr. 976, 978, 979; I. Moga, "Politica economica austriaca şi comerţul Transilvaniei in veacul XVIII" [Austrian Economic Policy and Transylvanian Trade in the 18th century], *Anuarul Institutului de Istorie Naţionala Cluj*, VII (1936-38), 106, 113.

8. Latin text published by E. Hurmuzaki, *Documente privitoare la istoria Românilor* [Documents concerning the History of the Romanians], (Bucharest, n.d.), XV², p. 1486.

9. The latin text of this Privilege is still unpublished. Greek and German translations by Ant. Moschatos, *Kripis Thespismaton* [Foundation of Statutes], (Braşov, 1858), 36-45.

10. Art. 2, Testa, *Recueil...*, IX, 83.

11. Testa, *ibid.*

12. Art. 6, Testa, IX, 140.

13. It coincided with the results of earlier efforts made by the Austrian administration to develop local industry and reduce imports, especially of textiles used by the less wealthy classes, I. Moga, 128-36.

14. N. Iorga, *Scrisori şi inscripţii ardelene ...*, X; A. Oţetea, "Casa de comerţ Hagi Constantin Pop din Sibiu" [The Trading Firm of Hagi Constantin Pop of Sibiu], *Comunicari şi articole de istorie*, (Bucharest, 1955), 29-44; D. Limona-

Elena Limona, *Catalogul documentelor greceşti din Arhivele Statului de la oraşul Stalin* [Catalogue of Greek Documents from the State Archives of Braşov], (Bucharest, 1958), vols. I-II; Elena Limona-D. Limona, "Catastifele casei comerciale Ioan Marcu din Sibiu" [The books of the Trading Firm Ioan Marcu of Sibiu], *Revista archivelor*, II, n⁰ 2, (1959), 225-43; idem, "Aspecte de comerţul braşovean in veacului al XVIII-lea" [Aspects of Trade in Braşov, in the 18th century], *Studii şi materiale de istorie medie*, IV (1960), 525-64; D. Limona, "Un catastih al unui companist Sibian din veacul al XVIII-lea" [A book of Accounts of a Member of the Sibiu Company in the 18th century], *Archivele Statului. 125 Ani de Activitate* (Bucharest, 1957), 407-15; D. Limona, *Catalogul documentelor referitoare la viaţa economica a ţarilor române in secolele XVII-XIX. Documente din Archivelor Statului Sibiu*, (Bucharest, 1966), vol. I; Elena and Dumitru Limona, "Negustori bucureşteni la sfîrşitul veacului al XVIII-lea. Relaţiile lor cu Braşovul şi Sibiul" [Bucharest Merchants at the end of the 18th century. Their Relations to Braşov and Sibiu], *Studii. Revista de Istorie*, XIII, n⁰ 4, (1960), 107-38; D. Limona, "Casa de comerţ Nicolae D. Paciura din Sibiu", *Revista Archivelor*, VIII, n⁰ 1 (1965), 265-85.

15. BAR, Mss. Gr. 976, f. 118ʳ.

16. For an analysis of the various forms of corporations of the Christians under Ottoman rule see N. Pantazopoulos, "Hellenon Syssomatoseis" [Greek Corporations], *Gnoseis* (Athens, 1958) 14-16, 18-19.

17. Sp. Focas, *Oi Hellenes eis tin potamoploïan tou Kato Dounaveos* [The Greeks in the Navigation of the Lower Danube] Salonika, 1975), 38-39, 63-66.

18. BAR, Mss. Gr. 976, ff. 206ᵛ-207ʳ for the Sibiu Company.

19. T. Bodogae, 650.

20. Cornelia Papacostea-Danielopolu and Lidia A. Demény, "Grecs, Roumains, Bulgares et Serbes dans la Compagnie Grecque de Braşov, 1777-1850," *Bulletin de l'Association Internationale d'Etudes Sud-Est Européennes*, X, n⁰ 2, (1972) 263-74; Cornelia Papacostea-Danielopolu, "L'organisation de la Compagnie Grecque de Braşov, (1777-1850)," *Balkan Studies*, XIV (1973) 313-23.

21. Chr. Ktenas, *Lefkoma tis en Stephanoupolei ethnikis hellenikis ekklissias tis Hagias Triados epi ti hekatonpentikontaetiridi aftis, 1787-1937* [Album of the National Greek Church of St. Trinity in Brasov, on its 150th Anniversary, 1787-1937], (Bucharest, 1937); idem, *Ai epigraphai kai oi aphierotai tis en Stephanoupolei hellinikis ekklissias tis Hagias Triados* [The Inscriptions and the Donators of the Greek Church of St. Trinity in Brasov], (Bucharest, 1938).

22. Eug. Pavlescu, *Meşteşug şi negoţ la Românii din sudul Transilvaniei* [Crafts and Trade of the Romanians of Southern Transylvania], (Bucharest, 1970), 98 ff.

23. I.e., prove their origin from "Greece or Macedonia."

V

Ports

Fulvio Babudieri

Maritime Commerce of the Habsburg Empire: The Port of Trieste, 1789-1913

The group of Triestine nobles, who, long ago in September 1382, went to the court of Habsburg Archduke Leopold, "Signore e patrone" [Lord and Patron] of the city, in Graz, to present him with an act of Trieste's submission to Austria, were certainly far from imagining that their action was decisive for the city's future. A reporter of the time wrote that the Austrians were anxious to possess Trieste, mainly for its production of excellent wines with which the inhabitants of the cold northern regions could warm themselves. But, for Archduke Leopold, the subjugation of Trieste, already planned by his predecessors, meant enlarging his dominions in Italy, completing the occupation of the subalpine region, which lacked only Trieste, and above all, the acquisition of a port. On learning of the archduke's acceptance, the city was suffused with joy, its citizens swarmed to the walls hoisting his red and white ensign, shouting "Long live the Duke of Austria!" Thus began a long association. The common history of Trieste and Austria, stretching over a period of five centuries, can be summarized in two fundamental considerations.[1]

To start with, there did not exist a direct ethnic conflict between the Adriatic city and the empire. Trieste never felt exposed to the risks of germanization. Even in 1780, when Joseph II was crowned, and 10,000 German-speaking Austrians, belonging to the mercantile or bourgeois classes were settled in Trieste as a result of his policy of germanization, the town did not fear it would be absorbed. The ethnic relationship was free from any sort violence, even if local resistance to a typically German feudal subjection was always as firm as its tenacious claim to autonomy.

Secondly, Trieste partook in the civil climate of the Habsburg empire and absorbed its processes, although maintaining its own national character. These characteristics mark Trieste even today and make it an Italian city which appears quite different from those of the peninsula.

In the eighteenth and nineteenth centuries, Trieste enjoyed privileged treatment from Austria, due to the fact the latter was interested in availing itself of its port for transit trade. Austria, however, was often obliged to subordinate its own economic and maritime policy to the pressures exercised by the imposition of internal and external forces, even at the expense of the port of Trieste itself. Evidence of this state of affairs is provided by Vienna's reluctance and delay in adopting measures favorable to Trieste during the nineteenth century. The construction of the southern railway line (*Sudbahn*) and of new port facilities were delayed and a concession of preferential tariffs at particularly difficult times was refused. However, it must be granted that the increasingly resolute and constant national claims of Triestine intellectuals before World War I were an added reason for Vienna to put a brake on concessions to the Adriatic commercial area.

Although the port of Trieste owed its development to its proximity to Central Europe, it must be admitted that the intervention of higher interests was necessary to turn it into a great maritime commercial center. Goods had to be conveyed along roads leading to the port, and these had heretofore been neglected. In addition, favorable trade conditions had to be created. If Austria was not prompted by any particular altruistic feeling when granting the port special favors at particular times, but rather by cold political and economic motives, it still deserves the credit for having led Trieste toward indisputable prosperity. The same applies to the port of Fiume which was considered the door to Hungary, but which, for reasons of space, can be dealt with only marginally in this paper.

The subject of the present study is the dynamics of the economic evolution of the Austrian coastal area (*Kustenland*) and of Trieste, its capital, from the end of the eighteenth century to the beginning of our century, an evolution substantially different from that of other bordering regions, both Austrian and foreign.[2]

To study the evolution of the port of Trieste in the eighteenth century, it must be understood that, although the natural characteristics of the local traffic had a predominant effect on the city's economy during the first decade of the century, later, the principal force became a political one; that is to say, one no longer depending on geographic environment and economic position, but rather determined on individual initiative prompted by political interests. The phenomenon was not new in the economics of Trieste.

Maria Theresa's Customs Edict of October 18, 1766 was of vital importance for the port of Trieste. As a result, the customs exemptions enjoyed by Trieste and Fiume were ever afterward considered general laws of state in matter of customs. Thus, the special regulations in favor of Trieste issued in previous times were not abrogated, and more privileges followed. In April 1769, Trieste was declared a "Free Maritime City," and the exemption from customs fees of the free port were extended to the whole city and its territory, that is, its "Umland." A larger "Lazaretto" [hospital] dedicated to St. Theresa, and intended to operate alongside an earlier one dedicated to St. Charles, was officially opened in the same year amid great rejoicing. Moreover, Maria Theresa had the satisfaction of seeing completed the new commercial highway which reached Trieste from Lubiana and Vienna, across the pass of Opicina, thereby reducing greatly the distance between Trieste and Vienna.

It was no doubt due to the Maria Theresa policy that Trieste attracted foreigners of all nations whose names were linked to major economic activities. The new commercial center needed capital, and the empress, among her various innovations, certainly, moved in the right direction when she turned Trieste into an "island of religious tolerance." Consequently, the city gave hospitality to merchants of all faiths and became the agent of commercial exchange between Central Europe and the Near East, absorbing the trade of areas that were being abandoned by Venice as well. New intermediate bodies came into existence within the social and political pattern of Trieste. These were ethnic and religious groups, endowed with their own institutional and juridical structures, and were called "nations." Although each was a corporation of its own, the nations did not hesitate to engage in profitable, mutual collaboration and combine their wealth to carry out important activities.

In spite of the comparatively small size of the vessels, their continuous arrivals and departures, the febrile rhythm of loading and unloading operations, and the piling of goods on the quays in the open air managed to convey a sense of prosperity and richness. In the space of 20 years, the value of the goods embarked and disembarked amounted to 15 million florins.

Inland traffic was effected by private firms using convoys made up of series of carts pulled by a varying number of horses that could carry several dozens of quintals. The journeys were long and difficult, for bad weather could cause accidents and heavy losses, nor were journeys not without risk from banditry and theft.

In 1780, the last year of Maria Theresa's reign, the port registered the movements of 10,000 ships with 82,000 grossregistered tons. The empress died without seeing her main plan realized, the conveyance via Trieste of all the traffic that normally proceeded from the Austrian Danubian states through Hamburg. Nor was the plan carried through by her successors.

The Port of Trieste in Habsburg Nineteenth Century Policy

In the last years of the eighteenth century, that is during Joseph II's reign, Trieste was politically a virtually independent province. Only a governor depending from the imperial court exerted his authority over the council of the nobles. The commune was run by a civil political and economic magistrate with executive power on matters concerning the city. The standing laws were the statutes and special bills passed by the Austrian government for Trieste. Economically, the city had experienced a visible growth in prosperity since the destruction of its walls in 1749 and the extension of free port privileges to its entire area. The free port of Trieste competed with the most important commercial European centers, thanks to its trade with the Near East, the Indies, Italy, Germany, and the northern countries in particular. Iron and steel products, lead, mercury, gemstones, goods from Nuremberg, canvas for sails, ropes, wool, firewood, building timber, cereals, glassware, livestock for slaughter, salted meat, medicines, alcoholic drinks, tar, and more passed through its port.

The items conveyed to Trieste from overseas proceeded by way of Ljubjana to reach, eventually, either Austria and the Germanies, or Hungary, or via Gorizia and Villach, Bavaria and Switzerland through Innsbruck and Salzburg. The north-south route that from then onward constituted, for many years, the almost exclusive way for Triestine traffic was already being frequently used for transit trade.

Triestine businessmen bound for the Near East or for the East and West Indies, visited the Italian towns along the coast, ports on the Aegean, Candia, Palestine, Egypt, the French coasts, and even the Barbary coast. At the end of the eighteenth century, merchants from Germany, Italy, Greece, Switzerland, Tyrol, Bohemia, Egypt, and the Near East worked in Trieste.

In the period from 1792 to 1812, three French invasions took place with drastic consequences for Trieste. The first of these occupations was very short, at the height of the revolution; the second and third coincided with Bonaparte's apogee. Three times the French flag flew over the town, and three times it was once more replaced by the Habsburg flag. The taxes levied by the French invaders on local businessmen, currency devaluation, and the suppression of the free port were harmful for the commercial interests of the city. Yet this was the time when Trieste began to attract general attention. Ships from all European nations, and even from the United States of America, dropped anchor in its port during the spells of truce. If trade underwent periods of inactivity during the French occupations, owing to financial hardship and restrictions on navigation in the Adriatic, its recovery was swift when the Austrian flag returned.

In the early nineteenth century alone, 5600 ships annually sailed in or out of the port of Trieste. In 1802, 115 firms registered with the Stock Exchange, and 140 wholesalers had their offices in Trieste. The population amounted to 28,000 inhabitants. In the same year, the turnover in trade amounted to 50,000,000 florins. In 1804, the number of carts used for imports and exports over land amounted to 70,000, a third of which were of three-ton capacity. In 1810, however, because of war, 64 firms had to close down and the population fell to 20,000. In 1798, the typical goods passing through the port included wines, tobacco, leather, skins, yarn, citrus and other fruits, sulfur, copper, and more, all discharged into the warehouses of Greek merchants along with 8000 pounds of currants, 80,000 barrels of oil, 20,000 bales of cotton, 7000 bales of wool, 26,000 bushels of wheat, 55,000 of oats, and 15,000 of barley.[3]

During the French occupation, imports and exports registered a conspicuous loss. The Peace of Schoenbrunn (1809), obliged Austria to hand over Trieste, the county of Istria, Fiume, and Carniola to France. By Napoleonic imperial decree, these new possessions on both sides of the Julian Alps constituted the Illyrian provinces of the French empire. A surveyor was appointed, who reported to the civil and military governor in Ljubjana. Napoleon, however, had no time to waste on the reorganization of the new provinces and they languished.

The Austrians returned to Trieste on October 13, 1813, and were received by the population with great acclaim as though they were liberators. In 1815, the Congress of Vienna assigned the territories which were to belong to each great power, so that Austria took permanent possession not only of the Illyrian provinces, with Trieste, but also of the Venetian provinces and Lombardy.

A royal bill of April 1, 1814 decreed that all the ports along the coast should be given back their former privileges. Trieste and Fiume were thus reestablished as free ports, and Istria once again enjoyed its former customs exemption. In 1815, a new form of commercial and provincial government was established in conformity with those of the other provinces of the Austrian empire. A "Coastal Province" (*Kustenland*) was established, including the territory between the rivers Aussa and Judrio and the Gulf of Quarnaro. It embraced the areas of Gorizia, Trieste, and Fiume and was administered by the Imperial-Royal Government in Trieste.[4]

The wars had left the maritime sector of Trieste in serious financial difficulties. Maria Theresa's far-reaching innovations had been left incompleted because of it. A desperate struggle for traffic after 1814 did not find the necessary backing in new maritime legislation. The first consequence of the long period of belligerency was the crisis that afflicted the whole of Europe and reached its climax in 1816.

Evidences of it could be traced practically everywhere: among impoverished, decimated, poorly nourished peoples; in houses either abandoned and decrepit or damaged by the requisitions; in neglected fields; and in ports full of half-sunken, rotting ships. Exhausted and insufficiently suppied as they were, nations demanded cereals and foodstuffs of all kinds. It would have been logical to resort to maritime transport, but the mercantile fleet had been reduced to a third of its prewar strength. The commercial fleets of Trieste and Istria had suffered heavily, restricted as they were under the French to a limited sea area, permanently under the menace of hostile ships and pirates.

Owing to dangers in navigation, freight rates were initially lower for the transport of goods by land, from Smyrna to Prussia, than by sea, via Trieste. In spite of this, all the vessels that could keep afloat were roughly repaired and made ready to sail. They carried supplies and wheat. The starving people of the Mediterranean basin received them as an act of providence. Thus, the city's maritime trade began to recover. Whereas Venice, on the opposite coast of the Adriatic, since the Treaty of Campoformio in 1797, no longer a state, sank into commercial decline, Trieste, favored by its reasserted status as a free port, inherited its trade with the Near East and consolidated its function as a commercial intermediary for Central Europe.

According to annual records, in 1821, movements through the port of Trieste totalled 6746 vessels. Fully 639 ocean-going vessels arrived, most under the Austrian flag, carrying 107,473 tons of cargo, and 613 ocean-going vessels sailed, with 89,152 tons of cargo. Coastal vessels were even more numerous, with 2933 arriving carrying 94,050 tons, and 2561 sailing carrying 88,010 tons, most of which wore Austrian, Neapolitan, or Papal colors.

After developing into a major commercial center, Trieste specialized in the importation of commodities from the colonies and the Indies by means of direct shipping lines. It became the primary port of the monarchy, as well as of a major part of the Levant, and particularly of Albania, the Ionian islands, and the Adriatic coast. Switzerland, Lombardy, and the Venetian provinces looked to Trieste for their goods and products from Egypt and the Near East, since there were usually large stocks available in warehouses at prices competitive with other markets. Trieste was also the only southern port from which Germany and northern Europe could obtain a supply of Mediterranean and Eastern products. These were forwarded to the purchasing countries not only by land, but also by sea, and so flowed to northern and western ports that, at the time, had little direct import trade. Owing to the absence of serious competition, a lack of rivals, and of an absence of unexpected events, Trieste could be ranked among the most flourishing commercial centers of continental Europe.

At the beginning of the nineteenth century, tourism did not exist, yet the demand for sea passages was heavy, though restricted mostly to commercial travelers. The early steam packets were rather simple, but reliable, and adhered to strict time tables, particularly after the Austrian Lloyd line (*Lloyd Austriaco*) entered the trade in 1836. Long-distance shipping lines were as necessary as coastal services. In the early part of the century, the commerce handled by the port of Trieste was either "negotiated transit" or on behalf of third parties, both of which brought high income. The latter involved mediation between producers and purchasers in distant countries, who were not represented on the local market, and also, between producers and purchasers of the Italian states and the Levant, who were present in Trieste when exchanging their products with those of the local maritime commercial sector.

This complex and rich trade activity was characterized by wholesale purchase in far-off foreign markets. Some of this was carried out by important mercantile firms with offices in Trieste, through their overseas agents, ship masters, and so forth, mainly for ready cash. In addition, in the port itself goods in whose trade the maritime commercial sector had specialized, for instance, colonial goods and coffee, were purchased directly from ships flying foreign flags. In short, the monarchy began to develop from an internal state into one of international dimensions, when Austria was persuaded that its numerous realms and provinces were destined to constitute a single economic unity, that is, as a unitary state capable of providing the stability to develop great political strength. This affected Austrian policy regarding commerce and maritime traffic, which increased Austrian influence over the seas.

This positive evolution, even if permanently directed to Vienna's profit — as was natural — was the cause of the importance of the port of Trieste.

It is necessary to stress here that the privileges granted to the port of Trieste (as well as to that of Fiume) were not occasional experiments destined to second the aspirations of the city, but only an aspect of the foresight of the Austrian policy.[5] Both Trieste and Fiume owed their development to the strategy of the House of Habsburg in the field of commerce, and not merely to their favorable geographic positions. The latter proved useful only when associated with the exigencies and political designs of the imperial authorities who considered these ports as the fittest instruments to favor and strengthen the monarchy as a whole. The merit for creating, in the eighteenth and nineteenth centuries, the basis for a strong maritime commercial sector in Trieste, a sector whose activity was not interrupted till the beginning of World War I, goes to the enlightened policy of the Austrian government.[6]

In the meantime, production and the search for new outlets were on the increase, owing to a constant rise in population all over Europe. New technological inventions, along with important scientific discoveries, opened new economic possibilities to more-evolved populations. New means of transportion widened commercial exchange and modified its flow. The transportation of goods was made easier, and international commerce was no longer concerned with small quantities of precious and exotic commodities, but rather with large quantities of consumer products. Around 1850, centers of production and of consumption became ever closer, due to the development of the railway networks among the various countries. The great progress in transportation by steam, both on land and on sea, afforded commerce facilities of supply and outlets which were lacking before, and so satisfied the demands of customers of larger geographical areas. As late as 1860, maritime commerce was still largely conducted by sailing ships. Little by little, however, the adoption of metal for shipbuilding contributed to the triumph of steam. At the same time, the conditions of transport were unified, time tables established, and the services of shipping companies carried through as regularly as those of the railways.

The new mechanical means made possible the transportation of large quantities of goods at minimal fuel costs; this permitted lower freight rates for the carriage of those cargoes that had heretofore been the monopoly of the sail. Decreased risk, regular voyages, and greater speed, resulted in reduced freight costs, in greater profits from the traffic.[7] The concept of a worldwide market prevailed over the regime based on closed economies and relationships restricted to bordering countries. Economic wealth began to be redistributed throughout Europe.

All of this caused the port of Trieste to face new, more complex problems, such as an increased competition by other European ports and a delay in the technological improvement of its facilities, most notably in terms of mercantile equipment and railway communications with the hinterland. Such deficiencies, which were both functional and structural, prevented the greatest Habsburg port from facing efficiently the new course of world economics. Added complications were depreciation and the instability of Austrian currency, owing to the permanent gap in the state budget caused by the military misfortunes of 1859, which forced Austria to give up Lombardy. It was then that the American Civil War chopped off one of the most flourishing branches of Trieste's trade, cotton imports. The port was also injured by a delay in the completion of the southern railway line, while northern ports, long since connected with Trieste's natural and economic hinterland, managed to absorb some of the Adriatic traffic. Moreover, the completion of the Ljubjana-Trieste branch of the Southern Railway in 1857, yielded disappointing results, for the advantages deriving from it were below expectations, principally because of high freight costs. Also, the slow development of Austrian industry, due mainly to the lack of capital, favored the rapid and easy sale of foreign manufactured goods on markets heretofore traditionally served by Adriatic carriers. Thus, the export trade of Trieste was deprived of the possibilities of any further development which the new general conditions of European economics would have otherwise favored.

This explains the decline in navigation experienced by Trieste in the middle of the nineteenth century in spite of the technical improvements throughout the shipping industry.

Meanwhile, Triestine merchants, who had up to then dominated economic transactions between groups materially and economically diverse and far apart, were reduced to a subordinate role. Specialized sales agents succeeded them and invaded their markets, and direct commercial contacts between industrialists and consumers prevailed. Businessmen were left with market dealings, transshipment, and the deposit of goods in transit. Later in the century, the situation was made even worse by the ever-strict application of the principles of free trade and the triumph of free competition. The enforcement of these principles and the gradual extension of a railway network all over Europe affected Trieste in a negative way. The port had to face often intolerable competition from other ports, while witnessing the slow but constant diversion of trade and customers who had previously contributed to its prosperity.

Trieste, a city that lacked the prerequisites for heavy industry, met the situation by building huge industrial establishments, which were to enjoy a worldwide reputation at a later date, in spite of the shortage of labor, buildings, water and fuel. Among these industrial establishments were a dockyard fit for a great maritime nation, the most up-to-date shipyards, and an engine factory equipped with a foundry. There were, in addition, facilities for producing beer, soap, and rope; chocolate factories; sugar refineries; a cotton mill; leather tanneries; metal foundries; and other establishments for the production of sundry manufactured goods. Nevertheless, crushed by serious competition, Trieste was supplanted by luckier, richer, and more powerful rivals and was unable to play an equivalent role on the stage of international commerce. This contributed even more to the gradual decline of its maritime commercial sector, and its commerce turned from negotiated transit into pure transit. Undoubtedly, negotiated transit had turned Trieste into a port of great prestige, endowed with such first class equipment and skilled labor, as to leave concrete traces of its efficiency in the years to come, during which it continued the same activity though on a reduced scale.

Around the middle of the nineteenth century, the crisis that had affected Trieste was overcome. A period of revival in traffic followed. An important event for the trade of the port of Trieste was the opening of the Suez Canal in 1869, which brought along new prospects for a more active commercial life: suffice to note that the distance between Trieste and Bombay was shortened by 7500 nautical miles. Moreover, the Middle and Far East, potentially extremely rich and until then almost unknown, offered themselves to new commercial and maritime initiatives. The opening of the canal marked also the fatal decline of sailing ships and the final adoption of engine-propelled vessels. In fact, the heavy tolls enforced on ships using the canal, as well as high towing costs, gales, and sand storms from the Red Sea prevented sailing vessels from profitably availing themselves of the new route. Maritime traffic from Trieste to the countries beyond Suez increased in value by 550 percent in only 20 years. Among other things, it meant the triumph of Austrian Lloyd, the greatest overseas shipping company in Trieste.

When the Suez Canal was opened, Austria realized that the possession of Trieste could be useful, not only to force Italy to accept tranquilly a policy of accommodation, even if permanently under the menace of an easy invasion, but also to reach, by means of the Lloyd vessels, those far-flung shipping routes that had, up to then, been the almost exclusive monopoly of English, French, and Dutch companies. The Austrian government came to the conclusion that it was necessary to carry out further improvements in the port of Trieste and to endow it with equipment apt to stand successfully the competition of rival ports, in consideration of the continuous increase in the movements of ships.

In 1863, there was held a competition for the construction of a new port. The project of a French engineer, Paul Talabot, who worked for the Southern Railway Company was chosen. He suggested the new port be constructed on the model of that of Marseille. Construction required many years. On December 19, 1883, the last stone of the new port was laid in the presence of many notables and a rejoicing city. The total cost amounted to 29,000,000 crowns, which underwent further increases when new quays and equipment were added. Later, the great increase in traffic that developed made even this port insufficient, and it was not unusual to see incoming ships waiting whole days off shore, owing to the lack of vacant quays.

As a result, in 1898 the Vienna government decided on the construction of yet another port to be added to the already existing one. The new port, named after Franz Joseph, was built in the San Andrea area, between the Lanterna lighthouse and Lloyd's dockyard. Between 1901 and 1914, Quays 5 and 6 were completed, as well as part of Quay 7, all with ample space. In addition, three new breakwaters were built.[7]

In April of 1880 the Trieste General Warehousing Corporation (*Magazzini Generali*) had been founded, at a time when the Commune and the local Chamber of Commerce had been allotted capital for the construction and management of some "general warehouses" to be built in the port area as part of the free port. The administration of these warehouses was initially handled by the two bodies mentioned above, which were turned into an autonomous Port Authority, even as the first warehouses were being built on quays and in open spaces.

The opening of the Suez Canal, so long awaited by all the civilized world and so rich in consequence for the economic and social life of a great part of humanity and for international shipping in particular, was also a milestone in the life of the Trieste's most important shipping company, Austrian Lloyd. New prospectives opened up, and Lloyd did not hesitate to make the most of them. As early as 1868, Lloyd had turned the run to Egypt into a weekly one, in order to stand the competition of Britain's powerful P & O and France's Messageries. At that time, Lloyd had begun an east Mediterranean circular service from Trieste to Trieste with calls at Alexandria, Beirut, Smyrna, Constantinople, Sira, and Corfu. The itinerary included also a short call at Port Said, which had grown in importance for transshipment of goods to and from the Indies. Any ship from the East Indies was entitled to take in goods for Trieste and deliver them at Port Said, from whence they were forwarded to Trieste by Lloyd's weekly steamer. The opening of the canal enabled Lloyd to expand its share of the Indies trade. In 1869, two fairly large, iron-hulled steamships were laid down. When ready, in the first months of 1870, they carried the Lloyd flag beyond Suez as far as India, opening a direct route between Trieste and Bombay. The daring and successful efforts of the Lloyd Company to secure for themselves the markets of India and the Far East date back to this time. The direct Trieste-Bombay run was soon extended as far as Columbo, Calcutta, Singapore, and Hong Kong, and to Japan in 1891. Asearly as 1880, when the new port facilities had to be completed, the position of Trieste was quite respectable when compared with that of other great Mediterranean ports, as the accompanying table bears out.

*Total Maritime Movements of the Principal Mediterranean Ports in
1880*

Ports	Net Registered Tons	Sailing Vessels and Steamers	
		Austro-Hungarian Flag Vessels	Foreign Flag Vessels
Marseilles	7,202,647	62.67%	37.33%
Genoa	3,751,437	54.31%	45.69%
Trieste	2,233,573	58.56%	41.44%
Venice	1,215,229	34.49%	65.51%

Source: Marchesetti, *Trieste il commercio orientale*

At the same time that port facilities were being improved in order
to reduce time lost lying at anchor in harbor, the creation of numerous
refueling points overseas diminished the dead weight of fuel which
ships had to carry during navigation. Progress in naval technology,
higher speeds, and the cutting of the Isthmus, shortened the time necessary to reach ports of destination, and thus added to the efficiency of steamers through an immediate increase in transport capacity.

A further step toward an increase in ship-size, safe navigation, and
reduced costs resulted from the substitution of iron for wood in ship
building. The weight of hulls was, thus, reduced and roomier holds
were obtained, the consequence being increased capacity. It was obvious that iron would be the material of the future, for in spite of its
higher specific gravity, an iron ship was considerably lighter than one
with a wooden hull of the same dimensions. Therefore, an iron ship,
besides being much sturdier, was endowed with greater transport
capacity, higher speed, and a higher potential profit than one of
wood. This transformation prompted what can be considered a
revolution in the field of steamers. The phenomenon affected positively both the volume and the value of the goods in transit through
Trieste from 1858 to 1888:

Value of Land and Sea Traffic
Into and Out of the Port of Trieste
1858 to 1888
(in millions of florins)

Year	By Sea	By Land	Total
1858	212.7	81.4	294.1
1868	216.4	156.6	373.0
1878	246.0	201.5	447.5
1888	331.8	301.4	653.2

Source: Fell, *Die Entwichlung des Handels von Triest*

From the latter part of the nineteenth century to the eve of World War I, port records registered a continuous progress which reached its peak in 1913 with 5,580,074 tons of inward shipping.

Two unfortunate potentially serious situations affected the economic welfare of Trieste at the end of the nineteenth century, and they were overcome only by the agile and prompt intelligence of local businessmen. The first, the suppression of the status of a free port in 1891: the second, the eleven-year delay in the completion of the new port at a very delicate time considering the competition from northern ports. The suppression of the free port did not influence local trade, which, after a period of uncertainty continued to progress. It did, however, affect the nature of the traffic which had, for some time, already developed from a profitable personal trade into the less profitable one of mere transit trade. The monarchy instituted a number of measures to mitigate the negative consequences of the suppression of the free port customs franchise. These included a preferential duty on sea imports, shipbuilding and shipping subsidies, completion of the Tauri Railway line in 1908, the fixing of railway freight rates at levels competitive with northern ports, a ten-year exemption from taxes and fees granted to newly constituted industries, and a franchise on outgoing goods. By virtue of these privileges and the efficiency of Austrian Lloyd, Trieste attained a position of prevalence in the Near

East and the old maritime nations began to look at it with ever-growing concern.

Trieste in the Era of the First World War

In a graph drawn to illustrate the mercantile fortunes of Trieste, one would note a constantly ascending line over many years in the eighteenth century followed by a more or less horizontal line throughout the early part of the nineteenth century, occasionally interrupted by a sudden drop, and then, from mid-century, a subsequent sharp rise until 1913-14. In those two years, the port of Trieste ranked fourth after Marseille, Naples, and Genoa in port movements in the Mediterranean, and first on the Adriatic. In 1913, the total maritime traffic of the Monarchy amounted to 51,779,089 quintals:

The Maritime Trade of Austria-Hungary, 1913

via Trieste	24,073,529	quintals
via Fiume	19,103,371	quintals
via other Austro- Hungarian ports	8,602,189	quintals
Total	51,779,089	quintals

Source: k. k. Statistische Zentralkommission, *Oesterr. statistisches Handbuch für das Jahr 1913.*

The total maritime traffic of Trieste actually amounted to 34,497,294 quintals in 1913, but only 24,073,529 quintals concerned Austria and Hungary, the remainder coming from, or being destined for, other countries. Moreover, as always, in 1913, 35,811,800 quintals of Austrian goods flowed toward the port of Hamburg.

At the beginning of 1913, the Austrian mercantile fleet had 306 vessels with 820,357 GRT, and fully 1,008,083 GRT including Hungarian vessels registered with the ports of the Austrian coast and Fiume, excluding Dalmatian ports. The capital invested in shipping amounted to 200,000,000 crowns. Crews for these vessels amounted to 12-13,000 men. An efficient long-sighted maritime policy had thus been able to create a notable commercial fleet in the space of a few years. Although Austria did not possess a large coast, it ranked seventh among European maritime countries as far as tonnage was concerned, Italy being sixth.

Besides the Austrian Lloyd, other shipowners managed to make themselves known overseas. There were, to cite some instances, the *Austro-Americana,* founded in 1895, which served North and South America, and the *Tripcovich, Gerolimich, Martinolich,* and *Premuda* companies, named for famed sea-faring families. Just before World War I, the transport capacity of the Austrian mercantile fleet exceeded 80,000,000 quintals per year. The annual income deriving from freights ranged from 150 to 200,000,000 crowns, a major part of which derived from the transport of goods essential to Austrian industry.

The institution of direct maritime connections, and the work of shipping agents, commercial agents, and brokers operating abroad in the interests of particular ports have always given a considerable impulse to commerce. The statistics concerning the port of Trieste prove this beyond doubt. Moreover the existence of maritime lines expanded knowledge of overseas territories within the mercantile area. To quote but one example, the improvement in the services for India on the part of Austrian Lloyd and the institution of a line to Argentina by the Austro-Americana line proved more useful to commerce than any other provision for the increase of exports.

In order to avoid handing over of profits to other countries and the spread of foreign influence at the expense of national interests, Vienna tried to prevent Austrian industries from availing themselves of ships flying foreign flags. Economic interests in Trieste knew that the merchant fleet not only procured hard currency, but also performed a valuable industrial function through the traffic it served. The development of shipping was the indispensable premise for an increase in the shipbuilding industry.

In 1913, the Austrian shipbuilding industry employed from 10-12,000 workers, with an annual output valued at many millions of crowns, money that would have otherwise gone abroad. Of course, the destiny of navigation ran parallel to that of its commerce. Commerce in overseas products or Austrian exports was an advantage for the Austrian economy only if the traffic was funneled through national ports. Only in this case would the income remain within the country.

Alongside the traffic in goods, passenger traffic also assumed remarkable proportions towards the end of the last century and the beginning of the present one. It was mainly formed of emigrants, and their sea crossings were governed by precise regulations likely to guarantee the utmost security. In 1913, for example, 50,693 emigrants embarked in Trieste, 43,521 bound for North America and 7172 for South America, the majority of them on vessels belonging to the Austro-Americana Company.

From the time the port of Trieste assumed worldwide importance, its functions were fully recognized, both in Austria and abroad, since it represented, above all, the best link of central Europe and the Balkans with the East. Trieste was in a more favorable position than other ports like Genoa, Marseille, Venice, or Fiume to traffic with the East, not only because of its Austro-Hungarian connections, but also because of its relationship with southern Germany and Switzerland. Although the German ports on the North Sea united against the competitive conditions afforded by the Tauri Railway Line (Trieste, Villach, Linz, Prague, etc.), the prevailing opinion in Germany was that traffic through Trieste was extremely important.[8]

By World War I, Trieste had achieved a key commercial position in the Balkans, the Levant, Turkey, Greece, Albania, Montenegro, Serbia, Bulgaria, and Romania. The import-export trade with Turkey, the Balkans, and the Near East amounted in 1913 alone to 5,959,000 quintals of goods carried for a value of 489,000,000 crowns. Thanks to the contacts and personal relations which the Trieste commercial firms had established in the East, to which should be added the progressive widening of Austrian maritime services and the enterprise of insurance and commercial agents, Trieste enjoyed the great privilege of possessing a very important and precious economic force in the East.

In 1913, its traffic with Asia alone amounted to 506,000,000 crowns (531,000,000 lire) against the 469,000,000 lire of the whole of Italy. These figures are sufficient to show how marvellously Trieste was equipped, from a technical point of view both in the commercial and maritime fields, for more voluminous trade than that carried out by the whole of Italy in traffic with the Levant, the Balkans, and Asia, before the war. Overall, during the last years of the Austrian government, the port of Trieste handled an average of 20 to 23 million quintals of imported goods per year and could have done even more.[9]

At the close of the last century, everyone considered Trieste the key to the economic domination of the Adriatic and saw in Trieste a means of European economic expansion in Asia Minor. No wonder then even Germany did not lose sight of Trieste in its imperialistic "Drang nach Osten" policy. It was clear that the most efficient way to put such a policy into effect was represented by the development of traffic between the Adriatic and the Levant. The Central Powers wanted the Balkans and the Levant for themselves, for their exclusive economic, demographic, and military exploitation. To this end, the Austro-Germans had conceived and enforced a system of communications that erected a barrier between those territories and the other European countries. It consisted of a network of railways running from north to southeast with no cross branches. Central European traffic from Hamburg to the Persian Gulf could thus be funnelled through this "channel," with the intention of absorbing the whole of the economic activity of the Balkans, Asia Minor, and Mesopotamia to the benefit of the Central Powers.

The plan was supposed to guarantee Austria, and above all, Germany the exclusive right of imposing their products, banks, railways, and enterprises upon the countries to be exploited in order to enrich the "Great German Country" with the resources of those territories. Trieste was included in this economic plan as it was considered a "springboard into the Levant." On the other hand, the economic life of the empire needed markets and raw material and it was therefore natural that it should do its utmost to widen its range of traffic. By its inclusion in the plan, Trieste suddenly acquired the essential premises for further economic development, as its port was the main maritime outlet of the central Danube hinterland, at the very moment when the latter's economic life experienced a rapid growth.

By the end of Austrian domination, the rise of Trieste proceeded as a result of developments along two fundamental lines:

1. The expansion of shipping was always the main goal of Austrian

policy which, by means of a well-organized and efficient bureaucracy, held as one the future of the empire and the interests of a
commercial and industrial sector that was rich, geographically
well-distributed, and in constant need of new markets with the
consequent reflected benefits for the economy of the country.
2. The history of Trieste, even in the more recent years, has proved
   that the geographic and economic factors, whose values it would
   be wrong to neglect, had to be linked to an essentially political coef-
   ficient in order to be fully productive.

Of no lesser importance is the assertion that, during the period
under consideration, the economic life of Trieste was always fundamentally connected with transit traffic, an activity which, together
with that of shipowners, insurers, and shipbuilders, constituted the
platform on which the economics of Trieste rested. It must be repeated that one of Vienna's main benefits in favor of Trieste was the
Adriatic Railway tariffs, which were competitive with those of the
north railways rather than based on kilometric distance. Maritime
subsidies were no less important, for they facilitated port communication with overseas markets. It was a great mistake on the part
of Rome, soon after World War I, not to have utilized to its full
extent the importance of the economic position and political function
of the Trieste commercial area, since it had inherited Triestine friend-
ship and appreciation throughout the Levant. This led to the loss,
beyond hope, of many important positions, so laboriously acquired
in the territories east of the Mediterranean, and in other international
areas, to the detriment of the Italian economy.

Conclusion

It is a matter of fact that Hapsburg politics developed along uncertain and often contradictory lines, occasionally torn between an
economic policy particularly favorable to Trieste and one of a wider
range, embracing the whole of the upper Adriatic areas in anticipa-
tion of that expansion which found a fertile ground only with the decay of the *Serenissima*. Economics were, therefore, subordinated to
politics, and this was but the beginning of a behavior typical of the

history of Trieste and the Julian region in general. The transformation of Trieste into a real maritime commercial center was not only due to its environment, but also to the psychological conditions, and to the mentality and traditions of the "new inhabitants" who had settled around the bulk of the "old town." The characteristics of commerce, therefore, were not only the result of the environment, but also of the qualities and tendencies of individuals. And, so it was that Trieste turned definitely into a center for commercial dealings, importation, redistribution, and preliminary work for an area reaching into the heart of Austria, the whole empire, and beyond. The geographical position of Trieste, so lengthily debated, theoretically speaking, is the best, so long as it had the presence of able businessmen prompted to act by political, economic, and social incentives, is not taken into consideration. But in politics, the position lies open to the ups and downs of the history of the world geographically gravitating around it, to the extent that the positive side of a "very good position" may turn into a negative one. At the turn of the century Trieste seems to have been an example of harmony among nations, as seen in the good relations among its varied populace aiming at a common economic welfare.

General speaking, and contrary to popular belief, the old Austria of the Habsburgs was an eminently law-abiding state. Laws were the constant guides of action. They were constitutionally voted and passed, later applied not so much according to their spirit as to the letter. Order and constitution were the two main concerns of rulers, but the Habsburg system was, at the same time, so modern as to anticipate governmental problems which, even nowadays, find no solution in certain countries. However, their rulers never knew how to choose the right method to articulate a multinational state between the extremes of federalism and centralism. Up to the constitution of the modern nation state, the relationship between Trieste and the Austrian empire was characterized by a vivid, mutual, structural, political, and economic convenience. It was the relationship between a world power which in 1866 stretched over a good portion of Italy, and the Adriatic port in its developing phase which, owing to its geographical position as a natural outlet to the sea, constituted a useful link between the possessions of the empire.

If Vienna was not prompted by any particular feeling when granting the port of Trieste special favors at particular moments, but rather by cold political and economic motives, it still deserves the honor of having led Trieste and Fiume toward indisputable prosperity. Convenience, therefore, was the only prompter of the relationship between Trieste on the one hand and Austria on the other, over a span of centuries. Although Trieste could live and prosper as a commercial market in the eighteenth and nineteenth centuries, it was never able to develop its dynamic potential to its full extent until the port was turned into the instrument of a political design fitting the superior interest of the monarchy. Certainly, the interests of Trieste were postponed, and sometimes even neglected by Vienna whenever polities suggested favoritism to other peoples or provinces, the Austro-Hungarian empire being formed by a shapeless violent aggregation of populations with different temperaments and needs.

A final essential point must, however, be stressed to clarify and fix the position and the status of the port of Trieste as a maritime commercial center serving Central European traffic: as long as the territories of the old Triestine hinterland belonged almost exclusively to Austria-Hungary, the political union proved most profitable for the port of Trieste and the industries depending on it, mainly that of shipping. The splintering of the monarchy into many independent states, also split the economic hinterland of Trieste, so that its successor states no longer favored Trieste for traffic, with the result that shipowners were the first to bear the consequences. During the postwar years, even if Italy did not substantially modify the range of activity of shipowners in the "redeemed provinces," certainly it was not prompt in utilizing profitably the precious and unique instrument of economic, commercial, and political penetration represented by the Trieste commercial community area, and thus, was actually going against its own interests.

Notes

1. Archival sources of importance for this study include: Oesterreichisches Staatsarchiv-Hofkammerarchiv, Vienna, Lit. Kom., rote 537, 582, 583, 585/A,

592-594, 606, 620-623, 685, 692; *Archivio di Stato*, Trieste, Intendenza Commerciale per il Litorale, covers 198, 199, 288, 390, 417, 478. Maritime Government, covers 2/14, dossier 318; Archivo Diplomatico, Trieste, covers 16 C 7, 7 G 15. Additional materials include: Girolamo Agapito, *Compiuta e distesa descrizione della fedelissima città e portofranco di Trieste* (Vienna, 1824); Johann Androvich, *Triest in seiner See- und Handelsentwicklung* (Trieste, 1918); Fulvio Babudieri, *La nascita dell'emporio commerciale e maritimo di Trieste* (Genoa, 1964), *L'industria armatoriaie di Trieste e della regione Guilia dal 1815 al 1918* (Roma, 1964), *I porti di Trieste e della regione Giulia dal 1815 al 1918* (Rome, 1965), *Considerazioni sulla potenzialità commerciale del porto di Trieste dopo la prima guerra mondiale* (Trieste, 1967), *Importanza del porto di Trieste alla vigilia della prima guerra mondiale* (Trieste, 1967), *Importanza del porto di Trieste per l'economia della città e della Monarchia absburgica dalla metà dell'Ottocento all'inizio del Novecento* (Trieste, 1968), *Le vicende economiche della Regione Giulia e del Friuli nei secoli XVIII, XIX e XX, con particolare riguardo al porto di Trieste* (Trieste, 1971), *I porti principali del Friuli-Venezia Giulia. La marineria di Trieste e della regione Giulia. Note storiche* (Udine, 1972), *Il porto di Trieste nel quadro della politica absburgica dell' Ottocento* (Innsbruck, 1977), *La funzione dell'emporio marittimo di Trieste nell' ambito della Monarchia absburgica nell' Ottocento* (Milan, 1980), *Industrie, commerci e navigazione a Trieste e nella regione Giulia dall'inizio del Settecento ai primi anni del Novecento* (Milan, 1982); Adolf Beer, *Die oesterreichische Handelspolitik im XIX. Jahrh.* (Vienna, 1891), *Geschichte des Welthandels* (II. Vol.) (Vienna, 1884), *Die Finanzen Oesterreichs im XIX. Jahrhundert* (Prague, 1877); Heinrich von Costa, *Der Freihafen von Triest* (Vienna, 1838); Alfred Escher, *Triest und seine Aufgaben im Rahmen der oesterreichischen Volkswirtschaft* (Vienna, 1917); Pietro Kandler, *Il porto franco di Trieste* (Trieste, 1864); Carlo de Marchesetti, *Trieste ed il suo commercio orientale* (Trieste, 1882); Franz Markitan, *Triest als Auswandererhafen* (Vienna, 1911); Richard Mayr, *Handelsgeschichte* (Vienna-Leipzig, 1921); Oesterreichische Reeder, *Denkschrift* (Vienna, 1903); and Giorgio Roletto, *Trieste ed i suoi problemi* (Trieste, 1952).

2. In 1784, the "Ces. Suprema Intendenza Commerciale" for the new "Provincia Meicantile del Litorale" [Mercantile Province of the Küstenland] was founded. It was subdivided into seven districts. Later it was dissolved and reconstituted in 1815.

3. *Source*: Oesterreichisches Staatsarchiv-Finanz- und Hofkammersarchiv Vienna.

4. Fiume formed part of the Küstenland till 1822. Then it passed under the Hungarian crown as a "Corpus separatum."

5. The Hapsburg legislation had a basic philosophy rooted in a global plan tending to the realization of the so-called "Reason of State," mainly during Maria Theresa's reign.

6. Insurance made its first appearance in Trieste as a coverage for risks of carriage by sea. In 1817 there were nine insurance companies in Trieste. On May, 1826 the Banco Adriatico, under the guidance of the Greek Angelo Gianni-

chesi opened with a capital of 200,000 florins. Giannichesi became the first director of the Riunione Adriatica di Sicurtà when the Banco Adriatico gave life to it. In 1831 the Assicurazioni Generali, the greatest among the twenty-one insurance companies then operating in the Trieste commercial area, was opened.

7. It is the present pier for containers.

8. When, in 1919, that Railway line was opened, the official representatives from Bavaria declared that it constituted a new important means of communication also for Germany.

9. Movement of goods through some of the main European ports in 1913.

(goods loaded and unloaded)
(in millions of quintals)

Ports	1913	change from 1912
Hamburg	254.579	+ 7.005
Marseille	98.475	+ 15.286
Genoa	74.282	+ 0.594
Bremen	71.669	+ 4.065
Trieste	34.497	+ 4.258
Venice	26.713	− 2.037
Fiume	20.984	+ 1.094

Source: Escher A., *Triest und seine Aufgaben.*

Vassilis Kardassis

The Port of Syra during the Nineteenth Century

Syros, an Aegean island in the center of the Cyclades, had been one of the most important trading centers of the eastern Mediterranean for a long period of time. Its port was the gathering place of merchant ships under Greek and foreign flags, which utilized the town's temporary warehouses to effect the movement of their goods. The island's great shipping and trading activity was unique for Greece in the first decades of the nineteenth century.[1]

First, let us examine the reason for Syros' development. That is, why Syros, and not any other place in the Aegean or in the eastern Mediterranean, became such an important maritime trading post. This question seems to grow in importance if one considers the fact that, before the Greek revolution, Syros played no large part in the economy, nor was it part of the spectacular development that shipping in the Aegean enjoyed by Hydra, Spetsai, and Psara.

The prerevolutionary economy of Syros was almost solely one based on farming and cattle raising.[2] The island's inhabitants, Catholics for the most part, lived on the high hill which dominates the port, in order to protect themselves from pirates. The local produce, consisting mainly of wine and vegetables, barely met the population's nutritional needs. Most of the island's sea-derived activities were confined to the art of fishing, and this involved only a small part of its workforce. The lack of shipping activity for the period has been confirmed. Pouqueville does not even list Syros among the top 26 Greek maritime trading centers in his book,[3] an account of prerevolutionary Greek maritime activity at the period of its greatest development — that is, 1813. Furthermore, the few huts depicted in their paintings by foreign visitors of the time were utilized for storage of comparatively small-volume merchandise that the island handled. We can, therefore, conclude that Syros had an economy geared to local consumption.

One fact that should not escape our attention is the nature of the island's political and administrational relations with the Ottoman empire. Since space does not allow me to go into the matter extensively, I shall mention here only two umportant facts: One, although the inhabitants of Syros were formally the Sultan's subjects, they enjoyed the protection of the French government because of special diplomatic accords between France and Turkey. One of the reasons they fell under French protection must needs be the fact that the inhabitants of Syros, being Catholic, favored friendly ties with, and feeling toward France. Two, the obligations of the local population to the Ottoman empire were few in comparison with those of the populations of other areas under Ottoman rule. Mainly, small tax contributions, characterized by weak administrational rule on the part of Kapoudan Pasha, the officer designated as governor of the Cyclades.

French capital allowed the Syrians to maintain a neutral attitude during the Greek-Turkish conflict of the period 1821 to 1828. The island's neutrality drew many people there from areas under attack by Turkish troops and later occupied by Ottoman armies, including Chios, Smyrna, Psarra, Kasos, Kydonies, and Crete, among others. By 1824, about 20,000 refugees had come to settle on its beaches, building thus Ermoupolis, the city of Kerdoos Hermes. The refugees, who, on the whole, were Chios merchants, flourished in commercial businesses as soon as they settled on Syros. Their noteworthy commercial activity was assisted and supported by the following factors:

a. Transfer of capital from their destroyed hometowns. An instructive example is the description of the activities of the Chios merchant Loukas Rallis in Vikelas' book, *Loukis Laras*,[4] ('Laras' being a corruption of the name Rallis).

b. The existence of commercial know-how among the refugee merchants — that is, the ability and skill to trade according to the technical methods of the period.

c. The granting of sizable loans by trading concerns belonging to Greeks living abroad. Relationship and common origins proved to be the strong tie which assured financial cooperation between the overseas Greek merchants and the refugee merchants of Syros.[5]

d. A sizable trade in contraband goods. The utilization of the state of war to their benefit assisted the refugee traders greatly in the amassment of commercial capital sums.

During the Greek war of independence Syros grew into an important center of economic activity. Trade in all its forms (import, export, transit), shipping, shipbuilding, insurance and credit agencies made considerable progress. In the newly founded Greek state of 1832, Ermoupolis was the economic capital of the nation.

At about the same time a commercial boom is observed in the eastern Mediterranean area. Wheat and similar staple commodities were the main exports of the East to the West. European wheat production was not sufficient to satisfy the nutritional needs of Western Europe. This steadily high demand of wheat became even greater at times of crisis and resulted in constant importation of wheat from Russia, the Ottoman empire, and Egypt. Russia, because of high volume and quality, was the most important supplier of wheat and other staples to Europe. In exchange, the developed countries of Europe — mainly England and France — exported industrial products to the huge market of the Orient, especially of the Ottoman empire. And, the British textile industry was the chief exporting industry of the West to the Orient at this period.

Syros was the chief beneficiary from this rise in commercial trade in the eastern Mediterranean, and from this intensive use of its sea routes. Its proximity to Asia Minor made it the natural link with Ottoman markets. But, its economy did not develop independently, based as it was totally on the commercial trading activities of the larger eastern Mediterranean.

Ermoupolis was mainly a society of merchants. These merchants did not only make up the greatest part of the economically active population, but they did hold key positions in the island's social and economic hierarchy. People from Chios made up the majority of the merchant class; they were also the most influential in local government and politics, thereby enjoying social domination. This dominant position in Ermoupolis led eventually to strife between them and the rest of the population. What, however, characterizes the political behavior of the merchant of Ermoupolis is indifference to the events in the wider political climate of Greece, and lack of participation in Greek political matters. This phenomenon, which certainly sets them apart from the other dominant social elements in the Greek world of the time,[6] calls for an explanation.

The merchant class on Syros drew its strength from economic activities that were in force mainly outside the confines of Greece. Syros, in effect, participated as a distributor of surplus produce from outside Greeces frontiers. Its income was, therefore dependent on foreign events and policies, which the leading class in Ermoupolis had no power to influence. This class did, however, show a strong interest in gaining and securing economic and social power in the area in which it controlled, that is, in Ermoupolis. Correspondingly, the merchants knew very well that the maintenance and extension of their political and economic power were almost independent of political developments at home. And, this rested on their ability to benefit from foreign trade. Thus, it will be seen that their indifference toward local politics and government was justified. In order to gain political power, the merchant class made every effort to gain influential posts in Ermoupolis.[7] Furthermore, Syros' chamber of commerce, the island's most important economic institution, became the meeting place of the merchant class. Finally, the most notable among Ermoupolis' bigger merchants had succeeded in holding the most powerful positions in the administration of many social institutions, such as cultural organizations, the hospital, the local high school, so on and so forth.

Syros' nucleus of economic activity during the first decades after the founding of an independent Greek state was foreign trade, particularly the import and transit trade. The various goods from overseas arrived at the port of Ermoupolis and were immediately stored in the transit warehouses there. The merchant then was obliged to pay a duty for transiting goods, which amounted to one percent of the value of the goods, or two percent in the case goods were voluminous, for a period of four months.[8] During this period, the merchant could sell his goods at the highest obtainable price, according to market demand. His representatives, both in the East and in the West, sent the Ermoupolis merchant regular information on the price of his goods in their local area. As long as the prices remained low, and, therefore, could not bring him profit, the merchant would renew his right to store his goods for an additional four months, paying additional customs fees, and he could continue extending his right of storage in this way up to a period of two years. This extension depended, however, on the nature of the goods. In other words, the merchant could extend the time for goods, such as textiles, ironware, leather, and such similar industrial products, but could not extend the time of storage for perishable goods in transit. In this latter instance, the merchant's negotiating powers were limited. Of note, also, is the fact that if the goods were sold within the country, they were liable to taxation; around 10-15 percent of the import tax on the value of the goods had to be paid to the state.[9] Finally, if the goods continued their journey toward some foreign market, Syros' customs collected only the initial transit duty that had been paid at the time of entry of goods for storage.

In order to appreciate correctly the importance of Syros' trading activities with those of the rest of Greece, we should note the following:

1. From 1840-55, we have information from Strong, Dakin, and the French consul which confirms that the trade of Syros made up two-thirds of the total Greek trading activities. In fact, Strong[10] estimates that the total trade of the country in 1840 amounted to 29 million drachmas, whereas Dakin's,[11] for 1845-55, gives us a value of 33-34 million drachmas. Furthermore, the French consul at Syros,[12] in his yearly reports, calculates the value of this trade during the same period at a figure of 21-24 million drachmas.

2. For 1851-58, import duties paid to the customs authorities of Syros constituted an average of 47.6 percent of the total sum of import duties collected throughout Greece.[13] And insofar as transit good duties are concerned, the percentage was even greater. Syros' customs authority collected a mean average of transit duties of 82 percent of the total sum of such duties collected throughout the Greek state.[14] The above information confirms that Syros was the main source of national revenue during this period. It also proves how important the transit-trade sector of Syros was, as it constituted more than four-fifths of the total value of the same sector of Greece.

Examining Syros trade over time, we should note the great stability which characterized it during the reign of King Otto, with the sole exception of the Crimean War (1853-56). The war in the banks

of the Danube and in Crimea had an adverse influence on the trade
of the eastern Mediterranean, and especially on the trade of Syros.[15]
A determining factor which contributed to this deterioration was a
decline in the wheat trade, as an embargo on wheat exports had been
imposed by the Russian government for 1854-55. Furthermore, at
this same time, Greek-Turkish commercial exchange was interrupted,
owing to a serious diplomatic rift. The recession in trade that the war
caused in Istanbul weakened the trade firms of Syros, with many
traders going bankrupt; thus, it also made it impossible for local
trade to regain its former strength and recreate the conditions of
development under which it had previously prospered. In the late
1850s, all the problems that plagued the Syro's trade and dealt it
final blow surfaced: these problems were also responsible for the
decline that followed in subsequent years. Now let us take a closer
look at the trade picture which Syros presented around 1860.

The degree of the participation of Syros in the total Greek trade
had greatly diminished. This decline lay in the creation and development of other competing trade centers in Greece. The export boom of
raisin trade in the Peloponnesos was a decisive factor in the development of the port of Patras, which became the center of the raisin export trade toward the West. Parallel to this, the transfer of the Greek
capital to Athens in 1834 played a key role in the development of
Piraeus, a relatively unimportant port up to that time, but which now
began to play a leading role in the import of capital. Thus, Syros lost
its privileged position as sole port and center to handle Greek foreign
trade.

Additionally, the development of Syros trade was always closely
influenced by the course of political and economic foreign events.
On the one hand, the island's trade was directly affected by the fierce
competition among the Great Powers of the time for domination in
the local politics of this crucial area of the Mediterranean; on the
other hand, the economic crises that plagued the countries with which
Syros had important trade links, also affected adversely its trade.

All these negative factors contributed to the gradual decrease of
Syros' share in the overall trade volume of Greece.

In the foreign sector, the trade of Syros was plagued by similar
circumstances. And its international trading activities diminished

accordingly. Hence, we draw the conclusion that trade in wheat products developed to the detriment of other products, especially Europe's industrial products. This fact of course, does not mean that Ermoupolis stopped shipping industrial goods to the markets of the East. It merely means that the flow of such products eastward — from Syros — gradually diminished.

The causes of these developments lay mainly in the growing use of the steamship as a means of shipping in the area. We shall now examine this new development in detail.

The Shipping Sector and Syros

The merchants of Syros invested their money in shipping, which seemed a natural way to invest their gains over the years. Construction of sailing ships at the local docks developed rapidly, especially during the period of Syros' economic boom. The growth in wheat trade in the Black Sea for 1845-55 (excepting Crimean War) contributed to the transport by sea of cereals, thus establishing the cereals sector as the most beneficial for the trading world of Syros. High shipping fares for the transport of cereals from East to West led many of Syros' shipowners to abandon transport of goods by sea from and to the coastal areas of Greece and turn their attention almost exclusively to shipping goods to and from various centers in the wider Mediterranean basin. As a result, the shipping register of Syros rapidly filled with ships of large tonnage, that is, ships in category "B" and weighing more than 30 tons.

Table I

Merchant Fleet Development: 1840-1855

| | Syros | | | | Rest of Greece | | | |
| | Ships | | Tonnage | | Ships | | Tonnage | |
Category	A	B	A	B	A	B	A	B
1840	211	257	2410	28560	2354	837	16549	94041
1848	200	449	2108	77306	2527	1456	17309	237914
1850	245	504	93289		2534	1482	18070	248131
1851	222	462	2307	85393	2890	1437	20011	237082
1852	240	460	83501		2825	1375	19696	228055
1853	634		96859		4153		247995	
1855	131	635	1400	119942	3538	1525	32396	264405

Sources: F. Strong, p. 159
"*Eolos*," no. 382, February 16, 1852, p. [2]
"*Enossis*," no. 289-156, June 10, 1854, p. [1]
"*Pandora*," no. 1-7, 1850-57
A.M.A.E., C.C.C., Syra, vol. 3, p. 203.

In the period 1840-50, total tonnage of the merchant fleet of Ermoupolis more than tripled. Furthermore, the tonnage of the sailing fleet of Syros, in 1855, was four times greater than that of 1840; the presence of ships of large tonnage is impressive. Thus, whereas in 1840, the Syros fleet consisted of 468 vessels, only 257 of these were above 30 tons; in 1855, the situation had changed drastically: among the 766 vessels in the port's shipping register, 635 belonged to Category "B", weighing over 30 tons. Of note is also the fact that Syros became the center of attraction of Greek shipping in the same period. In 1840, Category "B" ships from Syros represented, in terms of tonnage, 30.4 percent of the total tonnage of the whole Greek merchant fleet; in the year 1855, this figure had risen to 45.4 percent. At the same time, the second largest port of Greece, Spetsai, barely managed to represent in tonnage a figure of 10.5 percent of the total tonnage of Category "B" vessels in the whole Greek fleet.

Nature and Form of the Shipping Enterprise

Prerevolutionary shipping trade was based on the cooperative system.[16] A large number of smaller shipowners and entrepreneurs gravitated around the few big shipowners and participated in the ownership of vessels. Capital for the running of the ships was assured through the system of "sermagia," a Greek term signifying a partnership-derived form of capital for trade, the amassment of which merchants, shipowners, and sailors contributed a share. This kind of economic structure meant two things: One, a lack of distinction between shipowner and merchant; two, the payment of the crew's wages from the profits derived from the goods carried. It was also usual for the crew to participate in the "sermagia" system, that is, to contribute to the operative partnership capital.

In independent Greece, shipping took quite a different form. We conclude, therefore, after study of the various sources at our disposal that at the level of ownership,[17] the phenomenon of merchant and shipowner being the same person is repeated, although to a lesser extent. Many of the chief merchants of Syros were the sole owners of ships, or co-owners. They owned also the goods and determined the ways of loading and unloading the various cargoes. This meant that through the means of ship ownership, merchants retained full control of every phase of transportation by sea. This kind of mixture of commercial and shipping enterprise presupposed the purchase of the cargo and the sending of a ship to the point of loading. In other words, ownership facilitated greatly commercial activities on the part of the shipowner. Finally, this kind of operation allowed the ship to transport goods which did not fall under the sway of the shipowner, and thus, added to his profits. In times of high economic activity, however, the shipowner rarely bothered to transport additional goods, limiting his activity to the transport of his own proper cargo.

Apart from this special mixed class of shipowner-merchants, we also find the pure shipowner class developing at the same time on Syros. In this case, the shipowner owned only the vessel, but not its cargo. His profits depended on the shipping fares of the various ports, not on the sale of goods. At the period in question, shipowning capital was weak and divided, its collection depended greatly on loans for the construction of ships. This, in turn, made shipowners vulnerable to creditors, who supplied the loans. We could almost say that such creditors were the real owners of the ships. In a case of this kind, the shipowners were also the captains of the ships. The collection of substantial and real shipowning capital took place much later, when an economically strong class of Syros shipowners emerged on the scene.

Port Activity

The small Greek vessels had total control over the movement via sea lanes of products within the frontiers of Greece. In parallel, they sailed the transport route to and from Syros to the neighboring islands, as well as the eastern islands, such as Samos, Chios, Ikaria, and the Asia Minor coastal towns of Ephesus and Smyrna. Vessels of greater tonnage, and especially those of Syros, sailed the distant routes overseas. We should, however, note that the Greek flag had a much stronger presence in the coasts of the East than in the ports of Western Europe. It is indicative that during 1840, 2059 Greek vessels docked at least once in Constantinople, 1500 at the Dardanelles. 1000 at Smyrna, while only 230 reached Terjeste and about 100 Marseille.[18] In the same year, no Greek vessel seems to have reached a British port. However, examination of the frequency of arrivals and departures of vessels at the port of Ermoupolis is not the ideal method to appreciate the activity volume of trade originating in Syros. It would be more correct to examine the participation of the Greek merchant fleet in relation with the value of the goods shipped to and from Syros.

British vessels brought to Syros the greater part of imported, shipped goods. This resulted from the fact that imports of industrial products from Britain made up the largest volume in the total of imports arriving at the port of Syros. The main part of Greek shipping took second place because of the frequent journeys of the vessels of Syros to various provinces of the Ottoman empire. In the sector of export trade, the Greek flag occupied the first place, with the other flags lagging far behind.

Table II

Percentage of Participation in Sea Trade of Syros

Flag	Imports				Exports			
	1843	*1844*	*1845*	*1846*	*1843*	*1844*	*1845*	*1846*
	%	%	%	%	%	%	%	%
Greek	23	33.3	23.9	21.4	63.9	68.7	62.6	58.7
British	49.3	43	45.3	46.8	6.6	2.4	4.2	1.1
Austrian	8.5	5.3	7.2	8	12.4	11.3	10.8	13.1
Ottoman	5.7	6.9	6.8	6.2	11.9	11.9	11.6	15
Russian	4.2	1.8	6.4	7.6	3.4	1.9	4.5	2.4
Dutch	2.4	2.6	3.2	4	—	—	—	—
French	1	2.9	2.4	2.9	0.2	1.3	5.1	8.9
Others	5.9	4.2	4.8	3.1	1.6	2.5	1.2	0.8

Source: *AMAE, C.C.C.,* Syra, vol. 3, p. 172, dated November 25, 1848.

In conclusion, we can say that the picture of the port activities of Syros confirms the nature and kind of the foreign trade of the island. Ermoupolis, being a transit port of the eastern Mediterranean, received industrial products from the West and shipped them to Turkey. British trade goods were first destined for storage in Syros' warehouses. British ships brought their British-made industrial products to Syros. The continuation of the journey to Turkey proved impossible for two reasons. First, British products would remain in transit storage for some time in the warehouses of Syros until they were sold. Secondly, the Syros merchant owned the goods, and naturally, preferred to ship them to Turkey by ships registered in Syros. Thus, the great participation of the British merchant fleet in Syros imports as well as its total absence in exports can be understood rationally.

As far as vessels of other nationalities are concerned, we can see that Austrian shipping trade was quite active in both the import and export sectors of Syros trade. Austria ships controled direct trade exchange between Austria and Syros, and they also participated in the commerce between Syros and the Ottoman empire. The latter activity was largely due to journeys undertaken by Lloyd's steam vessels from Ermoupolis to certain Turkish ports. Finally, Ottoman shipping, comprised for the most part of ships owned by Greeks but being part of the empire, could not compete with Greek shipowners. As with the Syros trade, so with the Syros shipping activities: the Ottoman empire was the main area in which traders conducted business.

A chief factor which undoubtedly influenced Syros shipping and helped it develop rapidly — helping thus all of Greek shipping as a consequence — was the high freight rates for shipping cereals from Russian and Turkish ports to those of Western Europe. At least until 1847, the high fares and huge profits, as well as the widespread belief that this favorable state of affairs would continue indefinitely, decided a large number of traders to launch and ply their own vessels in the general framework of commercial activities. The cost of launching such ships was for the most part covered by maritime loans. The French consul offered the view that 75 percent of the large-tonnage vessels of Syros had been constructed with the aid of such loans. As will soon become evident, this factor was one of the determining factors for the crisis which plagued Syros shipping after 1850.

Perhaps at this point, some remarks are necessary in connection with the causes which provoked the fall in the freight rates, after 1848. One, there was a decrease of the prices of cereals in Western Europe in 1848-49. Two, an embargo was imposed on the port of Syros in January and February of 1850 by Britain, the result of a crisis in the diplomatic relations between Great Britain and Greece. Three, in the years 1851 and 1852, Western Europe became self-sufficient as far as demand of cereals was concerned. This five-year period, namely, from 1848 to 1852, was a painfully critical time for Greek shipping trade and affected greatly the Syros vessels which conducted most of the cereal trade in the Mediterranean.

Additionally, the decrease of Greek shipping activities in this period was the intentional scuttling of vessels. The non-activity of fleets in the period 1848-52 and the fall in prices brought the shipowners face to face with the impossibility of paying back loans to their maritime creditors. In their desire to free themselves from financial burdens, they resorted to illusory courses of action. Thus, they transfered the obligation to repay their loans to certain local insurance companies. These companies, in turn, received strong economic blows, and most of them declared bankruptcy. The crisis in the insurance sector of Ermoupolis, brought about by shipowners and captains, started to worry Western governments, which began to advise their own insurance companies not to insure the Greek vessels.[19]

At the same time, a lack of confidence in the dependability of the Greek merchant fleets reached its climax.

During the Crimean War, the activities of the merchant fleets showed fluctations, owing to the political events of the time. Freight rates, although they had risen somewhat in value, were still much lower than those of 1847.[20] The crisis almost but totally was overcome during the last phase of the war, when the Russian government lifted its embargo on cereal exports to neutral ports — among them those of Greece. Syros became the center of cereal trade. The ships of Syros seemingly undertook exports to Russia, for appearance's sake, even though the cargoes as such did not exist. In reality, the cargo ships, after stopping at Ermoupolis for a few hours, continued their journey not to Russia, but to various Western European ports instead. The profits of the Greek merchant marine, and particularly of the shipowners and captains of Syros, rose steeply for a while, but the onset of peace meant an end to this period of respite. Then, the fleets of the West resumed their trade activities in the eastern Mediterranean, with the steamer being now their principal competitive asset.

International steamer companies had direct connections between the ports of Western Europe and the great trading centers of the Middle East, and especially those of the Ottoman empire. The merchants of those cities could now order goods in the European market and have these goods reach them by steamer. They had no sound reason for Ermoupolis and its middlemen, in order to buy Western products. This reason was of great importance, as it meant the end of profit for the Syros' middleman and trader, while it had the effect of diminishing the price of the goods in favor of the Ottoman merchant. The higher steamer tariffs, in contradistinction to the lower sailing ship fares, did not stop the eastern traders from using the services of the steamer cargo ship, as the difference was much smaller than the Syros merchant's profit.

Although the steamship dictated the direct sale of Western goods to the markets of the East, this did not necessarily mean that it facilitated the transport of agricultural products, particularly cereals, from the East to the West. Steamships did not sail the banks and coast of the Danube and the Black Sea — and it was these areas that were the chief producers and exporters of cereals. The banks of the Danube did not allow for the passage of large ships, such as steamers. Furthermore, competition between Russia and Western nations contributed to the lack of the proper conditions for routing steamers toward Russian ports of call. Finally, many shipping companies avoided loading their ships with cereals, as the larger volume of such goods incurred more expense and less profit than other goods. Considerations of the kind just described ensured the survival of the traditional means to transport cereals — the sailing ship. This, in turn, allowed the merchant fleets of Syros to continue their activities, and it gave the Syros merchant the opportunity to expand and trade in cereals with the East. Thus, the turning of the Syros traders to cereal trade can be seen as a natural result of the development of the steamship. There were, of course, additional reasons, such as the lack of surpluses in wheat and the resulting high price that it fetched in the markets of the West. These factors, however, were temporary, whereas the consequences of steamers in the usual lines of the sea trade had a lasting and irrevocable effect.

Syros lost its leading role in trade with the East when the steamship routes expanded widely enough to connect the various trading ports of call of the Mediterranean — a development which made the activities of Syros as a transitory post and middle-stage post redundant. The merchant classes of Syros were, thus, forced to succumb to the latest in maritime technology which was responsible for the transfer of the Mediterranean centers of trade to other ports.

Notes

1. For a more detailed account of the economy of Syros during the stage of its development, see, B. Kardassis "Commercial activities on Syros, 1843-1857,"

Journal of Historical and Ethnological Society, (25, 1982), 321-94; also, by the same author, *Syros 1832-1857, Crossroads of Eastern Mediterranean* (Ph. D. diss Athens 1985).

2. For the history of the pre-revolutionary period of Syros, see, T. Ambelas, *History of Syros island*, (Hermoupolis 1874); also, A. Drakakis, *Syros under Turkish rule*, (Hermoupolis 1948; A. Fraggidis, *History of Syros island*, 2nd edition (Athens 1975).

3. See, the table Pouqueville published in G. Leontaritis, *Hellenic Merchant Marine (1453-1850)*, 2nd edition, (Society for Neohellenic Studies, Mnemon, Athens, 1981), 60.

4. See, D. Vikelas, *Loukis Laras*, (Athens).

5. See, *Archives du Ministere des Affaires Etrangeres*, *(AMAE)*, *Correspondence Consulaire et Commerciale (CCC)* (Syra), vol. 4, 55, where it is stated "The people of Chios help each other; they do business only with their fellow islanders, many of who are quite wealthy and counsil powerful commercial houses in Marseille, Livorno, Tergest, London, Odessa, etc. "Also see, I. Vlachogiannis, *Archives of Chios*, Vol. 5, (Athens, 1910), 361, where there is a relative excerpt from a letter from the Hermoupolis Chamber of Commerce. Finally, see, F. Thiersch, *Capodistrias's Greece* (titled originally: De l'etat actuel de la Grece et des moyens d'arriver à sa restauration), Vol. 2, (Athens, 1972), 71-73.

6. K. Tsoukalas, *Dependence and Reproduction. The sociological role of the educational mechanisms in Greece (1830-1922)*, (Athens, 1977), 218-20.

7. See, the two most important newspapers, *Eolos* and *Enossis* during the 1847-57 period, where articles on the local municipal elections are the main topics in the newspapers.

8. See, *Government Journal*, no. 3 (January 30, 1836), 4; also, F. Strong, *Greece as a Kingdom*, (London, 1842), 119-20; F. Thiersch, 85.

9. For matters concerning customs legislation at this period, see, A. N. Vernardakis, *On commerce in Greece* (Athens, 1885), 79; A. G. Mansolas, *Demographic Information about Greece*, 2nd edition (Athens, 1980), 171-73.

10. F. Strong, 133.

11. D. Dakin, *The Unification of Greece 1770-1923* (Athens, 1982), 447.

12. *AMAE, CCC*, vol. 3, 171.

13. B. Kardassis, 331.

14. *Ibid.*

15. For more details about the consequences of the Crimean War on the merchant marine and on commerce of Syros, see, B. Kardassis, 59-70.

16. B. Kremmydas, *Introduction to the History of Neohellenic Greek Society (1700-1821)* (Athens, 1976), 175-87, 128.

17. See, the shipbuilding tables concerning maritime construction in Hermoupolis for 1846-47, 1850-52, and 1857-59, in the *General Archives of the Nation*, in the I. Vlachogiannis collection, dossier 297, "Private Collections," Part V; also, the part "Of Chios and Hermoupolis;" the *Archives of the Municipality of Hermoupolis*, dossier "Shipbuilding."

18. F. Strong, 153.

19. See, *Athina,* no. 1706 (August 10, 1850), 3, where a relative directive issued by the French minister of Commerce has been published.

20. For information regarding shipping fares charged at the various shipping centers of the East during the years 1846-1857, see, B. Kardassis, 97-107.

Elena Frangakis

The Port of Smyrna in the Nineteenth Century

In 1883, the British consul in Smyrna noted the following:

> No other country of Europe is so dependent on other lands for the
> products of civilization as Turkey, and no portion of the Ottoman
> dominions is more dependent on foreign goods than Asia Minor.[1]

The integration of the economy of the western Anatolian region, the center of which was the city-port of Smyrna, into the world economy and the international market, which had begun in the eighteenth century, was well under way. Interregional trade, whilst flourishing, was no longer independent of international trade, and the domestic market of the region was fully linked to the foreign one. If we exclude the Pontos area in the Black Sea, with its ports of Trabzon and Samsun, and the immediate hinterland of Instanbul, the rest of Anatolia was linked to the world market through Smyrna.[2] It exported agricultural goods and other raw materials to Western Europe and imported and distributed Western manufactured goods and cloth in particular. And, this pattern of trade had not changed since the end of the seventeenth century.

The dominance of Smyrna in the foreign trade of Anatolia dates from the middle of the eighteenth century. It increased as the trade links between the Ottoman empire and the West were strengthened. It maintained a position of dominance during the early nineteenth century, at the same time expanding its network of trade within the empire. In 1817, a French diplomat proposed that French commercial activities in the Levant be centered in Smyrna, for all trade converged there.[3]

From the end of the eighteenth century, its greatest rival in the import trade was Istanbul. By the nineteenth century, the Ottoman capital was joined by Salonica as major import ports of the empire.

In export trade, Smyrna always enjoyed greater supremacy. In the 1840s, 24 percent of all imports to the empire and 57 percent of all exports passed through the port of Smyrna, whilst in 1900 the figures are 19 percent and 55 percent respectively. On the eve of World War I, this share fell even further.[4] Smyrna no longer enjoyed the monopoly of the Ottoman trade it once had.[5]

The higher the prices for agricultural goods and the lower the ones for manufactured goods in the international market, as was the case in the years 1820-40, the faster the process of integration of the Ottoman economy into the world economy.[6] Such an integration, however, had certain repercussions on the long-term growth of the economy. One such result was an overspecialization in certain agricultural products which led to an overdependency on the fluctuations of the international market. Lack of serious industrial growth was another. Pockets of industrial growth, as for instance textile factories in Lebanon and Syria that apparently grew and flourished in the nineteenth century, do not constitute a general pattern.[7] In the region of Smyrna, the only industry that survived and grew in the nineteenth century was the carpet industry.[8] In 1911, the British consul termed as "an industrial awakening" the establishment of a cotton factory in Smyrna which was an offshoot of the Oriental Carpet Manufacturers Limited.[9] Some industries did exist, but these were involved in the treatment of agricultural goods for export, such as factories for threading silk from cocoons or for spinning cotton.[10]

France had been the main trading partner of Smyrna since the 1740s, accounting for half the port's trade. The almost total destruction of the French trade by British naval action during the French Revolutionary and the Napoleonic Wars[11] and the great degree of insecurity in the Mediterranean for all merchant shipping other than British, caused major disruptions to the economic activities of Smyrna at the beginning of the nineteenth century.[12] By 1817, however, Smyrna had regained part of its former trade and was in a position to take a large share of the trade in the eastern Mediterranean, which was increasingly dominated by the British.[13] The outbreak of the Greek War of Independence in 1821, brought a new halt to economic activities, for a large number of Greeks, many of them from the nearby island of Chios, were forced to flee from the area.[14] They feared reprisals from the Ottoman government following the insurrection of their brethren. Since the French Revolution, a large part of the trade of Smyrna had passed into the hands of these Chiots.[15] The destruction of the island of Chios in 1822, due to the insurrection of the islanders against the Ottomans, had negative effects on the economy of the port.[16] The Greek War of Independence (1821-31) brought great disruption to the trade in the Aegean Sea. Privateering and piracy were so extensive that goods thus seized were sold in Smyrna at lower prices undermining the European merchants there.[17] Recovery was under way after the mid-1830s, and in particular after the 1838 Commercial Convention between Britain and the Ottoman Empire, which helped release exports from the interior of western Anatolia.

Before 1838, monopolies or prohibitions on the export of goods were irregularly and arbitrarily set by the Porte or by the biggest local landowner, and usually principal administrator in the area.[18] To annul these, European merchants had to bribe and protest and suffer interruptions to their trade.[19] This made Europeans reluctant to venture inland, confining their trade activities to the coastal areas instead. As a result, all inland trade was in the hands of Ottoman administrators and landowners and their merchants. These merchants, whether Muslim or *raya*, usually had bought the right to trade in a certain product from the Ottoman lord.[20] The 1838 Convention changed all that, abolishing monopolies and arbitrariness.

At the same time, the widespread use of *berats*, as well as the Tanzimat Reforms, strengthened the position of the *raya* merchants in Smyrna — Greeks, Armenians, and Jews. They took part in the international trade of the port acting either as agents for French, and subsequently British, houses,[21] or in cooperation with commercial houses of their compatriots established in Western Europe.[22] Finally, after 1838, local expertise, knowledge of the language and area on the part of the *raya* merchants, and capital resources and protection on the part of the British became a combination too powerful for the local Ottoman lords to compete against, and the terms of the Commercial Convention were vigorously applied.[23]

In the 1860s, following the construction of the Smyrna-Aydin railway, imports more than doubled, and exports rose between three and four times in value. The increase in trade continued through the 1870s to the 1890s despite a depression. In the late 1880s and early 1890s, a generally lower level of trade activity was recorded. Trade started to pick up in the early twentieth century, falling off slightly in the years immediately preceding World War I.

One way of explaining the recurrent fluctuations in the trade of Smyrna is by linking them to the economic cycle of Britain. Despite the fact that, after the 1870s, Britain did not dominate trade in Smyrna in the way it had done 30 years before, it still took almost half of the port's exports. So, that, whenever the British economy would experience a slump, demand for Smyrna's exports would fall. Conversely, as the cycle would rise, demand for Smyrna's exports would also rise and production would be stimulated. The time it took for production in Smyrna to adjust to shifts in export demand in Britain was two years. Hence there was a two-year time lag between the cycles of the British economy and those of the Anatolian port.[24]

Except for a few years to the contrary, Smyrna had an active balance of trade with Western Europe throughout the nineteenth century. For the period 1817-1912, Smyrna had an average annual surplus of 23.5 percent. The highest surplus, 40.3 percent, occurred in the 1830s and early 1840s. The following two decades had the smallest surplus in the century, 17.3 percent, closing with a deficit of 9 percent in 1857-60. This was the period of considerable economic growth of Smyrna and of expansion of its internal market. Other years with a passive balance of trade were 1873-74, 1878-81, and 1888. An active balance of trade need not signify that Smyrna was an net importer of capital. To determine this, one must look at the balance of payments. In the absence of readily available figures and at the present stage of research, one can only make the following tentative supposition. The European merchants did not necessarily export capital to the Ottoman port through their trade activities there. For apart from trade, there were other activities in which European merchants took part and which accrued them profit. For instance, it has been calculated British businessmen by repatriating their capital and profits from western Anatolia, transferred abroad an amount equal to their total investment in the Ottoman empire.[25] Apart from profits from investment, there were profits from banking, insurance, lending, and the carrying trade. These activities were to a large extent in the hands of Europeans. As a result, the balance of payments of Smyrna would be expected to be negative.[26] The only time the Ottoman empire became a net importer of capital was at the end of the nineteenth century when Germany, for political reasons, exported more capital than it got from the empire.[27]

Despite the growth of the Ottoman economy, the chronic problem of monetary scarcity continued to hinder the rapid growth of trade. Banking was very slow in developing. Little progress had been made since the late eighteenth century. A description of trade practices and banking in Smyrna in 1839-40 was similar to a report made by the French in 1821 which was itself reminiscent of late eighteenth century.

> Sales of imported goods are usually made on credits, seldom for cash, by the house broker to the street broker; that is, by the merchant's broker, to the outdoor or buyer's broker. Sales and bargains are made under some bond or other guarantee. The credits are for periods of 15 days. Payments are made by installments. Sales and purchases are also made partly for cash and partly on credit. Barter which is tedious in its process, must be considered as a speculative trade depending on the sale of the articles exchanged. Transactions, partly in cash and partly in barter are also common.[28]

In 1862, peasants in the area surroundung Smyrna were borrowing on a monthly rate of interest rate of 12 percent, in order to buy tools and make other necessary purchases. This coupled with competition from American cotton led them to cut back on their cultivation of the crop, which up to the 1830s was exported in great quantities and at large profits.[29] Having its revenue from trade greatly reduced after the 1838 Commercial Convention, the Porte further increased its taxation of the peasantry, thus depressing their purchasing power. Yet, the policy of issuing paper money as a means of alleviating monetary scarcity was not applied vigorously enough by the government in the middle of the nineteenth century. Shortly thereafter, the issuing of paper money came under the supervision of the European powers — a way in which the West in‘luenced and dominated the Ottoman economy.

In 1842, a number of British merchant houses in Smyrna set up a small, private bank, called *la Banque de Smyrne*, with an initial capital of five million Ottoman piastres in order to facilitate trade. They held current and deposit accounts for clients, who were mainly European merchants, cashed letters of exchange, and lent at moderate interest rates. Above all, they tried and succeded in keeping the exchange rates for European currencies from going too high by not letting the market of Smyrna be completely drained of foreign currencies during the buying season and intervening whenever this took place. Draining the market of currency was many times deliberate, designed to influence the exchange rate. Lack of money was usually followed by a frantic circulation of IOU's by local people, used to pay for European goods, which did not always reflect existing funds. Thus, European merchants could not recover their money easily. The bank's other aim was to put a stop to the speculative use of IOU's. Within two weeks of its establishment, these IOU's called *takas*, disappeared from the Smyrna market.

The bank also succeeded in keeping the exchange rate stable for three months. Foreign currency circulated at 1 percent less in the Frank quarter than in the Smyrna bazaar. Within a year, however, the Ottoman government, presumably bowing to pressure from local speculators, closed the bank claiming that it did not have permission to open in the first place.[30] In 1862, a small number of *raya* merchants, Greeks and Jews, set themselves up as small bankers on behalf of several commercial houses. They bought foreign paper money on three to four weekly installments, reselling them at a profit, also getting a greater percent brokerage commission on the transaction. However, this was done on a small scale and did not ease the need for paper money in Smyrna. Most of the import trade took place in the first six months of the year when there was a want for money to remit to Europe, and consequently, exchange rates were high. It was also the time when Ottoman merchants bought goods from the interior of Anatolia for export abroad, further increasing the need for money. From July onward, when the exports appeared in the market, money became abundant causing the exchange rates to drop. The exchange rates continued to fall till November, when they started to rise again.[31]

If an organized banking system could be installed that sold money

in the first half of the year and bought money for remittances in the
second half, as a British observer proposed, trade would have been
greatly facilitated. Two-and-a-half decades later, the Porte founded
the Agricultural Bank expressly for the needs of the peasantry, without
much success. In 1909, the British consul in Smyrna reported:

> There is a great need for a credit foncier or land bank for agricultu-
> ral districts..... The peasants are continuously indebted, through the
> exhorbitant interest on loans.[32]

In trade, things were better. There were seven public banks, besides
many private ones, most of them having been founded in the 1860s
and 1870s.

In 1848, debasing the coin as a means of financing budget deficits
was formally abandoned.[33] The Ottoman government was thereafter
unable to increase the amount of money circulating in the empire·
Usury became the means of increasing the money supply, with interest rates constantly at 60 percent or higher. The necessity to turn to
usury in the countryside led to disastrous results for the peasants.
Another way of increasing the money supply was though imports of
foreign specie. Since the eighteenth century, there circulated in the
market of Smyrna foreign specie which substituted for Ottoman coin-
age. In fact, it was a very lucrative trade.[34] In 1862, merchants still
had to bring money (gold and silver) from Western Europe to cover
purchases.[35]

As trade increased, loans from Western Europe were the only way
of alleviating the scarcity in the money supply. For the European in-
vestor, apart from loans, there were other possibilities for investment
in railways and other infrastructure projects, such as roads, the enlargement of the Customs House and the port quay. Railways were
the most important factor affecting the commercialization of agriculture in the area. In 1860, the British consul in Smyrna observed
that:

> The facility of communication with more civilized nations by steam
> and the introduction of Railways will probably do more for the general
> good of the country... than the introduction of new measures which the
> Turks cannot or will not understand.[36]

It is not coincidental that 40 percent of the railway lines constructed converged on Smyrna. Heavy investment by a European power meant an increase in its economic and political influence in the region.[37] In 1865, the British constructed the Smyrna-Aydin railway;[38] at the same time, Britain accounted for half the Smyrna trade.[39]

British predominance in the eastern Mediterranean dates from the French Revolution. During the French Revolutionary and Napoleonic Wars, British commercial might was backed by strong naval action. The only exception were the years 1801-1803, during which the Italian ports of Genoa, Leghorn, Trieste, and Ancona benefited from the general peace to take a large part of the Smyrna trade with Western Europe away from France and Britain.[40] After 1814, British commercial predominance was based on its increasing industrial strength and growing economy. After the Napoleonic Wars, France regained a part of its former economic strength. In the eighteenth century, it had been the first commercial power in the area, but, by the second half of the nineteenth century, Austria surpassed it as a commercial power in Smyrna. Together with Germany, Austria proved formidable rival to British trade activities in the Anatolian port in the closing decades of the nineteenth century. Britain, by then, looked to Suez and India for its economic and strategic interests.[41] The United States was particularly active in the Smyrna trade at the beginning of the century. In 1832, they accounted for 49.1 percent of its imports.[42]

Whoever the trading partner was, trade relations were the same as in the eighteenth century — with all the negative effects that this implied for the Ottoman economy. Owing to the low level of technology and the total absence of manufactured goods, excluding carpets, the volume of production and hence exports varied greatly according to weather conditions[43] and demand in the world market.[44] Certain changes took place among the exports within the category of raw materials since the eighteenth century, which showed the increasing integration of the Ottoman economy in the capitalist world market.[45] Whilst raw materials suitable for the manufacturing industry, such as cotton, cotton yarn, mohair yarn, silk, and wool dominated eighteenth century exports, in the next century, foodstuffs, such as raisins, figs, dried fruit, cereals, barley, wheat were the principal exports. Other raw materials, such as valonia, madder roots, opium, carpets, and sponges, which were minor export items in the eighteenth, figured prominently in the nineteenth century.[46]

One notable change was the decline in the export of cotton in the first half of the nineteenth century, which had accounted for 50 percent of Smyrna's exports in the second half of the eighteenth century.[47] The reason for this was the massive influx into the world market of American cotton. The American Civil War led to large areas of land in the *sanjak* of Aydin, which were brought under cultivation.

Despite the increase in cotton production, in 1863, the French consul in Smyrna calculated cotton exports to be 4-6000 bales. This figure shows a dramatic decrease compared to the pre-1830 figures of 70-90,000 bales.[48] Once the Civil War was over, the market in Smyrna was flooded with American cotton and exports dropped.[49] In the first half of the eighteenth century, small amounts of silk cloth were exported from Smyrna to the West. In the course of the century, these exports were replaced by silk thread. In the nineteenth century, it was mainly silk cocoons that were exported. Cotton yarn, an important export in the eighteenth century, was being imported in the nineteenth. American and British cotton yarn were cheaper and of a better quality.[50] Until the first half of the nineteenth century, Smyrna exported wheat; in the second half, it started to import it. It even imported carpets for domestic use, owing to their lower prices whilst its own renowned carpets went to a more expensive market in the West.[51]

As far as imports were concerned, there were fewer changes: cloth, interchanged with woolens, constituted the first import of Smyrna from the beginning of the eighteenth century right through the end of the nineteenth. These were followed by sugar and coffee, staple items of consumption, which could be afforded even by the peasantry in Anatolia. The increase in consumer goods such as fashionable clothes, furniture, cutlery, perfumes showed the growth of an internal market in Smyrna and the surrounding area.[52] Import of petroleum and machinery at the end of the nineteenth century testified to the further expansion of infrastructure, although this was largely in the hands of European firms.[53]

Throughout the eighteenth century, despite numerous fluctuations the population of Smyrna remained at 100,000. In 1909, it was estimated at 350-370,000.[54] The enormous increase in population testifies to the growth of Smyrna as a large urban and economically dynamic center. Whatever the effects on the Ottoman economy from its integration in the world economy were, for Smyrna, these were largely positive.

Notes

1. *Parliamentary Papers: Accounts and Papers* (London, 1883), vol. LXXIII, No. c3736, p. 1063. (Hereafter A & P.).

2. Lewis Farley, *The Resources of Turkey and Profitable Investments.* (London, 1862), 96-97.

3. Archives Nationales de France, Paris, AE B[iii] 243, Felix de Beaujour, Inspection générale du Levant, Smyrna, 5 Jan. 1817. Hereafter cited as ANF.

4. Trade figures for the nineteenth century exist on an annual basis only after 1830. See, Charles Issawi, *The Economic History of Turkey, 1800-1914* (Chicago, 1980), 110-13.

5. For the share of Smyrna in the total trade of the Ottoman Empire, see author's "Izmir - an International Port in the Eastern Mediterranean in the century, 1695-1820," *Actes du II[e] Colloque International d'Histoire* I (Athens, 1985), 107-108.

6. Sevket Pamuk, "Foreign Trade, Foreign Capital and the Peripheralization of the Ottoman Empire, 1830-1913." (Ph. D. diss., University of California, 1978), 65.

7. Roger Own, *The Middle East in the World Economy* (London, 1981), 93-94.

8. Dimitris Georgiades, *Smyrne et l'Asie Mineure au point de vue économique et commercial* (Paris, 1885), 63.

9. A & P, (1912), Vol. C, No. c 5011, 13.

10. Archives du Ministere des Affaires Étrangères, Paris, CCC, Vol. 50, Bentivoglio to Foreign Minister, Smyrna, Jan. 14, 1864, (Hereafter, AMAE).

11. David Syrett, "The Role of the Royal Navy in the Napoleonic Wars after Trafalgar, 1805-1814," *Naval War College Review*, XXXII, No. 2 sequence 275 (September-October, 1979), 75-76.

12. J. D. Nanninga, ed., *Bronnen tot de Geschiedenis van den Levantschen Handel, Vierde deel, 1765-1825* (Gravenhage, 1966), document No. 168.

13. AMAE, CCC, Vols 35-36.

14. Public Record Office, London, FO/78/136, Werry to Levant Company Smyrna, April 13, 1822. (Hereafter PRO).

15. ANF, AE B[iii] 243, Miège. Renseignements sur le commerce du Levant, Livorno, May 13, 1825.

16. AMAE, CCC, Vol. 8, David, Mémoire sur Scio, Chios, 1824; Fustel de Coulanges, *Mémoire sur l'île de Chio* (Paris, 1857), 152.

17. PRO, FO/32/39, Capt. Copeland to Parish, Nauplion, 31 Mar 1833; Despina Themeli-Katifori, "I dioxis tis piratias ke ton thalassion dikasterion kata tin protin kapodistriakin periodon, 1828-1829." [The Fight Against Piracy and the Admiralty Courts in the First Capodistrian Period, 1828-1829] (Ph. D. diss., University of Athens, 1973), 41.

18. PRO, SP/105/129, Werry to Levant Company, Smyrna, June 2, 1804.

19. PRO, FO/32/39, Wilkinson to Palmerston, London, January 28, 1833.

20. PRO, SP/105/135, Werry to Levant Company, Smyrna, August 17, 1815.

21. Elena Frangakis, "The *Raya* Communities of Smyrna in the 18th Century (1690-1820). Demography and Economic Activities, "*Actes du Colloque International d'Histoire*, (Athens, 1985), 27-42.

22. Huseyin Ramazonglu, *Turkey in the World Capitalist System* (Aldershot, England, 1985), 50.

23. PRO, FO/195/128. J. A. Werry to Charnaud, V-C, Smyrna, September 10, 1839.

24. Orhan Kurmuş, "The Role of British Capital in the Economic Development of Western Anatolia, 1850-1913" (Ph. D. thesis University of London, 1974), 280-82.

25. *Ibid.*, 80.

26. Charles Carrière & Marcel Courdurié, "Un sophisme économique. Marseille's enrichit en achetant plus qu'elle ne vend. (Réfléxions sur les mécanismes commerciaux levantins au XVIIIe siècle)," *Histoire, Économie et Societé*, (Ier trimestre, 1984), 36-48.

27. Çağlar Keyder, "The Dissolution of the Asiatice Mode of Production," *Economy and Society*, Vol. 5, No. 2, (1976), 193.

28. *Parliamentary Papers: Tariffs* (London, 1843), Vol. 2, 98.

29. AMAE, CCC, Vol. 50, Bentivoglio to French Minister, Smyrna, March 26, 1863.

30. PRO, FO/195/178, J. F. Hanson *et al.* to the Porte, Smyrna, June 23, 1843.

31. Lewis Farley, 81.

32. A & P, (1910), Vol., CIII, No. 4598, 18.

33. Sevket Pamuk, 139.

34. Charles Carrière, "Réflextions sur le problème des monnaies et des metaux precieux en Mediterranée Orientale au XVIIIe siècle," *Cahiers de la Mediterranée* (1976), 1-10.

35. Lewis Farley, 83.

36. PRO, FO/78/1533, Blunt to FO, Smyrna, July 28, 1860.

37. PRO, FO/78/2255m Meeting of Shareholders of the Ottoman Railway Company, London, July 17, 1867.

38. PRO, FO/78/2255, Purser to Ottoman Railway Company, Smyrna, September 14, 1868.

39. A & P, (1873), Vol. LXVII, No. c. 824, 739-40.

40. Elena Frangakis, "The Commerce of Izmir in the Eighteenth Century, 1695-1820" (Ph. D. diss., University of London, 1985), 182-88.

41. On the decline of British trade in Smyrna see A & P, (1873), Vol. LXVII No. c. 824, 744-45.

42. AMAE, CCC Vol. 43, Exportation et Importation de Smyrne, 1832.

43. A & P, (1868), Vol. LXVIII, No. c. 3953, 224.

44. A & P, (1890), Vol. LXXVII, No. c. 1354, 10-13.

45. Fernand Rougon, *Smyrne, situation commerciale et économique* (Paris, 1892), 131.

46. A & P, (1867), Vol. LXVII, 157.

47. Archives de le Chambre de Commerce de Marseille, Marseilles, I, 26-28, États des marchandises venant du Levant et de Barbarie, 1700-1789.

48. AMAE, CCC, Vol. 50, Bentivoglio to French Minister, Smyrna, March 26, 1863.

49. Donald Quataert, "The Commercialization of Agriculture in Ottoman Turkey," *International Journal of Turkish Studies*, I, No. I (1980), 38-55.

50. PRO, FO/195/177, Cotton Yarn Guild to Brant, Smyrna, July 30, 1840.

51. A & P, (1883), Vol. LXXIII, No. c. 3736, 1069.

52. AMAE, CCC, Vol. 42, Exportation et Importation de Smyrne, 1828.

53. A & P, (1914), Vol. XCV, No. 5247, 11.

54. A & P, (1910), Vol. CII, No. 4598, 24.

Théano Tsiovaridou

The Commercial Development and Economic Importance of the Port of Thessaloniki, from the End of the Eighteenth Century to the End of World War I

The present paper hopes to give an idea of the importance of the port of Thessaloniki from the Crimean War to World War I.[1] So, I shall begin by examining the decade after 1860, the port's "gold decade."[2]

In that period, many political and economical events influenced positively or negatively the commercial development and the economic importance of the Port of Thessaloniki. Sometimes, different events compensated each other, or went in the same direction, thereby magnifying the results.

But, it should be emphasized that, in general, often, the repercussion of the West European business cycle during periods of depression was corrected or even attenuated by some international events — usually wars — of economic importance.[3]

The most important historical events that influenced the port's economic position were:

1. The American Civil War (1861-66).
2. The Orient Crisis (1875-78).
3. The Constitution of the Young Turks (1908).
4. The Balkan Wars (1912-13).
5. World War I (1914-18).

The American Civil War increased the export of cotton, the main export after the cereals, especially to Massalia, and it gave rise to renewed contacts between the two Mediterranean ports. So, whereas in 1862, the total value of Thessaloniki's cotton exports amounted to 2.788.000 francs, in 1863, after a rude ascent, they fluctuated around 15.220.000 francs,[4] that is, an increase of 545 percent, which was also the result of increases in price. According to the law of supply and demand, the price of cotton in the European markets rose considerably although its quality was not so good as the American one.

In 1864-65 the total annual value of cotton produced in Serres, and exported from Thessaloniki amounted to about 16.000.000 francs. From the December of 1865, export of cotton was directed not only toward France and England, but also toward Germany and Transylvania.

Thus, the American Civil War saved Thessaloniki from the ravages of the European depression[5] of that time.

During the period 1863-65, more than two-thirds of the total value of Thessaloniki's exports were absorbed from France; England came first in its imports, though.

The end of the American Civil War, in 1866, diminished considerably the demand of Macedonian cotton in the European markets, and thus, caused a gradual fall in its price. So, the annual average value of 150 kg of cotton was about 500 francs in 1865, it fell to 300 in 1867, although this price was higher than the pre-Civil War one. Also, the production and export of cotton continued to be important, and this was one of the reasons that the balance of trade for 1866-68 was positive and the port's commercial movement presented a special development. France continued to be the first country for its exports.

The construction of the Suez Canal[6] influenced the export trade in these years. After exhausting the timber from nearby regions, the canal's administration turned to deliveries from Thessaloniki. Thus, the export of timber until the inauguration of the Suez Canal, in September 1869, contributed for a while to the increase of the port's export volume. Flour, dairy products, and so on, were also exported for the needs of the canal's workers.

The increase in the number of shipping companies which maintained more or less regular ties with Thessaloniki, although of smaller significance, was another reason for the rise in the volume of exports.

All these factors helped to overcome the negative influence of the continuing European depression, and thus, did not lead to a further decline in port activity after 1866.

During 1870-75,[7] Thessaloniki's foreign trade knew very important fluctuations as a result, first of all, of the Ottoman empire's very bad economic situation, and secondly, of political reasons. The Franco-Prussian War (1870-71) considerably decreased its export activity to Massalia, and, so, this explains the vertical fall of the total value of the port's export trade. Of course, after the recovery of the French economy, commercial relations began again, and France absorbed the bigger part of Thessaloniki's external trade.

Another political event with an unfavorable repercussion was the revolution in Voznia and Erzegovini in 1875. The well-known fairs of Serres and Perlepe were completely deserted, because they, too, were provisioned from these revolutionary provinces. This situation became even more aggravated because of bad crops, considerable fall in local industrial production, and the devaluation of the Ottoman money, which had a very unfavorable effect on the value of Thessaloniki's exports, calculated in francs.

The 1875 depression in Thessaloniki was brief, and even in 1876, we have a new upward tendency in the value of imports and exports, which lasted until 1878. Thus, once again we see that the crisis in the major European states had minimal impact.

Following market prices, the nominal increase in the port's turnover, in current prices, in 1876-77, did not reflect a real increase in the physical volume of the imports and exports.

The development of Thessaloniki's trade with its hinterland increased considerably after the construction of railways, that began in 1869,[8] because the port could play, finally, a special role for the foreign trade. So, between 1886 (=100) and 1889, the index of the ship tonnage increased to 151 and the value of goods exported and imported went to 150.

The line between Thessaloniki and Skopje was completed in 1871;[9] that between Skopje and Belgrade in 1888; the Thessaloniki-Monastir line in 1894; and in 1895, completion of another line from Thessaloniki via Alexandroupolis to Constantinople. The coming of the railway brought an end to the old caravan trade and a decline in the importance of fairs.

So, the railway rapidly crisscrossed the hinterland, but, for the transportation of goods, the results were not very satisfactory, as fares remained high. For this reason, in 1889[10] a conference between the representatives of the Ottoman empire, Serbia, Bulgaria, and

Austria-Hungary took place in Constantinople, and a unitary price was adopted, one which favored especially Austria-Hungary.

The Treaty of Berlin (1878) changed the map of the Balkan peninsula and increased the role of Thessaloniki in its hinterland: the trade of the Ottoman Balkan provinces, Serbia and eastern Macedonia and Thrace, and Albania, were directed to the port of Thessaloniki.

According to the treaty,[11] Balkan states were obliged to construct railway lines, in order to facilitate the connection of Thessaloniki and Constantinople with the rest of Europe. So, a contract was signed between Austria-Hungary and Serbia, Bulgaria, and the Ottoman empire in 1883, and so, began the construction of the Skopje-Niš line.

In 1885,[12] an effort at decentralization of the Porte's foreign trade took place, and as a result, Thessaloniki in Europe and Smyrna and Beirut in Asia prospered. This, of course, was possible, as a good land communications already existed.

Thessaloniki's new harbor opened for navigation in 1901[13] while the Turks were still in control. Its facilities were further enlarged between 1903 and 1907. In 1904,[14] a contract was signed between Turkey and France for the construction of new port facilities. The French company, "Societé Ottomane d'Exploitation du port de Salonique" was responsible for this project. And, consequently, transit and external trade increased continually.

The transit trade with Serbia, before the conference of 1889, was restricted, as the fares on Serbian and Ottoman lines were very high; but, since fares decreased by almost half price in February 1890, followed by lower custom duties, the transit trade via Thessaloniki increased considerably. In 1906,[15] an economic war between Austria-Hungary and Serbia, in which Serbia directed its exports to Thessaloniki, brought increased trade to Thessaloniki. For, Serbia was the only Balkan country that extensively used its port facilities.

After the proclamation of the Constitution, July 24, 1908,[16] the Ottoman empire, and especially Macedonia, entered a new economic and social life.

Freedom of the press, of association, the right to strike, and all other constitutional liberties, had a vivid effect on Thessaloniki's commercial activities.

Strikes were declared the day after the proclamation of the constitution, for an increase in wages or a decrease in working hours were communicated from one profession to another, and they were the cause, for a certain time, of a stoppage in some branches of the port's economical activity.

Also, the strikes of stevedores, boatmen, porters, cartmen, and tobacco workers ended in partial or total satisfaction of the strikers' demands.

The conclusion of all strikes came a year after the constitution's promulgation, thereby increasing the prices of products as well as the cost of life, and with these changes, stagnation set in, in 1910.

The relationship between a port and its hinterland has usually been reflected in the traffic flow between the port and its hinterland, the total turnover in trade, and the size of the port, its efficiency of operation, including the services of one or more free zones. The larger and closer the relationship, the freer the flow of the trade, the more important is the position of the port.

As it is well known, in European Turkey, there were only three towns, Constantinople,[17] Thessaloniki and Alexandroupolis that were connected to the hinterland. Thessaloniki's was considered more wide than Constantinople's,[18] although Constantinople constituted a bigger urban agglomeration.

From commercial point of view, Thessaloniki's geographical position was considered unique, and its commercial life played the prime role in the Balkan peninsula for maritime communications and relations with the hinterland.

Thessaloniki organized relations with its hinterland from a central point.[19] European economic penetration was developed, and Thessaloniki had a tendency to be coordinator of European influence within the framework of the Ottoman empire. It was the main agency — εμπόριο with the ancient Greek meaning, or "ville-comptoire" — from where the already industrialized Europe sent its products, and thereby, expanded its economical and political presence.

Thessaloniki's relationship to its hinterland has changed constantly and has depended upon the territorial extent and peacefulness of the hinterland.

Between 1878 and 1920,[20] the politico-geographical map of the hinterland was completely redrawn. Greece expanded its territory to include Thessaloniki, and the hinterland was divided among several countries; Turkey was left with only a small territory in Europe; and Thessaloniki itself became separated from its hinterland by a boundary which left the city with only a small trading area. Nevertheless, the city remains the principal natural port of entry for a rather large region.

To combat the impact of the territorial changes of the hinterland after World War I, a free zone was established in 1923. After difficult negotiations between Greece and Serbia — Yugoslavia later — a Yugoslav free zone was officially established in 1929, serving exclusively Yugoslav transit trade.

The history of Thessaloniki at various times has advanced or impeded the natural relationship between the port and its hinterland. The creation of new states and new boundary lines has altered its position with respect to the hinterland, but we have seen from the example of Rotterdam[21] that the free flow of trade between a port and its hinterland is possible, in spite of boundary lines, provided that all neighboring countries are convinced of the economic advantage offered by the port and are prepared to place these economic advantages above political expediency.

During the second half of the nineteenth century, Thessaloniki served as a sea outlet to a population of at least 2 million people —despite the transit of goods from and to Serbia and partly from the Sofia district. No wonder some nineteenth century observers called it the *lung* of a vast economic region, which covered the largest part of Macedonia, part of the Aegean, and part of Thessaly. The good functioning of this "lung" showed, to a certain extent, the general health of the economic body it served.

Notes

1. The first part of this paper, through the Crimean War, was prepared by Dr. Vacalopoulos, and the second by Prof. Tsiovaridou.

2. Κ. Α. Βακαλόπουλος, *Οικονομική λειτουργία του Μακεδονικού και Θρακικού χώρου στα μέσα του 19ου αιώνα στα πλαίσια του διεθνούς εμπορίου,* Εταιρεία Μακεδονικών Σπουδών (Θεσσαλονίκη, 1980) 75.

3. See, Lueben Berov, *The course of commodity turnover at the Port of Thessaloniki and the West European Economic Cycle in the Nineteenth and early Twentieth Century,* elsewhere in this volume.

4. Κ. Α. Βακαλόπουλος, 76.

5. L. Berov, *op. cit.*

6. *Ibid.*

7. Κ. Α. Βακαλόπουλος, 82 *et passim.*

8. Γ. Κ. Χριστοδούλου, *Η Θεσσαλονίκη κατά την τελευταία εκατονταετίαν, Εμπόριον - Βιομηχανία - Βιοτεχνία,* Εκδοτικός Οίκος η «ΕΝΩΣΙΣ» (Θεσσαλονίκη 1936), 113.

9. George W. Hoffman, "The impact of a changing hinterland," *East European Quarterly,* Volume 2, Number 1 (March, 1968), 22; Ι. Κ. Βασδραβέλλη, *Ο λιμήν της Θεσσαλονίκης* (Θεσσαλονίκη 1959), 48.

10. Γ. Κ. Χριστοδούλου, 115.

11. *Ibid.*

12. Milan A. Todorovich, *Salonique et la Question balkanique,* Challamel (Paris, 1913), 9.

13. G. W. Hoffman, 23.

14. Ι. Κ. Βασδραβέλλη, 12, 29.

15. M. A. Todorovich, 48.

16. Γ. Κ. Χριστοδούλου, 151.

17. M. A. Todorovich, 6.

18. *Ibid.,* 14.

19. Κ. Μοσκώφ, *Θεσσαλονίκη 1700-1912, Τομή της μεταπρατικής πόλης,* Στοχαστής (Αθήνα 1973), 31 et *passim.*

20. G. W. Hoffman, 22.

21. G. W. Hoffman, 26.

Liuben Berov

The West European Trade Cycle and Price Movement in the Salonika Economic Region during the Nineteenth and Early Twentieth Centuries

The study of price formation, and particularly of the directions and causes of its changes, is an important element in forming a comprehensive picture of the economic-historical development of every country in the epoch of capitalism. This requires study of the directions and amplitude of the fluctuations of formation of prices of the home market and investigation of their effect on the general trends of development of the economy of a particular country. Of no less importance, however, is the establishment of the ratio of internal and external causes of these fluctuations inasmuch as every country in this epoch still joined more actively the international division of labor and became a link in the world capitalist economy with the cyclic developments which have characterized it since the industrial revolurion.

The problems of price formation in Salonika and its economic region (which, particularly after the construction of the first local railway lines, to a large extent, coincided with Macedonia as a geographic concept) in the epoch of premonopoly capitalism have so far remained inadequately researched in Bulgarian, Yugoslav, and Greek literature, although a number of sources, especially reports of foreign consulates, Turkish court and administrative documents that contain quite a lot of information, albeit fragmentary, about the level of the prices of individual items in the nineteenth and the early twentieth centuries have appeared in the past two decades. It is true that Katardjiev's 1951 monograph offers a cursory review of the changes that occurred in the volume of production, export, and prices of several types of farm produce in the nineteenth century in Macedonia; they were generally linked with the repercussions of wars or other events on the supply of Europe with these commodities.[1] Attempts in this respect are partly present also in the recent studies of Rushkov[2] and Zografski.[3] All this, however, remains in the sphere of more or less general findings with respect to the principal direction of evolution of foreign trade or the economic development of the region as a whole in the nineteenth century. The specific movement of the prices of the principal articles of trade at that time (except the occasional mention of individual examples) is not followed up with a view to reveal the internal and external factors of price formation in Macedonia in the last century, nor to outline the boundaries of the effect of the changing conditions in the world market. There are considerable gaps, and sometimes inaccuracies, in the general characterization of the conjuncture of the basic export goods of Macedonia at that time. No general market price index, or at least a separate group index, for some of the more important items is given, so as to establish the general trends of price movement in the area, the changes taking place in the price structure, the presence or absence of cyclical fluctuations under the impact of the crises of European capitalism, etc.[4]

This paper has set itself the task of contributing to the more specific study of general market conditions, especially the combination of some basic export articles of the Salonika economic region with the change in direction of the prices of the important trade items at that time, recalculated from different sources into a comparable currency and measure, and by approximately outlining the boundaries of the effect of changes in the market in the developed capitalist countries as a factor of price formation in Macedonia. It does not aim at putting into scientific circulation new historical facts; its purpose simply is to give meaning to the information already published on the prices, transportation costs, and other trade conditions, combining it with the available data on the market situation at that time in the main capitalist countries.

Along with the establishment of the changes in the level of the prices of the individual items in nineteenth century Macedonia, an attempt will also be made to compile a general price index in an unchangeable currency (in the actual silver equivalent of the coins then in use) with the level at the end of the eighteenth century taken as a base of 100. The working out of such an index inevitably comes up against great difficulties, owing to fragmentary information, different dates, incomplete geographical homogeneity, differences in the quality of sources in some of the cases, discrepancies in wholesale and retail prices, etc. In this sense, the initial statistical material is far from meeting the formal requirements of accurate statistics. But, as in many similar cases, the economic historian, if he adheres only to the strict requirements of statistics of mass phenomena, should, in all likelihood, sit arms folded, and give up the quantitative study of the past. In such a situation, the attempt to get closer to historical truth should be preferred to the lack of even an approximate knowledge of indicators of the economic reality of that time.

An important prerequisite for achieving these objectives is the necessary comments on the reports of the foreign consuls in Salonika concerning the price level. The inaccuracies in these reports, as to the local capacity and weights, turnover, and prices are not rare; they are due to lack of reliable Turkish official statistics and to inadequate direct knowledge of newly appointed consuls concerning market conditions and local customs. Noticeable, too, are cases of negligence, owing perhaps, to errors of printing or translation.[5] Mistakes encountered have been corrected wherever possible. In the cases where this is not possible,[6] the erroneous data (on the basis of the logic of the market price movement in adjacent years), concerning the unit of measure or the sum and amount of individual sales of some of the commodities studied have been eliminated.

The present study does not set itself the task of following up in greater detail the movement of wages of hired labor in Macedonia, since data in this respect are extremely scanty and do not permit anything more than a tentative outline of a trend of development in the nineteenth century. Scarcity of information as regards wages is easy to explain, given the widespread use of illegal forced or semi-forced labor by the *çiftliks* of the Turkish beys (sometimes paid, but at half the customary rate). Foreign consuls' reports did not pay attention to wages (with only one exception), since they tried to supply merchants in their countries with information about Macedonia as a market of important industrial goods and source of raw materials, but not as a sphere of productive investment of capital.

We exclude from this study the first 75 years of the eighteenth century, and we refer the reader to Svoronos' general index of prices in Salonika,[7] as well as to available group indices for those years. We can do nothing more for that period, in this respect.

The survey of the changes in the market conditions in Macedonia during the nineteenth century is based on an analysis of the movement of prices of 26 items most often encountered in the trade of that time, and for which there is information. Among them are six types of cereals (wheat, maize, rye, barley, oats, and rice), five other agricultural and forestry products (cotton, tobacco, peas, wine, and firewood), eight products of animal origin (wool, cheese, butter, meat, sheep skins, lamb skins, sheep, and eggs), six imported commodities (coffee, sugar, good-quality soap, olive oil, olives, and black pepper), and iron as a competitor of local metallurgy.

This study is based chiefly on data found on the prices of individual goods in different years, scattered among the various reports of the British, French, Belgian, and Italian consuls in Salonika[7] (including a small number of reports of the British consuls in Bitolja),[8] some local commercial almanacs,[9] and travel books,[10] geo-economic studies on Salonika or parts of Macedonia,[11] Turkish court documents from Macedonia,[12] and some other specialized research of Yugoslav and Greek historians concerning the history of tobacco in Macedonia, the evolution of tithes, and so on.[13] These sources, in most cases, provide information about price levels of individual goods in Salonika. Sometimes, they also fix the level of prices in some near or more distant towns in this economic region like Kavalla, Bitolja, etc. It may be generally assumed that the price level in Kavalla did not differ markedly from that in Salonika (except in cases of different grades of the tobaccos exported or other goods). The prices registered in Bitolja and in rare cases in Prilep, Prizren, Seres, and certain other villages sometimes have been recalculated, whenever possible, as probable selling prices in Salonika on the basis of adding the likely transportation costs to the port of Salonika. But, this is not always possible, owing to the absence of information about the level of transportation costs to Salonika for each year and for all types.

In comparisons with the price levels for specific items in Great Britain, France, the USA, Germany, and Austria-Hungary, countries connected with the Salonika commerce during the epoch studied, we have proceeded from the official statistical year books of the countries concerned from the late nineteenth and early twentieth centuries (including some surveys in authoritative economic periodicals of the time),[14] and for the earlier decades of the nineteenth century—from some official retrospective publications of French and American statistics,[15] British statistical periodicals of the second half of the century,[16] and some special studies of individual authors.[17]

The largest amount of information about the movement of prices can be systematized with respect to Salonika's principal export items in the nineteenth century — cotton, tobacco, and cereals.

At the end of the eighteenth century, cotton prices were relatively stable, but not high (recalculated in stable currency they fluctuated around 1.1 French francs for 1803-14 for one kg of unginned cotton). The cause for this was the weak demand of Europe's industry. During the Napoleonic Wars, restrictions of cotton exports from the United States were removed and prices in Salonika soared temporarily. In the 1820s and 1830s, the demand for cotton on the European market was strong, but it was met chiefly by the rapidly growing export of comparatively cheap cotton from the plantations in the American south. This led to a fall in prices in Salonika (especially in the 1840s).

During the first half of the 1860s, again, a favorable market situation was reached, thanks to the American Civil War. This made it possible for the price, calculated in stable currency, at times, to reach 5.3 francs per kg of cotton. During the second half of the decade, prices were again back to normal, owing to fierce competition by Egyptian cotton. After a temporary rise in prices, because of local conditions in 1876-78, they stabilized in the 1880s approximately at the same level of a century earlier.

In the 1890s the price of Macedonian cotton in Salonika dropped under pressure from a prolonged worldwide crisis in production, thereby causing a drop in the price of American and Egyptian cotton, but local competition in Macedonian agriculture kept prices from dipping to the degree it did in London. From the end of the 1890s, owing to the growing consumption of the developing local cotton textile industry, export of cotton from Salonika was almost discontinued, and the price of Egyptian cotton (burdened by the corresponding transportation costs to Salonika) became the limiting factor for the cotton price level on the local market.

Analysis of the information leads to the conclusion that the commercial capital in Salonika, on the whole, read correctly its bearings on the European nineteenth century cotton market and made good use of temporarily favorable conditions.

It is more difficult to follow up the evolution of the tobacco prices in Salonika, owing to the presence of the much greater differences in the quality of the leaf by areas. Tobacco prices in Macedonia at the end of the eighteenth century were satisfactory and were equal to about 1.3-1.4 French francs per kg of dry tobacco. After that, however, there appeared a downward trend (although with fluctuations in certain years) which went on until the second third of the nineteenth century. Even the American Civil War did not create conditions for raising Macedonian tobacco prices, since the export of American tobacco (which from the 1830s had begun to play a role in the commerce of the Levant) was not considerably reduced and continued to compete with Macedonian tobaccos in Italy, Austria, and even North Africa. A more considerable, temporary rise in prices in the Salonika economic region occurred only in the turbulent years from 1876 to 1881, when some tobacco-growing areas were temporarily taken out of production. The growing tobacco consumption in Europe, especially during the stages of cyclic industrial upturn in the 1880s and 1890s and the 1900s in the developed capitalist countries, contributed to this raise in prices of Macedonian tobaccos, reaching an average export price of up to 3 francs per kg. Village producers, however, failed to take full advantage of changes in tobacco taxation.

Basic cereal prices were at first comparatively low, largely owing to the presence of a system of obligatory state deliveries in the Ottoman empire up to 1837-42 (although ever more liberally applied in Salonika at the end of the eighteenth and the beginning of the nineteenth centuries). After a temporary upward turn during the Napoleonic Wars, wheat in the Salonika economic region during the second quarter of the nineteenth century, once again, fell to a comparatively low level under pressure from cheap Russian and Indian wheat. This, along with the abolition of the system of obligatory state deliveries for the needs of Constantinople and the army, seems to have brought about a certain reduction in the areas sown with principal cereals, and a shift to such industrial crops as tobacco, raw opium, sesame, hemp, cotton, oleaginous seeds, and so on. Despite this, the export of cereals from Salonika fell considerably in comparison with the situation at the end of the previous century.

In the 1860s prices rose somewhat as a result of the weakened competition of Russian wheat, which was very cheap until the emancipation of serfs in 1861, and the rising price of the competitive Romanian wheat after the mildly radical agrarian reform of 1864. Of less importance was the drop in the rate of the freight at least in the eastern Mediterranean, which facilitated the access of Macedonian wheat to Greek and Italian ports. In the last quarter of the century, there followed a downward trend, owing to the 1873 depression in Western Europe and the continuous crisis in agriculture in the whole of Europe up to the last years of the nineteenth century; the push downward was further strengthened by the sharply increased competition of cheap American wheat; Russian wheat continued to be a dangerous competitor as well. The sharp drop in freight from the beginning of the 1870s played an important role in strengthening the competitiveness of American, and even of Russian, wheat. The net effect was, however, offset by years of poor harvests, uprisings, and local wars. Only with the end of the European agricultural crisis at the dawn of the twentieth century did wheat prices in Salonika rise again.

Our analysis shows that the prices of wheat and other export cereals in the economic region of Salonika were as a rule considerably higher than those in northern Bulgaria and Thrace. This can be explained by the closer proximity of Salonika or Kavalla as the principal ports of Macedonia for exports to Italy, France, and other Mediterranean countries.

The evolution of the prices of the other more important cereals was to a large extent analogous to that of wheat, although their position in the market was sometimes distinguished by certain specific features. The ratio between foreign and domestic price factors differed from those of wheat since foreign competition and changes in European market conditions usually played a more restricted role.

The prices of imported vegetables, such as coffee, olive oil, olives, etc., fluctuated, owing to fluctuating conditions in the exporting countries, changes in transport to Salonika, and so on. Ultimately, they did not account for lasting changes in price levels calculated in a stable currency (silver equivalent).

More specific was the change in the price of animal products, which could be divided into two subgroups: export articles and those for domestic consumption. For exports of animal origin, the growing demand on the European market led to a price rise. On the domestic scene, no change occured in the supply-and-demand ratio.

The picture was different in the prices of industrial products. As a rule, they fell as the industrial revolution advanced in Western and Central Europe, although changes were not always in the same direction. A typical example is provided by the prices of sugar and iron. Similar phenomona can be observed in studies of other regions.

In sum, the individual items studied lead to some general conclusions about the level of prices in the Salonika economic area, and in Macedonia in general during the nineteenth century. In the first place, it should be noted that, for the majority of goods, price levels in a silver equivalent was on an average higher than in the seventeenth century. This is seen from the following comparison of the recalculated silver equivalent of prices of some items in Macedonia in 1623-39 and in 1888-91 (in grams of pure silver per kilogram of commodity):[18]

	1623-39	*1888-91*
Rice	0.39	1.37
Barley	0.40-0.25	0.52
Wheat	0.71	0.75
Olives	1.80	2.34
Non-melted butter	2.51-3.10	7.10
Soap	2.14-2.80	3.90
Honey	3.12	4.55[19]
Wax	3.12-3.51	5.00[20]
Milk	0.31-0.39	0.45-1.11[19]
Candles, wax	3.12	4.09[19]
Grapes	0.25-0.58	0.28-0.33[20]
Cabbage	0.19	0.22[19]
Cheese	0.98	0.98
Coffee	17.90	8.60
Meat	0.58-1.74	0.62
Cotton	7.50	5.10
Olive oil	4.18	3.70
Apples	0.48-0.58	0.22[20]

The results in silver equivalent show that the degree of the rise in price for individual goods was quite different, and a decrease in some cases. This testifies to the considerable instability of the price structure over a two-hundred-year period. No law governed regularities, however, for some general relative outstripping or lagging of prices by groups of commodities did occur.

In the second place, it should be pointed out that the level of the prices during the nineteenth century, with the exception of cereals, was, as a rule, fairly lower than that in northern Bulgaria and Thrace. This is seen from the following comparison of the prices of some items in Macedonia in 1886 and in Bulgaria in 1887 (recalculated in grams of silver per kilogram of commodity):[21]

	Macedonia	*Bulgaria*		*Macedonia*	*Bulgaria*
Rice	1.37	2.25	Sugar	2.02	3.47
Cheese	0.98	3.02	Wheat	0.76	0.66
Butter	7.10	7.22	Rye	0.52	0.48
Wool	5.37	6.07	Barley	0.56	0.47
Olive oil	3.70	6.30	Oats	0.57	0.40
Wine	0.78	1.17	Maize	0.50	0.49
Coffee	8.05	13.30			

The equalization of price levels between the two regions did not take place until the end of the nineteenth century, since they were actually two regions economically separated from each other, and the economic links between Macedonia, on the one hand, and northern Bulgaria, Thrace, and even the Sofia region, on the other, were limited. Northern Bulgaria, as far as exports were concerned, was oriented toward the Danube and partly toward Varna, and Thrace — toward the port of Burgas and partly toward that of Dedeagach (particularly after the construction of the Constantinople-Belovo-Nova Zagora railway line with a branch to Dedeagach in 1873-74). But, Macedonia, as far as exports were concerned, was oriented chiefly southward to Salonika and partly northward across Serbia to Austria-Hungary (the importance of the port of Durazzo as a maritime outlet for part of the output of Macedonia declined a great deal from the beginning of the eighteenth century onward). Import routes were also correspondingly different. It is true that up to the gradual decline in importance of the big fairs as intermediaries in supplying the Bulgarian lands with imported goods, a large part of the import trade of the Sofia region passed through Salonika and Seres. But after the construction of the railway from Constantinople to Belovo, this link began to weaken quickly, and after 1886, was fully abolished. The limited export production of the Sofia region (including the areas of Dupnitse, modern Stanke Dimitrov, Samokov, Pernik, and Kyustendil) was not practically directed to the south. Samokov iron was sometimes sold in the northern part of Vardar, Macedonia, and occasionally reached Prilep, but southward it found no real outlet, owing to the iron from Nevrokop. Until the mid-nineteenth century, there also existed certain links in the supply of wool and fabrics between Macedonia and Thrace, but, later, they ceased completely, and the corresponding trade routes through the Rhodope Mountains became deserted. Seldom and in small quantities was the artisanal production of the settlements in the valleys south of the Stara Planina Range directed to Macedonia. It is true, nonetheless, that Bulgarian merchants from Karlovo and Samokov sold kerchiefs, braid and woollen cloth worth 2 million piastres at the Prilep fair in August 1864,[22] but this constituted a mere one-tenth of the total turnover of the fair.

The relatively low level of the prices of animal products was a characteristic feature of the price structure in the Salonika economic region and in Macedonia generally. According to evaluations of 1801 estate registers, one Bitolja kilo of 75 okkas (96.51) of wheat cost from 1320 to 1800 aspers, whereas an ox cost 3000-3600, and a cow 1800-2640.[23] This means that, at the beginning of the century, an ox cost only as much as 133-159 kg of wheat and a cow — 80-117 kg. Again, in 1800-1801, one okka of cheese cost 18 paras as compared with 1200-2040 paras for one Vardar kilo of 85 okkas of wheat.[24] This meant that one kilogram of cheese cost almost as much as one kilogram of wheat. This state of affairs did not improve much over the century, since, in 1891, again, one kilogram of cheese cost as much as 1.3 kg of wheat. The relatively low level of the prices of animal products can be seen from the fact that, in 1887, in Bulgaria, one kilogram of cheese cost as much as 4.7 kilograms of wheat, an ox — 655 kilograms and a cow 405 kilograms of wheat.[25] It was only about 1910 that the relative level of animal products in the Salonika economic region and generally in Macedonia improved considerably.

Compiling a general statistical index of the results obtained concerning the prices of the studied goods, converted into a silver equivalent and a metric measure, is connected with great difficulties and inevitable traditional assessments of the heterogenous and fragmentary data. Difficulties also arise in choosing a base year, since a year is lacking in which all the items studied are present. As a conditional base year, we chose 1888, but, for some items, the index includes the closest year.[26] For other commodities, it is based on hypothetical projections.[27] Thus, we find:[28]

End of the nineteenth century - 85 (7)[29]	1828 - 140 (2)	1861 - 139 (10)
	1829 - 97 (3)	1862 - 154 (17)
1800 - 135 (12)	1830 - 131 (2)	1863 - 149 (14)
1801 - 112 (9)	1831 - 72 (6)	1864 - 141 (19)
1802 - 132 (3)	1832 - 86 (9)	1865 - 103 (4)
1803 - 139 (7)	1833 - 100 (11)	1866 - 154 (7)
1804 - 124 (5)	1834 - 124 (2)	1867 - 116 (7)
1805 - 151 (4)	1835 - 76 (11)	1868 - 113 (2)
1806 - 160 (4)	1836 - 123 (2)	1871 - 118 (2)
1807 - 142 (7)	1837 - 83 (9)	1875 - 130 (4)
1808 - 135 (7)	1838 - 107 (3)	1876 - 257 (8)
1809 - 150 (7)	1839 - 106 (3)	1877 - 219 (7)
1810 - 180 (4)	1840 - 106 (3)	1878 - 130 (2)
1811 - 190 (4)	1841 - 106 (3)	1879 - 181 (7)
1812 - 157 (5)	1842 - 112 (2)	1880 - 158 (7)
1813 - 189 (12)	1844 - 118 (2)	1881 - 130 (6)
1814 - 189 (6)	1847 - 118 (2)	1882 - 136 (2)
1815 - 184 (4)	1848 - 131 (7)	1883 - 109 (10)
1816 - 176 (4)	1849 - 207 (4)	1884 - 117 (4)
1817 - 249 (4)	1850 - 145 (4)	1885 - 148 (7)
1818 - 198 (4)	1851 - 115 (2)	1886 - 104 (12)
1819 - 183 (3)	1852 - 203 (3)	1887 - 146 (2)
1820 - 178 (3)	1853 - 183 (4)	1888 - 106 (14)
1821 - 185 (2)	1854 - 197 (4)	1889 - 112 (8)
1822 - 177 (2)	1855 - 202 (3)	1890 - 151 (2)
1823 - 169 (2)	1856 - 202 (3)	1891 - 132 (11)
1824 - 162 (2)	1857 - 201 (3)	1896 - 105 (7)
1825 - 116 (10)	1858 - 111 (2)	1902 - 89 (3)
1826 - 149 (2)	1859 - 127 (12)	1907 - 120 (12)
1827 - 145 (2)	1860 - 142 (8)	1909-1910 - 183 (13)

It is true that the results obtained in this way inevitably contain a considerable dose of conditionality. In reality, the changes in the general level of prices in some years probably were not so abrupt as they look. But, even the occasionally inaccurate statistical generalization provides a certain knowledge about the phenomena studied, and in the absence of a possibility of something better, it should be preferable to the lack of any knowledge whatever.

Clearly, the results obtained outline the trend toward a rapid rise in the cost of living in the Napoleonic War years, with a peak in 1811 and 1813-14, which was followed by a still greater jump in 1817. After that, the general level of prices dropped rapidly, and the downward trend continued up to the beginning of the 1830s. At that time, prices fell below the level at the end of the eighteenth and the first years of the nineteenth centuries. About the middle of the second half of the 1830s, the downward trend fluctuated, and in the 1840s, was again replaced by an upward thrust which peaked during the Crimean War, and a new jump of prices around 1863-64. The very hesitant development from the middle of the 1870s, in the ultimate analysis, was, nevertheless, directed to a downward trend of prices at the end of the century. It continued up to 1902 inclusive, and only after that was it replaced by a rise in prices up to the Balkan Wars. This shows that, unlike West European countries, but like the case with Bulgaria,[30] Macedonia underwent a few years later the prolonged crisis fall in prices in capitalist Europe, until the last years of the nineteenth century.

The general price index obtained allows us to evaluate, albeit in most general terms, the trend in the development of nominal and real wa es in the Salonika economic area and generally in Macedonia. If we systematize the isolated pieces of information available, the following picture emerges (wages recalculated in the silver equivalent of grams of pure silver):

	unskilled workers	*master bricklayers*
1819[31]	40 to 45 paras	1.63 to 2 piastres
	(2.26-2.54 g silver)	(3.67-4.52 g silver)
1834[32]	2.5 piastres	4 piastres
	(1.79 g silver)	(2.85 g silver)

1839[33]	1.5 to 3 piastres	4 to 5 piastres
	(1.06-2.13 g silver)	(2.85-3.55 g silver)
1883[34]	1.3 to 2 piastres	3.25 to 4 piastres
	(1.30-2.00 g silver)	(3.25-4.00 g silver)

If this evolution of the silver equivalent of wages in Salonika and other towns of Macedonia at the beginning and the end of the nineteenth century is compared with the movement in the general price index, it should be generally assumed that real wages did not change substantially, or that there was a trend toward an increase.[35] At first glance, 1819 nominal wages in a silver equivalent exceeded by 15-30 percent those in 1883, but, the 1819 price index was considerably higher as well.

The question then arises of the domestic and foreign factors in the fluctuations of market prices. It is admittedly absurd to think that the market fluctuations were due to some autonomous cycle of development of Macedonian capitalism. The weak beginnings of capitalist enterprises in Salonika and some other towns of Macedonia during the last third of the nineteenth century, and even up to 1912, could in no way be regarded as sufficiently economically complex to claim an autonomous capitalist cycle of its own, and independent of the West European economy. And yet, without fully denying the role of some extremes in local harvests, in the final analysis, the conclusion gains ground that the chief factor for the changes in Macedonia was the influence of the West European economy through foreign trade, and in part, credits connected to it. This is sufficiently clear from the following chart where the general price index of the Thessaloniki economic region is compared with the general indices of wholesale prices in Britain and France.[36]

The three graphic lines show a considerable degree of parallelism in market conditions, although, sometimes, from a more general point of view. Until the end of the Napoleonic Wars, this phenomenon was inevitably disrupted by the almost complete interruption of the maritime trade of Salonika and its economic region with Western Europe and Italy. But, the parallelism worked both in the movement of prices downward in Britain in 1816 as in their turn upward in 1817. A notable exception, the fall of prices in the Salonika economic region and generally in Macedonia during the early 1820s (when Britain enjoyed an upsurge in price around 1822-23) can be explained by the disruption of trade in connection with the Greek Uprising of 1821. The fall in prices in the 1830s echoed that in Britain and France. Salonika responded to an upturn in Britain in 1836, as it did to a slump in the following year, and then to a temporary rise in the prices in 1838-39 (but not to the crisis in 1840). We see, too, a discrepancy between changes in the Salonika economic region and Western Europe at the end of the 1840s, but a considerable degree of parallelism appears with an ascending movement in the mid-50s.

Very clearly, upon the Salonika economic region and generally in Macedonia, is the slide in prices in Western Europe in 1857-59. After the mid-1860s[37] there again appears a parallelism in Salonika and Western Europe during the crisis of 1865-66. Fairly parallel, too, the upturn in the capitalist economy up to 1873 (but, the depression in fall of 1873, however, had no visible effect in Macedonia). The political events in the Balkans (the April Uprising, the Russo-Turkish War of Liberation, etc.) temporarily disturbed the synchronization of price movements in the Salonika economic region and Western Europe. But, by the 1880s, the similarities are, once more, apparent in the general downward trend in prices (despite certain fluctuations in Salonika). We see the same mechanism in the upward turn of prices on the eve of the 1890 depression in Western Europe, as well as the ensuing fall up to 1896. But, recovery came only to Salonika at the turn of the century, though.

All this means that, for the last two-thirds of the nineteenth century, the Salonika economic region and Macedonia generally forged an indivisible link with the world capitalist economy, and for this reason, market conditions, notwithstanding the country's considerable backwardness, in general, moved in unison with the cyclic fluctuations in the developed countries of Western and Central Europe. It is very difficult, indeed (owing to the absence of studies on the national income or the national product of Macedonia up to 1912), to assess what part of the gross national product of Macedonia passed through the foreign-trade channels, but obviously this part was sufficient to exercise, thanks to its linkage to world prices, a strong influence on local market conditions. The most approximate calculations for

1910 show that up to 20 percent of the national product of Macedonia passed through import or export channels (in the mid-nineteenth century, this percentage was much lower).

We should also raise the question of how this linkage made itself felt on the Macedonian economy. Some authors claim that trade with Western Europe had a negative effect on agriculture and led to the impoverishment of the peasants.[38] This is an oversimplification of propaganda importance. The results obtained about the movement of prices of basic Macedonian farm exports in a stable currency, do not testify to a fall in prices below the level of the late century (with the partial exception, perhaps, of tobacco).

Moreover, in this case, another elementary consideration is forgotten. Every country, if it wishes to join the international division of labor and use the products of other peoples it lacks, should manage with the aid of some products of its own national labor to win its place in the international market and thereby, with the inevitable equalization with labor productivity of more developed countries and with the existing level in value and prices of individual commodities. Nineteenth century Macedonia might have not exported its agricultural produce to Western or Central Europe, but in this situation (owing to the lack of funds), it would not have had a chance to import from Europe products of more developed industry, or agricultural produce not produced, or insufficiently produced, in Macedonia, such as coffee, spices, rice, olive oil, olives, etc. Here, Tokugawa Japan as an unsuccessful example of economic and political isolation serves our purposes. For, in Macedonia, although the peasants would not have been ruined (everyone would have produced cereals and other types of farm produce for his own needs and for an elementary exchange of artisan articles), the country as a whole, in splendid isolation, would have remained at a low artisanal level of consumption that was characteristic of Europe up to the seventeenth century. Macedonia's shortcoming in the nineteenth century was not in its participation in international trade, but in its very slow adaptation under Ottoman domination to the newer conditions of an ever-expanding industrial revolution, and therefore backward in industry and agriculture, it became an appendage to developed European capitalist countries.

Notes

1. Iv. Katardzhiev, *Serskata oblast, 1870-1879. Ekonomski, politichki i kulturen pregled* (= The Seres region, 1870-1879), (Skopje, 1961), 60-87.

2. T. Rushkov, "Obsti Karakteristiki na nadvoreshnata trgovija na Makedonia vo vtorata polovina na XIX vek" (= Common characteristics of export trade in Macedonia in the second half of the 19th c.), *Godishnik na Pravniot Fakultet* (Skopje, 1965), 225-54.

3. D. Zografski, "Nadvoreshnata trgovija na Makedonija od srednata na XVIII vek do pochetokot na XX vek" (= Export trade in Macedonia from the end of the 18th to the beginning of the 20th century), *Godishnik na Ekonomskiot Fakultet* (Skopje, 1962), 53-56.

4. The absence in the literature so far of an index of the market prices in Macedonia is to a large extent due to objective reasons. Among them, stress should be laid on the greater fragmentariness of the available data on the prices in Macedonia in the still incomplete process of publishing certain sources in this respect. True, from the beginning of the 1860s, some Macedonian historians engaged in a most useful work, which for Bulgaria in the past was done by the eminent bibliographer N. Mihov: the retrieval and publication of the consular reports and some other official documents of the nineteenth century. As far as the wealth of specific information (especially about the prices and changes) is concerned, the reports of the consuls in Salonika, Kavalla, and Bitolja are considerably inferior to those of the foreign consuls in Ruse and Varna. In ansolute and relative terms, less numerous and poorer in information about prices is the historical literature about inhabited localities in Macedonia in which one does not come across works of the kind of Tsonchev's valuable monograph on the economic past of Gabrovo.

5. In some instances are encountered translator's errors which may be removed by checking up on the archival original published in parallel. E.g., in the text of one of the reports of the British consul in Salonika of 1835 the measure quarter is erroneously translated as "kilolitre" (cf. *Britanski dokumenti za istorijata na makedonskiot narod* (= British documents on the history of the Macedonian people), v. 1. 1797-1839, Skopje, 1968, 88 and 247). But in most cases of publishing such reports only the translation is given without the original text.

6. Some cases of obvious negligence where outside indications are lacking do not permit the establishing of the actual situation. E.g., in the report of the British consul in Salonika of March 1835 according to the data in piastres and a local measure, a ratio of the price of barley to that of wheat of 1:2.64 is obtained, whereas according to the data in British currency it is 1:3.52. The ratio of the prices of barley and sesame according to the same report in Turkish currency is 1:4.55, and in British 1:5.26. It is impossible to establish which of them is more correct.

7. N. Svoronos, *Le commerce de Salonique aux XVIIIe siècle* (Paris, 1956), 80-81. The author does not include wheat in the general price index owing to difficulties in weighing its higher specific gravity and to the great fluctuations in its prices in poor harvests.

8. *Britanski dokumenti za istorijata na makedonskiot narod* (= British documents on the history of the macedonian people), v.I. 1797-1839g. (Skopje, 1968); v.II. 1840-1847 g. (Skopje, 1977); v.III. 1848-1856g. (Skopje, 1982); *Francuzski dokumenti za istorijata na makedonskiot narod* (= French documents on the history of the Macedonian people), v. I. 1878-1879g. (Skopje, 1979); Al. Matkovski, P. Angelakova, "Izveshtai na francuzkite konzuli od Solun od 1887 do 1889 godina" (= Reports of the French consuls in Salonika from 1887 to 1889), *Glasnik* INI, XVI, Skopje, 1972, no 1, 212 *et passim*; Al. Matkovski, P. Angelakova, "Izveshtaina belgiiskite konzuli izprakani od Solun od 13. IV. 1859 do 8. VIII. 1871g." (= Reports of the Belgian consuls sent from Salonika from 13.IV.1859 to 8.VIII.1871), *Glasnik* INI, XV, Skopje, 1971, no 3, 227 *et passim*; Al. Matkovski, P. Angelakova, "Izveshtai na italjanskite konzulio od Solun za 1861, 1882 i 1863 godina" (= Reports of the Italian consuls in Salonika from 1861, 1882 and 1863), *Glasnik* INI, XVII, Skopje, 1978, no 3, 190 *et passim*; D. Zografski, "Izveshtai na britanskite konzuli vo Bitola od sheesettite godini na XIXv." (= Reports of the British consuls in Bitola in the 60s of the 19th century), *Glasnik* INI, XX, Skopje, 1976, no. 1, 219 *et passim*. Some data from consular reports in later years of the 1890s and the beginning of the 1900s are published in *Preussisches Handelsarchiv* (later *Deutsches Handelsarchiv*, Berlin).

9. *Annuaire commerciale et administratif du vilayet de Salonique.* Publié par I. S. Modiano, I (Salonika, 1908).

10. V. Kŭnchov, *Izbrani proizvedenija* (= Selected works), v. 1. (Sofija, 1970); P. Koruev, *Selo Gabrovo, Ksantijsko* (= The village Gabrovo, Ksantijsko), (Sofija, 1964) et al.

11. At. Ishirkov, *Grad Solun* (= The city of Salonika), (Sofija, 1911); I. G. Senkevich, "Kon prashanjetop za ekonomskiot zhivot na Bitolskiot vilaet vo 80-90 godina na XIX vek" (= On the question of economic life in the vilayet of Bitola in the 80s and 90s of the 19th century), *Glasnik* INI, 11, Skopje, 1967, no. 3, 167; Hr. Andonov-Poljanski, "Kon istorijata na trgovijata na Bitola i Bitolsko v 1856 godina" (= About the history of the trade in Bitola and its region in 1856), *Glasnik* INI, 16, Skopje, 1972, no. 3, 203; Gl. Todorovski, "Selskoto stopanstvo vo Vardarska Makedonija po Balkanskite vojni 1912-1913 g." (= Rural economy in Vardar Macedonia after the Balkan wars, 1912-1913), *Glasnik* INI, 21, Skopje, 1977, no 1, 135.

12. *Turski dokumenti za makedonskata istorija* (= Turkish documents on Macedonian history), v. I. 1800-1803 (Skopje, 1951); v. II. 1803-1808 (Skopje, 1953); v. III. 1809-1817 (Skopje, 1955); v. IV. 1816-1827 (Skopje, 1957); v. V. 1827-1859 (Skopje, 1958).

13. Kr. Bitoski, "Za dvesetokot i zemjedelskoto proizvodstvo vo Makedonija kon krajot na XIX i pochetokot na XX vek" (= On the dime and agricultural production in Macedonia at the end of the 19th and the beginning of the 20th century), *Glasnik* INI, 11, Skopje, 1967, no. 3, 83; Zl. Biljanovski, "Nekoi podatoci za nadvoreshnata trgovija na Mekedonija vo vremeto od Krimskata do Balkanskata vojna" (= Notes on the export trade in Maçedonia at the time of the

Crimean and the Balkan wars), *Glasnik* INI, VI, Skopje, 1962, nos 1-2, 195; N. Gheron, *Die Handelsbeziehungen zwischen Leipzig und Ost- und Südosteuropa bis zum Verfall der Warenmessen*, Zürich, 1920; L. Lape, "Prilog kon izuchavanjeto na drushstveno-ekonomskite i politichki priliki na Makedonija vo XVIII vek" (= Contribution to the study of the socio-economic and political conditions in Macedonia in the 18th century), *Glasnik* INI, 2, Skopje, 1958, no 1, 91; L. Berov, "Roljata na zadŭlzhitelnite dŭrzhavni dostavki vŭv vŭtreshnata i vŭneshnata tŭrgovija na bŭlgarskite zemi prez XVI-XIXv." (= The role of the compulsory state commission in the domestic and foreign trade in the Bulgarian countries in the 16-19th century), in *Istorija na tŭrgovijata na bulgarskite zemi prez XV-XIXv*, Sofija, 1978; Al. Matkovski, *Gurchin Kokaleski 1775-1863g.* (= Gurchin Kokaleski, 1775-1863), Skopje, 1959; Kl. Dzhambazovski, "Za karavanskiot transport vo Makedonija" (= On the caravan transportation in Macedonia), *Glasnik* INI, 4, Skopje, 1959, nos 1-2, 274.

14. E.g., *Zeitschrift für Nationalökonomie und Statistik* (Jena).

15. *Historical Statistics of the United States* (New York, 1949); *Annuaire statistique de la France 1937*, Apercu retrospectif (Paris, 1937).

16. *Journal of the Statistical Society* (London).

17. P. Guetter, *Statistical Tables to the Economic Growth of the United States* (Philadelphia, 1924); Th. Tooke, W. Newmarch, *Die Geschichte und Bestimmung der Preise Während der Jahre 1793-1857* (Dresden, 1862), I; I. G. Esteban, "Trends and Cycles in the U.S. Trade with Spain and the Spanish Empire 1790-1819," *The Journal of Economic History*, vol. XLIV (June, 1984), no. 2; M. N. Sobolev, *Tamozhennaja politika Rossii vo vtoroj polovine XIX veka* (= Customs policy of Russia in the second half of the 19th century). Tomsk, 1911; R. Al. Barani, *Ekonomicheskoe razvitie Egipta v novoe vremja* (= Economic development of Egypt in modern times), Moskva, 1954.

18. For 1623-39 recalculated from initial data of *Turski dokumenti* (= Turkish documents)..., v. I, 141; v. II, 157-58; v. III, 62-64, 180. The prices have been recalculated on the assumption that the "akçe" coin of that time weighed 0.33 g of a 750/1000 standard and contained 0.25 g of pure silver.

19. The data refer to 1801-1803 (there are no data for 1888-91).

20. The data refer to 1831 (there are no data for 1888-91).

21. For Bulgaria recalculated from *Statisticheski godishnik* (= Statistical yearbook) ..., 4, Sofija, 1914, 261-263. For the cheese, butter, olive oil, and wine the comparison is for the prices in 1890 in Bulgaria and 1891 in Macedonia (for Bulgaria there is no information for 1891 since in the special publication of the chief Department of Statistics *Statistika na cenite na stokite na edro i drebno* (= Statistics of wholesale and retail prices), Sofija, 1937 (the earliest data are of 1895). For 1887-94, only the general price index has been preserved.

22. D. Zografski, *Izveshtai* (= Reports)...., v. I, 243-45.

23. *Turski dokumenti* (= Turkish documents) ..., v. I, 95-97, 98.

24. *Turski dokumenti* (= Turkish documents) .., v. I, 101-102.

25. Calculated after *Statisticheski godishnik na Bŭlgarskoto carstvo* (= Statistical yearbook of the Bulgarian kingdom), IV. 1912, 6., 1914, 259-61,

26. As base of the index, we have chosen 1888 since this is a year for which information is available about the greater part of the articles studied (13 of a total of 25 commodities). For those items about which there is no information concerning their 1888 prices, as base of the individual indices has been taken one of the neighboring years with available information (for olive oil — 1863, tobacco — 1861, sheep — 1860, cheese — 1833, rice and oats — 1883, wine and meat — 1891). This slightly violates the formal requirements for the calculation of a general price index but it is the only way of surmounting the already noted great fragmentariness of information. The general price index in Macedonia in the nineteenth century is an unweighted one, since with the sketchy statistical information concerning the quantity of production and the sum of sales by items and by years, it is impossible to do some weighting of the individual indices.

27. For some imported goods with prices almost stable during a particular decade (e.g., soap and sugar in the 1850s and 1860s) where there are gaps in the information of but a few years, it has been assumed that the price in the intermediate years with missing information was at the level of the middle between the two results for the close years with available information. The price of firewood was relatively stable in individual places in the sense that it did not depend on some foreign competition or on local market fluctuations and was a function primarily of the level of the wages of unskilled labor, the growing demand of the urban population and the worsening conditions of wood production with the diminishing forests (the competition of coal in the last third of the nineteenth century played a limited role). On account of that, we assume that during the years between 1801 and 1910, for which specific information is lacking about the prices of firewood, the index of their prices changed evenly according to the difference between the close years with available information (the price for 1803 is taken as valid for the three earliest years of the index). The position was similar with the prices of meat which went up more only in years of a general high cost of living. Their index has been supplemented similarly to that of wood (the price of 1891 is taken as valid up to 1910). This has not been done with respect to cheese and butter, since they have always been also goods exported to Constantinople and Greece.

28. In the recalculation of the prices, the adjustment of the foreign gold and silver coins to a silver equivalent has been carried out in accordance with their official content of pure gold or silver, and not with their current rate to the Turkish piastre, since information is lacking for this rate for each separate group. Some prices of individual items, sharply deviating from the results for close years (probably due to errors in the source), such as the price of tobacco in 1888, of rice in 1847, wool in 1891 and sheep skins in 1885, have not been taken into account in calculating the general index. Where a minimum and a maximum price are indicated for a particular year in the sources, the arithmetical mean of these two prices has been accepted. Where possible, the relative geographic homogeneity of the data has been taken into consideration and in the case of major price differences between Salonika and the interior of Macedonia, only the data for Salonika have been taken (if there is parallel information). In the absence of parallel information,

sometimes no approximate adjustment has been made of the Bitolja prices to the probable Salonika price, since the relative value of the differences between the prices in the two towns was rather unstable by years and items.

29. The number of items about which there is information is given in brackets

30. In Bulgaria, the fall in prices at the end of the nineteenth century reached its lowest point in 1901, after which a rise in prices began.

31. *Turski dokumenti* (= Turkish documents) ... v. IV, 36-37. The fixing refers to stone carriers and "mud mixers" in Bitolja. There is no information about the wages of master bricklayers (the information is about "master builders" and "master house-painters").

32. *Turski dokumenti* (= Turkish documents) ... v. V, 80. The data refer to master and apprentice bricklayers in Bitolja.

33. *Ibid.*, 122. The data refer to master and worker carpenters and stonemasons employed in the building of Turkish barracks. The fixing was of the *kadi* of Bitolja of March 1839 when the money reform had not yet been carried through.

34. Al. Matkovski, P. Angelakova, "Izveshtai i....." (= Reports), *Glasnik* 1972, no 1, 240. The data refer to Salonika. The consul gives the wages in French francs, but it seems that they are in local currency (piastres).

35. A trend toward an increase was noticeable in the nineteenth century also in other regions of the Balkans. See, L. Berov, "Wages in the Balkan Lands during Manufacturing Capitalism and the Industrial Revolution," *Bulgarian Historical Review* (1978), no. 4, 39-58; L. Berov, "Le salaire des ouvrieres qualifiés dans les pays balkaniques au cours de 1 periode du cpitalisme manufacturière et de la revolution industrielle," *Etudes Balkaniques* (1976), no 1, 30-54; L. Berov, "Le salaire des fonctionnaires d'état et communales dans les pays balkaniques au course de la periode du capitalism manufacturière et de la revolution industrielle," *Etudes balkaniques* (1980), no. 2, 36-62.

36. For Britain (base 1913 = 100) after E. Wageman, *Struktur und Rythmus der Weltwirtschaft* (Berlin, 1931), appendix; for France, (base 1901-10 = 100), according to *Annuaire statistique de la France, 1937*. Resumé retrospectif (Paris, 1938), 440. The data on France for 1857-1900 cover the prices of 43 imported commodities (for 1820-56-45 commodities). In both countries many of the items observed during the period of one century are not identical (there are many cases of changes of the sort, replacement of a commodity by another, etc.). There are no generalized data on Austria. We do not include Germany because this would make difficult the following up of the chart with many interweavings of the lines with a considerable degree of parallelism with the evolution of the conjuncture in Britain and France.

37. The big fall in prices in Macedonia observed in 1863-64 did not coincide with the continuing economic pickup in the principal capitalist countries at that time, but was one of the first crisis warnings of glutting the market primarily with imported goods "more than can be sold" (D. Zografski, "Izveshtai..." (= Reports) 243).

38. Al. Matkovski, *Gurchin Kokaleski 1775-1863g.* (= Gurchin Kokaleski, 1775-1863), 25,

Constantin A. Vacalopoulos

Commercial Development and Economic Importance of the Port of Thessaloniki from the Late Eighteenth Century to 1856

Various events, of political import, of the eighteenth century, such as the Treaty of Kioutchouk Kainardgi (1774), the French Revolution, the Napoleonic Wars, and the breaking of the English blockade of France by Greek ships transformed the port of Thessaloniki into one of the most important trading centers in Central Europe.[1] However, from the beginning of the Revolutionary and Napoleonic Wars, commercial activities there underwent a remarkable decline. The considerable decrease in exports brought stagnation to the local market, and life in Macedonia became dear. French trade was particularly paralyzed.[2] Thessaloniki was, at that time, the center of the German trade, too. Germans bought considerable quantities of cotton which were then transferred via Semlin and the Danube to Vienna.[3]

At the end of the eighteenth century and the beginning of the nineteenth, the foreign goods most in demand at Thessaloniki were clothes from wool and silk, paper, coffee, and so on. In 1810, Greek ships transhipped via Thessaloniki English sugar and wool and cotton clothes coming from Smyrna and Malta. By the end of the Napoleonian Wars the ports of Thessaloniki and Marseille began to develop trade relations, and the value of exports to Marseille soon tripled. The French Consul of Thessaloniki, Félix Beaujour, reported on July 16, 1817 on the fall in the Thessaloniki trade and observed that export goods varied in their destination: silks to France, wool to Germany, paper and silk to Italy, silk, coffee, and sugar to England. At that time, the most important trading houses established in Thessaloniki were Austrian, such as Vianelli, Loëhley, Goch, Beyer, Werbeil, and Barahell. England was represented by the houses of Abbott, Chassaud, and Charnaud, and France by those of François

Tavernier and Thomas Vailhen. The leading Greek traders were the brothers Kaftandzoglou, Paikos, Rogotis, Skambalis, Papatheos, Kakos, and Balanos; the major Jewish interests were those of Misrahi and Fernandez.[4]

On the eve of Greek independence the city's foreign trade seemed to be on an even keel. But revolutionary events of 1821 and 1822 in Macedonia affected imports and exports adversely, which became especially noticeable at the end of 1823 and the beginning of 1824. The fall in trade was due mainly to military operations and piracy in particular in the Aegean. After 1824, the value of imports remained at a steady level, but exports fluctuated as a consequence of war in Greece. Thus the considerable difference between the value of imports and exports which existed at the end of 1810-20 had been sensibly reduced.[5] As a result of revolutionary turmoil, Thessaloniki's foreign trade was a mere shadow of the city's commercial prosperity, as the French consul suggested in his report of January 1, 1834. He saw as the principal causes of its decline the flight of the wealthiest Greek merchants during the war of independence and the new tax system imposed by Turkish authorities, which was characterized by a continual increase in tariffs. Traditionally, inhabitants of Macedonia travelled for their provisions to Thessaloniki. But, extraordinary Turkish taxes on imported and exported goods diverted trade to Austrian borders, to Dyrrachion, and other outlets where no custom duties existed. Additionally, the French consul noted the steady diminution of production of wool, tobacco, cotton, cereals, and skins. The reduction in wool was very important. It dropped from 350,000-400,000 to 150,000-170,000 okas annually. Tobacco suffered from lack of systematic cultivation and heavy taxes, but sericulture and cereals marked continual increase.[6]

The decade 1830-40 saw a slight acceleration in the value of imports and exports.[7] But by the 1840s the political situation in Europe, the new Turkish-Egyptian crisis followed by the Treaty of Unkiar-Skelessi (1833), the plague in Macedonia and the burning of Thessaloniki in 1839, and internal unrest combined with an increase in acts of brigandage in Macedonia took their toll on the development of the city's foreign trade.[8] Yet, by the mid-nineteenth century, Thessaloniki had close relations with many commercial centers of Western

Europe. For, Macedonia never ceased to be both a rich source for materials for the international market and an outlet for European manufactured articles.[9]

The local production was regulated by the demands of the European capital, and especially of the English market.[10] Therefore, foreign trade preserved a certain flexibility; it adapted to international events financial and political. European markets imported agricultural products and exported manufactured and colonial wares.[11] English cotton products took advantage of the favorable terms of the Treaty of Balta Liman, thereby flooding Ottoman markets with its products. This 1838 treaty between Turkey and England imposed minimum custom duties on the value of imported goods in the Ottoman empire, and thus, opened the doors to Western exploitation of Turkey.[12]

It must be stressed that the value of imported English manufactured articles during 1840-50 covered 40 percent of the total value of imports at the port of Thessaloniki. The penetration of English cotton was facilitated by cheap prices, excellent quality, and the low freight rates of British ships.[13] So, in short time, in spite of primitive transportation facilities, English cotton managed to enter in the most important trade fairs in Macedonia, such as Serres, Vodena, Kozani, Nevrokopi, Petritsi, Jannina, and Perlepe.[14] On the eve of the Crimean War, Austrian trade became highly competitive in the Macedonian region.[15] In 1849, the value of the Austrian imports at the port of Thessaloniki reached 2.641.400 francs and those of the English 3.138.988.[16] But France's trade was inactive during 1840-60. Insignificant, too, were French trading firms in Thessaloniki; in 1844, for example, only two French ships entered its port. As early as 1821, a gradual decline of trade between Thessaloniki and Marseille had set in and by 1850 it had ceased to exist. Nevertheless, the Crimean War revived this trade, and it became very active during the American Civil War. Once, Marseille imported Macedonian cotton, cereals and tobacco, and Thessaloniki French silk, wool, and fezes. But now, the situation had changed. German industry replaced French wool; Italian factories traded in lower priced fezes. The same thing happened with cotton, clothes, colonial wares and yarns imported from Trieste, and basically from English ports.[17]

Silk was the most important export of the port of Thessaloniki, until 1845. It covered 40 percent of the total value of exports. Year after year silk production grew in the Macedonian region, and its fine, quality silk, we add, surpassed Proussa's exports to France, Austria, and England for 1841-45.[18] Cotton had also lost its leading place in the export trade and until 1860 remained insignificant.[19]

Eighteen forty six, on the eve of the depression of 1847, saw the considerable development of the foreign trade, with a parallel rise in imports and exports, especially in cereal exports. Silk production would be gradually reduced, as cereals' increased.[20] During 1846-75, cereals was Thessaloniki's most important export, replacing wool and cotton. Its dominant position is due to the introduction of monoculture in the fertile plains of Thessaloniki for the production of wheat. Economic crisis in Europe in 1847 gave the impetus to a significant growth in the production and export of cereals[21]. In 1847, the total value of exported cereals surpassed 800,000 livres sterlings.[22] It must be added that the important increase in cereals and cotton exports, especially during the Crimean War and the American Civil War, depended on external economic and political events.[23]

Undoubtedly, the most important push to the commercial development of cereals in Macedonia was war in the Crimea and the closing of the Russian ports on the Black Sea.[24] Thus, this tremendous demand contributed greatly to Thessaloniki's prosperity. Just before Russia's Black Sea ports closed down in 1853, the freight of commercial ships which loaded there for Western ports of call doubled. Serious problems arose by the stationing of troops in Wallachia and Moldavia; shortages paralyzed Greek production. Therefore, Macedonia as a whole had to cover the enormous demand of cereals.[25] Macedonia took on an enhanced commercial importance, but the lack of concrete statistical data makes it impossible to measure quantitatively Thessaloniki's foreign trade during the Crimean War. Anyhow, as to the growth of the cereal trade, total exports before the war was fixed at 300,000-350,000 hecatoliters a year of which 75,000 were wheat. This number shot up tenfold in 1853-54, and in 1856, in spite of a decline, wheat surpassed in quantity prewar total exports of cereals.[26] Here, it must be mentioned that during the war, prices of agrarian products of the Macedonian region fluctuated, owing to elasticity of demand and to instability of supply. The average annual price of wheat during 1840-50 moved between 5.5 francs to 8 francs. On the eve of war, it had reached 4 francs, and during the war, it rose spectacularly, stabilizing at 20-25 francs. Noteworthy, in spite of this considerable increase, the price of wheat in France in June 1854 was 40 percent higher than at Thessaloniki.[27]

At the end of the 1850s, Thessaloniki had become Turkey's most important European port after Constantinople. In 1857, its total exports reached 51,000,000 francs (23,000,000 in exports, 28,000,000 in imports).[28] In the middle of the nineteenth century, about fifteen important trading houses, Greek, foreign, and Jewish, were established there with a total capital of five million francs and an annual turnover of twelve million. The greatest part of these gains was directed to Constantinople and to other European centers such as Smyrna, Marseille, Vienna, Trieste, and Genova. It must also be mentioned that most of the city's houses were represented by the "protected" subjects of England, Russia, France, and Austria. Among the Greeks' houses worthy of mention were those belonging to Argiri Matheos with a capital of 100,000 francs and an annual trade of 250,000, and close commercial relations with London, Liverpool, Trieste, and Marseille; of Theagenis Charissis with a capital of 250.000 francs and transactions with London, Smyrna, Alexandria, and Constantinople; of P. Rogottis, Dimitris Blatsis, Ioannis Pavlides, Petrokokkinos and Mavrodordatos. Jews distinguished themselves in houses of Allatini and Modiano with a capital of 1,000,000 francs and an annual circulation of 2,000,000 and of Fernandez and Misrahi. The old English house of Abbott which had been in Thessaloniki since the end of the eighteenth century, possessed a capital of 1,500,000 francs, and traded with London, Marseille, Amsterdam, Vienna, Genoa, Trieste, Malta, Syra, Smyrna, and Constantinople.[29]

Notes

1. N. Svoronos, *Le commerce de Salonique au XVIIIe siècle* (Paris, 1956), 349-53; Constantinos Vacalopoulos, «Το εμπόριο της Θεσσαλονίκης, 1796-1840, Σύμφωνα με ανέκδοτες εκθέσεις των Ευρωπαίων προξένων», *Makedonika*, 16 (1976), 74.

2. William Martin Leake, *Travels in Northern Greece* (London, 1835), vol. 3, 252-54; Apostolos E. Vacalopoulos, *History of Macedonia, 1354-1833* (Thessaloniki, 1969), 495.

3. Félix Beaujour, *Tableau du commerce de la Grèce* (Paris, 1800), vol. 2, 53.

4. C. Vacalopoulos, *Το εμπόριο της Θεσσαλονίκης, 1796-1840*, 97-100.

5. *Op. cit.*, 102-104.

6. *Ibid.*, 106-10.

7. *Ibid.*, 111.

8. Constantinos Vacalopoulos, *Οικονομική λειτουργία του μακεδονικού και θρακικού χώρου στα μέσα του 19ου αιώνα στα πλαίσια του διεθνούς εμπορίου* (Thessaloniki, 1980), 14.

9. Z. Biljanovski, "Nekoi podatoči za nadvoresnata trgovija na Makedonija vo vremeto od Krimskata do Balkanskata vojna," *Glasnik* VI (1962): 195-216; K. Djambazovski, "Za Razvitokot na Makedonskata trgovija vo tekot na prvata polivina na XIX vek," *Glasnik* VI (1962): 217-20; Hristo Andonov Poljanski, "Ekonomskite aspekti vo odvosite na imperialističkite državi kon Makedonija i Makedonskoto Nacionalosvoboditelno dviženie od krajot na XIX vek i početokot na XX vek," *Glasnik* XVII 2(1973): 27.

10. C. Vacalopoulos, *Οικονομική λειτουργία του μακεδονικού και θρακικού χώρου*, 19.

11. *Ibid.*, 19.

12. George Hoffman, "Thessaloniki: the Impact of a Changing Hinterland," East European Quarterly 2(1968): no. 1; Lewis Farley, *The Resources of Turkey* (London, 1863), 267-71; V. J. Puryear, *International Economics and Diplomacy in the Near East*. A Study of British Commercial Policy in the Levant, 1834-1853 (Stanford, California, 1935), 84-92, 123-25; Oya Köymen, "The Advent and Consequences of Free Trade in the Ottoman Empire (19th Century)," *Etudes Balkaniques* 2(1971): 48-50; C. Vacalopoulos, *Οικονομική λειτουργία του μακεδονικού και θρακικού χώρου*, 17 annot. 3, 10 annot. 2, for further bibliography on Balta Liman treaty and Anglo-Turkish political and economic relations in the middle of the nineteenth century.

13. C. Vacalopoulos, 23.

14. Nicolas Michoff, *Contribution à l'histoire du commerce de la Turquie et de la Bulgarie*, III, Rapports Consulaires Français, Documents officiels et autres documents (Svichtov, 1950), vol. 3, 300; analytically Dančo Zografski, *Razvitokot na kapitalističkite elementi vo Makedonija za vreme na turskoto vladeenje* (Skopje, 1967), 265-87.

15. Virginia Paskaleva, "Ikonomičeskoto pronikvane na Avstrija u nas ot 30-te godini na XIX v. do Krimskata vojna," *Istoričeski Pregled*, XII² (1956): 19-20, 33.

16. C. Vacalopoulos, 69-70.

17. *Ibid.*, 20-21.

18. *Ibid.*, 16, 65.

19. *Ibid.*, 17.

20. *Ibid.*, 66.

21. Constantin Svolopoulos, "Les effets de la Guerre de Crimée sur la condition de Salonique: l'exportation des céréales," *Actes du IIe Congrès International des Etudes du Sud-Est Europé en (Athénes, 7-13 1970)* (Athens, 1974), 4-5.

22. Lewis Farley, *Modern Turkey* (London, 1872), 230.

23. N. Michoff, *Contribution à l'histoire du commerce de la Turquie et de la Bulgarie*, vol. 3, 631.

24. Irina Dostian, "Les échanges commerciaux par la mer Noire et les Détroits pendant le XVIIIe et la première partie du XIXe siècle," *Association Internationale des Etudes du Sud-Est Européen*, Bulletin XII 2(1974):190.

25. C. Svolopoulos, *Les effets de la Guerre de Crimée sur la condition de Salonique*, 5-6.

26. *Ibid.*, 9; C. Vacalopoulos, Οἰκονομικὴ λειτουργία τοῦ μακεδονικοῦ καὶ θρακικοῦ χώρου, 16.

27. C. Svolopoulos, *ibid.*, 74.

28. C. Vacalopoulos, Οἰκονομικὴ λειτουργία τοῦ μακεδονικοῦ καὶ θρακικοῦ χώρου, 75.

29. *Ibid.*, 49-54.

VI

Maritime Law, Quarantine and Piracy

Nicholas J. Pantazopoulos

Greek Contributions to Maritime Laws
and Commercial Customs in the Eastern Mediterranean
during the Eighteenth and the Nineteenth Centuries

Events in the Mediterranean from the early eighteenth century up to the present day, by their very nature, revolve around the axes of a multifaceted and slow-moving process: the rivalry of West and East to control the Mediterranean. The Greeks have been at the epicenter of this intense competition and a decisive factor in its development. This article deals especially with this aspect of Mediterranean history.

Until the end of the eighteenth century, the Greek shipping was at a distinct disadvantage compared with its European rivals. According to the capitulations prevailing at that time, the subjects of the European powers (*soudenten*) enjoyed preferential treatment economically (through customs duties relief) and politically (extra-territoriality). Ships belonging to these powers sailed freely in the Mediterranean, while those owned by *rayahs* need permits, (non-Muslim subjects of the Ottoman empire).

Greek ships were obliged to sail under an Ottoman "*rayah* flag." However, since they feared reprisals from Ottoman enemies, Greek seamen preferred to fly a foreign, preferably neutral, flag. Greek merchant shipping benefited particularly from the right to fly the Russian flag, conferred on Greek captains by a secret protocol of the Treaty of Kutchuk Kainardji (July 1774). Despite initial objections on the part of the Turkish government, the Russo-Turkish alliance played a part in the temporary alignment of all Greek merchant vessels under the Russian flag.

In the middle of the eighteenth century, Greek merchant shipping began to develop into an independent force for the first time, in the western regions of Greece, Mesolongi, Aitolikos, Galaxidhi, and the Ionian Islands.In these areas,there was a surplus of exportable produce and liquid capital available for investment in maritime operations. This period saw the development of a system of collaboration between merchants and seamen, and also, at the same time, an opening toward the English, who, because of fierce commercial rivalry with the French, gave the Greeks the opportunity to invest capital within the framework of the British merchant marine.

Merchant-marine activity opened up unprofitable regions of Greece on the mainland and in the islands, where looting and smuggling were confused with merchant trading, thereby creating a somewhat peculiar life style. For, proverty and piracy, permanent features in the Mediterranean, offered a source of revenue for the local economy, in the Cyclades (Mykonos, Milos, Tinos, Amorgos, Kasos, Kea, and Paros) and other regions, such as Psara in the northeastern Aegean, Mani in the Peloponnese, Trikeri in Thessaly, and Sfakia in Crete. In Mykonos, when nautical activity was at its height, piracy was openly practiced. Agreements between pirates and sailors were signed in the chancellery of the community, and the pirate crews circulated freely and were held up as examples worthy of imitation (*leventes*), not only on Mykonos but elsewhere as well. This is, perhaps, the reason why some islands (Mykonos, Santorini, Kythnos, and Naxos), although they had codified local laws, avoided taking measures against piracy, and also avoided building ships large enough for the seafaring trade, since smaller vessels served smuggling better.

Collaboration between capital and labor dating from the time of Rhodian marine law formed the basis for the institution of associate-seamanship, the co-operative participation of the crew, paid on a percentage basis, in commercial enterprises. The three seafaring islands of Hydra, Spetses, and Psara modernized and perfected this system and converted it into a legislative model (Hydra, in 1804-18; Spetses, in 1814-33), so that they were in a position to play an important part in international commercial competition in the Mediterranean. The tasks involved in building and equipping vessels were shared, and the profits were apportioned after each voyage, just as the booty was distributed among pirates.

Collaboration between capital and labor was also based on the general principles of good faith, solidarity, mutual interest, and arbitration, and it was firm enough to allow this system to function both in the oligarchical communities of Hydra and Spetses and in the democratic community of Psara, where the name "sailor" was thought to be disparaging, but where the word "associate" had no such overtones and denoted no financial dependence but equal participation in the enterprise. There is evidence that the institution extended to other areas, too. A variation of it was in practice in the sponge-fishing industry, indeed in two forms (Trikeri and Kalymnos). Yet, there was a certain deviation from it when the roles of shipowner, captain, and capitalist were united in one and the same person, a phenomenon which coincided with the decline of the institution of associate-seamanship.

Although the Sublime Porte forbade Greek seamen to come under the protection of a foreign flag, an entirely different policy was in force regarding another important category of *rayahs*, the merchants. After endeavors made by the great dragomans Jacob Argyropoulos (1806) and Dimitrios Mourouzis (1808), Greek wholesale merchants of Constantinople, Thessaloniki, Smyrna, and Halepio were granted permits (*peratia*), which allowed them various privileges, such as customs-duties relief, the right to wear special uniforms, and to keep representatives (*firmanlis*) in Smyrna and Salonika, to conduct their affairs and to appeal personally to the Sultan on behalf of their private interests.

By the end of the eighteenth century, these merchants had systematically organized themselves into chambers of commerce. Through a network of representatives in the most important European commercial centers, they carefully monitored any developments in commercial law, and in their own rules, they recognized customs that had the force of unwritten law in the Mediterranean, even before they were included in the French Commercial Code. Hence, sequestration was put into commercial practice by means of Article 6 of the Regulations of the Smyrna Chamber of Commerce in 1806. In this guild's legislation for the first time in Modern Greek law, the term *driton* of commerce was used instead of *diritto* (law) of commerce. Other up-to-date practices which filled the gaps in popular law were those concerning promissory notes and bills of exchange, limited-liability companies (sociétés anonymes), the necessity for agreements of all types (the general principle of good faith), and the law of copyright and patent. These were applied according to each case within the context of the general stipulations of Greek law. They had not yet been dealt with systematically, however.

The development of commercial legislation was so rapid that the Constantinople Chamber of Commerce had to revise its regulations, three times in quick succession. But in 1814 "by common consent, the last (legislation) was approved and a new organization was set up." Unfortunately, further evidence which would complete our knowledge has been lost or has not come to light yet.

Commercial Shipping Codes

1. Official Law

During the period of Turkish domination, three contradictory legislative systems were in effect in Greek zones and the eastern Mediterranean: the Byzantine, the Ottoman, and common law. In practice, none of them was able to satisfy the whole gamut of needs. Hence, each was confined, or extended, to one sector of exclusive or concurrent jurisdiction, while the other contradictory systems were abandoned or served to fill the gaps where necessary.

The rules of official law were chiefly found in Armenopoulos's *Hexabiblus*, a summary of *Basilika* (imperial) decrees, which was compiled in 1345, printed in 1540, translated into the vernacular by Alexios Spanos in 1744, and frequently republished thereafter. This collection gained the stature of an official code and contained 23 nautical provisions under the title "On sea-faring vessels." But, these were not applied, having been abandoned in favor of common law.

2. Popular Law

a. Regions with unwritten nautical law

On the eve of the Greek Revolution, according to one source, Greeks had 615 vessels in allo. Of those, 240 belonged to the islands of Hydra (120), Spetses (60), and Psara (60), while the other 375 belonged to other areas. Regions and islands which had small fleets, such as Psara (60), Skopelos (35), Kastelorizo (30), Crete (60), Andros

(40), and Galaxidhi (50) did not feel it necessary to codify their laws, but Mykonos (with 22 vessels in its fleet) and Santorini (32) did not include maritime provisions in their codes. This meant that, in practice, common law, albeit unwritten, met every need. An obvious distinction between civil and maritime law appeared for the first time in 1804 in the "Provisions" or Maritime Law of Hydra, and later, in 1818, in Article 1 of the Merchant Maritime Law of Hydra.

b. Regions with written maritime law

Of all the seafaring islands, only two, Hydra and Spetses, gradually codified their merchant marine law. Recording began with a series of provisions which first appeared on Hydra on February 1, 1804, under the title, "Provisions or Maritime Law of Hydra." These provisions regulated the relations between shipowner, captain, and associate-seamen (*syntrofonaftes*), and the settlement of damages in the event of shipwreck and salvage, paying special attention to bottomry-loan and interest. Codification of hitherto unwritten law was undertaken by captains and shipowners, who, it seems, had earlier formed a sort of guild, consisting of 37 members, with economic, administrative, and legal jurisdiction. This guild exercised its powers in the guise of a civil community.

Codification took more concrete form in the 65 articles of Law of Hydra (1818). This legislation included local civil laws, which, according to the legislators, corresponded to maritime commercial laws. Despite its conservative and conformist/regressive nature, it included seventeen provisions concerning associate-seamanship, that unusual institution, which from the time of the Rhodian maritime law, held sway in the Mediterranean in different forms, one of which was piracy. Hydra's social system was based on the collaboration of capital and labor. With the acceptance of associate-seamanship, a realistic effort was made to iron out social contradictions, these being irreversibly settled by the *boule*, that is, the council of judges elected each year to govern the community. Spetses' codification of maritime customs was set down in a similar way; work began on May 15, 1814 and finished in 1833, with a basic catalog of the existing customs. As to content, the customs of Spetses were no different from those of Hydra.

As we have seen, the official, that is Byzantine, law, which during this period was in force side-by-side with Ottoman law and common law, did not contain provisions which met the needs of contemporary commercial practice. We cannot speak of Ottoman merchant marine law as such at that time. It was usually limited, by means of firmans, Kapudan Pasha's decrees, and orders of the Dragomans of the Fleet, to the ratification of the islands' customary laws, such that they may be considered to have become part of Ottoman legislation. The Greek merchants' chambers of commerce noticed this gap in time and were quick to fill it by translating the French *Code de Commerce* of 1807. This legislation, which put into concrete form the centuries-old experience of Mediterranean peoples, had been published a few years earlier and had started to be disseminated throughout Europe.

The first translation was undertaken by Nicholas Papadopoulos, on the initiative of the "System of Greek-Roman Merchants of Constantinople" (Chamber of Commerce). It was completed in 1815 and published in Vienna in 1817. A second translation was done by Theodore Rakos for the merchants of Marseille, and was printed in Vienna in 1820. The more up-to-date translation was that of Papadopoulos, who, in his foreword and translator's notes, shows how well informed the Greek commercial element was about the sensitive issues of the time. It is also worth mentioning that Papadopoulos did not propose a complete replacement of common law, which had traditionally regulated commercial relations, with foreign, i.e., French, law, but confined himself to suggesting that the latter should have a purely supplementary function, where and when practice demanded it, thereby recognizing the equal status of custom and law. Papadopoulos also published in Vienna in 1815 a four-volume supplement, remarkable for its time, entitled *Ermis o Kerdoos* (Hermes the Profitable). He set down in encyclopedic form all the information and practical experience necessary to promote commerce internationally.

In 1817, in Vienna, Captain Nicholas Kefalas published "Every Seaman's and Merchant's Guide to Maritime Legislation Collected from Various Legislators and Sea-faring Europeans, Supplemented by Various Customs Still Observed."

These publications show the degree of awareness existing in the organized, progressive *rayah* classes and attest their ability to adapt to the legislation which was developing in the Mediterranean. Greek legislation was to follow the exact same policy. During the revolution, the Capodistrian period, and the Modern Greek period, it recognized the force of the French code as a supplementary source for Greek law. Article 99 of the Constitution of Troezen (1827), however, deviated from this, by providing for the total application of French legislation in Greece.

In order to facilitate the application of the French *Code de Commerce*, which was being applied by the Commercial Tribunal of Syra — a court which the merchants of Syra had established independently in 1826 — the Greek government published an official translation of the French *Code de Commerce* and printed it together with the "Law Regarding the Jurisdiction of Commercial Tribunals." The first edition came out in 1835, the second and third in 1837 and 1838. The decision by the System of Greek-Roman Merchants to adopt the French *code* (1817) was taken shorthly after its publication in France (1807), but it was another 50 years before Ottoman legislation followed suit with the publication of the Ottoman Commercial Law (1869).

Conclusions

From this analysis, we can draw the following conclusion: the French commercial code ushered Western legislation into Greece, and consequently, Greece entered Europe. The secret of the code's unchallenged supremacy in the Mediterranean region lies in the fact that it embodied the maritime experience of the Mediterranean peoples, and consequently, corresponded to their own collective conception of the law. It was embraced, with particular warmth, by the Greeks, because it helped to embody their complex desire "to be counted among the civilized nations of Europe." For these reasons, it was accepted by the Greek merchants, who customarily applied it as a complementary source for their own common law before it was officially incorporated into Greek legislation.

The total application of French legislation in the three maritime regions of the country (the Ionian Islands, Crete, and Samos) revealed the wide scope of the Mediterranean judicial spirit. This spirit set great store by custom and collective will of the people, in contrast to the pressure exerted by the pandectic science of the north, which aimed at the formal application of the law and the total imposition of Roman law in the form in which it had become accepted in Germany.

As we have seen, Greek seamen and merchants played a significant role in the momentous process of bringing Greece into Europe. To-ing and fro-ing across the Mediterranean as slaves, they felt the liberal spirit of the French *Code de Commerce*, became aware of its message, which was an echo of their own ancestral heritage, and used it as a means of securing their own freedom.

Select Bibliography

Αθηναίου Ε., *Το δίκαιον της προεπαναστατικής ναυτιλίας των Ελλήνων*, Αθήναι 1973.

Βισβίζη Ιακ., «Νομικά τινα έθιμα των νήσων Σπετσών, Ύδρας, Πόρου και Σαμίνος», *Επετ. Αρχ. Ιστορ. Ελλην. Δικαίου*, τ. 3 (1950) 8-16.

Γκίνη Δ., *Περίγραμμα ιστορίας του μεταβυζαντινού δικαίου*, Αθήναι 1966.

Γκόφα Δ., *Η φόρτωσις επί του καταστρώματος*, Αθήναι 1965.

Gofas, D., *Esquisse d'une histoire du droit commercial grec dans la domination ottomane*, "*Affi de terzo congresso internationale della società italiana di storia dell diritto*", Vol. III, Firenze 1977, 1087-1104.

Δ.Α. - Σ.Π., «Το εμπόριο και η ναυτιλία όπως το είδαν οι περιηγητές», *Ελληνική Εμπορική Ναυτιλία, Πανηγυρικός Τόμος Εθνικής Τραπέζης* (1972) 316 επ.

Θεοφανίδη Ι., *Ιστορία του Ελληνικού ναυτικού*, Αθήναι 1932.

Κεφαλά, Καπετάν Νικολάου, *Θαλάσσιος Νομοθεσία*, Βιέννη 1817.

Κιάντου-Παμπούκη Αλ., *Εμπόριον και εμπορικόν δίκαιον επί Τουρκοκρατίας ως συντελεσταί της επαναστατικής συνειδήσεως των Ελλήνων*, Θεσσαλονίκη 1971.

Κοντογιάννη Π., «Οι προστατευόμενοι», περιοδ. *Αθηνά*, τ. 29 (1917).

Κοτσίρη Λ., *Κοινωνική και νομική μορφολογία του Ελληνικού Εμπορικού Ναυτικού κατά τους χρόνους της Εθνεγερσίας*, Θεσσαλονίκη 1983.

Κριεζή Γ., *Ιστορία της νήσου Ύδρας προ της (Ελληνικής) Επαναστάσεως του 1821*, Πάτραι 1860.

Κωνσταντινίδη Τρ., «Η πειρατεία και καταδρομή και οι Έλληνες», *Ναυτική Επιθεώρηση*, τεύχ. 214, Αθήναι 1949.

Κωνσταντινίδη Τρ., *Καράβια, Καπετάνιοι, Συντροφοναύται*, Αθήναι 1954.

Λεονταρίτη Γ., «Ελληνική Εμπορική Ναυτιλία (1453-1850)», *Ελληνική Εμπορική Ναυτιλία, Πανηγυρικός Τόμος Εθνικής Τραπέζης*, Αθήναι 1972, 13-48· 472-487.

Λιγνού Αντ., *Αρχείον Κοινότητος 'Υδρας*, τ. 1-16 (1921-1932).

Λιγνού Αντ., *Ιστορία της νήσου 'Υδρας*, Αθήναι 1946-1953.

Λιγνού Αντ., «Περί τινων προεπαναστατικών εθίμων της 'Υδρας», Περιοδ. *Το μέλλον της 'Υδρας*, τ. 6 (1938) 99-100.

Μανιατοπούλου Ι., *Το ναυτικόν δίκαιον της 'Υδρας (1757-1821)*, Αθήναι 1939.

Νικοδήμου Κ., *Υπόμνημα της νήσου Ψαρών*, τ. 1-2, Αθήναι 1862.

Μανίκη Α., «Τα συνάφια της προεπαναστατικής 'Υδρας», *Το μέλλον της 'Υδρας*, τ. 5 (1937) 189-193.

Μαξίμου Σερ., *Το ελληνικό εμπορικό ναυτικό κατά τον XVIII αιώνα*, Αθήναι 1976.

Μοσχοβάκη Ν., *Το εν Ελλάδι δημόσιον δίκαιον επί Τουρκοκρατίας*, Αθήναι 1882 (ανατύπ. 1973), 117-148.

Ορλάνδου Αναστ., *Ναυτικά*, τ. 1-2, Αθήναι 1869.

Πανταζοπούλου Νικ., «Ελλήνων Συσσωματώσεις κατά την Τουρκοκρατίαν», ανατ. από το περιοδικόν *Γνώσεις*, Αθήναι 1958.

Πανταζοπούλου Νικ., *Από της «Λογίας» Παραδόσεως εις τον Αστικόν Κώδικα* (1965)², 235.

Πανταζοπούλου Νικ., *Τα «προνόμια» ως πολιτιστικός παράγων εις τας σχέσεις Χριστιανών-Μουσουλμάνων. Συμβολή εις το εθιμικόν κοινοδίκαιον της Εγγύς Ανατολής και της Νοτιοανατολικής Ευρώπης*, Θεσσαλονίκη 1975, 836-879.

Παπαδοπούλου Νικ., *Εμπορικός Κώδιξ της Γαλλίας*, Βιέννη 1817.

Παπαρρηγοπούλου Κωνστ., *Τα διδακτικώτερα πορίσματα της ιστορίας του Ελληνικού 'Εθνους*, Νέα Υόρκη 1915, 440-452.

Pardessus J. M., *Collection des lois maritimes anterieures au XVIII siècle*, τ. 5, Paris 1839.

Pleionis L., "The influence of the Rhcdian Sea Law to the other Maritime Codes," *Revue de Droit International*, 1967, 171 επ.

Pouqueville F.C.H.L., *Voyage dans le Grèce*, τ. 5, Paris 1821, 68-71.

Savary J., *Le parfait negotiant*, Paris 1745.

Σβολοπούλου Κ., «Ο Ελληνικός εμπορικός στόλος κατά τάς παραμονάς του αγώνος της Εθνικής Ανεξαρτησίας. Ανέκδοτος πίναξ του F. Pouqueville», περιοδ. *Ερανιστής*, έτος Γ, τεύχ. 55, 187 επ.

Shaw Stanf. J., *Between old and new. The Ottoman Empire under Sultan Selim III, 1789-1807*, Cambridge, Mass. 1971.

Stoianovich Tr., Conquering Balkan Orthodox Merchant, ανατ. από το *Journal of Economic History*, June 1960, 234-313.

Φιλαρέτου Γ., *Συνεργατικοί συνεταιρισμοί Αμπελακίων, 'Υδρας-Σπετσών-Ψαρών*, Αθήναι 1927².

Χατζηαναργύρου Αναργύρου Ανδρ., *Σπετσιωτικά*, τ. Α΄, Αθήναι 1861, τ. 2-3,
Πειραιεύς 1925/6.

Zakythinos D., "Corsaires et pirates dans le mers grecques au temps de la domination turque," περιοδ. *L'Hellénisme Contemporain*, τ. 10 (1939) 695 επ.

Ζέπων Ιω. και Π., *Συλλογή Τοπικών Ελληνικών εθίμων*, *Jus Graeco romanum*,
τ. 8 (1831) 441-573.

Ronald E. Coons

Austrian Maritime Quarantine Reform during the First Half of the Nineteenth Century

In the space of a few years during the 1840s, the Austrian government carried out a policy of maritime quarantine reform that belies the frequently-held notion that the Habsburg monarchy during the reign of Emperor Ferdinand I was "stagnant and immobile."[1] Between 1841 and 1847, the *Hofkanzlei,* that bureau of the central government primarily responsible for public health policy, progressively reduced quarantines against plague for vessels arriving from the Levant at ports in the Adriatic. As a result of this policy of gradual reform, by the time revolution overthrew the Austrian old regime in 1848, such vessels and their passengers were subjected to the minimum of delay and inconvenience that practical considerations and scientific knowledge as understood by the monarchy's medical experts and bureaucrats would allow. In this reforming enterprise, Austria was by no means alone during the first half of the nineteenth century. Yet, Austrian policy differed significantly from that pursued by the monarchy's major commercial rivals in the Mediterranean. British and French quarantine reforms were influenced by public opinion and reflected the strength of anticontagionist thought concerning the nature of plague.[2] In contrast, the officials who implemented Austria's reforms were loyal servants of absolute monarchy who believed that plague was contagious and that quarantines were efficacious. If these officials, nevertheless, accepted the need for reform, it was not as a result of political pressure or of a major shift in medical thought. Austrian quarantine reform instead represented a cautious response to commercial, political, and medical realities.

Even a cursory description of the Austrian maritime sanitary code as it existed on the eve of reform suggests the heavy burdens it imposed upon commerce and travel. Initially decreed in 1755 and only slightly modified before 1841, the code was especially harsh in its treatment of ships arriving from the Levant. Like sanitary codes elsewhere in Europe, Austrian legislation recognized bills of health in three denominations — *patente netta* (clean), *patente tocca* (suspicious), and *patente brutta* (foul) — and classified merchandise as susceptible, doubtful, or non-susceptible, according to its alleged ability to transmit plague. Because the disease was held to be a constant danger in the Levant, however, no ship arriving from the eastern Mediterranean carried a clean bill of health. Even under the most favorable of circumstances, a vessel arrived from any port in the Ottoman empire or Egypt carrying *patente tocca* was subjected, along with its passengers, to a quarantine of 28 days; susceptible merchandise underwent purification for 32 days in a lazaretto. Ships that arrived from a port that was actually infested with plague, on the other hand, carried *patente brutta* and underwent a quarantine of 40 days, as did susceptible merchandise, while passengers spent 28 days in quarantine. For arrivals from the Ionian Islands and Greece, moreover, a quarantine of fourteen days was proscribed unless susceptible merchandise was on board, in which case the period was extended to 21 days for ships, passengers, and cargo.[3] At best, these provisions of the Austrian code proved vexatious, dilatory, and costly. At worst, the administration of the code could be inefficient, capricious, inhumane, and even corrupt.[4]

The burdens and deficiencies of Austrian maritime quarantine legislation during the early nineteenth century were similar to those caused by the sanitary codes of all European states bordering on the Mediterranean.[5] What was peculiar and exasperating about Austrian public health policy was the existence of a separate sanitary code for the monarchy's land border with the Ottoman empire, the terms of which were less severe than those enforced at ports in the Adriatic. Both codes were firmly based upon the conviction of the government and the monarchy's medical community that plague was contagious. Notwithstanding this cardinal principle of Austrian sanitary policy, however, in 1785, Emperor Joseph II acted to promote commerce by land by quietly establishing a 20-day maximum for quarantines along the Austrian Military Frontier. The major figure in this reform was Adam Chenot, a physician born in Luxemburg who had gained considerable experience in Austrian service along the sanitary cordon

in the Balkans. On the basis of that experience, Chenot concluded
that humans were poor carriers of plague. He also argued that since
the incubation period of the disease did not seem to exceed four days,
quarantines in the traditional length of 40 days were unreasonable.
According to him, even under the worst of epidemiological circumstances a quarantine of 20 days was fully adequate to protect the
health of the monarchy.[6]

The Austrian reforms of 1785 were initially implemented as mere
administrative instructions in order not to alarm either an uneducated
public fearful of plague or foreign governments that failed to share
Chenot's conclusions. Only after years of experience showed that reduced quarantines had not exposed the monarchy to increased danger
from plague did Chenot's reforms receive public status when they
were incorporated into a new Plague Ordinance (*Pest-Polizey-Ordnung*) for the military frontier, which was published in 1838.[7] To the
consternation of merchants in the monarchy's ports, however, neither in the late eighteenth nor in the early nineteenth century did
Vienna seriously consider applying the 20-day maximum to maritime
commerce.[8] The result was an anomaly. Even when plague claimed
victims throughout the Levant and even on the very borders of the
monarchy, a traveler from the Ottoman empire to Vienna could, by
journeying by land rather than by sea, endure a quarantine eight days
shorter than that imposed at Trieste. If, moreover, plague was confined
to distant parts of European Turkey, or to Anatolia, Syria, or Egypt,
the quarantine imposed at the land border amounted to only ten days,
in comparison with the 28 days required in the Adriatic for passengers arriving on any ship from the Levant. The discrepancy between
the two codes was particularly glaring when the Balkans and the Levant were entirely plague-free. On such an occasion no quarantine
was required at the land border, whereas passengers arriving at
Trieste or other ports were still forced to undergo the minimum quarantine of 28 days required under the code of 1755.[9]

The explanation for this apparent absurdity is to be found in a
single word — "Italy." Out of a combination of loyalty to the ancient
sanitary code of Venice and extreme fear of the ravages of plague, the
several governments of the peninsula independently and obstinately
pursued highly conservative quarantine policies. By so doing, they

long exercised a *de facto* veto power over maritime quarantine reform in the Habsburg monarchy. Austrian officials, aware of the importance of the monarchy's maritime trade with Italy,[10] feared that liberalization of their own code might convince Italian states that ships leaving Austrian ports were potential carriers of plague and should, therefore, be subjected to discriminatory treatment.[11] Their fear was by no means irrational. During Europe's first expeience with cholera in the early 1830s, for example, the Austrian government accepted the advice of the Viennese medical faculty that quarantines against the disease were useless.[12] When, however, Emperor Franz I ordered the withdrawal of the special cholera quarantines the government had initially imposed, his decision evoked in Italy precisely the sort of discriminatory measures the monarchy wished to avoid.[13] When cholera next struck Europe in the late 1840s, therefore, Vienna found itself forced to protect Austrian maritime commerce with Italy by imposing minimal cholera quarantine in whose efficacy it did not believe.[14]

Austrian policy toward quarantines against cholera suggests that neither the bureaucracy nor the Viennese medical faculty, which served as the government's official advisor in sanitary affairs, regarded quarantines as ends in themselves. The same conclusion can be drawn from the support diplomats and consular officials of the United States received in Vienna in their attempt to gain the abolition of quarantines against yellow fever which were imposed in the Adriatic upon arrivals carrying clean bills of health and shipments of cotton from North America. Prince Clemens Metternich, the foreign minister, Count Francis Kolowrat, the emperor's chief advisor for internal affairs, and *Hofkammer* President Baron Peter Eichhoff, who supervised the administration of financial and commercial policies, were all led to recognize an unpleasant commercial reality. Long quarantines in Trieste only drove American cotton bound for the monarchy to ports in northern Europe, where liberal policies against yellow fever prevailed. From here, cotton could often reach markets in Bohemia or Austria before the period of detention to which it would have been subjected at Trieste had expired.[15] The deliberations generated by the American request for changes in Austrian sanitary policy were admittedly slow, as was all too characteristic of the monarchy's antiquated administrative apparatus.[16] They were also successful. After duly consulting with the medical faculty and with officials at the central and provincial levels, in May 1838, the *Hofkanzlei* ordered that all ships arriving at the monarchy's ports directly from the United States with clean bills of health should be received in free practic and should, therefore, undergo no quarantine.[17] Beginning in 1840, similar treatment was also accorded such ships even if they called at Gibraltar or Malta before arriving in the Adriatic.[18]

Austria's liberalization of the sanitary code as far as yellow fever was concerned serves to place the monarchy's sanitary policy in perspective. However conservative their political and medical principles, Austrian officials recognized that commerce generated wealth and prosperity promoted power. They also recognized the negative effect sanitary legislation had upon the monarchy's maritime trade. The importation of yellow fever by ships with clean bills of health from North America was, to be sure, only a remote threat to central Europe, so that a liberalized policy on quarantines against the disease hardly exposed the monarchy to danger. If, however, it could be shown that quarantines against plague could also be safely reduced, Vienna would have every reason seriously to entertain proposals for more liberal treatment of vessels arriving from the Levant.

In 1838, developments at a number of levels created an atmosphere that enabled and even forced the government to devote attention to the need for further sanitary reform. The first of these developments was the financial crisis that afflicted the Steam Navigation Company of the Austrian Lloyd shortly after its founding. Less than a year after its steamships opened routes to Constantinople, Alexandria, and intermediate ports, the company in which Vienna placed high hopes for improved ties with the Levant faced impending doom.[19] To save the company, there was much the government could do, most notably by guaranteeing a loan from the House of Rothschild in the amount of 500,000 florins.[20] In dealing with the company's plea that steamships making regularly scheduled voyages to the Levant required special quarantine favors, however, the government declared itself unwilling to make major concessions in the sanitary code for the benefit of a single economic enterprise.[21] The conclusion was obvious. If the Lloyd's steamers were ever to receive the maximum freedom of movement that medical opinion would allow, *general* reform of the maritime sanitary code would have to be undertaken.

A second development was closely connected with the Lloyd's financial situation. In 1838, the possibility existed that Great Britain would fill the company's coffers by granting it a contract to transport official East Indian mail between Alexandria and the continent by way of Trieste. Although the hope that the monarchy's premier port might emerge as a major point on Britain's vital route to the Far East ultimately proved illusory,[22] it, nevertheless, moved the government to action. Earlier proposals for reduced quarantines against plague had in fact emerged from within the bureaucracy but had only resulted in minor reductions that essentially reaffirmed the terms of the code of 1755.[23] In 1838, however, the opportunity for the improved commercial — and political — ties with Great Britain which might result from a contract for the Lloyd created a willingness hitherto lacking on the part of the central government to contemplate significant change. Recognizing that the harsh provisions of the existing sanitary code might well discourage Her Majesty's Government as well as British merchants and travelers from choosing Trieste over competing ports, in August 1838, the *Hofkanzlei* ordered authorities in Trieste to consider to what degree it might be possible to reduce plague quarantines in periods of satisfactory public health in the Levant.[24] Against the background of earlier inaction by the bureau, the decree represented a fundamental breakthrough in the direction of the sort of sanitary reform desired by merchants and shippers in the monarchy's ports.

A third development concerned negotiations at the international level. In the course of 1838, both the British and French governments approached Metternich in independent attempts to gain changes in Austrian quarantine legislation. For their part, the British requested that their warships be assigned shorter periods of quarantine than merchant vessels and that they be allowed to count towards these reduced periods the number of days they spent at sea since their last port of call.[25] The French were more ambitious. On July 4 their chargé d'affaires in Vienna forwarded to Metternich a proposal from Paris that the governments of the Italian peninsula, including Austria, send sanitary experts to a conference to be held at a French port to discuss the creation of a uniform quarantine code for the Adriatic code for the Adriatic and the Mediterranean.[26]

Austria responded negatively to both initiatives. In the case of London's search for special favors for the Royal Navy, Metternich faced the problem that Austrian legislation did not distinguish fundamentally between naval and merchant vessels, although he shared his colleagues' fear that Italy would retaliate against any liberalization of the monarchy's sanitary code. As the *Hofkanzlei* explained, if the British request were granted, a warship that called at an Austrian port after a long voyage from the Levant might easily escape quarantine altogether. If this were to happen the danger existed that Italian governments would conclude that Austrian ports were medically unsafe.[27] Accordingly, Metternich informed the British ambassador that Austria could only accede to London's request if "the British Government should obtain and place in the hands of the Austrian Government, formal assurances from other States bordering on the Mediterranean that any concessions to Great Britain in favour of her ships of war, should not be made the pretext for increased severity upon goods and vessels arriving from Austrian ports."[28] Because no such guarantees could be expected from Italy, Metternich's response amounted to a polite refusal to embark upon negotiations with the British.

For more complex reasons, Metternich also imposed upon Paris conditions that could not be fulfilled. In his initial response to the French chargé, Metternich agreed that a uniform quarantine code "would unquestionably be a boon to mankind."[29] Metternich's subsequent efforts on behalf of domestic quarantine reform give every reason to believe that he meant what he wrote. Yet, Metternich was unwilling to sacrifice vital Austrian political interests merely for the sake of humanity. On the basis of diplomatic reports from Italy, Metternich appears to have concluded that the French, by inviting only governments of the Italian peninsula to their planned conference, were delibarately seeking to insinuate themselves into the affairs of an Austrian sphere of influence.[30] Metternich, therefore, insisted that any international conference be held in Vienna rather than in a French port, and that it include representatives from Great Britain, Greece, and Russia, whose governments also had an interest in international quarantine reform.[31] He further proposed that instead of assembling sanitary administrators in an attempt to arrive at a uniform code, the congress bring together medical experts from all over Europe in order to settle for once and for all the hotly disputed question whether or not plague was contagious.[32] Metternich was right to doubt the chances of success of the conference the French wished to convene. Since European sanitary officials generally accepted the principle that the closer a port lay to the Levant, the greater the danger existed that any ship arriving from that area could import plague, it could be expected that the Italians would argue for lengthy,the French for moderate, and the British for minimal quarantines. Metternich's counterproposal was open, however, to an equally serious objection. As the French perceived, any conference of physicians was likely to degenerate into a futile debate between contumacious contagionists and anticontagionists.[33]

Unfortunately, the archival record of Vienna's correspondence with foreign governments concerning the French proposal is incomplete. All that can be said with certainty is that the conditions Metternich imposed upon Paris for Austria's participation prevented a sanitary conference from being held.[34] On the one hand, Metternich feared the political implications of French leadership in sanitary reform; on the other hand, he seems to have hoped to establish Austrian leadership in a worthwhile enterprise by changing the locale of such a conference, expanding its membership, and imposing his own agenda. As a first step in the direction of collective action in the area of maritime sanitary policy, the French project was a disappointing failure.[35] In the context of the history of Austrian sanitary legislation, however, that very failure had an important consequence. The collapse of negotiations forced upon Vienna the realization that any amelioration of the burdens imposed upon commerce by maritime quarantines would have to be achieved at the level of domestic rather than foreign policy.

Progress toward internal reform was made possible by a fourth development of 1838. Early in the year, the Sultan of Turkey, Mahmud II, announced his determination to establish a sanitary code for the Ottoman empire.[36] Contrary to what might have been expected given the threat plague had long posed to Europe, not all the Powers greet-

ed the Sultan's announcement with enthusiasm. The British in particular opposed the creation of any obstacle to the free movement of
navigation in the Mediterranean, in part for economic reasons, in
part because they doubted the ability of the Turks effectively to administer any quarantine code that might be promulgated. In consequence,
on July 5, Lord Palmerston instructed the British ambassador in
Constantinople to remonstrate "against the incoevenience of all kinds
to which the establishment of this quarantine will give rise, both in
impeding commerce, and in obstructing the intercourse of travellers."[37]
When the Turks, nevertheless, proceeded with drafting sanitary legislation, Palmerston sought to weaken their power of enforcement by
claiming that treaty rights enjoyed by the European powers prevented
Ottoman officials from entering the houses of foreigners to conduct
searches or from firing upon European ships that might seek to evade
control.[38]

Far removed as they were from the assumed source of plague, the
British could afford to raise objections. The Austrians could not.
It was the common assumption in Austrian medical and bureaucratic circles that ships arriving from the Levant could at any time import plague into central Europe that forced the monarchy to maintain
quarantines in the Adriatic. If, however, the danger of importation
could be diminished through improved public health in the Ottoman
empire, it might then be possible to effect quarantine reductions at
home. Sanitary legislation had already been enacted by the Pasha
of Egypt, Mehemet Ali.[39] Announcement of the Sultan's plans gave
further indication that Islamic governments were abandoning their
traditional fatalism in matters of public health.[40] In consequence,
in the same period that Metternich effectively torpedoed France's
proposal for a Mediterranean sanitary conference, he also encouraged
the Porte to take steps to combat plague by creating a quarantine
code of its own. Not only did Vienna advise the British "to avoid
treating the matter [of quarantines] as a violation of the capitulations,"[41] but it aided the Turks in creating a maritime sanitary code
by providing medical advice and diplomatic support.[42] Once the
Ottoman code was in operation, moreover, Austrian diplomats
did everything in their power to encourage the Turks to improve its
administration and effectiveness.[43]

There is yet a fifth reason why 1838 marks a turning point in the history of Austrian maritime quarantine policy. As the year opened, a public health official receptive to modified contagionist views on the etiology of plague was beginning his activity as chief medical officer of the Austrian Littoral. Dr. Franz Weber is an obscure figure in Austrian administrative history,[44] but he emerges from the records of the provincial government in Trieste as one of the major proponents of quarantine reform within the Austrian bureaucracy before 1848. It was he, for example, who was charged with overseeing the deliberations in Trieste occasioned by the *Hofkanzlei* decree of August 1838, while it was from his pen that the most persuasive arguments in favor of reform flowed. Weber was no medical innovator, but he was in close touch with the lively debate being conducted in European medical circles on the nature of plague. Drawing in particular upon the work of Carl Lorinser, published as recently as 1837,[45] Weber held that all European sanitary codes were based upon the false assumption that plague was *inherently* contagious. Rather, he argued, experience with the disease in Egypt since the beginning of the century suggested that plague only became contagious under the primitive, unsanitary conditions that had long been allowed to prevail in its presumed homeland in the Nile Delta. Now that the cause of civilization was advancing under the leadership of Mehemet Ali, Weber expressed the hope that plague would no longer succeed in developing into its contagious stage.[46] Should this be the case, European quarantines could be safely reduced. In March 1839, the provincial government in Trieste incorporated these views into a lengthy justification for a number of sanitary reforms, the most important of which was the proposal that the category of *patente netta* be allowed for ships leaving uninfected ports in Turkey. If adopted, this single reform would reduce the minimum quarantine for ships and passengers from European Turkey and Anatolia from 28 to sixteen days.[47] Ships leaving ports in Syria and Egypt would continue, however, to be refused clean bills of health.

To ensure success for this program Weber recommended, good fortune and decisive leadership were required. The former came from the most unlikely of sources. Beginning in the late 1830s, plague staged a biological retreat so dramatic that by the middle of the following decade it had disappeared as a present danger in the Levant and as a direct threat to Europe.[48] Leadership was provided by Count Francis Stadion, an energetic bureaucrat who was appointed governor of the Austrian Littoral late in February 1841.[49] Stadion was not an administrator who tolerated the normal lethargy of the monarchy's central bureaucracy. When he assumed office, the quarantine reforms that Weber and his colleagues had proposed in March 1839 had sat at the *Hofkanzlei* for two years without resolution. Eager to promote the commercial and maritime interests of Trieste, Stadion embarked upon a determined campaign to gain speedy acceptance of the 1839 recommendations and to pressure Vienna into effecting further changes in the maritime sanitary code inherited from the eighteenth century.

In that campaign, Stadion showed initiative and skill. In cooperation with Weber, for example, he seized upon the incontrovertible fact of the decline of plague in the Levant and erroneously but understandably credited that fortuitous development to the sanitary codes recently introduced by the Pasha of Egypt and the Sultan of Turkey.[50] He also exploited the response of other Mediterranean states to improving conditions in the Levant. Involved as they were in an intense competition to establish their ports as major centers for European commerce with the Near East, even medically conservative Italian states occasionally introduced moderate quarantine reductions as circumstances warranted. These actions Stadion effectively used to support his claim that if Austria's hopes for Trieste were to be realized, Vienna would have to outpace the monarchy's commercial rivals in quarantine reform.[51] He sought to avoid alarming the still timorous Italians, however, by advocating gradual reductions in the existing code rather than radical change.

In each stage of his campaign, Stadion, knew how to mobilize pressure on the *Hofkanzlei*. He collected evidence on conditions in the Levant from the monarchy's diplomatic and consular officials;[52] he engineered calls for reform from the merchants of Trieste;[53] he argued his case vigorously in corresponding with Vienna; and he mobilized support in high places. Most importantly, at critical moments in Vienna's deliberations on recommendiations from Trieste, he turned to his friend and patron at the *Hofkammer*, Baron Car

Friedrich Kübeck von Kübau,[54] who impressed upon the *Hofkanzlei* the commercial and financial implications of quarantine policy.[55] Kübeck, president of the *Hofkammer* since November 1840, proved a powerful ally. Not only did he occupy a major administrative post, but he also enjoyed during the 1840s an increasingly close relationship with Metternich, whose aid he enlisted in the cause of reform.[56] Although Kübeck and Metternich could not themselves determine quarantine policy, they could nevertheless offer advice that was difficult for the *Hofkanzlei* to ignore.

Thanks to determination and a favorable constellation of circumstances, Stadion, Weber, and their successors[57] gained each of their limited objectives, until by late 1847 the monarchy's maritime quarantine code had been significantly revised as far as plague was concerned. Although the entire administrative apparatus created by the eighteenth-century code was allowed to survive in case plague should reappear in full vigor in the Levant, quarantines were reduced from being a major impediment to commerce and travel to being a tolerable inconvenience. In times of satisfactory public health in the Levant — that is, when no cases of plague were reported by European consular or diplomatic agents — ships and passengers arriving from ports in the Ottoman Empire, Syria, or Egypt with *patente netta* were subjected merely to a five-day period of observation in port; susceptible merchandise underwent a relatively short quarantine of seven days. Furthermore, the category of *patente tocca* had been abolished, as had been quarantines for ships arriving with clean bills of health from Greece and the Ionian Islands. As for quarantines for ships arriving from the Levant with *patente brutta*, these had been reduced to fifteen days for passengers and 22 days for merchandise.[58] Since the issuance of clean bills of health became the norm owing to the absence of plague, these changes meant considerable savings in time and money for travellers, merchants, and shipowners.

Austrian reforms also had an impact upon other maritime states. On the positive side, in France, those reductions which the *Hofkanzlei* began to enact in 1841 combined with growing anticontagionist sentiment and with fear of the increasing commercial importance of Trieste to produce major reductions in the quarantines of the July Monarchy in 1845 and again in 1846.[59] In turn, these reductions provided powerful arguments for officials in Trieste in pressing for still further modifications in the Austrian code, which were enacted in September 1847.[60] On the negative side, however, this final stage in Austria's program of quarantine reform at long last provoked Italian governments to retaliate. In the final weeks of 1847, and again, in early 1848, Metternich's foreign office, already hard pressed by an increasingly threatening international situation, found itself forced repeatedly to protest discriminatory measures taken against ships arriving from Austria in Sardinian, Neapolitan, and Papal ports.[61] That the Habsburg Monarchy had so significantly reduced its quarantines against plague and was also showing itself reluctant to take stringent measures against a renewed threat of cholera convinced Turin, Naples, and Rome that Vienna was irresponsibly endangering the health of Europe.[62]

In an influential article published in 1947, the distinguished historian of medicine, Erwin H. Ackerknecht, discerned a close connection between anticontagionism, hostility to quarantines, and political liberalism on the one hand, and contagionism, support of quarantines, and conservative ideology on the other.[63] His thesis may hold true for England and France, upon whose experience it is based. But, it is not applicable to the Habsburg monarchy. Whatever may have divided them in their political views, Stadion, Kübeck, and Metternich were not liberals in Ackerknecht's sense of the term. Nevertheless, each would cheerfully have abolished quarantines in their entirety had it been possible for them to do so. Such freedom did not exist. The medical community upon which the government depended for advice was contagionist,[64] while Italian governments would not tolerate radical reform in Austria. Under these circumstances, it is noteworthy that of the two leading continental Mediterranean powers, it was not constitutional France, but absolutist Austria that assumed the lead in reducing quarantines against plague in the first half of the nineteenth century. Precisely why the French government should have been slow to reform is uncertain and requires further investigation.[65] No uncertainty exists concerning the Habsburg monarchy. From the archival record, it is clear that Austrian quarantine reforms were based upon the realization by key officials in Trieste and Vienna that the monarchy's strength in a changing technological and commercial world required improved ties with the Levant. To attain that goal, during the 1840s, the monarchy reduced maritime quarantines against plague as far as medical knowledge and practical considerations would allow. For the government of a "stagnant and immobile" state, it is a record worthy of rescue from obscurity.

Notes

* Research for this article has been supported by grants from the National Institutes of Health, the Gladys Krieble Delmas Foundation, and the University of Connecticut Research Foundation.

1. William L. Langer, *Political and Social Upheaval, 1832-1852* (New York, 1969), p. 119. At the level of high politics the generalization has considerable merit. In the area of economic history, however, it is misleading. Despite political reaction, Ferdinand's reign experienced economic growth and modernization; see, e.g., the recent study by David F. Good, *The Economic Rise of the Habsburg Empire, 1750-1914* (Berkeley / Los Angeles / London, 1984), 38-73.

2. Charles F. Mullett discusses British quarantine policy in "A Century of English Quarantine (1709-1825)," *Bulletin of the History of Medicine*, XXIII (1949), 527-45; "Politics, Economics and Medicine: Charles Maclean and Anticontagionism in England," *Osiris*, X (1952), 224-51; *The Bubonic Plague and England: An Essay in the History of Preventive Medicine* (Lexington, 1956), 335-62. See also, J. C. McDonald, "The History of Quarantine in Britain during the 19th Century,"*Bulletin of the History of Medicine*, XXV (1951), 22-44.French quarantine policy is discussed briefly in Paul Masson, ed., *Les Bouches-du-Rhône: Encyclopédie départementale* (Paris, 1913-1937), IX, 53: *La grande encyclopédie: Inventaire raisonné des sciences, des lettres et des arts* (Paris, 1885-1902), XXVII, 107-108.

3. The major provisions of the code are reproduced and discussed in Loris Premuda, "Regolamenti e istruzioni degli Uffici di Sanità di Trieste e Litorale negli anni 1755 e 1764," *Rassegna giuliana di medicina*, IX (1947), 293-303; X (1948), 338-53; preparation of the code is discussed in Erna Lesky, *Österreichisches Gesundheitswesen im Zeitalter des aufgeklärten Absolutismus* ("Archiv für österreichische Geschichte," vol. 122/1; Vienna, 1959), pp. 32-40. For the provisions of the maritime sanitary code following minor modifications in August 1837, see, John MacGregor, *Commercial Statistics: A Digest of the Productive Resources, Commercial Legislation, Customs Tariffs, Navigation, Port and Quarantine Laws and Charges, Shipping, Imports and Exports, and the Monies, Weights, and Measures of all Nations* (2nd ed.; London, 1850), I, 59-60.

4. An example of apparent corruption in the Austrian maritime sanitary service is provided by the charges brought against the president of the Maritime Sanitary

Office in Venice, Dr. Angelo A. Frari; see the extensive report prepared by the protomedicus of Trieste, Dr. Franz Weber, in March 1843 (Archivio di Stato di Venezia, Atti dell' I. R. Governo, fascicolo XIII, busta 2/22) and the Hofkanzlei Vortrag of August 24, 1843 (Haus-, Hof- und Staatsarchiv, Vienna [hereafter cited as HHStA], Staatsrat-Akten 4846/1843).

5. European quarantine legislation of the 1830s is summarized in tabular form in MacGregor, *Commercial Statistics* I, 1262-1263, and in *Rapport adressé à son exc. le Ministre du Commerce, par M. de Ségur-Dupeyron, secrétaire du conseil supérieur de santé, chargé de procéder à une enquête sur les divers régimes sanitaires de la Méditerranée, et sur les modifications qui pourraient être apportées aux tableaux qui fixent la durée de quarantaine en France* (Paris, 1834), pp. 90-91. For an example of contemporary criticism of quarantine legislation in the Mediterranean see, Arthur T. Holroyd, *The Quarantine Laws, their Abuses and Inconsistencies* (London, 1834); for brief histories of quarantines see Neville M. Goodman, *International Organizations and their Work* (Edinburgh / London, 1971), pp. 23-42, and L. Fabian Hirst, *The Conquest of Plague: A Study of the Evolution of Epidemiology* (Oxford, 1953), pp. 378-88.

6. Erna Lesky discusses Chenot's reforms in "Die österreichische Pestfront an der k. k. Militärgrenze," *Saeculum*, VIII (1957), 99-101, and "Die josephinische Reform der Seuchengesetzgebung," *Sudhoffs Archiv für Geschischte der Medizin und der Naturwissenschaften*, XL (1956), 67-88. Also of value is Iosif Spielmann, "Über den Einfluß der Chenotschen Seuchenordnung auf Siebenbürgen," *Medizinhistorisches Journal*, VI (1971), 200-206.

7. "Pest-Polizei-Ordnung für die k. k. österreichischen Staaten, "*Medicinische Jahrbücher des k.k. österreichischen Staates*, XXIV [N. F. XV] (1838), 257-63, 398-469, 556-95. The preparation of the code is discussed briefly in Gunther E. Rothenberg, "The Austrian Sanitary Cordon and the Control of the Bubonic Plague: 1710-1871,"*Journal of the History of Medicine and Allied Sciences*, XXVIII (1973), 21-22.

8. For an example of extreme dissatisfaction with the discrepancies between the land and maritime quarantine codes see the complaint lodged by the Steam Navigation Company of the Austrian Lloyd to the central government on August 23, 1837 (Finanzarchiv, Vienna, Präsidial-Akten [hereafter cited as FA, Präs.] 5128/1837), after one of its vessels had received especially harsh treatment upon its return from the Levant.

9. The terms of the quarantines enforced at the land border are stated in "Pest-Polizey-Ordnung für die k.k. österreichischen Staaten," pp. 398-399, 428, and 433 in §§ 18, 59, and 66.

10. Figures published in Austria, k.k. Direktion der administrativen Statistik, *Tafeln zur Statistik der Oesterreichischen Monarchie* (Vienna, 1829-1851) show that in 1834 the value of goods exported to the Kingdom of the Two Sicilies, Sardinia, and the Papal States amounted to 28% of the total exports of Trieste and 51% of those of Venice (*Tafeln zur Statistik*, 1835, Table 40); for 1845 the respective figures are 20% and 47% (*ibid.*, 1845-1846, Table 6, pp. 14-15). See also

Fulvio Babudieri, *I porti di Trieste e della ragione giulia dal 1815 al 1918* (Rome, 1965), Table I.

11. In 1785 the Austrian foreign minister, Count Wenzel Kaunitz, insisted that the reforms proposed by Chenot be restricted to the land border with the Ottoman Empire because he feared Italian retaliation if they were applied at the monarchy's ports in the Adriatic; see Lesky, *Österreichisches Gesundheitswesen,* p. 137. Over sixty years later the provincial government in Trieste, in a review of Austrian quarantine policy since the late eighteenth century, observed: "Hitherto the only consideration that justified this distinction [between maritime and land quarantines] was the timidity of the Italian maritime bureaus, the pertinacity with which they resisted any relaxation in quarantine regulations, and the threat to deny Austrian arrivals immediate admission to free pratique if Austrian authorities did not act with greater severity." See Gubernium in Trieste to Handelsministerium, February 5, 1849 (Archivio di Stato di Trieste [hereafter cited as AST], Atti dell'I.R. Governo del Litorale [hereafter cited as Governo], Atti generali, busta 653, fasciolo 4/7.1, 1681/1849).

12. See, e.g., Virgilio Giormani, "La linea a vapore della Dalmazia e il colera del 1831," *La rivista dalmatica,* LIII (1982), 327-28.

13. On February 14, 1838, the American consular representative in Trieste, Alexander Murray, wrote the United States' chargé d'affaires in Vienna: "In the late removal of all sanitary restrictions during the prevalence of cholera, ships from this place became subject to severe quarantine regulations in the Neapolitan and other ports, occasioning thereby considerable loss and inconvenience to trade." *Document Number* 246, in vol. 4 of United States Senate Documents, 27th Congress, 2nd Session, 1841-1842 (hereafter *Doc. No. 246*), p. 24.

14. See, e.g., Hofkanzlei to Staatskanzlei, January 14, 1848 (HHStA, Administrative Registratur [hereafter cited as Adm. Reg.] F 50/3, Convolut "Contumazmaßregeln gegen Österreich." Under Italian pressure, the Hofkanzlei after some delay reluctantly instituted a five-day cholera quarantine even though it agreed with the Viennese medical faculty that such a measure was "reprehensible;" see Hofkanzlei to Gubernium in Trieste, December 13, 1847 (AST, Governo, Atti generali, b. 653, f. 4/7.1, 22914/1847).

15. The negotiations can be followed from the American side in *Doc. No. 246,* pp. 8-12, 16-24, 31-43; for Austrian responses to the American initiative see, e.g., Hofkanzlei to Hofkammer, April 21, 1838 (FA, Präs. 2654/1838), Hofkammer to Hofkanzlei, May 12, 1838 (*ibid.*), and Meteernich to Hofkammer, March 25, 1838 (FA, Präs. 1667/1838).

16. Egon Radvany, *Metternich's Projects for Reform in Austria* (The Hague, 1971) provides a useful discussion in English of the Austrian administration during the first half of the nineteenth century.

17. Moore to Forsyth, May 29, 1838 (National Archives, Washington, D.C., Records of the Department of State, Despatches from United States Consuls in Trieste [Microfilm No. T-242, Roll 2].)

18. Metternich to Muhlenberg, January 10, 1840 (*Doc. No. 246,* pp. 68-69).

19. On the Lloyd's financial crisis see Ronald E. Coons, *Steamships, Statesmen, and Bureaucrats: Austrian Policy towards the Steam Navigation Company of the Austrian Lloyd 1836-1848* (Wiesbaden, 1975), pp. 63-78.

20. *Ibid.*, pp. 90-94. The value of the Austrian florin in contemporary United States currency was approximately SO. 48.

21. *Ibid.*, pp. 83-84.

22. The diplomatic history of Austrian efforts to direct the East Indian mail over Trieste is discussed in Ronald E. Coons. "Das Dampfschiff als diplomatisches Mittel: Österreich und die englisch-ostindische Post," *Mitteilungen des Österreichischen Staatsarchivs*, XXIII (1970), 147-79.

23. In 1837 quarantines for ships arriving from the Levant with *patente brutta* had been reduced from forty to thirty-five days; otherwise the provisions of the 1755 code had been reaffirmed. See Hofkammerarchiv, Vienna, Commerz-Akten 116/Sept. ex 1836, Fasz. 22, rote Nr. 1308, and AST, I.R. Luogotenenza del Litorale (hereafter cited as Luogotenenza), Normalien, vol. 3349, 20918/1837.

24. Coons, *Steamships, Statesmen, and Bureaucrats*, pp. 79-82; Hofkanzlei to Gubernium in Trieste, August 16, 1838 (AST, Governo, Atti generali, b. 619, f. 4/7.1, 20396/1838).

25. Palmerston to Lamb, June 11, 1838 (Public Record Office, London, Foreign Office [hereafter cited as PRO, FO] 412/1, p. 6).

26. Langsdorff to Metternich, July 4, 1838, and Molé to Langsdorff, undated (HHStA, Adm. Reg. F 50/2, Convolut "Verhandlungen wegen Aufstellung eines Quarantine Systems für das Mittelmeer").

27. Hofkanzlei to Gubernium in Trieste, July 24, 1838 (AST, Governo, Atti generali, b. 620, f. 4/7.4, 18072/1838), and Gubernium to Hofkanzlei, September 2, 1838 (*ibid.*, 19283/1838).

28. Metternich to Lamb, November 5, 1838 (PRO, FO 412/1, p. 17).

29. Metternich to Langsdorff, July 13, 1838 (HHStA, Adm. Reg. F 50/2, Convolut "Verhandlungen wegen Aufstellung eines Quarantaine Systems").

30. On Austrian suspicions of possible ulterior motives on the part of France see, e.g., Lebseltern to Metternich, Naples, June 22, 1838, and Prokesch-Osten to the Greek State Secretary for Internal Affairs, Athens, October 14, 1838 (HHStA, Adm. Reg. F 50/2, *ibid.*).

31. See Metternich to Langsdorff, July 13, 1838 (HHStA, Adm. Reg. F 50/2, *ibid.*).

32. See, e.g., Metternich to Hofkanzlei, October 24, 1838 (HHStA, Adm. Reg. F 50/2, Convolut "Sanität & Quarantine 1843").

33. St. Aulaire to Metternich, Vienna, June 20, 1839 (HHStA, Adm. Reg. F 50/2, Convolut "Verhandlungen wegen Aufstellung eines Quarantaine Systems").

34. In December 1841 the British consul in Trieste, Sir Thomas Sorell, reported to the Foreign Office: "When Prince Metternich visited Trieste in 1838, he expressed himself strongly in favour of a general re-construction of the quarantine code, as regards the Mediterranean, but he justly observed that no system would work well which should not be established with the concurrence of all the Powers

which have possessions either on or within that sea. The Prince told me that it had been in contemplation to hold a Congress to regulate this matter, but that the project went off in consequence of a difference of opinion as to the place of the meeting, and of objections, on the part of France, to the admission of Great Britain as a party in the discussion." Sorell to Bidwell, December 8, 1841 (PRO, FO 7/300).

35. MacGregor, *Commercial Statistics*, I, 1256-1257; Norman Howard-Jones, "The Scientific Background of the International Sanitary Conferences, 1851-1938," *WHO Chronicle*, XXVIII (1974), 161; and Goodman, *International Health Organizations*, pp. 42-43.

36. Ponsonby to Palmerston, Therapia, April 19, 1838 (PRO, FO 412/1, p. 276).

37. Palmerston to Ponsonby, July 5, 1838 (*ibid.*, p. 285).

38. Palmerston to Milbanke, February 22, 1839 (*ibid.*, p. 19).

39. The establishment and the early history of the Egyptian sanitary code are discussed in Laverne Kuhnke, "Resistance and Response to Modernization: Preventive Medicine and Social Control in Egypt, 1825-1850." (Ph. D. diss., University of Chicago, 1973), pp. 116-165; Robert Tignor, "Public Health Administration in Egypt under British Rule, 1882-1914." (Ph. D. diss., Yale University, 1960), pp. 27-48.

40. Islamic fatalism vis-à-vis plague is discussed in William H. McNeill, *Plagues and Peoples* (New York, 1976), pp. 166-167, and M. W. Dols, "The Black Death in the Middle East." (Ph. D. diss., Princeton University, 1971), pp. 23, 297-98.

41. Milbanke to Palmerston, Vienna, March 19, 1839 (PRO, FO 412/1, p. 20).

42. Max Neuburger, "Österreichische Ärzte als Pioniere der wissenschaftlichen Medizin und des Sanitätswesens in der Türkei (1839-1856)", *Wiener medizinische Wochenschrift*, LXVII (1917), 1685. For an example of Austria's moderating role in negotiations between the European Powers and the Porte, see Stürmer to Metternich, January 9, 1839 (Kriegsarchiv, Vienna, Hofkriegsrat 1839, B-1/63).

43. See, e.g., Stürmer to Metternich, September 11, 1844, with numerous attachments (HHStA, Adm. Reg. F 50/4, Convolut "Reform des türkischen Quarantänewesens 1844-1845").

44. Weber was born in Laibach in 1791, graduated from the University of Vienna, and was appointed protomedicus of the Austrian Littoral on December 22, 1837, in which post he died on March 26, 1844. The author is indebted to Dr. Ugo Cova, director of the Archivio di Stato di Trieste, for supplying this information.

45. Carl Ignatz Lorinser, *Die Pest des Orients, wie sie entsteht und verhütet wird; drei Bücher* (Berlin, 1837), pp. 115-251.

46. Weber's views are expressed in a report to a meeting of the provincial government of Trieste held on March 16, 1839 (AST, Governo, Atti generali, b. 638, f. 4/7.1, 5430/1839). For a published version of the report see "Ansichten

über das Zeitgemässe von Modificationen im gegenwärtigen See-Sanitäts - und Contumaz-System, mit Hinblick auf den Vorschlag des Dr. Bulard," *Medicinische Jahrbücher des k.k. österreichischen Staates,* XXXIV [N. F. XXV] (1841), 18-27, 161-72.

47. Gubernium in Trieste to Hofkanzlei, March 23, 1839 (AST, Governo, Atti generali, b. 638, f. 4/7.1, 5430/1839).

48. See, e.g., Robert Pollitzer, *Plague* ("World Health Organization, Monograph Series," N.o. XXII; Geneva, 1965), p. 14; Hirst, *Conquest of Plague,* p. 386, who observes: "During the greater part of the nineteenth century, plague showed no tendency to diffuse from its ancient haunts in Africa and Asia. After 1844 it seemed to have disappeared from the Levant and Egypt."

49. On the career of Stadion, who served as governor of the Littoral until April 1847, see Rudolph Mattausch, "Franz Graf Stadion," *Neue Österreichische Biographie ab 1815,* XIV (1960), 62-73.

50. Stadion to Hofkanzlei, June 17, 1841 (AST, Governo, Atti generali, b. 638, f. 4/7.1, 12298/1841); Stadion to Hofkammer, November 6, 1842 (FA, Präs. 8087/1842); and Stadion to Hofkanzlei, October 6, 1846 (FA, Präs. 10268/1846). For an example of a modern scholar who gives the Turkish sanitary establishment greater credit for liquidating plague than it in fact deserves, see Jean-Noël Biraben, *Les hommes et la peste en France et dans les pays européens et méditerranéens* (Paris / The Hague, 1975-1976), II, 175.

51. See, e.g., Stadion to Hofkanzlei, May 4, 1841 (AST, Governo, Atti generali, b. 638, f. 4/7.1, 9968/1841), following minor reductions in the Tuscan quarantine code, and Stadion to Hofkanzlei, April 20, 1844 (*ibid.,* b. 653, f. 4/7.1, 7397/1844), following changes in the Sardinian code.

52. Stadion to Stürmer, November 5, 1841 (AST, Governo, Atti presidiali, b. 42, f. 4/7.3, 1757/1841), and April 27, 1846 (*ibid.,* Atti generali, b. 653, f. 4/7.1, 10201/1846).

53. Stadion to Kübeck, June 5, 1841 (AST, Governo, Atti generali, b. 638, f. 4/7.1, 12298/1841).

54. See, e.g., Stadion to Kübeck, June 5, 1841 (*ibid.*), February 12, 1843 (FA, Präs. 1405/1843), and December 8, 1846 (FA, Präs. 10268/1846). Stadion's close relationship with Kübeck is stressed, e.g., in Joseph Alexander Freiherr von Helfert, *Geschichte Oesterreichs vom Ausgange des Wiener Oktober-Aufstandes 1848* (Prague, 1869-1886), III, 25. When in 1848 Kübeck found it necessary to resign his post as Minister of Finance for reasons of health, he initially proposed as his successor Stadion, who declined the position; see Maria Woinovich, "Philipp Freiherr von Krauß, Finanzminister im Jahre 1848," *Mitteilungen des Österreichischen Staatsarchivs,* XIV (1961), 550.

55. For important examples of Kübeck's intervention on behalf of quarantine reform see his notes to the Hofkanzlei of July 20, 1841 (FA, Präs. 4543/1841), November 29, 1842 (FA, Präs. 8087/1842), and February 22, 1843 (FA, Präs. 1405/1843).

56. Kübeck's cooperation with Metternich during the 1840s is discussed in my

forthcoming article "The Pre-Revolutionary Origins of Kübeck's Neoabsolutism,"
to be published under the auspices of the Institut für Europäische Geschichte,
Mainz. Kübeck was particularly successful in gaining Metternich's support for
a proposal advanced by the Austrian physician Ferdinand Gobbi to have the European Powers contribute funds annually towards the operation and improvement
of the Ottoman sanitary establishment. Gobbi argued that improvements in Turkey would ultimately save European governments money by enabling them gradually to dismantle their own quarantine establishments. On Gobbi's scheme see
his *Beiträge zur Entwicklung und Reform des Quarantaenewesens* (Vienna, 1849),
pp. 1-74; on Kübeck's search for Metternich's cooperation in this ultimately unsuccessful venture see, e.g., Kübeck to Metternich, June 19, 1845 (FA, Präs.
3066/1845), and Staatskanzlei to Hofkanzlei, July 31, 1845 (Kriegsarchiv, Vienna,
Hofkriegsrath 1845, B-1/92). Kübeck also enlisted Metternich's aid in gaining the
emperor's approval to send a commission of Austrian physicians to the Balkans
and the Near East to investigate quarantine establishments there, in the hope that
a favorable report might justify further Austrian reform, especially along the sanitary cordon in the Balkans; see Metternich's Vortrag of September 30, 1847 (FA,
Präs. 8549/1847). The observations of one of the members of the commission,
which did not set out until after Metternich's fall, are published in Karl Ludwig
Sigmund, *Die Quarantäne-Reform und die Pestfrage* (Vienna, 1850).

57. Following Stadion's appointment as governor of Galicia, the final changes
in the maritime code during the pre-revolutionary period were proposed by the
acting governor, Joseph Edler von Fölsch; Weber's successor as protomedicus
was Dr. Octav Edler von Vest (1807-1861).

58. The major stages in Austrian quarantine reform between 1841 and 1847
can be described briefly. By a decree of July 29, 1841, the category of *patente
netta* was created for arrivals from Turkey, while quarantines for arrivals from
all ports in the Levant carrying *patente tocca* or *patente brutta* were reduced by
approximately one week (Pillersdorf to Gubernium in Trieste, AST, Governo,
Atti generali, b. 638, f. 4/7.1). On February 16, 1843, moreover, the Hofkanzlei
accepted the provincial government's recommendation that three health zones be
established for the Levant — Turkey, Syria, and Egypt — with quarantines appropriate to conditions in each. On this occasion the bureau also created the category of *patente netta* for arrivals from Syria and Egypt and abolished quarantines
for arrivals with clean bills of health from the Ionian Islands and Greece,
except for those ships carrying shipments of rags (Hofkanzlei to Kübeck, FA,
Präs. 1751/1843). Then, on December 13, 1846, a further decree instituted a five-
day period of observation for arrivals with clean bills of health from the first zone
in the Levant — i.e., Turkey — and reduced quarantines for arrivals with *patente
netta* from Syria and Egypt (Hofkanzlei to Gubernium in Trieste, AST, Governo,
Atti generali, b. 653, f. 4/7.1, 669/1847). Finally, a decree of September 17, 1847,
applied the five-day period of observation to all arrivals from the Levant with
patente netta, abolished the category of *patente tocca*, and reduced quarantines
for ships and passengers with *patente brutta* from twenty-four to fifteen days

(Hofkanzlei to Gubernium in Trieste, AST, Governo, Atti generali, b. 653, f. 4/7.1, 22427/1847).

59. See Stadion to Kübeck, December 8, 1846 (FA, Präs. 10268/1846), and Fölsch to Hofkanzlei, May 25, 1847 (AST, Governo, Atti generali, b. 653, f. 4/7.1, 10672/1847). French quarantine reforms are discussed in *The Times* (London), April 24, 1847, p. 8, and Abroise Auguste Tardieu, *Dictionnaire d'hygiène et de salubrité ou répertoire de toutes les questions relatives à la santé publique* (Paris, 1854), III, 270.

60. See Fölsch to Hofkanzlei, May 25, 1847 (AST, Governo, Atti generali, b. 653, f. 4/7.1, 10672/1847), and Hofkanzlei to Gubernium in Trieste, September 17, 1847 (*ibid.*, 22427/1847).

61. The diplomatic correspondence concerning Italian measures against arrivals from Austrian ports is preserved in HHStA, Adm. Reg. F 50/3 in the folders "Sardinien, Neapel, Malta, Rom: Quarantaine-Meßregeln" and "Contumazmaßregeln Italiens gegen Oesterreich."

62. On Italian objections to Austrian quarantine reforms see, e.g., Kübeck to Metternich, November 1, 1847 (FA, Präs. 9307/1847), and Schwarzenberg to Metternich, Naples, December 10, 1847 (HHStA, Adm. Reg. F 50/3, Convolut "Sardinien, Neapel, Malta, Rom: Quarantaine-Maßregeln").

63. Erwin H. Ackerknecht, "Anticontagionism between 1821 and 1867," *Bulletin of the History of Medicine*, XXII (1947), 567, 589-92; see also, George Rosen, *A History of Public Health* (New York, 1958), pp. 289-90.

64. Governmental correspondence indicates that information supplied the bureaucracy by the Austrian medical establishment was overhelmingly contagionist as far as plague was concerned. Contrary views were, however, expressed in the monarchy. The most notable opponent of quarantines was the Viennes physician Carl Sigmund, who in 1847 and 1848 published in the *Österreichische medizinische Wochenschrift* a series of articles criticizing the existing system. The views expressed in these article were later incorporated into Sigmund's *Die Quarantäne-Reform und die Pestfrage* (Vienna, 1850). On Sigmund's career see Erna Lesky, *The Vienna Medical School of the 19th Century* (Baltimore/London, 1976), pp. 257-60; Constant von Wurzbach, *Biographisches Lexikon des Kaiserthums Oesterreich* (Vienna, 1856-1891), XXXIV, 272-75.

65. Discussions of French maritime sanitary legislation against plague approach the topic from the viewpoint of anticontagionist reformers rather than contagionist governmental officials; see, e.g., Ann Elizabeth Fowler La Berge, "Public Health in France and the French Public Health Movement, 1815-1848" (Ph. D. dissertation, University of Tennesse, 1974), pp. 115-32. For an excellent discussion of governmental policy towards quarantines against yellow fever and cholera, however, see George D. Sussman, "From Yellow Fever to Cholera. A Study of French Government Policy, Medical Professionalism and Popular Movements in the Epidemic Crises of the Restoration and the July Monarchy." (Ph. D. diss., Yale University, 1971), *passim.*

Konstantinos K. Hatzopoulos

The U.S. Navy in the Aegean during the Greek War of Independence, 1821-1829

The arrival of the U.S. Navy in the Aegean during the Greek War of Independence (1821-29), because of its importance in understanding American foreign policy toward the "Greek Question," has been the object of research of many historians, Greek and non-Greek. They come, however, to different conclusions for Washington's real intentions in sending U.S. warships to such a remote part of the world which remain, even today, obscure in certain aspects.

I cannot possibly, in this paper, discuss in detail all the opinions expressed in the past, but, nevertheless, I would like to stress here their main points, before expressing my own views on this subject. According to certain historians, the arrival of the American squadron in the Aegean during the Greek War of Independence proves definitely the interest of the American government in the case of Greece, and is closely related to the philhellenic movement developed during that period of time in the U.S. known as *Greek Fever*.[1] On the other hand, an opposing point of view says that the American presence in the Aegean served exclusively the commercial interests of the U.S. in the eastern Mediterranean and the Black Sea. Consequently, it had nothing to do at all with the Greek War of Independence and the philhellenic feelings of the American people.[2]

The discordance of opinions expressed so far, both so absolute in their expression, has spurred me to study the available sources, convinced that there might exist a third interpretation, one much closer to the historical truth. I think that the results of my research, which I am going to discuss later in this paper, have justified my doubts.

Therefore I first intend to give a short account of the activities of the U.S. Navy in the Aegean during the Greek War of Independence, and then, to clarify why the American government was led to undertake these naval missions there.

To begin with, it is proper to remark here, I think, that the appearance of the American warships in the Mediterranean dates from the beginning of the nineteenth century. Their main purpose was, as is well known, to protect American commercial vessels from attacks by Barbary pirates of North Africa. During the first 20 years of the century, we find an American naval squadron patrolling the western and central Mediterranean, especially near the shores of North Africa; on many occasions it had successfully undertaken military action.[3]

The American Navy's presence in the western and central Mediterranean for these years was continuous. However, the first American warship appeared in the Aegean only in October 1820.[4] Consequently, the repeated missions of American warships in these waters during the 1820s should not be considered as common.

Besides, we must pay special attention to the status of the Aegean during the 1820s when American warships made their first appearance there. Immediately after the outbreak of the Greek War of Independence (March, 1821), the Greek revolutionary navy blockaded the shoreline from Dyrrahium to Euboea (Negropont). Consequently, the waters of the Aegean changed status *de facto*, that is, under the control of Greek insurgents it gradually became a "Greek Sea." A few years later this status was recognized by the Great Powers with the exception of Austria. Thus, the U.S. could not overlook this new reality by sending American warships in the Aegean. America's neutrality, however, all through the war in the archipelago, meant nothing more than an indirect recognition of the new status the Greeks imposed on the Aegean.

American Warships in the Aegean, 1821-29

According to the sources I have at my disposal, the U.S. Navy arrived in the Aegean on special mission. Let us look at the chronology of events.

1) *June-July 1822:* Three ships of the American Mediterranean Squadron — the frigate *Constitution*, the sloop of war *Ontario*, and the schooner *Nonsuch* — on their way to Smyrna witnessed the destruction of the flagship of the Turkish admiral (Captain Pashaw) by Konstantinos Kanaris at the straits of Chios on June 6-7, 1822.[5] A

little later, on June 17, 1822, the squadron arrived in Hydra,[6] the well-known island on the northeastern coast of the Peloponese. Its arrival in Hydra had neither a ceremonious purpose nor was it connected with the provision of supplies for its ships. On the contrary, the American admiral, Commodore Jacob Jones, had formal discussions with Greek authorities on the island regarding the Greek War on Independence. In the second part of this paper I shall expound on the significance of these discussions.

2) *Winter 1824-25:* The U.S. warship *Erie* arrived in the troubled Grecian waters of the Aegean with orders to protect a convoy of commercial vessels heading for Smyrna.[7] The USS Erie, it should be emphasized, neither arrived in a port controlled by the Greeks nor did its commander come in any contact with the Greek authorities.

3) *August-September 1825:* The squadron consisting of the ship-of-the-line *North Carolina*, the frigate *Constitution*, the sloops of war *Ontario* and *Erie*, and the brig *Cyane*, under the command of Commodore John Rodgers, arrived in the Aegean. At first, the squadron anchored for five days near Paros, an island controlled by the insurgent Greeks (August 1825).[8] Later, the American ships visited Smyrna for a brief period of time. At the end of August 1825, they left Smyrna for Nafplio (known as Napoli di Romania as well), the capital of the liberated Greece, where they remained till September 6, 1825 (o.s.).[9] While there, Commodore Rodgers had official meetings with the representatives of the Greek revolutionary government and discussed with them the "Greek Question." As we shall see in the third part of this paper, the arrival of Americans in Nafplio was the most important political act of America's foreign policy as to the "Greek Question."

4) *September-November 1825:* After the squadron's departure from Nafplio, the *Ontario* was ordered to remain in the Aegean for the protection of the American commercial vessels sailing in these waters. Despite its formal mission, the USS *Ontario* repeatedly visited Greek ports. At that time, Captain John B. Nicholson, commander of the *Ontario*, apparently interested in the case of Greece, came in contact with the Greek authorities.[10]

5) *March-April 1826:* The *Erie* sailed the Aegean once more, protecting American commercial vessels from the pirates' raids, which

had intensified during this period. I would like to point out that, though the American warship arrived many times at ports controlled by the Greek insurgents its commander did not come in any contact — official or unofficial — with the Greek authorities.[11]

6) *June-August 1826:* The squadron, consisting of the ship-of-the-line *North Carolina*, the frigate *Constitution*, the sloop of war *Ontario*, and the schooner *Porpoise*, under the command of Commodore Rodgers, arrived again in Grecian waters. The ships, after having anchored for a few days near the Greek islands of Milos, Paros, and Anti-Paros, arrived in Smyrna, where they also remained for a few days.[12] Later the squadron sailed toward the Greek islands of Tenedos and Mitilina, where an official meeting between Commodore Rodgers and the Captain-Pashaw Khosrew took place at the beginning of July 1826. The only subject discussed was the conditions of a possible American-Turkish commercial treaty.[13] Finally, in the middle of August 1826, the U.S. ships departed westward to the naval base of Port Mahon, leaving behind the *Ontario* to protect the American commercial vessels.[14] I would like to point out here that during this visit, Commodore Rodgers avoided sailing to Nafplio or Hydra; on the other hand, the American ships, upon return to Port Mahon, sailed round the eastern coast of the Peloponnesos.

7) *April 1827-beginning of 1828:* The American warships *Constitution*, *Warren*, *Lexington*, and *Porpoise* sailed in succession toward Grecian waters, with the mission to protect U.S. commercial vessels from the "piratical" raids of Greek insurgents. However, while the commanders of the *Warren*, *Lexington*, and *Porpoise* followed orders to the letter, and pursued vigorously, and at times brutally, "pirates,"[15] Captain Daniel Patterson of the USS *Constitution*, it seems, either understood his orders in a different light or was on a different mission. Consequently, the *Constitution*, on patrol in the Aegean, sailed round the coast of eastern Greece, visiting frequently many ports controlled by the Greek insurgents. During these visits Captain Patterson came in contact with the Greek authorities and military leaders, including the famous hero, Konstantinos Kanaris. It must also be pointed out here that the USS *Constitution* sailed toward Nafplio, where Captain Patterson was informed by the Greek revolutionary government of the course of the War of Independence.[16]

8) *August-September 1828:* The American squadron, consisting of the warships *Java, Delaware, Lexington, Porpoise,* and *Warren,* under the command of Commodore William Crane, the new American admiral in the Mediterranean, sailed down the Aegean heading for Smyrna. His mission was the undertaking of a new round of negotiations with the Captain-Pashaw with the view of concluding an American-Turkish commercial treaty.[17] I would like to point out, once again, that the American admiral avoided sailing to the ports controlled by the Greek insurgents, and in particular, skirted every possible meeting with the Greek revolutionary government, just as Commodore Rodgers had done in 1826.

The American Squadron of the Mediterranean and Insurgent Greece

I would like to proceed now to the analysis of the reasons which led the U.S. government to send the American squadron to the Aegean during the 1820s. At this point I shall not refer, it should be mentioned, to the American-Turkish negotiations regarding the conclusion of the commercial treaty between the two powers, because, on one hand, I have nothing new to add,[18] and on the other, this is not the subject of the present paper.

The problem of an American naval base in the Mediterranean

In the beginning of the nineteenth century, Washington realized the need for a naval base in the Mediterranean, because of: a) the great distance between the American warships patrolling in the Mediterranean and naval bases in the U.S.; b) their prolonged stay in the Mediterranean (usually from February or March up to November or December); and c) the growth of American maritime commerce in the Mediterranean, which required the continuous protection of the American commercial vessels from pirates.

The port of Mahon on the Spanish island of Minorca was considered both by the American admirals and the U.S. government to be the best choice.[19] The American government, beginning in 1815, tried to persuade the King of Spain to accept its proposals regarding the port. But he only granted, in February 1821, a six-month use of

Port Mahon as a naval base, after which he refused to renew the agreement. The king reacted thus because of U.S. recognition of the newly independent nations of Latin America, once Spanish colonies.[20]

In June 1822, the American Mediterranean Squadron, under the command of Commodore Jacob Jones, reached, for the first time, the Greek island of Hydra, as I have already mentioned. The American admiral in his meetings with the Greek authorities discussed, among other things, the U.S. Navy's need for a naval base in the Mediterranean. It is worth quoting here, from a letter, dated June 24, 1822, sent by the authorities of Hydra, just after their meeting with Commodore Jones, to the Greek revolutionary government: "The U.S. wishes to obtain a naval base in the Mediterranean, as it has been known for a long period of time, and has been reported to us by the admiral himself; we encouraged him in believing that our government could easily accept this proposal, on condition that we receive support when we urgently need it."[21]

The first Greek-American discussions regarding the American proposals obviously were not continued after the squadron's departure in June 1822. And they were held in abeyance, the more especially since, in 1825 Commodore John Rodgers, the new American admiral, managed to overcome the King of Spain's objections and succeeded in obtaining again the use of Port Mahon as a naval base for the U.S. Navy.[22]

Despite this agreement, I believe that Washington's problem regarding the naval base in the Mediterranean was not definitely resolved because: a) nothing prevented the King of Spain from changing his mind as he had already done in 1821-22; b) the base at Port Mahon was far away from the eastern Mediterranean and the Black Sea, where the ships of the American squadron had started patrolling since 1820 to protect American commercial vessels; and c) the possibility of a commercial treaty between the U.S. and the Ottoman empire created favorable conditions for the growth of the American commerce in the eastern Mediterranean.

Under these circumstances a naval base in the Aegean would certainly serve American interests. Thus, I believe that we cannot overlook the possibility that the U.S. Navy was looking for a naval base in the Aegean in spite of the 1825 American-Spanish agreement.

Here I wish to introduce a piece of information which refers to America's interest in the Greek Aegean islands. The British newspaper, *Morning Post* (October 23, 1825), made mention of official meetings between the Greek government and Commodore Rodgers during his visit to Nafplio in September 1825: "Commodore Rodgers was charged by his government to negotiate with the provisional government of the Greek insurgents the conclusion of a Greek-American commercial convention, and at the same time, to deliver six American frigates to the Greek Navy. On the other hand, the Greek government would have to concede to the U.S. Navy the use of a naval base either on the island of Milos or Paros."[23]

The *Morning Post's* claim is in a way confirmed by the French historian Edouard Driault. Referring to meetings between Commodore Rodgers and the French Admiral de Rigny in the Aegean in summer 1825, he noted: "Cependant on remarquait que les Américains levaient avec soin le plan de Paros, ou les Russes aprés 1770 avaient fondé un établissement."[24] I have to stress here that the American interest in Paros is beyond dispute, because the American squadron heading for Smyrna in August 1825 anchored near Paros for five days, and the American officers "visited" the island "and the adjacent islands of Anti-Paros, Delos, and Naxos."[25]

A further confirmation of the *Morning Post's* article is in Commodore Rodgers' report of August 31, 1825 to Henry Clay, the American secretary of state: "This (report) will inform you of my having left Gibraltar on the 10th ultimo on a cruise of observation among the Greek Islands, having for its object the protection of our commerce.. ..."[26]

Nevertheless, the information mentioned above is not confirmed by other sources, especially Greek ones, as proof positive that the American government charged Commodore Rodgers, among other duties, to discuss with the Greek authorities the possibility of using a Greek island as a naval base for the U.S. Navy.

The correspondance of the Greek notables, Lazaros and George Koundouriotes, who played an important role in Greek politics during this period, contains interesting information concerning the arrival of the American squadron at Nafplio in the beginning of September 1825.[27] However, it does not give us any information about discussions with the Greek revolutionary government. Nevertheless, I think it is proper to quote here from a letter written by George Koundouriotes in Nafplio on September 5, 1825 (o.s.) and addressed to his brother Lazaros in Hydra: "My most beloved brother. I include herewith a draft of the discussions which Mr. Trikoupes held with the American admiral."[28] This "draft," which would throw light to the content of the discussions has not been found to date.

Unfortunately, no information concerning the same subject is given by Spyridon Trikoupes, who, as mentioned above, had official discussions with the American admiral as the representative of the Greek revolutionary government. Strangely enough in his book on the Greek War of Independence he does not even mention the visit of the American Mediterranean Squadron to Nafplio in September 1825.[29]

No information is also included in the Greek newspaper of Missolongi, *The Greek Chronicles*, even though in issue no. 73 (September 12, 1825), there is a detailed account on the American squadron's arrival in Nafplio, as well as the meetings of Commodore Rodgers with the delegates of the Greek revolutionary government.[30]

The sole Greek source, which offers important information as to American interest in the Greek islands of the Aegean, is the newspaper *General Gazette of Greece*, published, as is known, in Nafplio. And the issue of December 12, 1825, commenting on information published in several British newspapers concerning the American squadron's visit to Nafplio in September 1825, as well as on the possibility of concession by the Greeks of a naval base to the U.S. noted: "Neither the Americans have asked for, nor the Greeks have conceded to them, any harbor in the Aegean Sea. The appearance of the American flotilla in the Mediterranean had no special purpose for the Greeks..."[31]

The *General Gazette of Greece's* article should, it seems, settle the question of a U.S. Navy base in revolutionary Greece once and for all; the more especially since the *General Gazette of Greece* was the official voice of the Greek revolutionary government.[32]

Personally, I feel such a conclusion somewhat hasty. We should, however, not forget that at that time the Greek revolutionists had clearly turned toward Great Britain for help, so that the newspaper may have been echoing a pro-British point of view.[33] Consequently, it had every reason to deny any relation with the U.S. which had become a visible threat to the British interests because of its expanding naval activities in the eastern Mediterranean.[34]

In conclusion, based on the available information, I believe that it must be accepted *in principio* that the American government expressed an interest in exploring the possibility of obtaining naval accommodations on an island of the Aegean, controlled by Greek insurgents. This interest initially was demonstrated during the arrival of the American squadron in the Grecian waters in 1822 and 1825; but that interest diminished during the second phase of the Greek Revolution (1825-29).

After Commodore Rodgers' departure from Nafplio on September 7, 1825, I could not find any further sources on the matter at hand. Hence, during the squadron's next visit in summer 1826, Rodgers avoided visiting Greek ports or islands, and mainly, avoided coming into any contact with the Greek revolutionary government. The same holds true for Commodore William Crane, two years later, in summer 1828.

This change in American foreign policy after 1825, in my opinion, was due to the following reasons: a) to the more active intervention of the Great Powers, who could not, in any case, tolerate an American naval presence in the Aegean; b) to the Greek revolutionary government's policy that such a presence clearly outweighed its advantages for Greece's cause; and c) to the progress of negotiations between the U.S. and the Ottoman empire concerning the conclusion of an American-Turkish commercial treaty.[35]

The problem of U.S. Recognition of Greece's Independence

The philhellenic movement in the U.S. represented by Edward Everett, Daniel Webster and other distinguished Americans, had already publicly raised the question of recognition of independent Greece early after the outbreak of the Greek Revolution.[36] But the American government, as it is well known, ignored the call of American supporters of the Greek cause; finally, in 1837,[37] seven years after the creation of the independent Greek state, did it recognize Athens.

Before I proceed in my analysis of the role admirals of the American

Mediterranean Squadron played as representatives of the State Department,[38] I would like to point out three important factors which influenced the American foreign policy toward the "Greek Question".: a) the Monroe doctrine forced Washington to adopt a neutral policy regarding the Greek War of Independence; b) the coincidence of contradictory moves on the part of American philhellenes pushing for official recognition of an independent Greece and the U.S. government seeking a commercial treaty with the Ottoman empire; and c) the hostility of the Great Powers against the presence of the U.S. Navy in the Mediterranean, and especially in the Aegean.

I come now to examine the significance of the arrival of the American Mediterranean Squadron in the Aegean.

During the first visit of the American squadron to Hydra, in June 1822, Commodore Jacob Jones discussed with the Greek authorities the possibility of the U.S. recognizing Greek independence. However, he stressed that what he said was his own personal opinion, and that it in no way reflected the official position of his government.[39] Thus, the talks cannot be placed within the context of American foreign policy regarding recognition of Greek independence.

However, Rodgers' mission, I realized, was closely tied to the "Greek Question." There is no doubt, of course, that the American admiral was instructed by the U.S. State Department to negotiate with Captain-Pashaw an American-Turkish commercial treaty. But, this was not realized in 1825, owing to the Ottoman fleet's naval operations in the Aegean. Consequently, the commodore remained in the Grecian waters until September 19, 1825, when he finally left for Port Mahon, leaving behind the warship *Ontario* with the formal mission of protecting American commercial vessels.

While the American squadron remained in the Aegean, it visited the capital of liberated Greece — Nafplio — from September 1-6, 1825. In his report of October 14, 1825 and addressed to Henry Clay, secretary of state, Commodore Rodgers, justifying the squadron's arrival in Nafplio, claimed that he had taken this decision in order to be informed by the Greek revolutionary government the whereabouts of Captain-Pashaw.[40] The American admiral's justification proves, according to some historians, that the American squadron's visit there had no relation to American's recognizing an independent Greece.

Analyzing Rodgers' visit one may ask himself: a) was it really necessary for him to sail to Nafplio with the entire American squadron just to receive information he could have gotten by sending only one ship? b) was it necessary for the squadron to stay six days in Nafplio since, right after its arrival, he found out that it was not possible for the Greek revolutionary government to provide him with the information he was asking for? and c) was it necessary for him to exchange formal visits and hold official discussions with the Greek authorities in order to receive information which, at least at that period of time, was not of military importance, nor of a secret nature?

Unable to give a satisfactory answer to those questions, I carefully studied the commodore's reports to the American government about his mission in the Aegean in August-September 1825.[41]

According to these reports: a) the American admiral, after his arrival in Smyrna toward the end of August 1825, realized that meeting Captain-Pashaw would be very difficult, because of the Ottoman fleet's naval operations in the Aegean and Ionian Sea. His report of August 31, 1825, from Smyrna, to the Secretary of State Henry Clay noted: "At the time of leaving Gibraltar I was led to believe I should find the Capt. Pashaw at the Island of Mitilina, but on entering the Archipelago I found he was with the whole fleet at Misolongi, at the entrance of the Gulf of Patrasso, engaged in besieging that place by sea, in cooperation with the Pashaw of Scutari, commanding the Albanian forces by whom it had been invested by land. Finding the Captain Pashaw so situated I deemed it impolitical to attempt an interview so long as he continued thus employed, and according put into this port for refreshments with the intention of continuing here until a more favorable moment presented itself of communicating with him than I should have had any prospect of, had I gone directly to Misolongi."[42] b) Commodore Rodgers had no need of the information provided by the Greek authorities in connection with the whereabouts of Captain Pashaw, because, as he stated in his report to Henry Clay of October 14, 1825, he was able to locate Captain Pashaw without the help of the Greek revolutionary government ("... I had learnt where to find him....")[43] c) Furthermore in the same report, he expressed his belief that a meeting with the Captain Pashaw at that time would have had undesirable consequences for U.S.

foreign policy. He also noted: "... his situation, wherever he was, would have been such, in all probability as to have precluded a communication without giving rise to a variety of speculations and conjectures which however absurd they might be, it was desirable to avoid giving the slightest grounds for consequently instead of making any further attempt to obtain a personal interview, I determined at once that the most prudent course left for me to adopt now would be to communicate by writting..."[44]

Thus, I come to the conclusion that Commodore Rodgers did not decide to visit Nafplio in the beginning of September 1825 with the entire American squadron, under the guise of seeking information from Greek authorities about the whereabouts of Captain Pashaw. His real purpose was completely different from the one he gave in his October 14, 1825 report.

Unfortunately the American admiral's reports do not reveal the true reasons for visiting Nafplio. However, from the context of Commodore Rodgers' and Captain J.B. Nicholson's, commander of the USS *Ontario*, reports[45] the real reasons for the squadron's arrival in Nafplio can be easily explained.

A careful reading of Commodore Rodgers' reports show that they are obviously dealing extensively with the Greek War of Independence. Specifically, these reports included the following information which was significant for the American State Department: a) the course of the Greek Revolution; b) the possibilities of the successful prosecution of the war by the Greeks; c) the attitude of the Great Powers toward the "Greek Question"; and d) the foreign policy of the Greek revolutionary government.

Also, Nicholson's reports to Rodgers reaffirm the interest of the American government in the course of the Greek War of Independence. Furthermore, Nicholson's report of October 30, 1825 explicitly confirms the American squadron's mission in Nafplio: "I shall then look into Napoli (*sic*) and endeavor to get some information and will do myself the honor to keep you informed as often as opportunity offers."[46]

Keeping this in mind, I conclude that the American Secretary of State, John Quincy Adams, ordered in February 1825 Commodore Rodgers to sail to the Aegean with the mission to meet Captain Pashaw and discuss with him the possibility of a commercial treaty between the U.S. and the Ottoman empire.[47] At the same time, the American admiral was ordered *to sail to Greece on a research mission*, in order to gather information regarding the course of the Greek War of Independence.

In order to understand Adams' interest in the "Greek Question," we must bear in mind the following: a) the statement the American secretary of state made on August 18, 1823 in answer to the Greek delegate in London, Andreas Louriotes, who had asked the U.S. to recognize the insurgent Greece as an independent state. "If, in the progress of events, the *Greeks* should be enabled to establish and organize themselves as an independent Nation, the United States will be among the first to welcome them, in that capacity, into the general family, to establish diplomatic and commercial relations with them suited to the mutual interests of the two countries, and to recognize, with special satisfaction, their constituted State in the character of a sister Republic."[48] b) the constantly increasing pressure exerted by American philhellenes on the American government in order to recognize Greece as an independent state; this philhellenic movement already had much influence on American public opinion; and c) Washington's decision to send to Greece in 1825 an American diplomatic agent on a mission of gathering information about the course of the Greek War of Independence, and at the same time, of protecting American commercial interests.[49]

In conclusion, I believe that in 1825 the American government was faced with the possibility of recognizing Greece's independence. But it considered the gathering of information about the course of the Greek Revolution and the policy of the Great Powers toward the "Greek Question" essential, before making any further decisions. This essential information could only be obtained by sending the American Mediterranean Squadron to the Grecian waters. And, that is why Commodore Rodgers visited *officially*[50] in September 1825 the capital of the liberated Greece and held formal meetings with the Greek revolutionary government.

During the years that followed, the American government's interest in the "Greek Question" diminished. So, when the American squadron arrived again in the Grecian waters in 1826 and 1828, it neither visited ports controlled by the Greeks nor did the American admirals meet members of the Greek revolutionary government.

This change in American foreign policy after 1825 was due, in my opinion, to the following reasons: a) the discouraging information sent by Commodore Rodgers to the American government in 1825, regarding the possibilities of the successful conclusion to the Greek War of Independence;[51] b) the complexity, from the diplomatic point of view, of the "Greek Question," because of the interference of the Great Powers; c) the American policy of nonentanglement in European matters adopted by the new American President, John Quincy Adams; and d) the improvement of the climate in the American-Turkish negotiations of a commercial treaty.[52]

In sum, American foreign policy toward the insurgent Greece after 1825, for all the reasons I have mentioned so far, was strictly neutral even after Greece's autonomy in 1827 and independence in 1830.

Notes

1. Andonis N. Manikes, «Κατάπλους αμερικανικής μοίρας εις το Ναύπλιον το 1825» [The Arrival of the U.S. Squadron at Nafplion in 1825], *Νέα Εστία* XXIX (1941), 341-43; S. F. Argyros, *Η πειρατεία από το 1500 π.Χ. ως το 1860. Ιστορία και θρύλος* [The Piracy from 1500 b.c. to 1860. History and Legend] (Athens, 1956), 154; El. Tr. Raftes, *Σχέσεις της Οθωμανικής Αυτοκρατορίας, της Αυστρίας και των Ηνωμένων Πολιτειών της Αμερικής προς την Ελληνικήν Επανάστασιν (1821-1825)* [The Relations of the Ottoman Empire, Austria, and the United States of America with insurgent Greece, 1821-1825] (Thessaloniki, 1975) 195-97; St. A. Larrabee, *Hellas, Observed. The American Experience of Greece (1775-1865)* (New York, 1957), 65.

2. James A. Field, Jr., *America and the Mediterranean World (1776-1882)* (Princeton, 1969), 125-26, 134-35; Kyriakos Simopoulos, *Πώς είδαν οι ξένοι την Ελλάδα του '21* [How the Foreigners Viewed Insurgent Greece of 1821] II (1822-1823) (Athens, 1980), 158-59; Chr. D. Lazos, *Η Αμερική και ο ρόλος της στην Επανάσταση του 1821* [America and Its Role in the Greek Revolution of 1821] I (Athens, 1983), 305, 335-36.

3. J. A. Field, 49-58.

4. *Ibid.*, 119-20.

5. St. A. Larrabee, 59-61.

6. Andonios Lignos, *Αρχεία Λαζάρου και Γεωργίου Κουντουριώτου (1821-*

1832) [Lazaros and George Koundouriotis' Archive, 1821-1832] I (1821-1823) (Athens, 1920), 63-64; idem., *Αρχείον της Κοινότητος 'Ύδρας (1778-1832)* [The Archives of the Island of Hydra, 1778-1832] VIII (1822) (Piraeus, 1927), 276-77; St. A. Larrabee, 61-62.

7. St. A. Larrabee, 63-64.

8. *Ibid.*, 75-76; J. A. Field, 134.

9. An. Manikes, 341-43; St. A. Larrabee, 78. Interesting information concerning the arrival of the U.S. squadron at Nafplion (Napoli di Romania) are included in Lazaros and George Koundouriotis' correspondence; see, An. Lignos. *L. and G. Koundouriotis' Archive....*, 183-207.

10. St. A. Larrabee, 79-80.

11. *Ibid.*, 81; Chr. D. Lazos, 335.

12. St. A. Larrabee, 81-82; J. A. Field, 135.

13. St. A. Larrabee, 83-84; G. T. Kolias, *Αι ΗΠΑ εις την Μεσόγειον (1775-1830)* [The USA in the Mediterranean Sea, 1775-1830] (Athens, 1960), 52-57; Chr. D. Lazos, 326-31.

14. St. A. Larrabee, 84.

15. *Ibid.*, 89-90; Chr. D. Lazos, 333.

16. St. A. Larrabee, 87-89.

17. *Ibid.*, 90; G. T. Kolias, 76-77; J. A. Field, 148.

18. Concerning the long-term and laborious American-Turkish negotiations of 1820-30 for the conclusion of the commercial treaty, see, the well-informed studies of G. T. Kolias and J. A. Field mentioned above.

19. J. A. Field, 105, 108-109, 110-111.

20. *Ibid.*, 109.

21. An. Lignos, *The Archives of the Island of Hydra....*, 277. This letter includes interesting information concerning the discussions held by the American admiral and the notables of the Greek island. More information, however, can be found in a letter sent from Hydra on June 20, 1822, signed by L. and G. Koundouriotis and addressed to J. Orlando at Argos; see, An. Lignos, *L. and G. Koundouriotis' Archive...*, 63-64.

22. J. A. Field, 109-10.

23. Demetrios Loules, «Η Ελληνική Επανάσταση και ο Βρεττανικός τύπος. Η περίπτωση της 'Morning Post', 1821-1827" [The Greek Revolution in the British Press — The Case of the "Morning Post," 1821-1827], *Δωδώνη* XII (1983), 108.

24. Ed. Driault, M. Lheritier, *Histoire diplomatique de la Grèce de 1821 à nos jours* I: *L'insurrection et l'independance (1821-1830)* (Paris, 1925), 289.

25. In his report sent from Smyrna (August 30, 1825) and addressed to Samuel L. Southard, secretary of the Navy, the American Admiral of the Mediterranean Sea Commodore Rodgers noted: "... having on my passage touched at Tunis and the Island of Paros, where I remained five days for the purpose of filling up the water of the squadron, and affording the officers an opportunity of examining the relicks of Antiquity still to be met with in it, and the adjacent Islands of Antiparos, Delos and Naxia." See, K. K. Speliotakes, «Αμερικανικαί εκθέσεις εκ του Αιγαίου (1825-1827)» [American reports sent from the Aegean Sea, 1825-1827],

Ελληνικά XXV (1972), 157. Rodgers' claim, that he" afforted the officers an opportunity of examining the relicks of Antiquity, does not diminish, I believe, the American greater interest in the military importance of Paros.

26. *Ibid.*, 164.

27. An. Lignos, *L. and G. Koundouriotis' Archive....*, 183-207.

28. *Ibid.*, 207.

29. Sp. Trikoupes, *Ιστορία της Ελληνικής Επαναστάσεως του 1821* [History of the Greek Revolution of 1821] (Thessaloniki, 1935²) II, especially chapters LIV and LVI, where the political and military events of 1825 are analyzed.

30. *Τα Ελληνικά Χρονικά.* Εφημερίς πολιτική εκδοθείσα εν Μεσολογγίω υπό του Δ. Ι. Μάγερ. Μετατυπωθέντα επιστασία και δαπάναις Κ. Ν. Λεβίδου [Greek Chronicles. Political newspaper, published at Mesolongi by D.I. Mɪyer. Republished by C. N. Levides] (Athens, 1840), 96.

31. *Γενική Εφημερίς της Ελλάδος* [General Gazette of Greece] December 12, 1825, 79.

32. K. Mayer, *Ιστορία του ελληνικού τύπου* [History of the Greek Press] I (1790-1900) (Athens, 1957), 30-32; N. E. Skiadas, *Χρονικό της ελληνικής τυπογραφίας* [The Chronicle of the Greek Press] I (1476-1828) (Athens, 1976), 276.

33. As is well known, in July 1825, the Greek revolutionary government approved an act signed by the greatest number of the political and military leaders of the revolutionary Greece, known as the "act of submission," asking officially for British protection (the text of this act is published in Ap. Daskalakes, *Κείμενα-Πηγαί της ιστορίας της Ελληνικής Επαναστάσεως* [Text-Sources concerning the History of the Greek Revolution] II (part 1) (1821-1826) (Athens, 1967), 445-47.

34. For the reactions of the Great European Powers, and, especially of Great Britain, toward the increasing naval presence of the U. S. in eastern Mediterranean but, mainly, toward the prospect of an American-Turkish commercial treaty, see, G. T. Kolias, 17, 100-101; Chr. D. Lazos, 287-288; J. A. Field, 120, 150-51.

35. As I have already noted, after Commodore Rodgers' second visit to the Aegean and his meeting with the Captain Pashaw near the Greek island of Mytilini (July 1826), the American-Turkish negotiations for the conclusion of a commercial treaty went through a particularly favorable phase for the American interests; see, J. A. Field, 141-51.

36. S.Th.Laskaris,*Ο φιλελληνισμός εν Αμερική κατά την Ελληνικήν Επανάστασιν* [The Philhellenic Movement in America during the Greek War of Independence] (Athens, 1926), 17-33; G. G. Arnakis, "Everett and the Question of Recognition of Greece in 1823-1824," *Neo-Hellenika*, II (1975), 155-58; Chr. D. Lazos, 155-243 (in this study the author cites, in Greek translation, the full proceedings of January 1824 of the American Congress).

37. El. Tr. Raftes, 207. The complete text of the Greek-American treaty of commerce and navigation of December 22, 1837, is published in *Treaties and Other International Acts of the United States of America*, edited by Hunter Miller (Washington, 1933), IV (1836-1846), 107-24.

38. The fact that the American government charged the admirals of the American Squadron of the Mediterranean with missions of a purely diplomatic charac-

ter should not be considered strange because: a) at this time the U. S. had no diplomatic representatives to the Ottoman empire; b) during the negotiations of the American-Turkish commercial treaty, the Ottoman empire was represented by the Captain-Pashaw (admiral of the Ottoman Navy). So, it was essential that the American government should send his equivalent, that is, the admiral of the American Squadron of the Mediterranean. The diplomatic character of this mission is also stated by Commodore Rodgers himself in his report of August 31, 1825, sent from Smyrna, to Henry Clay, American secretary of state. In this report he wrote: "this will inform you of my having left Gibraltar on the 10th ultimo on a cruise of observation among the Greek islands, having of its object the protection of our commerce and the attainment of an interview with Captain Pashaw of the Turkish fleet, *in the discharge of certain duties entrusted to my execution by the Department of State...*" (Italics mine), K. K. Speliotakes, 164. Concerning the diplomatic character of this mission, see also, G. T. Kolias, 41-43; J. A. Field, 134.

39. An. Lignos, *The Archives of the Island of Hydra....*, 276.

40. K. K. Speliotakes, 167-68.

41. Commodore Rodgers sent to the American government the following reports: a) from Smyrna, on August 30, 1825, addressed to the Secretary of the Navy, Samuel L. Southard; b) from Smyrna, on August 31, 1825, addressed to the Secretary of State, Henry Clay; c) from Gibraltar, on October 14, 1825, addressed to the secretary of state as well; and d) from Port Mahon, on December 25, 1825, addressed once more to the secretary of state. Those reports were published for the first time by K. K. Speliotakes, 156-72, 179-80, and in Greek translation by Chr. D. Lazos, 306-19, 325-26.

42. K. K. Speliotakes, 164.

43. *Ibid.*, 168.

44. *Ibid.*

45. The Commander of the USS *Ontario*, Captain John B. Nicholson, during his mission in the Aegean, sent to Commodore Rodgers two reports: a) from the Greek island of Milos, on October 30, 1825, and b) from Port Mahon, on December 21, 1825; see, K. K. Speliotakes, 172-79; Chr. D. Lazos, 320-25.

46. K. K. Speliotakes, 174.

47. John Quincy Adams' orders of February 7, 1825 to Commodore J. Rodgers, as well as the orders of September 6, 1825, sent by the new Secretary of State, Henry Clay, to the American admiral are published in G. F. Martens (continué par Fr. Murhard), *Nouveau Recueil des Traités* XII (Goetingen, 1837), which I had not the opportunity to consult. As regards to those two important documents, see also, G. T. Kolias, 41-43.

48. S. Th. Lascaris, 14; El. Tr. Raftes, 176ff.

49. This decision materialized, as it is known, in September 1825, when the new American Secretary of State, Henry Clay, appointed William C. Somerville commercial agent of the U. S. to Greece. Unfortunately, W. C. Somerville never reached his destination, because he died in France on January 1826 on his way to Greece. The American government avoided to appoint another commercial

agent to Greece until 1837; see, J. A. Field, 126-27; El. Tr. Raftes, 199-200; Chr. D. Lazos, 267-68.

50. It must be mentioned here that, during their visit to Nafplion, the American warships were the first to salute the Greek national flag and hoist it on their masts according to the international law. This event was greatly appreciated by the Greek rebels because it gave the impression that the U. S. was, indirectly, acknowledging the Greek Independence; see, An. Lignos, *L. and G. Koundouriotis' Archive....*, 185; *The Greek Chronicles...*, 96; El. Tr. Raftes, 194-97.

51. Commodore Rodgers, in his report of August 30, 1825 from Smyrna, addressed to the secretary of the Navy, noted: "Indeed from what I have seen myself and heard from others, I am induced to think their cause so desperate, that nothing short of a miracle can sustain them much longer..." "I have come to the conclusion that without the interposition of some one or more of the European powers, they (the Greeks) will be unable to sustain themselves twelve months longer." K. K. Speliotakes, 161.

52. As is well known, the American-Turkish negotiations of 1828-30 led to the first American-Turkish treaty of commerce and navigation on May 7, 1830. According to this treaty the Ottoman empire would accord the U.S. the same privileges that other European Powers had already obtained. The text of the treaty is published in *Treaties and Other International Acts of the United States...* III (1819-1835), 54ff.

Name Index

Adams, John Quincy (1767-1848), Secretary of State (1817-25), sixth President of the United States (1825-29).

Clay, Henry (1777-1892), American statesman, secretary of state (1825-26).

Crane, William (1784-1846), American naval officer, commander of the Mediterranean Squadron (1827-29).

Driault, Edouard (1864-1947), French historian.

Everett, Edward (1794-1865), American orator, educator, and public official.

Jones, Jacob (1794-1865), American naval officer, commander of the Mediterranean Squadron (1821-24).

Kanaris, Konstantinos (1790-1877), Hero of the Greek War of Independence (1821-29), admiral, and statesman.

Koundouriotis, Gheorghios (1782-1858), Greek shipowner and statesman, prime minister of revolutionary Greece (1825-26).

Koundouriotis, Lazaros (1769-1852), Greek shipowner and politician.

Louriotis, Andreas (1789-1894), Greek statesman, representative of revolutionary Greece to Great Britain (1823-25).

Monroe, James (1758-1831), Fifth President of the United States.

Orlandos, Ioannis (? -1852), Greek statesman, representative of revolutionary Greece to Great Britain (1823-25).

Rigny de, G.H.D. (1782-1835), French naval officer.

Rodgers, John (1771-1838), American naval officer, commander of the Mediterranean Squadron (1825-26).

Somerville, William C. (? -1826), First American agent to Greece.

Southard, Samuel L. (1787-1842), Secretary of the U.S. Navy (1823-29).

Topal Khosrew Mehmet (? -1859), Ottoman naval officer and statesman.

Trikoupis, Spyridon (1788-1873), Greek statesman, orator, and historian.

Webster, Daniel (1782-1892), American orator and statesman.

Apostolos E. Vacalopoulos

Piracy during the Last Years of the Greek War of Independence

Piracy increased to a very dangerous extent during the Greek War of Independence. This was particularly so after Kasos and Psara were devastated, and after the Greek governments started to issue their sailors with numerous raiding documents — inspection warrants for foreign trading vessels[1] — in an attempt to keep the navy from dispersing, because many ships were flying foreign flags, as the Secretary for Foreign Affairs G. Glarakis told Capodistrias on his arrival in Greece.[2] This situation was aggravated by the invasion in Peloponnese of Ibrahim Pacha of Egypt and by the increasingly wretched situation of the Greek population in various areas. True, the raids carried out by the Greek fleet, who were enraged by the false documents presented to them by foreign shipowners who were transporting supplies to the enemy and by the hostile attitude adopted by one or another of the Great Powers, easily turned into the seizure of the merchant ships' cargoes. Essentially they were acts of piracy. In an attempt to deal with this situation, that is, to ascertain the real destination of the cargoes and to avoid misunderstandings, the government established the tribunal "of plunder" (of the seized cargoes) on April 24, 1825; it operated under various titles until 1829 at Nafplion, Trizina, Poros, and Aegina.[3] However, as usually happens in small states, the force of political circumstances and the influence and pressures of powerful individuals forced the judges to revise their decisions and to release confiscated cargoes, even when the shipowners had been taking them to the enemy, and ought, therefore, to have been sentenced. These shipowners were English, Heptanesians, among others, with whose governments the revolutionists were on good terms.[4] To begin with, the raiders behaved honestly and handed their plunder over to the competent authorities; but, they soon began dipping into it themselves, having seen that Christian Europe, on which their hopes were pinned, was adopting a disappointing attitude.[5] They turned to piracy out of their own desperate financial need, out of the harsh necessity for survival, and after seeing that those who dared to commit the illegal deed went unpunished. Such were, above all, the people of Psara, who had lost all they possessed in the flames which had engulfed their island home.[6] Now, their ships were blockading Turkish ports, of course, but they were straying into piracy.[7] Nor did the people of Hydra linger far behind.

After 1824 (and European travelers provide abundant information about this), pirates in the Aegean had attained such a degree of effrontery that they were using deserted Aegean islands as their bases: Gyaro (Gioura),[8] Antiparos, Heracleia (west of Amorgos between Naxos and Ios), Donousa, now Denousa (east of Naxos), Kero, and the Upper and Lower Koufonisia.[9] From these islands, they also carried out raids on inhabited islands: Yorgos Spiliotopoulos, for example, raided Andros, Dimitrios Marinos raided Ios, and others raided Sifnos.[10] The fact that many of the raiders turned to piracy, however, damaged the financial interests of the Europeans who were trading or smuggling weapons and supplies to the Near East.[11] In a report to their government, the French merchants of Alexandria observed that as the Greeks' own supplies gradually dwindled, so they behaved more arbitrarily against the merchant ships, simply because the latter could fulfill their immediate needs. They, consequently, demanded that appropriate steps be taken quickly to avert disastrous results, for the cotton alone exported from Alexandria represented a liquid capital of 833,705 francs a month, quite apart from the value of the other merchandise. It should be noted that from 1824 to 1825, 145 French ships sailed from Alexandria, an average of seven per month.[12]

Two statements by Captains Embry and Celly concerning the plundering of their merchandise, and a deposition by a third ship's captain concerning the seizure of four Turkish passengers by pirates, who subsequently drowned them off the coast of Milos, led the French Consul in Alexandria, Drovetti, to inform his minister, Baron de Damas, of the intolerable situation that had arisen in the Aegean. On July 13, 1825, he reported that the French trading ships were being terrorized to such an extent that he did not know how best to advise them. He hoped, however, that Vice-Admiral de Rigny would deem it necessary to take severe measures to intervene effectively and give some relief to the merchants.[13]

It must be said again, however, that many of the arrested European ships, and in particular the numerous Austrian vessels,[14] were engaged in shameless smuggling to the detriment of the interests of the Greek nation. The captains of Austrian ships concealed the provisions and munitions they were carrying, produced false manifests declaring that the ships had been loaded by Europeans for the benefit of Europeans and that they were bound for the Ionian Islands, or for Free Greece, or for neutral countries and ports. Sometimes the traders sailed with a protective escort of warships and openly supplied the blockaded areas, and sometimes the same warships took back from the raiders by force the merchandise that had been seized. Indeed, Spiliadis accused that, on occasion warships, too, transported war supplies to the ports of Methone and Korone. Mavrokordatos, Secretary-General of the Executive — that is, the government — wrote indignantly to Orlandos: "The Austrians have virtually declared war on us. Not only is there no neutrality, but they do not even conceal the fact — and defend themselves with violence — that they are carrying illegal cargoes of supplies and munitions to the enemy. What is the use of our burning the enemy's ships, when they have the supposedly neutral powers, whom we are not allowed to harm, transporting both their provisions and munitions and go scot-free?"[15] The captains of Austrian ships turned on the Greek raiders with particular violence, in defense of both their own and their compatriots' ships.[16] Indeed, the Austrian Ambassador in Constantinople, Ottenfels, wrote to Gentz, Metternich's adviser, proposing even harsher conduct toward the Greek raiders: he stated that Greek piracy was increasing, that under the pretext of inspecting a ship they noted everything of any use, and returned at night to seize it, and that in this way they had plundered six Austrian ships in a short space of time without their captains daring to resist, because the shipowners forbade them to. Ottenfels' opinion, therefore, was that they would be vindicated only by meeting violence with violence, for they could expect no compensation or satisfaction from the Nafplion government.[17]

Admiral de Rigny and the English deputy governor of Malta complained bitterly to Mavrokordatos about the piracy against French ships in the Mediterranean, even around Malta, by ships flying the Greek flag. Consequently, the Greek government wrote to the notables of Hydra on October 10, 1825, emphasizing the disastrous consequences of these activities, and calling on them to investigate which captains were guilty of these abuses, so that innocent seamen would not pay for them.[18]

Indeed, the sailors of Hydra were pursuing and capturing the merchant ships of neutral countries that were carrying, or at least accused of carrying, supplies to the enemy; they seized the cargoes, divided up amongst themselves the plunder, the *bonnes prises*, or *bona prezes* as they called it, and thus illegally came by the necessary means of survival for their unemployed and impoverished families, for the island's economic situation was worsening year by year. In a letter from Lazaros Kountouriotis to his brother Yeorgios, the president of the government, dated January 13, 1826, we read that after the ships had sailed from Hydra for Mesolongi «ὁ ἐναπολειφθεὶς ἐνταῦθα λαὸς» —that is, the remaining seamen — came to his house shouting that they were suffering privations and asking permission to cope with their difficulties by conducting raids for "booty". And, Lazaros suspected that this commotion had been instigated by their captains, who had been left unemployed.[19]

The poverty that had overtaken the crews, the lucrative piracy that many islanders engaged in, combined with the inaction of the government officials, caused the piracy to spread. The Commander of the English squadron in the Aegean, Hamilton, behaved inconsistently toward the pirates, according to contemporary witnesses: sometimes he was harsh and sometimes very lenient and indulgent with them, which undoubtedly contributed to the increase in piracy.[20]

Dismayed by this unruliness, which blackened Greece's name and defamed the Greek cause, Ignatius, bishop of Hungaro-Wallachia, who was residing in Pisa in Italy, wrote to Yeorgios Kountouriotis on December 1, 1825: "Europe has seen no virtue, justice, probity, and moral serenity in the Greeks to make her think that we are better than the Turks and to prefer us to them; it is therefore to be hoped that the Administration will suppress this unruliness and punish the greed of these sailors, so that there will be no reason for the foreigners to punish them and the affair to lead to excesses."[21]

The raiders even attacked ships from the Ionian Islands, which so enraged Hamilton that he ordered the notables of Hydra to hand over the culprits. He blockaded the island for two days (July 13/25 and 14/26, 1826) with his flagship, the *Cambrian*, and with the *Naiad*, demanding that the pirates be handed over and that the price of an Ionian ship be paid. The warships were stationed outside the harbour so that the "mistika" (pirate ships) and caïques could not escape into the Aegean for piracy. The notables, divided as they were into factions by jealousy and suspicion, were afraid to take on the responsibility of meeting the English squadron commander's demands. Some of them, indeed, had by now begun to despair of the outcome of the revolution against the Ottomans and wanted to leave the island and save their property, while others insisted on continuing the fight, since they now had weapons in their hands and more means than before. This irregular situation and the lack of unity and agreement amongst the islanders saddened the enthusiastic Scottish philhellene Edward Mason, who had settled on the island as a pedagogue and English teacher and had dedicated himself to the Greek cause. The matter of the piracy was finally solved on July 17/29, when the notables paid compensation and handed over two pirates. The rest were killed.[22]

The sailors divided the spoils amongst themselves, but the captains took the lion's share, which infuriated sailors and skippers alike. When the loot was not shared out in accordance with established custom, much displeasure and scheming arose amongst the crew. On August 2, 1825, Miaoulis the Greek Admiral, wrote to the notables of Hydra: "Try to collect it (the plunder) so that it may be divided fairly amongst all, and use all prudent means of preventing trouble so that it does not happen in future; for this sort of thing is enough to break up our fleet, on which the nation's salvation depends."[23]

This aberrant situation, which brought turmoil into the fleet's operations, was recounted in tragic tones two days later by the admiral: "All our sailors and the rest are murmuring because a number of our ships ... instead of rising to the occasion (fighting, like us), turned back before their month was up, or took loot only for themselves, as if they had been sent for this purpose alone, and as if they too were not ships of the fleet. And some profiteers thus take the opportunity to grab double or triple monthly salaries/engagements solely in order to go around stealing more...."[24]

In the summer of 1825, the cliff of Gramvousa on the northwest coast of Crete became a pirates' hideout, when it was seized by 200 bold Cretans; most of them had been recruited in Monembasia, and their leader was the young Dimitrios Kallergis. They turned the cliff into an impregnable base and amassed fabulous riches there.[25] Rumors and legends about the treasures collected there attracted a great rush of sailors, from the islands Psara, Crete, Kasos, etc., who all applied themselves to piracy, quite fearlessly by now.[26] And so the cliff of Gramvousa became what the steep cliffs of Korakonisi in Cilicia had once been in antiquity.[27] The raiders and pirates of Gramvousa, like the buccaneers of the West, devastated the central Aegean.

A motley crowd gathered in this pirates' retreat. To begin with, the raiders and pirates sailed forth in small "navettes," which had a limited sphere of action. Later, however, having saved money, they obtained government sanction to buy communications vessels to ply between Gramvousa and Nafplion; they bought schooners or larger ships, expanded their predatory operations, and became the most fearful pirates in the east Mediterranean.[28]

It was chiefly Cretans who were in communication with Gramvousa, having fled to the Greek islands in a lamentable state. A French visitor to Milos, Charles Deval, observed that the island's caves were full of women, old men, and children from Crete, wretched creatures lying on the ground, almost naked, sighing and groaning in their despair, their faces wan, their eyes morose, their lips white; skeletally thin, these exhausted, shrivelled creatures were dying of hunger and illness, with little or no chance of survival.[29]

Other islands, too, became refuges for persecuted refugees, and also, targets for the pirates. On the coast of Amorgos were some miserable hovels occupied by wretched people from Crete, Psara, Chios, etc. Many had once been prosperous two years before, with houses, fields, and all the creature comforts; now, they were living in hovels or caves, without beds, tables, or chairs, sleeping on rags. It was with these rags that they covered their nakedness whenever they went out to collect a few shellfish to relieve their hunger.[30]

In view of all this, it is understandable that simply in order to survive, the refugees, too, became an unruly element in the Aegean. Many cf them, but above all the men of Sfakia, who sought refuge on the beautiful and peaceful Sifnos, whither others were constantly arriving, having no other resources, took to piracy. Very quickly, these spirited and restless refugees not only turned Sifnos into the base for their raids, but also began to behave despotically and insultingly toward the hospitable islanders who had received them so kindly. Eventually, an elder of Sifnos, Nikolaos Prokkos, arrived in Nafplion, bringing with him a report from the islanders, dated November 16, 1825, addressed to the government. He himself recounted their tribulations: his compatriots had been reduced to "helots and slaves and bondsmen of the former recipients of their benevolence, their co-religionists from Sfakia," who seized the laborers they encountered in deserted places, took them to Gramvousa, and there sold them as slaves; they even sank so low as to snatch girls from their mothers' arms, "a brazen act which not only a sentient soul, but not even a stone, could endure." Generally, the islanders' only hope of salvation was to flee to caves and hideouts where they trembled like rabbits at the voice, or even, the name of the Sfakians. The elder's report ended with an appeal to the government to send soldiers to expel these undesirable strangers from the island by force.[31] However, the government was unable to help them. And so, their tribulations continued and they were cut off from the outside world, for no ship dared to approach the island's shore. The Sifniots also suffered terribly from the consequences of a crop failure, not daring to go to nearby Syra to obtain supplies of the bare necessities of life. The same sort of thing was happening on othe1 islands, too, where Cretans had settled, on Naxos, Paros, Milos, and Ios, where the refugees became the real lords of the place and created anarchy with the collaboration with some of the locals.[32]

The Eparch of Mykonos and Syra, Dritsas, described the frightful situation in the Aegean most elegantly in his report to the Naval Ministry December 29, 1825:

The islands of Skyros, Psara, Fourni, Kalymnos, Antiparos, Koufonisia, and others besides, have become the most grievous and frightful lairs of the robbers, the refuges of inhuman and damnable piracy, and the workshops of criminality, whither all who chance by are mercilessly dragged, and stripped not only of their belongings and apparel, but even of their lives. The crossing between Syra and Tinos and Mykonos has now become dangerous, and likewise the crossings between many of the aforementioned islands and places. These unpunished and unrestrained robbers and criminals hold up ships and sailing boats, strip them bare, and then abandon them, as they did a few days ago at Kalymnos, and even yesterday at Mykonos and Fourni, where they stripped two Austrian ships and various other small boats.[33]

Equally terrible, if not worse than the Cretans, were the Kasiots, who, as the elders of Naxos reported on May 11, 1826:

Have attained such a degree of audacity and effrontery that they even strip the pirates of Hydra, who are the terror of the sea; imagine, then, how ill they have treated us poor Aegean people. They have left us no oxen, nor sheep or goats, our agriculture has ceased because of the lack of oxen, the sheep and goats are seized daily and we have none left to pasture. These abuses both by land and by sea have plunged us into utter despair...[34]

The Kasiots must have been largely responsible for the raids on the coasts of Syria and Egypt. The French Consul in Alexandria wrote to his minister on May 20, 1826 that no ship entered or left the port without being visited or more or less plundered by the pirates who patrolled the sea outside Alexandria.[35]

The Aegean communities appealed to the government, which sent Konstantinos Metaxas with a substantial military force to patrol between Naxos and Paros.[36] A number of pirates sent a letter to Metaxas, having gathered on Gioura to deliberate on ways of dealing with this new situation. In their letter, they complained of their persecution, saying that through their piracy they not only ensured the survival of their own and many others' families, but also performed a service to the nation in general, because they would eventually force the European powers to recognize Greece's independence. Consequently, Metaxas ought to reach a compromise with them.[37] Although it seems irrational at first sight, the pirates' second argument contained a dash of realism. For piracy to be wiped out and peace to prevail in the east Mediterranean, a satisfactory solution would have to found for the Greek Question.

In 1826, the three-member Governing Committee was set up to wipe out piracy. The president was Metaxas himself, who, after a savage chase, captured the notorious Psarian pirates Moros, Voyos, and Karoulias. They and other pirates had established their refuge on Andros.[38]

The refugees in the north Sporades, who were Thessalian and Macedonian veterans of 1821, were also dangerous pirates; they served under well-known chiefs, amongst whom were Yeros Karatasos, Gatsos, Yorgos, Zorbas, Diamantis Nikolaou, Konstantinos Binos, Mitros Diakopoulos, Konstantinos Doumbiotis, the Thessalian brothers Gogos, Alexandros, Apostolos, and Stefanos Kalamidas, their brother-in-law Yorgos Grizanos, and others.[39] They operated chiefly in the Thermaïc Gulf and all along the coast of Macedonia, Thrace, and Thessaly as far as the entrance to the Dardanelles, and also the whole of the Aegean from the north Sporades northward. Indeed, they even had the effrontery, with the help of agents from Salonika, to penetrate that city in order to impose a tribute on the Jewish fishermen of the Gulf. Skopelos seems to have been their main base.[40]

The Psarians also became dangerous pirates, particularly after their island home was occupied and ravaged by the Turks. Their base was Mykonos, with the tolerance and certain collaboration of the island's notables. Their closest victim was Tinos, which they frequently harassed with their raids. Other, even smaller, islands were turned into pirates' retreats — Antiparos was the base of the archpirate Yorgos Xekoukoulotos, and Kythnos that of Stravodimos Papafingos.[41]

The Psarian pirates grew so bold that they even used the island Aegina as a base, the seat of the Psarian Committee (many Psarian refugees had fled there, chiefly the richest people), which had been set up to replace the old Council of Elders after Psara was destroyed. They carried out their deeds of piracy undisturbed, under the very noses of the committee, until eventually the committee began to deliberate as to how they were going to deal with this irregular situation. The threatening communication sent to them on May 3, 1826 by the Commander of the English naval forces in the Aegean, Hamilton, forced them to take drastic measures: they organized a garrison of Psarian citizens and set fire to the pirate ships in the harbor. Nevertheless, piracy continued on the island. And so, following a secret proposal by the committee, the government sent a company of regular soldiers to Aegina. But as soon as they landed, the pirates fled or went up and hid in the mountains, while the committee and the people once again set fire to whatever pirate ships they found in the harbor.

For the third and last time the French Admiral de Rigny repeated the same in Aigina and Poros (he used as base the island of Milos to surpress piracy in the Aegean Sea and to secure the navigation) upon the request of the ship burner and hero Kanari, concerned over his compatriot's situation and indignant over this dissoluteness, which was destroying the Greek cause in the eyes of Europe, and who in this case played a leading part in banishing piracy from the island.[42] Kanaris' sentiments were shared by almost the whole Greek nation. De Rigny subsequently returned to Syra, whence he had been summoned.[43]

Following these events, and after the Psarian Committee had issued orders to its fellow citizens, Psarian pirates virtually disappeared, for they either entered the government's service or went into commerce. Most of the Psarians gathered on Aegina and became the masters of the island, whither they transplanted their manners and customs as though to a new homeland.

Unlike the Olympians in the north Sporades and the Cretans on some of the Aegean islands, who forced themselves on the locals with violence and were agents of disorder and turmoil, the Psarians won the island over peacefully, and through the authority and strength of their committee they managed to impose absolute order. The Psarian Committee was exceptionally active with regard to both the relief and rehabilitation of its compatriots and the wider interests of the nations, which exalted it in the eyes of all the Greeks.[44]

Although the Psarian pirates disappeared and became law-abiding citizens of the new Greek state, nevertheless, piracy still continued to devastate the Aegean.

Equally fierce pirates, notorious since the last centuries of Turkish domination, were the Maniots, who turned to piracy even more furiously after 1825, when the Egyptians spread over most of the Peloponnese and cut off their land communication with the capital. Then the deputy governmental committee itself ordered the President of the Ephorate of Sparta, Ioannis Mavromichalis, to issue raiding documents (countersigned by the high priest or other eminent inhabitants of Mani) to various Maniots to allow them freedom of action against enemy transport ships and European ships carrying supplies to the Turks and Egyptians. The president himself and his sons were the first to take advantage of this order, followed by other Maniot chiefs, such as the powerful Dion. Mourtzinos Troupakis, Panayotis Kapetanakis, and Paschalis Yerakaris, who was later to give evidence before the Maritime Committee to the effect that Konstantinos Mavromichalis had embezzled from his plunder what should have been deposited with the National Fund. Consequently, Codrington was not incorrect when on August 7 (new style) he charged that the notables of Mani were owners of pirate vessels.[45]

European trade suffered heavy losses at the hands of the pirates. It is estimated that the European merchants established in the Near East suffered heavy losses from 1821 to 1826: the Austrians 4 million francs, the English 900,000, the French 300,000; and the Sardinians, the Dutch, and the Americans suffered losses as well.[46]

The European governments made efforts to control the piracy in the Aegean by using convoys — that is, warships accompanying trading vessels — but not always with much success: they usually delayed despatching the merchandise for days (in order to collect the ships together) and then burdened the state with the expense of maintaining strong naval squadrons, without even then completely safeguarding the merchandise, because bold pirates did not hesitate to take advantage of darkness or storms to attack merchant vessels. This situation led to increases in freight charges and marine insurance, and consequently, the prices of merchandise went up and the merchants' profits down.[47]

The Administrative Council or temporary government of Greece took spasmodic measures and did what it could to smite this latter-day Lernaean Hydra, either alone or in collaboration with the admirals of the Great Powers.[48] Act no. 854/May 27, 1826 declared that only the ships of the Greek fleet (and they had to be supplied with the necessary documents - war certificates, regular raiding or blockading documents, etc.) were entitled to fly the nation's warflag or to carry out raids. Any others would be deemed to be pirate vessels. It forbade the construction of ferry boats and κλεφτρινῶν and other such vessels which were evidently built with piracy in view, and it imposed sanctions (fines and imprisonment) on those caught building such ships thenceforward, and also, on the communities of the islands or coasts concerned if they did not prevent it. It also forbade Greek warships to seize the cargoes of neutral ships carrying war supplies to the enemy or to ill-treat their crews or passengers. The Greek warships were required to escort these neutral freighters to the headquarters of the Maritime Tribunal, where they would be investigated and tried. Otherwise, not only would they forfeit all rights to conduct raids, but they would be deemed to be pirate ships and be subject to the appropriate penalities.

At the end, the Greek government in a proclamation called once again for the effective assistance of the admirals and commanders of the foreign naval squadrons in stamping out the piracy that was damaging not only the commerce of the neutral countries, but also "that of the Greeks, whose houses, property, and often lives have not remained untouched by these criminals." And what was worse, they attracted a "general outcry and indignation against the innocent Greek people, against the whole Greek nation."[49]

Cooperation between the squadrons of the Greek fleet and those of the English, French, and Russian fleets provided the only solution capable of ridding the Aegean of the scourge of piracy. It started at the beginning of January 1828, when its first governor of Greece, Ioannis Capodistrias, arrived in Greece. Greek crews cleared up the north Sporades, while crews of the Great Powers did the same for Gramvousa. However, the piracy in the Aegean lingered like a bad dream with the islanders and provided the material for Jules Verne's novel, *L'Archipel en feu*.

Notes

1. M. Οικονόμου, *Ιστορικά της Ελληνικής Παλιγγενεσίας* (Αθήναι, 1874), 658.

2. Capodistrias, *Correspondance* (Paris, 1839), vol. 1, p. 553. About the causes of the piracy, see also, V. Fontanier, *Voyages en Orient* (Paris, 1829), 192-202.

3. E. Georgiou, *Le Tribunal Maritime en Grèce pendant la guerre de l'Indépendance 1825-1829* (Athens, 1971), 45; Fontanier, 209-210; *Μονόφυλλα του Αγώνος 1821-1827*, vol. 2, H-51.

4. D. Urquhart, *The Spirit of the East* (London, 1839), vol. 2, 186-87.

5. Georgiou, 256.

6. Charles Swan, *Journal of a Voyage up the Mediterranean* (London, 1826), vol. 2, 140-41.

7. Swan, vol. 2, 147-49, 150-56.

8. Jourdain, *Mémoires historiques et militaires sur les événements de la Grèce depuis 1822* (Paris, 1828), vol. 2, 229.

9. Δ. Πασχάλη, *Η Άνδρος κατά την Επανάστασιν του 1821* (Αθήναι, 1930), 45.

10. Ανδρ. Δρακάκη, «Η πειρατεία εις τας Κυκλάδας», *Μνημοσύνη* (1974-75), 342-46.

11. Jourdain, *Mémoires*, vol. 2, 229.

12. Ed. Driault, *L'expédition de Crète et de Morée 1823-1828* (Cairo, 1930) 166-68.

13. Driault, 3.

14. Εμμ. Γ. Πρωτοψάλτη, *Ο Γεώργιος Χριστιανός Gropius και η δράσις αυτού εν Ελλάδι* (Αθήναι, 1947), 8; Αντ. Λιγνού, *Αρχείον Λαζάρου και Γεωργίου Κουντουριώτου (1821-1832)*, vol. 5, 300; Γεωργίου Θ. Ζώρα, *'Έγγραφα του Αρχείου Βατικανού περί της Ελληνικής Επαναστάσεως*, «Μνημεία της Ελληνικής Ιστορίας» 10, Α' *1820-1826* (Αθήναι, 1949), 549

15. Πρωτοψάλτη, *Gropius*, 55.

16. Κωνστ. Νικοδήμου, *Υπόμνημα της νήσου Ψαρών* (Αθήναι, 1862), vol. 2, 333-41.

17. Anton Prokesch-Osten, *Zur Geschichte der Orientalischen Frage. Briefe aus dem Nauchlasse Friedrichs von Gentz, 1823-1829* (Vienna, 1877), 102, 119. Cf. p. 122, 142-44; Fontanier, *Voyages*, 191-92.

18. Αντ. Λιγνού, *Αρχείον της κοινότητας Ύδρας 1778-1832* (Πειραιεύς, 1928), vol. 11, 582-83.

19. Κωνστ. Α. Διαμάντη, *Αρχεία Λαζάρου και Κωνστ. Κουντουριώτη* (Αθήναι, 1967), vol. 7, 25 et *passim*.

20. Κ. 'Αιδεκ., «Τα των Βαυαρών φιλελλήνων κατά τα έτη 1826-1829», *Αρμονία* (1900), 447-48, Νικολάου Δραγούμη, *Ιστορικαί Αναμνήσεις*, 4th editior, (Αθήναι, 1966).

21. Λιγνού, 5, 488.

22. Swan, *Journal*, 2, 139-50.

23. Λιγνού, Αρχ. 'Υδρας, 11, 461.

24. Λιγνού, Αρχ. 'Υδρας, 11, 463-64, 470-71, 473-74.

25. Jourdain, *Mémoires*, 2, 207-208; Jurien de la Gravière, *La Station du Levant* (Paris, 1867), vol. 1, 14; G. G. Gervinus, *Geschichte des neunzehnten Jahrhunderts* (Leipzig 1862), vol. 6, 83.

26. Γ. Ασπρέα, «Κουρσαρόκαστρα και κουρσαροφωλιές. Η Γραμβούσα και τα Κουφονήσια», *Ναυτική Ελλάς*, 8 (1936), 3399-3400.

27. Gervinus, *Geschichte*, 6, 83.

28. Ασπρέα, *Ναυτική Ελλάς*, 8 (1936), 3400.

29. Charles Deval, *Deux années à Constantinople et en Morée (1825-1826)* (London - Paris 1828), 9-10.

30. Σάμουελ Χάου, *Ημερολόγιο από τον Αγώνα 1825-1829* (Αθήνα, 1971), 125.

31. Δρανδάκη, «Η πειρατεία εις τας Κυκλάδας», *Μνημοσύνη* 5 (1974-75), 334-38.

32. Δρανδάκη, 339-40; Χάου, *Ημερολόγιον (20 Οκτωβρίου 1825)* 173; Κωνστ. Μεταξά, *Ιστορικά απομνημονεύματα περί της ελληνικής επαναστάσεως* (Αθήναι, 1878), 216-18. About the disorders of the refugees of Kreta in Milos, see also, Ζαφειρίου Αντ. Βάσου, «Κρήτες αγωνισταί ιδρυταί του Αδάμαντος Μήλου», *Επετ. Εταιρείας Κυκλαδικών Μελετών,* 5 (1965-66), 215-17.

33. Δρανδάκη, *Μνημοσύνη* 5 (1974-75), 341, Fontanier, *Voyages,* 285-86.

34. Δρανδάκη, *Μνημοσύνη* 5 (1974-75), 341-45.

35. Driault, *L'expédition de Crète et de Morée*, 165-216.

36. Μεταξά, *Απομνημονεύματα*, 212-13; Δρανδάκη, *Μνημοσύνη* 5 (1974-75), 336, 640; see also, Κωνστ. Α. Βακαλόπουλου, «Νέες ειδήσεις για τα νησιά Σύρα, Σάμο, Σίφνο και Νάξο στα 1822», *Μνημοσύνη* 6 (1976-77), 278.

37. Μεταξά, *Απομν.,* 218.

38. Jourdain, *Memoires,* 242-43, 257; Δ. Πασχάλη, *Η 'Ανδρος κατά την Επανάσταση του 1821* (Αθήναι, 1930), vol. 2, 305, Δρακάκη, *Μνημοσύνη* 5 (1974-75), 345, 347, 349-50.

39. Δ. Κατηφόρη—Θέμελη, *Η δίωξη της πειρατείας και το θαλάσσιον Δικαστήριον κατά την πρώτην καποδιστριακήν περίοδον (1828-1829),* (Μέρος πρώτον) (Αθήναι, 1973), 21-22.

40. Θ. Μαλαβέτα, «Δύο επιστολαί του Στεφάνου Καλαμίδα», *Θεσσαλικά Χρονικά* 1 (1930), 102-103.

41. Δρακάκη, *Μνημοσύνη* 5 (1974-75), 352.

42. Νικοδήμου, *Υπόμνημα* 2, 94-95, 169-50; Gravière, *Station*, 2, 18-20; Ζώρα, *Έγγραφα του Αρχείου Βατικανού Α' 1820-1827,* 557, 623.

43. Ζώρα, 623.

44. Νικοδήμου, *Υπόμνημα,* 2, *passim*, especially 1-2, 14, 94-95, 149, 235, 344.

45. Henry A. V. Post, *A Visit to Greece and Constantinople in the Year 1827-1828* (New York, 1830), 68 notice; *Renseigrements sur la Grèce et sur l'administration du comte Capodistrias* (Paris, 1833), 123; Archives of Kapodistrias, dossier 1, document 11, Brief of Fred. Adam, 16-1-1828, to Kapodistria: Θέμελη-Κατη-

φόρη. Rich material about piracy, especially document, see, in C. G. Pitcairn Jones, *Piraey in the Levant 1827-1828. Selected from the Papers of Admiral Sir Edward Codrington* (1934).

46. Gravière, *La Station*, 2, 8.

47. Θέμελη-Κατηφόρη, 43-49.

48. Λιγνού, *Αρχείον 'Υδρας,* vol. 12, 24-28, 54-56, 151-52, 434-35, 480.

49. Αναργύρου Α. Χατζηαναργύρου, *Τα Σπετσιωτικά* (Αθήναι, 1862), vol. 1, 1043-46; Jourdain, *Memoires,* 2, 242, 252, 426-42.

VII

Conclusions

Theodore A. Ropp

Maritime War and Trade and Southeastern Europe, 1740-1920: The Setting, the Issues, and the Results

Our colleague Thucydides, who lost his command when Brasidas took the Athenian stronghold of Amphipoulis (424 B.C.) some hundred kilometers from here, saw land and naval war, trade, and piracy as similar arts. Whether an Athenian served as a horseman, hoplite, or rower depended on his net worth, not his personal preference. By 1740, however, most European states represented landed elites, who protected what Thucydides would have called their "resources" behind legal barriers which enclosed rivers, lakes, coasts, and even entire seas. A weak state, as in Thucydides's day, might still be penetrated politically or economically before it could be conquered, but concepts of land and maritime conquest had now so diverged that they were practiced by separate guilds of soldiers, sailors, and traders. What Europe's Christian states wanted in the Turkish eastern Mediterranean were legal protections for their men, ships, and goods. But these would eventually be translated into lands for themselves or their client Christian nationalities. Those which lay to the north of the old Greek trading empires of the eastern Mediterranean were now so land-minded that this Program's previous studies of war and social change in East Central Europe have assumed that goods, men, ideas, and blows were largely exchanged between states with definable land objectives. Even though smugglers, pastoralists, and refugees often penetrated the resulting legal barriers, the idea of a homogeneous, self-sufficient national state was a goal which seemed increasingly achievable in Northwestern Europe.

To examine this particular Missing Link in Southeast European history, we must first open a Pandora's Box of changing Geopolitical Settings, Issues, and Results. To cover some two centuries, we must also reconcile Paul Ricoeur's view that narration is explanation, with time slices which roughly correspond to those disjunctures in Europeans' ideas and values by which they judged results as war or peace-breeding in international relations.[1] These are, thus, the major themes of a Conference about peoples seeking access to the sea for goals of city or national sovereignty or empire over a particular means of transportation within "a particular civilization, an integral part of Europe, yet substantially different [in its Setting and ideas] from the West."[2] What we find may suggest analogies for other areas — such as Southeast Asia — which were also overwhelmed by Western Europe's sailors, traders, soldiers, techniques, goods, and ideas — but are now struggling for national independence within, or in opposition to, that international oceanic alliance which still dominates the sea's trade, resources, and transportation. To any military-maritime historian, it is, thus, an honor and a challenge to return to the amphibious world of Herodotus, Thucydides, Xenophon, and Polybius of Megalopolis (together ?485-?125 B.C.).

Our setting is within the Inner Margin of what the British geographer Sir Halford J. Mackinder (1861-1947) defined in 1904 as the Inner or Marginal Crescent between the world's Pivot Area or Heartland, and the lands of its Outer or Insular Crescent. Southeast Europe was to be one testing ground for twentieth-century European military and maritime institutions and strategies. After the Great Powers had fought one another to a standstill, air power was to give them even more sweeping promises of victory. But, while technology was to upset the geopolitical balances twice in one 60-year era, some South Europeans' ideas about their shares of this Inner Crescent's resources want back to the days when the Greeks had "collected a vast armament, invaded Asia,... destroyed the kingdom of Priam," and divided Europeans and Asians into "distinct and separate" civilizations.[3] They were still issues in both waves of total war and revolution in Southeast Europe before the usual great power pause for peace and reconstruction.

This geopolitical arena is, thus, a classic example of issues changing with time and circumstances. Those involving access to the sea have changed with sovereigns' ideas for directing, blocking, or enlarging traffic on what the American naval theorist Alfred Thayer Mahan (1840-1914) had seen in 1890 as "a wide common, over which men may pass in all directions, but on which some well-worn paths show that controlling reasons have led them to choose certain lines of travel rather than others. These lines ... are called trade routes; and the reasons which have determined them are to be sought in the history of the world." But his study of sea power's influence from 1660 to 1783 had been too time-bound. Although "travel and traffic by water" had "always been easier and cheaper than by land," he did not ask how the industrial era's literate citizens, factories, railways, roads, and weapons might have changed the technological, economic, and political balances between land and sea-going nations and empires.[4] Farmers, craftsmen, mariners, traders, and bankers have always been subjected to self-appointed protectors. The question for them was which elite could protect them best over the widest area without taking too much of their product. For pastoral, hydraulic or irrigated, agrarian, trading, industrial, and postindustrial societies, the political and military answers have been historically different.

Insofar as long-range transportation and communications are concerned, which nations would benefit the most from free access to those "wide commons" of the land, sea, air, and literate and visual communications which smaller nations would later declare to be "the common heritage of mankind?" Is this best secured by a world empire, a responsible consortium of great powers, or by a community of nations? At the end of the nineteenth century's total wars and revolutions, nearly every nation was sovereign, but liberty, equality, and fraternity were still being applied as unequally to nations as to individuals. So the posthistoric resolution of these issues seems to involve technological, economic, and political problems just as complex as those left over from that Era of Revolutions which this project dates at 1775-1856.[5] Although the nations of Southeast Europe are now fully sovereign, there are still constraints on the movement of their people, goods, and ideas over the "wide common."

If narratives are explanatory, they are judged from lengthening hindsight. Montesquieu (1689-1755) and Voltaire (1694-1778) saw the *Age of Louis XIV* and Peter the Great in different terms from those used by Lord Acton (1834-1902), Mahan, or the survivors of the next round of peoples' wars and revolutions.[6] Historical periodization is not mere numerology. That which best fits the changing balances of power in modern Europe is in the 60-year slices suggested in Quincy Wright's 1942 *Study of War*. Whether one starts with those Crises in the balance of power which — from the French invasion of Italy in 1494 to the outbreak of the Great War in 1914 — form the agreed framework of diplomatic history, or from the origins of these eruptions is immaterial. Here, if only because it fits a decadal system a bit better, we will sound the relatively peaceful international waters of 1720-80 and 1840-1900 and the more turbulent ones of 1780-1840 and 1900-1960, for changes "caused" by Southeast Europe's reemergence onto mankind's "wide common."[7]

That the issues of such adjustments to Europe's great power balances changed with time is, thus, a historian's firm grasp of the obvious. What connects our Missing Links of maritime war and trade, revolutions and counterrevolutions, and political and military leadership selection and education in the national successors of four dismembered empires is the persistence of feudal, monarchist, and imperial ideas and ideals. Like Thucydides, Mahan thought of maritime-military power in terms of land, labor production, and communications, and leaders' will and ability to marshal and use them. Well after they had a power technology to manage, Europe's *Philosophes* had been wordsmiths, manipulators of political, national, or class reason and passions. Even in 1900, few intellectuals were mechanics, much as they admired the latter's artifacts in Denis Diderot's (1713-84) *Encyclopédie ou Dictionnaire Raisonné des Sciences, des Arts et des Métiers* (1751-80). Britain's military-maritime elite still combined the Roman and feudal military traditions with their experiences of overseas wars, trade, and banking. Free trade, enterprise, ships, and land would produce military power as they had already produced peacetime prosperity. That mechanized industry demanded a new regimentation of warfare and communications, as well as of the work force and business was more ignored by British and American politicians, soldiers, and bureaucrats than by those in conservative East Central Europe. Throughout Europe, soldiers, politicians, bankers, bureaucrats, and manufacturers were still drawn from quite different social and educational backgrounds. In Southeast Europe in particular, this Conference will find more literary and less statistical evidence of nations re-emerging into the commercial and industrial revolutions as we go backward into a past in which 1900 is now as distant from us, as 1815 then was from 1900. Even the most "modern" Victorian powers were still ruled by elites which had grown out of those feudal, monarchist, and imperial elites which had traditionally governed Europe's illiterate, isolated, largely agrarian masses.[8]

In the Age of Reason Europe's feudal elites were still adapting to the Commercial Revolution. During the relatively limited wars of 1720-40 and the more violent ones of the Era of Revolutions, 1780-1840, overseas trade had little appeal to the powers dominating Southeast Europe. So, its peoples got few economic benefits from the access to the sea, which their sovereigns won for them between the Treaties of Utrecht and Kuchuk Kainardji (1713-74) and between that Treaty and the Convention of Münchengrätz (1774-1833). Britain had become, in Mahan's view, the paramount maritime power, and was to reenforce her position during the Era of Revolutions. French overseas interests now lay in the Mediterranean. Kuchuk Kainardji opened the Black Sea and the Straits, made Russia the protector of Orthodox Christians, and gave her the same consular rights as Britain and France. But her naval victory in the Aegean at Chesme (1774) did not spark a Greek insurrection. Turkey had resettled the Morea, won from Venice in 1718. In 1739, Austria had returned Servia and Oltenia (Western Wallachia), while retaining the right to protect Roman Catholics and of "free commerce for both parties." And, increased overland trade did not greatly benefit the peasants in the land corridors to Salonika and Istanbul. Hence, not until the Industrial Revolution, 1840-1900, affected both land and water transport and communications, is there much statistical evidence of the economic benefits to these agrarian peoples of access to the sea.

Lines on eighteenth — and early nineteenth — century Southeast European maps are not, thus, too indicative of economic modernization. Voltaire, who died in 1778, saw Southern Europe as politically and culturally backward as when he had shown French civilization to be more advanced than that of Renaissance Italy. The Habsburgs and Turks were still exhausted by their long struggle. Bourbon Spain was a backward French ally. Prussia, which had suffered greatly from plague and famine during the last decades of the Century of Louis XIV, had invested more successfully than Austria in economic and military development. Neither had invested in oceanic trade and colonies, far more risky than in contiguous territories in Europe. Overseas profits were far too dependent on powerful non-European monarchs, and on Creoles' continued willingness to funnel their goods and specie to the Mother Country. Lines on overseas maps were, thus, even more militarily speculative than those on maps of Europe. How, in 1720, could anyone compute Britain's maritime gains from the Treaty of Utrecht: Gibraltar, Acadia, Hudson's Bay, and the Asiento? Or, in 1783, those which were eventually to internationalize the Great Lakes-St. Lawrence route, while retaining primacy in the Indian Ocean?

We must, therefore, use what few figures there are for the economic development of the isolated, subject, agrarian peoples of Southeast Europe. On Robert R. Palmer's map of "European Civilization in the Eighteenth Century: the Enlightenment, Spread of Science, Growth of the Press, Deism, Tolerance, Reform," the Russian and Ottoman empires are buff, the rest of Europe green. Boundaries are those of 1721. The sizes of cities are indicated.[9] The areas most affected by war — though insurrections are not shown and casualties from plague and famine cannot be calculated before modern transport and medicine began to mitigate them[10] — appear on William R. Shepherd's 1929 maps of "Principal Seats of War in Europe:" 1672-1721 (two maps), 1740-63, 1788-1815, and 1914-18.[11] Southeast Europe was heavily involved in all but the wars of 1740-63. But only in 1672-1721, 1914-18, and 1939-45 was that area one epicenter of general war. So, for gauging the effects of war on these isolated subjected peoples' contacts with the sea before the industrialization of land and sea transport, war, weaponry, and empires, we have only isolated and largely anecdotal bits of evidence.[11]

Palmer has no map of European civilization during the "Revolutions in the Atlantic World, 1776-1826," or our 1780-1840, which gave Britain her lead in the Industrial Revolution. Changes in sovereignty in Southeast Europe were again wholly related to the great power balance. By 1840, small Serbian and Greek states, a Russian-supported Montenegro, and an autonomous Russian-protected Wallachia and Moldavia held river and maritime choke-points. Britain protected the Ionian Islands. Austria had gained Venetia and Dalmatia. But Shepherd's maps of the American Revolution and War of 1812 and of the Seats of War in Europe and India, 1788-1815, mainly show the campaigns of imperial armies and fleets.[12] Király's *Era of Revolutions* is primarily concerned with armies. Naval forces are noted in George A. Kourvetaris's "Greek Armed Forces and Society in the Nineteenth Century, with Special Emphasis on the Greek Revolution of 1821." Yet, we know far more about Napoleon's Army of the Orient, or the Allied fleets at Navarino in 1827, than about the transformation of the Greek navy from 300 armed merchantmen with 12,000 sailors in 1821 to one with 1025 "regular" sailors in 1840.[13]

This Conference must deal with the commercial and naval interests, policies, doctrines, strategies, equipment, and personnel of both old imperial and new national powers. But the Northern and Western powers' 1780-1840 campaigns on the Danube, and in the Black and Mediterranean Seas have been so well studied that we may find little new evidence on the battles summed up in R.C. Anderson's *Naval Wars in the Levant 1559-1853* (1952), the last of the sailing era.[14] But, our evidence of the effects of the European consortium's decisive opening of this part of the "wide common" on the subject peoples who lived near this land and water crossroads of Southeast Europe may well be anecdotal. In 1840, the landlocked peasants of Serbia, Montenegro, Wallachia, and Moldavia were still largely landlocked. Still more important, we may have largely anecdotal evidence on the many Greek seamen who had traded, trafficked, and fought for the Turks since Mohammed the Conqueror and Suleiman the Magnificent (*regnant* 1451-1566). We can also note that the Greeks' irregular navy had had as little effect on their War of Independence as had that of the American colonists. Or even less effect. The Greeks had been fighting the nearby forces of Mehemet Ali (the Albanian Viceroy of Egypt, 1805-48), a survivor of the Turkish forces defeated by Napoleon at Abukir (1799). The European-trained "regulars" he sent to Greece in 1825-28 were about as numerous as the British armies captured at Saratoga (1777) or Yorktown (1781), or the Spanish regulars defeated at Ayacucho in Peru (1824).

At the dawn of the era of blood, iron, and steam, 1840-1900, Greek access to the sea was barely reflected by the volume of trade into the new, poverty-stricken monarchy's ports, or of shipping under its flag. A well-known bit of anecdotal evidence comes from a 26-year-old English law student. Alexander Kinglake (1809-91) never went to the monarchy at all. His account of the East in 1835, published in 1844 as *Eothen, or Traces of Travel Brought Home from the East*, is typically romantic and condescending. With an equally condescending Edwardian Introduction by Harold Spender, it made Everyman's Library in 1908. Kinglake's East began at plague-threatened Belgrade, "at the end of this wheel-going Europe," from which nobody went "down to look upon the stranger race dwelling under the walls of that opposite castle." The "hyper-Turk-looking fellows" who met his boat, the Pasha who complimented him on "the cutlery of England, and also the East India," his Janissary courier, gypsy horsemen, and the poverty-stricken Bulgarian peasants whom they occasionally met during their fifteen days from Belgrade to Stamboul, were what King-lake and his readers expected.[15]

"Nowhere else," Kinglake remarked of Stamboul, "does the sea come so home to a city." Why was it so hard for a trader to find "the fair market value of his property? ... In England," goods went "through the hands of a wholesale dealer,... [who] bargains with an entire nation of purchasers by entering into treaty with retail sellers;... but in Turkey, from the primitive habits of the people, and partly from the absence of great capital and great credit, the importing merchant, the warehouseman, the wholesale dealer, the retail dealer, and the shopman, are all one person." A nation of seamen, traders, and shop-keepers (a term from Adam Smith) knew its need for legal protections at both ends of the chain to "universal opulence." From "Infidel Smyrna," with its "Jews offering services, and receiving blows," and "fussy" Europeans "adopting the East," Kinglake and an English yachtsman avoiding the law set out for Syria with a Greek skipper who felt "that there is a greater field for commercial enterprise, and even for Greek ambition, under the Ottoman sceptre than ... in the dominions of Otho [of Greece]." Those ideals of legality which "act so advantageously upon the mere clay of the Russian serf, ... hang like lead upon the ethereal...Greek.» His ventures were so sur-rounded by real and imaginary nautical and political dangers, and "conducted in a manner so wholly determined by the wayward wishes and fancies of the crew, that they belong to enterprise rather than to industry." In their War of Independence their goal, as in Thucydides's day, had been plunder. But their tactics "as naval warriors, were so exceedingly cautious, and their habits as commercial mariners are so wild," that their capacity for "mischief" was "far wider even than that...in our more civilised countries," whose borrowed flags they preferred to fly.[16]

By 1908, Harold Spender was to note, "the Balkan States have been freed," and the eastern Mediterranean pacified. But the Levant's romance had faded "before the prose commonsense of Milner [Alfred, 1st Viscount, 1854-1925, undersecretary for finance in Egypt, best known as administrator in South Africa, 1897-1905], Cromer [Evelyn Baring, 1841-1917, 1st Earl, Egyptian administrator, 1883-1907], and "a hundred and one ingenious inquirers and observers." If Spender now found Kinglake's massive Crimean War history dull, overstrained, and metallic, the reason was that the author had been forced to devote to "an inferior war and a second-rate issue, the research and style that was worthy of another Peloponnesian struggle."[17] As for modern Greece's contributions ro "European Civilization in the nineteenth century (to 1913)," with the political boundaries of 1871, Palmer was to list the founding of the University of Athens (1837), and of five great power Schools of Classical Archaology from the French in 1846 to the Italian in 1910.[18]

By 1900, Europe had a new German empire, Italian, Hungarian, Rumanian, and Bulgarian kingdoms, and an autonomous Crete. The Danube, internationalized since 1856, was open to ocean shipping to Braila, just above the junction of its outlets. But Hungary, trying to funnel Serbian trade through Habsburg ports, had set canal and towage dues so high around the Iron Gates that Romanian oil went to Bavaria by sea.[19] Palmer's maps of industrialization in 1850 and 1910 do not reveal the effects of steam land and sea transportation on Southeast Europe. Hungary's railway mileage per head was now above Germany's, twice as great as that of Italy or Congress Poland, and over twice as large as Russia's. But these ratios did not hold for pig iron production or port tonnage. And Greece was now as urban as Poland, Sweden, or Spain, but her foreign trade had not grown as fast as that of Austria-Hungary or Russia.[20] The Great Powers had not, from

1840 to 1900, put any new Southeast European nation in direct contact with an imperialistic world with new Indian, American, and Japanese empires, or weakened their grip on Southeast Europe's polities and resources. Again, we need only to note the results of the Concert's armed diplomacy there. In no case had indigenous armed forces been decisive factors, although Southeast Europe was beginning to bristle with modern people's armies, navies, and weapons.

To the American Ralph Waldo Emerson (1803-82) and the German Karl Marx (1818-83), things had been in the saddle and riding mankind since the 1840s. But the feudal-capitalist elites which were guiding the Victorian-Bismarckian Concert of Europe did not understand the dangers of those power technologies which had helped to restore and expand law and order after the climate changes, plagues, and near anarchy of the fourteenth century. Their new monarchs had first to control their nobles, peasants, and workers, then their religious passions, and, increasingly, their lawless national monarchs. Adam Smith's "nation of shopkeepers" had so helped to defeat Bonapartism that most political economists took for granted that the forces which had destroyed mercantilism would not become as repressive as mercantilism had been overseas. By 1900, industrial capitalism had annexed the Russian and Habsburg elites, while continuing to change the West's own internal and external power balances. The Victorian-Bismarckians' limited experiments with industry's new weapons and communications systems were now obsolete, but the great imperial powers could not believe that their own ambitions, weapons, and complacency would destroy them in two generations of total violence.

More railways, rifles, telegraphs, explosives, and literate conscripts promised quicker and more Napoleonic victories for empires who used their General Staffs' abilities to mass men and guns at the right times and places. And in the Balkan Wars of 1912-13, every Southeast European army used some version of Franco-German military organization, education, strategy, tactics, and weaponry. Victoria's empire was not, after the Crimea, involved in a major European war. But the long American Civil War (1861-65) had shown that armored steamships, railways, and mass armies could cut up a large underpopulated agrarian state along water and land routes defended by fixed or field fortifications. Imperial forces with modern transport, arms, and medicine had pushed open the Ottoman and Chinese empires, carved up Africa, opened new lands for European miners, ranchers, and farmers, before meeting their first checks at Majuba (1881), Lang-Son (1885), and Aduwa (1896). And Southern and Eastern Europeans were leaving for new lands from the imperial powers' ports by their ships and trains. They were sorted out by their mothers' tongues when they arrived at their overseas destinations.

In 1882-83, Sir Thomas Brassey, civil lord of and then secretary to the Admiralty, published five volumes on the world's sea powers as *The British Navy: Its Strength, Resources and Administration*. Greece had two armored ships, a dozen unarmored ones, and was buying British torpedo boats. The Turks had more ironclads and "old-fashioned" ships. Brassey's 1914 *Naval Annual* showed both with more modern fleets, but it was the arrival of the battle cruiser *Goeben* at Istanbul which helped to tip Turkey into the German alliance. German seamen were deserting in British and American ports to escape "the dreaded maritime conscription"; a similar system was just as unpopular in Italy. He did not note the political radicalization which accompanied the industrialization of maritime transportation, nor the growing number of lascars [1614, an Indian sailor or artilleryman] in tramp shipping. And, Turks were still reluctant to serve "in the Navy" the "most useless extravagance of the late Sultan [Abdul Aziz]."[21]

During the industrialization of naval warfare the lessons of the Crimean, American, and German wars were as important to navies as those of battles from Sevastopol (1854-55) to Plevna (Pleven, 1877) were to armies. But, neither of these great sieges convinced the victors of Königgrätz (1866) and Sedan (1870) that their new Alexanders, such as Alfred von Schlieffen (Chief of the German General Staff, 1891-1905) could not win more-than-Napoleonic victories. In 1899, the Russian industrial promoter Ivan Bloch predicted a stalemate leading to economic collapse and political and social revolution in a six-volume statistical study of *The Future of War in its Technical, Economic, and Political Relations*. The possibilities for Southeast Europe included a war of attrition and blockade, with amphibious forces tipping the Continental military balances, if the war on shipping suggested by French and American naval theorists after the American Confederacy's *Alabama's* depredations in the American War did not starve out industrialized Britain.[24]

Schlieffen (1833-1913), Bloch, Brassey, Mahan, and the American psychologist William James (1842-1910), whose "Moral Equivalent of War" was published in 1910, had all come of age in the Crimean-and-American-Civil-War decade (1854-63). They were all concerned with the effects of industrialization on military technology, economics, and politics. But Mahan derived his "principal conditions affecting the sea power of nations" from a "century," 1660-1783, in which the "advantage" of water transport "was yet more marked ... when roads were few and very bad, wars frequent and society unsettled" than in 1890. Not all his comments on "I. Geographical Position" and "II. Physical Conformation,... natural productions and climate" reflected changing geopolitical conditions. His "III. Extent of Territory" in relation to "IV. Number of Population" ignored the growth of land transport and, in a more literate age, overvalued the "number following the sea, or...available for employment on shipboard and for the creation of naval material. Traditional sailors distrusted the engineers who had made their lives so hot and noisome, and the iron coffins which were soon to be built by Rosie the Riveter. How industrialization had changed the "V. Character of the [American] people" and "VI ...Government" was not apparent until his imperial formula was taken up by such populist politicians as Theodore Roosevelt and the German Emperor William II. Those strenuous lifers had come of age in 1879 and 1880, when Victoria's sea power had seemed as unassailable as her still expanding empire.[23]

Mahan never claimed that "production, with the necessity of exchanging products, shipping, ...and colonies" which multiply "points of safety" were the only keys to maritime "history and policy." American mercantilists did not stress the fact that everyone's "freedom of the seas" had partly depended on Britain's ability to force doors open overseas, and as an island "neither forced to defend itself by land, nor induced to seek territory" there,[24] to use diplomacy to preserve the Concert of Europe. In their "splendid isolation" of the 1880s, Victorian statesmen did not stress this. When they abandoned isolation after 1900, to check an increasingly powerful and imperialist Germany, this was not stressed by American imperialists alarmed by William II's blackmailing naval diplomacy.

Europe's best army knew as little about navies as the Royal Navy knew about landing an army against its. The former's confidence in a short war kept it from thinking about blockades or amphibious surprises. Once steam had "bridged the Channel," the British army's worries about home defense kept them from thinking about such operations. Germany's landlocked War Lord would not risk his "Parade Fleet" in battle, and Her Majesty's *Dreadnought's* commanders acted with the caution which Sir Julian Corbett, a lawyer turned historian who had come of age in the 1870s, had suggested in *Some Principles of Maritime Strategy* (1911). By that time, however, all the great powers had imperialist fever. Even a dreadnought on order was a status symbol, like a national airline, for emerging nations.[25]

The great powers' technical failures left postwar military and maritime thought in confusion. But Bloch's economic crisis did not occur until a decade after Central and Eastern Europe's empires had been split into national pieces. In a 1919 preliminary study for James T. Shotwell's cooperative *Economic and Social History of the World War*, an American economist, Ernest L. Bogart, tried to estimate the costs of liberation. An industrial ranking suggested by a French economist indicated the costs of creating new industrialized national armies and navies. Bogart capitalized a dead American worker at $4720, a Briton at $4140, a German at $3380, a Frenchman or Belgian at $2900, an Austro-Hungarian at $2720, and other Eastern and Southern Europeans at $2020. With the losses of neutrals and from famine and disease, Bogart's totals of $337,946,179,647 were "incomprehensible." As for "human relationships...the present disturbances in Europe" suggested the "breakdown of modern economic society."[26]

This was most obvious for the nationalization of maritime trade in goods, funds, ideas, and people. By 1936, David Mitrany's Shotwell study of *The Effect of the War in Southeastern Europe* saw that this was particularly tragic for its peoples' "relentless striving ... to reach the open sea." Hungary's efforts to impede river traffic around the Iron Gates had hampered the Central Powers' efforts to plunder Romania, while Hungarian, Czech, and Croatian peasants' food hoarding had aided the Allied blockade. The postwar treaties restricted "regional and national contact and intercourse.... More states are without sea outlets;...once active ports have been assigned to countries which have no...use for them." After losing her Aegean port at Dede Agach (Alexandroúpolis), Bulgaria would not invest in an international port there. The Treaty of Neuilly did not internationalize its railways.[27]

The freed nations' hopes of national discipline, political authority, and machine weapons — which the British strategist J.F.C. Fuller added to economic autarky as needed for modern war — were not attained during the era, 1914-45, in which the Great Powers twice made most of Europe into a desert and called it *peace*. The Central Powers twice blocked traffic into the Baltic and Black Seas and through the Mediterranean. Southeast Europe remained part of the "inner" or "marginal crescent" of Eurasia's "pivot area." Germany's efforts to penetrate it had carried little farther than those of the First and Second French empires. And, how best to protect commercial and military operations over oceanic distances was as much in doubt as ever, especially after the development of air and shipborne weapons of apocalyptic power.[28]

In our discussions of the details of maritime trade and war, 1740-1920, we might, finally, look at the programs of the international, interdisciplinary commissions set up at Berne to examine the future of war. The eventual sponsors of the Shotwell series, these commissions were to deal "scientifically, and as far as possible without prejudice either for or against war: " I. The Economic and Historical Causes and Effects of War, and II. Armaments in Time of Peace. Military and Naval Establishments. The Theory, Practice, and History of Modern Armaments, including "military airship & c,." and the "effects of recent inventions upon offensive and defensive war." Anyone who has survived since 1911 may have learned something on those topics. We have perforce paid less attention to "III: The Unifying Influences in International Life," and to maritime nations' efforts at modernization without overdependence on outside technical, economic, and political assistance.[29]

Social change has been sparked by war, revolution, imperialism, international public and private institutions, and the fading of Victorian ideas and institutions. European overseas empires have vanished. Japan's has been converted into an economic thalassocracy. That mechanization of alienation and homogenization which converted Europe's townsmen and villagers into nationalists now threatens maritime nationalism's future. So, while this may be the cloudiest concept in Pandora's Box of International Science, Technology, Socialism, and Capitalism, we might look at it with the eyes of those Greek fathers of history, science, and empire their ingrown maritime cities to the older and newer agrarian cultures which surrounded them. None of them were Athenian. They came from Halicarnassus (Bodrum) in Caria, and Stagiros and Pella in Macedonia. We are as fortunate to be here as Octavian was when he won Philippi (42 B.C., between Amphipolis and Alexandroúpolis) and Actium (31 B.C.). And so, we have returned to those Augustan Benevolent Despots whose Concert hoped to recover the peace and prosperity of the longest-lived Western classical empire.[30]

Notes

1. Paul Ricoeur, *Time and Narrative*, Translated by Kathleen McLaughlin and David Pellauer, Volume I (Chicago, 1984). These time slices reflect priorities, paradigms, or mind-sets according to which — in an expanding economy with internal and external balances of power — literate elites governed the classical and modern agrarian masses.

2. *War and Society in East Central Europe: Special Topics and Generalizations on the 18th and 19th Centuries.* Vol. I. Edited by Béla K. Király and Gunther Rothenberg (New York, 1979), p. xi.

3. *The History of Herodotus*, Translated by George Rawlinson (Chicago, 1952), p. 2. Frederick Jackson Turner's (1861-1932) Frontier thesis appeared in 1893, only three years after Alfred Thayer Mahan's *Influence of Sea Power upon History, 1660-1783* (Boston, 1890). Both theories were basically geopolitical. Both, like Mackinder's, assumed progress in conquering time and distance. A classical political theory which assumed essentially static mind-sets was that of the great Berber historian Ibn Khaldun (1332-1406), of the wandering pastoralist or trader about the corruptions of the farm or city. A closed economic system, like that of irrigated or hydraulic agriculture also strongly circumscribes or channelizes the movement of people, goods, and, eventually ideas.

4. Mahan, *Influence of Sea Power*, p. 25. This is not the place to discuss "whales'" or "elephants'" empires. But they should be noted, because these small

nations' fate was to be largely determined by powers which held these theories.

5. *East Central European Society and War in the Era of Revolutions, 1775-1856* Edited by Béla K. Király, *War and Society in East Central Europe*, Vol. IV (New York, 1984).

6. Voltaire's *History of Charles XII, King of Sweden* was printed in 1731, his *Century of Louis XIV* in 1751. The dates of Montesquieu's *Persian Letters* and *The Spirit of the Laws* were 1721 and 1748. Acton's "Letter to the Contributors" to *the Cambridge Modern History*" was written in 1898.

7. Quincy Wright, *A Study of War*, Abridged by Louise Leonard Wright (Chicago, 1964), pp. 343-45. My *History and War* (Augusta, Ga., 1984) suggests that sixty-year paradigm-changes in international relations do fit "epochs dominated by an expanding economy and a balance-of-power system." The "causal" factors are generational struggles for power between competing literate elites, in the sixty-year life span which was normative in classical and modern career patterns. The quite recent extension of people's consuming lives seems to be a brake on "progress." For those linked revolutions which produced classical Greek civilization, with its changing economic, political, military, and intellectual priorities, see Anthony Snodgrass, *Archaic Greece: The Age of Experiment* (Berkeley, 1980). For this Conference, dates of 1715-75, 1835-95, 1775-1835, and 1895-1955, would be as good for the periodization of international relations as those chosen.

8. My view of emerging nations' dependence on the ideas and procedures of the great powers may be too sweeping. But neither the Old nor the New Schools of land and naval warfare had "solved" some of the tactical problems of land, naval, and combined operations. Britain's governing elites knew that they faced new problems of defense of their commerce and against invasion, and by 1900 were again aware of the old problem of checking a Continental imperialist coalition.

9. Robert R. Palmer, ed., *Atlas of World History* (New York, 1957), pp. 81-83.

10. The basic works on human costs do not cover the Napoleonic Wars, or try to deal with the effects of plague and famine on "innocent" civilians. They are Lewis Fry Richardson, *Statistics of Deadly Quarrels*, Edited by Quincy Wright and C. C. Lienau (Pittsburgh, 1960), and J. David Singer and Melvin Small, *The Wages of War 1816-1965: A Statistical Handbook* (New York, 1972).

11. William R. Shepherd, ed., *Historical Atlas* (7th ed., New York, 1929), pp. 121, 125, 129, 132, 153, 168b. The Wars of Louis XIV may have been as exhausting for the Empire as the Thirty Years War. Christopher R. Friedrichs, *Urban Society in an Age of War: Nördlingen, 1580-1720* (Princeton, 1979), pp. 292-97.

12. Palmer, *Atlas of World History*, pp. 86-92, 99, 102. Shepherd, *Historical Atlas*, pp. 153, 195, 200. Shepherd's map of the American West and South, p. 195, gives the reader no idea that George Rogers Clark took 175 frontiersmen about the distance from Königsberg to Moscow.

13. Király, ed., *Era of Revolutions*, pp. 290-97. Kourvetaris concludes that, "like other institutions imported from Western [and Central] Europe the Western military model was at best structural and artificial. These models were based on rational bureaucratic and centralized notions of uniformity and convergence which

were contrary to Greek, Byzantine, and Ottoman models of local autonomy and cultural diversity." p. 299. This is the tragic legacy of exchanging one form of imperial dependency for another.

14. R. C. Anderson, *Naval Wars in the Levant 1559-1853* (Princeton, 1952). This work, like his *Naval Wars in the Baltic during the Sailing Ship Epoch, 1522-1850* (1910; London, 1969), may need revision in some details, but focuses on operations rather than on the broader question of access to the sea. The Russian Navy was paramount in the Black and Baltic seas after the Napoleonic wars, but lost control of them both to Germany in the Era of Total War, 1900-60. The Levant was hard to treat in "definite alternations of war and peace." Before the 17th Century, "there was a constant state of irregular warfare with no obvious stage where a historical survey ought to begin." Naval Wars in the Levant, pp. vii-viii.

15. Alexander William Kinglake, *Eothen* (1844; London, 1908), pp. 1, 9.

16. Kinglake, *Eothen*, pp. 23, 28, 42-44, 19.

17. Harold Spender, Introduction to Kinglake, *Eothen*, pp. xi-xiii. Kinglake's "picture is so vivid" because he was "so sincere" about "the haughty, brainless" Turk, the clever, calculating Levantine, the crafty Jew, the slow, simple Bedouins." p. xi. Forty-nine years later Britain's Prime Minister resigned after a final failed Anglo-French landing in the Levant.

18. Palmer, *Atlas of World History*, pp. 106-108. None of his "European Civilization" maps cover the whole Levant from Western Greece to Western Egypt. "The American Robert College at Constantinople" helped to spread "Western ideas in Turkey."

19. David Mitrany, *The Effect of the War in Southeastern Europe* ("Economic and Social History of the War," ed. James T. Shotwell [New Haven, 1936]), p. 44.

20. Palmer, *Atlas of World History*, pp. 102-105. The external trade and transport statistics for South East Europe in B. R. Mitchell, *European Historical Statistics 1750-1970* (New York, 1975) are quite unrevealing for these years.

21. Sir Thomas Brassey, *The British Navy: Its Strength, Resources and Administration* (5 Vols.; London, 1882-1883), Vol. I, pp. 582-83; 601-602. The first of his authoritative *Naval Annuals* appeared in 1886.

22. Jean de Bloch, *The Future of War in its Technical, Economic and Political Relations* (Boston, 1899). See, Michael Howard, "Men Against Fire: Expectations of War in 1914," *International Security*, IX, No. 2 (Summer, 1984), 41-57. On naval theories see my forthcoming *Making of a Modern Navy: French Sea Power, 1870-1905*.

23. Mahan, *Influence of Sea Power*, pp. 28-29.

24. *Ibid.*

25. The best and most recent general works on sea power and naval theory are Clark G. Reynolds, *Command of the Sea* (rev. ed., 2 vols.: Malabar, Fla., 1984), James L. Stokesbury, *Navy and Empire* (New York, 1983), and D. M. Schurman, *The Education of a Navy: The development of British naval strategic thought, 1867-1914* (repr.: Malabar, Fla., 1984). On Anglo-German and interwar naval matters

see the essays in Arthur J. Marder, *From the Dardanelles to Oran* (London, 1974) and in A.M.J. Hyatt, ed., *Dreadnought to Polaris: Maritime Strategy since Mahan* (Toronto, 1973).

26. Ernest L. Bogart, *Direct and Indirect Costs of the Great World War* ("Preliminary Economic Studies of the War," ed. David Kinley, No. 24, [New York, 1919]), pp. 275, 299.

27. Mitrany, *The Effect of the War*, pp. 171-183. "Modern war calls for economic needs and forms differing widely from those of peace.... The extent to which national production had to be reorganized during the War is ... a measure of the extent to which modern economic life had rested on the free international exchange of services and materials and goods," p. 183.

28. J. F. C. Fuller, *Machine Warfare* (London, 1943), p. 35.

29. Gaston Bodart, *Losses of Life in Modern Wars: Austria-Hungary; France* (Oxford, 1916), General Appendix, pp. 1-4.

30. On economic nationalism as a tragically romantic ideal for small powers seeking access to the "great common," see Dudley Seers, *The Political Economy of Nationalism* (New York, 1983). To replace the current neo-colonial system, he proposes one of "large regional economies" in which "none would dominate, though some would be stronger than others," p. 185. Well before Aristotle and Alexander, Herodotus's *History* was to prevent "the great and wonderful actions of the Greeks and the barbarians from losing their due meed of glory; and withal to put on record what were their grounds of feud." Preface to "The First Book, Entitled Clio," p. 1.

BIOGRAPHICAL   INDEX

Binos, Konstantinos, Greek military chief.

Birago, Karl Freiherr von (1792-1845), Colonel I & R Army, Pioneer.

Bolfras, Arthur Freiherr von (1838-1922), Generaloberst I & R Army, Adjutant
   General of Emperor Francis Joseph I.

Bonaparte, Napoleon (1769-1821), First Consul, 1799-1804; Emperor of France,
   1804-15.

Capodistrias, John (1776-1831), First President of Greece, 1828-1831.

Caravia M., Greek river vessel owner, Braila Romania.

Carol I (Charles of Hohenzollern-Sigmaringen) (1839-1914), Prince of Romania,
   1866-81; King of Romania, 1881-1914.

Carp, Petru (1837-1918), Romanian statesman.

Celly, Captain of a menchant-ship.

Chenot, Adam (1721-1789), Physician and Austrian sanitary official.

Chrissoveloni, M. Z., Greek river vessel owner, Braila.

Clausewitz, Karl von (1780-1831), Prussian military theoretician and general.

Codrington, Edward (1770-1851), English Admiral during the Battle of Navarino
   (1827).

Constantine A' (Gluksbourg) (1868-1923), King of Greece, 1913-22.

Cosulich, Name of a family of famous shipowners and shipbuilders from Lussin-
   piccolo (Quarnaro Gulf).

Cuza, Alex., Ion (1820-1873), Prince of Romanian Principalities.

Damas, Baron, Minister of Foreign Affairs of France.

Deval, Charles, French traveller in Greece.

Doumbiotis, Konstantinos, Greek military chief.

Dritsas, Elefterios, Eparch (Sub-perfect) of Mykonos and Syra.

Drovetti, French Consul in Alexandria.

Eichhoff, Baron Peter Joseph (1790-1866), Hofkammer President, 1835-40.

Ekl, Paul (1883-1967), Linienschiffsleutnant, I & R Army, Commandor of Bodrog.

Embry, Captain of a merchant ship.

Fanciotti, Eo. Italian ship chandler, Braila Romania.

Ferdinand I (1783-1875), Emperor of Austria, 1835-48.

Francis I (1768-1835), Austrian monarch, 1792-1835.

Franz Ferdinand (1863-1914), Austrian archduke; heir to the throne of Austria-
   Hungary.

Gatsos, A., Greek military chief.

Gattorno, L., Italian ship chandler, Braila Romania.

Gentz, Frederic (1764-1832), German Diplomat, Counsellor of Metternich in Vienna.

George, Christian, Wilhelm, Ferdinand, Adolf (Gluksbourg) (1845-1913), King of Greece, 1863-1913.

Gheorghiadis, D., Greek river cuner, Braila.

Giannichesi, Angelo, General Manager of the Riuniore Adriatica de Sicurta, Trieste (Insurance Company), 1838-63.

Glarakis, G. (1789-1885), Secretary for Foreign Affairs in Greece in 1827.

Grizanos, Yorgos, Greek military chief.

Grotius, Hugo (1583-1645), Dutch statesman and jurist.

Hamilton (commodore), Admiral of the English squadron in Aegean (1821-1828).

Heideck, Karl, Wilhelm (1788-1861), One of the three Bavarian regents of Greece when King Otto was still a minor, 1833-36.

Ibrahim Pasha of Egypt (1780-1848), Son of Mehemet Ali Pasha of Egypt.

Ignatius (1765-1828) Greek Bishop of Hungaro-Wallachia.

Istrate, Panait, Romanian writer.

Jelleacic de Buzim, Josef Graf von (1801-1859), Feldzeugmeister I & R Army.

Joseph II (1741-1790), Austrian monarch, 1780-1790.

Kalamidas brothers: Alexandros, Apostolos, Gogos, Stefanos, Greek military chiefs.

Kallegris, Dimitrios, Greek officer during the Greek Revolution (1821-1829).

Kanaris, Konstantinos (1790-1877), World known officer, hero of the Greek Revolution, 1821-29.

Kapetanakis, Panayotis, Military chief and notable of Mani.

Karatasos, Yeros, Greek military chief.

Karatzas, George (1803-1882), Director of the Greek Military Academy, 1844-62.

Karoulias, Greek pirate in Aegean.

Kolourat, Court Francis (1778-1861), State and Conference Minister, 1826-48.

Kountouriotis, Lazaros (1769-1852), Eminent notable of the Island Hydra.

Kountouriotis, Georgios (1782-1858), Eminent notable of the Island Hydra.

Krankovsky, Eduard, Linienschiffsleutnant, I & R Army, Commander of Szamos.

Krieghammer, Edmund Freiherr von (1831-1906), Feldzeugmeister I & R Army, Reichkniegsminister.

Kubeck von Kubau, Baron Carl Frienich (1780-1855), Hofkammer President, 1840-48.

Kuhn von Kuhnenfeld, Franz Freiherr von (1817-1896), Feldzeusgmeister I & R Army, Reichkriegsminister.

Leopold II (1747-1792), Emperor of Austria 1790-1792 (called Leopold I as Grand Duke of Tuscany).

Levantines, Foreign subjects living in the Ottoman Empire until 1920.

Lloyd, L., British Vice Consul, Braila, Romania.

Lobkouitz, Rudolf Prinz von (1840-1908), Feldmarschalleutnant I & R Army.

Lobl, H., Jewish river vessel owner, Braila, Romania.

Rigny, Henry-Daniel de (1782-1867), French Admiral during the Battle of Navarino (1827).

Rodinis, Karl, Linienschiffsleutnant I & R Army, Commander of Maros.

Speromilios, Mihail (1800-1880), Hero of the Greek War of Independence and Director of Military Academy (1840-44).

Spiliadis, Nikolaos (1785-1867), General Secretary of the State (1829-31) under Capodistrias.

Spilotopoulos, Yorgos, Greek pirate in Aegean.

Stadion, Count Francis (1806-1853), Governor of the Austrian Littoral (1841-47).

Talabot Paul, French engineer who planned the Port of Trieste at the end of the nineteenth century.

Topin, Karl, Linienschiffsleutnant I & R Army, Commander of Leitha.

Tricoupis, Harilaos (1832-1896), Greek Prime Minister and statesman (1882-85, 1887-90, 1892-95).

Troupakis, Mourtzinos, Military chief and notable of Mani.

Venizelos, Eleftherios (1864-1936), Greek Prime Minister and statesman (1910-20, 1924, 1928-32).

Verne, Jules (1828-1895), Well-known French novelist.

Victoria (1819-1901), Queen of Great Britain (1837-1901).

Vok-Collins, Johann, Linienschiffsleutnant, Commander of Temes.

Voyos, Greek pirate in Aegean.

Weber, Franz (1791-1844), Protomedicus of the Austrian Littoral (1837-44).

Wulff, Olaf Richard (1877-1955), Vizeadmiral I & R Army, Commander of the Austro-Hungarian Danube flotilla in World War I.

Xekoukoulotos, Yorgos, Greek pirate in Aegean.

Yerakaris, Paschalis, Military chief and notable of Mani.

Zehden, Franz, Captain, Danube Shipping Company (DDSG).

Zorbas, Yorgos, Greek military chief.

List of Contributors

Babudieri, Fulvio, Professor, University of Trieste.
Berov, Ljuben, Member of the Bulgarian Academy of Sciences Sofia.
Coons, Ronald E., Professor, University of Connecticut, Storrs, CT.
Damianov, Simeon, Director, National Museum, Balkan Institute, Academy of Sciences, Sofia, Bulgaria.
Delivanis, Demetrius J., Professor Emeritus, University of Thessaloniki.
Fischer-Galati, Stephen, Distinguished University Professor, University of Colorado, Boulder.
Focas, Spiridon G., Brooklyn, NY.
Frangakis, Elena, Queens College, New York.
Frucht, Richard Charles, Professor, Northwest Missouri University, Maryville, MO.
Hatzopoulos, Constantinos, Institute of Balkan Studies, Thessaloniki.
Hunt, Barry Dennis, Professor, Royal Military College of Canada, Kingston, Ontario.
Jonás, Paul, Professor, University of New Mexico, Albuquerque.
Kardassis, Vassilis, National Bank of Greece, Athens.
Moschonas, Nikos G., National Research Foundation, Athens.
Palotás, Emil Reader, Eotvos Lorand University, Budapest, Hungary.
Pantazopoulos, Nikolaos J., Professor Emeritus, University of Thessaloniki.
Papathanassopoulos, Constantinos, Panteios School of Political Science, Athens.
Paskaleva, Virginia, Balkan Institute, Academy of Sciences, Sofia, Bulgaria.
Rauchensteiner, Manfred, Professor, University of Vienna.
Ropp, Theodore A., Professor Emeritus, Duke University, Durham, NC.

Tsiovaridou, Theano, Assistant Professor, Institute for Balkan Studies, Thessaloniki.

Tsourka-Papastathis, Despoina, University of Thessaloniki.

Vacalopoulos, Apostolos E., Professor Emeritus, President, Institute of Balkan Studies, Thessaloniki.

Vacalopoulos, Constantinos, Institute of Balkan Studies, Thessaloniki.

STUDIES ON SOCIETY IN CHANGE

PUBLISHED VOLUMES

BROOKLYN COLLEGE STUDIES ON SOCIETY IN CHANGE

1. *Tolerance and Movements of Religious Dissent in Eastern Europe.* Edited by Béla K. Kiràly. (Brooklyn College Studies on Society in Change No. 1). 1977. (ISEN C-914710-06-0), (LON 75-6229), East European Monographs No. XIII.

2.* *The Habsburg Empire in World War I.* Edited by R.A. Kann, B. K. Kiràly, P. S. Fichtner (Brooklyn College Studies on Society in Change No. 2). 1978. (ISBN C-914710-16-8), (LON 77-47779), East European Monographs No. XXIII.

3.* *The Mutual Effects of the Islamic and Judeo-Christian Worlds: The East European Pattern.* Edited by A. Ascher, T. Halasi-Kun, B. K. Kiràly. (Brooklyn College Studies on Society in Change No. 3). 1979. (ISBN C-930888-00-6), (LON 77-90629), Brooklyn College Press.

4.* *Before Watergate: Problems of Corruption in American Society.* Edited by A. S. Eisenstadt, A. Poogenboom, R. L. Trefousse. (Brooklyn College Studies on Society in Change No. 4). 1979. (ISBN C-03-888-01-4), (LON 77-90630), Brooklyn College Press.

5.* *East Central European Perceptions of Early America.* Edited by B. K. Kiràly and G. Barany. (Brooklyn College Studies on Society in Change No. 5). 1977. (ISBN 90-316-014-62), Lisse, The Netherlands: Peter de Ridder Press.

6.* *The Hungarian Revolution of 1956 in Retrospect.* Edited by B. K. Kiràly and Paul Jonas. (Brooklyn College Studies on Society in Change No. 6). 1978. (ISBN 0-914710-33-8), (LON 77-82394), East European Monographs No. XL.

7.* *Brooklyn U.S.A.: Fourth Largest City in America.* Edited by Rita S. Miller. (Brooklyn College Studies on Society in Change No. 7). 1979. (ISBN C-930888-02-2), (LON 78-62275), Brooklyn College Press.

8. *Prime Minister Gyula Andrassy's Influence on Habsburg Foreign Policy.* Janos Decsy. (Brooklyn College Studies on Society in Change No. 8). 1979. (ISBN C-914710-44-3), (LON 78-73122), East European Monographs No. LII.

9.* *The Great Impeacher: A Political Biography of James M. Ashley.* Robert F.

NOTE:

 * No longer sold by Columbia University Press. Currently sold by Atlantic Research Publications.

Horowitz. (Brooklyn College Studies on Society in Change No. 9). 1979. (ISBN C-930888-03-0), (LON 78-62276), Brooklyn College Press.

10.* *Special Topics and Generalizations on the Eighteenth and Nineteenth Century.* Edited by Béla K. Kiràly and Gunther B. Rothenberg. (Brooklyn College Studies on Society in Change No. 10-War and Society in East Central Europe Vol. 1). 1979. (ISBN C-030888-04-9), (LON 79-51780), Brooklyn College Press. (Volume I**)

19. *At the Brink of War and Peace: The Tito-Stalin Split in a Historic Perspective.* Edited by Wayne S. Vucinich.(Brooklyn College Studies on Society in Change No. 19 - War and Society in East Central Europe Vol. X). 1982. (ISBN C-1914710-98-2), (LON 82-80756), Brooklyn College Press. (Volume X)

21.* *Germany and America: Essays on Problems of International Relations and Immigration.* Edited by Hans L. Trefousse. (Brooklyn College Studies on Society in Change No. 21). 1980. (ISBN C-930888-06-5), (LON 80-66797), Brooklyn College Press.

22.* *Brooklyn College: The First Half Century.* Murray M. Horowitz. (Brooklyn College Studies on Society in Change No. 22). 1981. (ISBN 0-930888-11-1), (LON 81-65408), Brooklyn College Press.

28. *A Question of Empire: Leopold I and the War of Spanish Succession,* 1701-1705.Linda and Marsha Prey. (Brooklyn College Studies on Society in Change No. 28). 1983. (ISBN C-88033-038-4), (LON 83-80628), East European Monographs No. CXLVI.

29A. *A Grand Ecole for the Grands Corps: The Recruitment and Training of the French Administration.* Thomas R. Osbourne. (Brooklyn College Studies on Society in Change No. 29A). 1983. (ISBN 0-88-33-037-6), (LON 83-60780).

34. *War, Revolution and Society in Romania: The Road to Independence.* Edited by Ilie Çeausescu. (Brooklyn College Studies on Society in Change No. 34 - War and Society in East Central Europe vol. XV). 1983. (ISBN 0-88033-023--6), (LON 82-61911), East European Monographs No. CXXXV. (Volume XV)

NOTE:

** Volume Nos. I through XXVIII refer to the series War and Society in East and Central Europe.

ATLANTIC STUDIES /

BROOKLYN COLLEGE STUDIES ON SOCIETY IN CHANGE

11. *East Central European Society and War in the Pre-Revolutionary 18th Century.* Edited by Gunther B. Rothenburg, Béla K. Kiràly, and Peter F. Sugar. (Brooklyn College Studies on Society in Change No. 11 - War 0-930888-19-7), (LON 81-50886), East European Monographs No. CXXII. (Volume II)

12.* *From Hunyadi to Rakoczi: War and Society in Late Medieval and Early Modern Hungary.* Edited by Janos N. Bak and B. K. Kiràly. (Brooklyn College Studies on Society in Change No. 12 - War and Society in East Central Europe Vol. III). 1982. (ISBN 0-930888-13-8), (LON 81-65694), Brooklyn College Press. East European Monographs No. CVI. (Volume III)

13. *East Central European Society and War in the Era of Revolutions:* 1775-1856. Edited by B. K. Kiràly. (Brooklyn College Studies on Society in Change No. 13 - War and Society in East Central Europe vol. IV). 1984. (ISBN 0-930888-17-0), (LON 81-52736), Brooklyn College Press. East European Monographs No. CL. (Volume IV)

14. *Essays on World War I: Origins and Prisoners of War.* Edited by Samuel R. Williamson Jr. and Peter Pastor. (Brooklyn College Studies on Society in Change No. 14 - War and Society in East Central Europe Vol. IV. 1983. (ISBN 0-930888-05-7), (LON 80-66798), Brooklyn College Press, East European Monographs No. CXXVI. (Volume V)

15. *Essays on World War I: Total War and Peacemaking, A Case Study on Trianon.* Edited by B. K. Kiràly, Peter Pastor, and Ivan Sanders. (Brooklyn College Studies on Society in Change No. 15 - War and Society in East Central Europe Vol. VI). 1982. (ISBN 0-930888-18-9), (LON 82-62855), Brooklyn College Press, East European Monographs No. CV. (Volume VI)

16. *Army, Aristocracy, Monarchy: War, Society and Government in Austria,* 1618-1780. Thomas M. Barker. (Brooklyn College Studies on Society in Change No. 16 - War and Society in East Central Europe Vol. VII). 1982. (ISBN 0-930888-14-6), (LON 81-85645), East European Monographs No CVI. (Volume VII)

17. *The First Serbian Uprising* 1804-1813. Edited by Wayne S. Vucinich. (Brooklyn College Studies on Society in Change No. 17 - War and Society in East Central Europe Vol. VIII). 1982. (ISBN 0-930888-15-4), (LON 81-52690), East European Monographs No. CVII. (Volume VIII)

18. *Czechoslovak Policy and the Hungarian Minority* 1945-1948. By Kalmar Janics. Edited by Stephen Borsody. (Brooklyn College Studies on Society in Change No. 18 - War and Society in East Central Europe Vol. IX). 1982. (ISBN 0-914710-99-0), (LON 80-67487), East European Monographs No. CXXII. (Volume IX)

20. *Inflation Through the Ages: Economic, Social, Psychological and Historical Aspects.* Edited by Edward Marcus and Nathan Schmuckler. (Brooklyn College Studies on Society in Change No. 20). 1981. (ISBN 0-930888-12-X), (LON 81-65409), Brooklyn College Press.

23. *A New Deal for the World: Eleanor Roosevelt and American Foreign Policy.* Jason Berger. (Brooklyn College Studies on Society in Change N0. 23). 1981. (ISBN 0-930888-07-3), (LON 80-67486), Brooklyn College Press.

24. *The Legacy of Jewish Migration: 1881 and Its Impact.* Edited by David Berger. (Brooklyn College Studies on Society in Change No. 24). 1982. (ISBN 0-88033-026-0), (LON 82-61913), Brooklyn College Press.

25. *The Road to Bellapais: Cypriot Exodus to Northern Cyprus.* Pierre Oberling. (Brooklyn College Studies on Society in Change No. 25). 1982. (ISBN 0-88033-000-7), (LON 82-61912), Brooklyn College Press, East European Monographs No. CXXV.

26. *New Hungarian Peasants: An East Central European Experience with Collectivization.* Edited by Marica Pollos and Bela C. Maday. (Brooklyn College Studies on Society in Change No. 26). 1983. (ISBN East European Monographs No. CXXXIV.

27. *Germans in America: Aspects of German-American Relations in the Nineteenth Century.* Edited by Allen McCormick. (Brooklyn College Studies on Society in Change No. 27). 1983. (ISBN 0-88033-02502), (LON 82-61910), Brooklyn College Press.

29. *The Beginning of Cyrillic Printing - Cracow, 1491. From the Orthodox Past in Poland.* Edited by Lucwik Krzyzanowski. (Brooklyn College Studies on Society in Change No. 29). 1983. (ISBN 0-88033-027-9), (LON 82-62806), East European Monographs No. CXXXVI.

30. *The First War Between Socialist States: The Hungarian Revolution of 1956 and Its Impact.* Edited by Béla K. Kiràly, Barbara Lotze, Nardor Dreisziger. (Brooklyn College Studies on Society in Change No. 30 - War and Society in East Central Europe Vol. XI). 1984. (ISBN 0-88033-044-9), (LON 83-50184), Brooklyn College Press. East European Monographs No. CLII. (Volume X)

31. *The Effects of World War I, the Uprooted: Hungarian Refugees and Their Impact on Hungary's Domestic Politics.* Istvan I. Mocsy. (Brooklyn College Studies on Society in Change No. 31 - War and Society in East Central Europe Vol. XII). 1983. (ISBN 0-88033-039-2), (LON 83-60781), Brooklyn College Press, East European Monographs No. CXLVII. (Volume XI)

32. *The Effects of World War I: The Class War After The Great War: The Rise of Communist Parties in East Central Europe, 1918-1921.* Edited by Ivo Banac. (Brooklyn College Studies on Society in Change No. 32 - War and Society in East Central Europe Vol. XIII). 1983. (ISBN 0-88033-028-7), (LON 82-63191), East European Monographs No. CXXXVII. (Volume XIII)

33. *The Crucial Decade: East Central European Society and National Defense, 1859-1870.* Edited by Béla K. Kiràly (Brooklyn College Studies on Society in Change No. 33 - War and Society in East Central Europe Vol. XIV). 1984. (ISBN 0-88033-043-0), (LON 83-50183), Brooklyn College Press. (Volume XIV)

35. *Effects of World War I: War Communism in Hungary, 1919.* Gyorgy Peteri. (Brooklyn College Studies on Society in Change No. 35 - War and Society in East Central Europe Vol. XVI). 1984. (ISBN C-88033-059-7), (LON 84-50533), Brooklyn College Press. East European Monographs No. CLXCII. (Volume XVI)

36. *Insurrections, Wars, and the Eastern Crisis in the 1870s.* Edited by B.K. Kiràly and Gale Stokes. (Brooklyn College Studies on Society in Change No. 36 -

War and Society in East Central Europe Vol. XVII). 1985. (ISBN 0-88033-089-9), (LON 85-50469), East European Monographs No. CICVI. (Volume XVII)

37. *East Central European Society and the Balkan Wars, 1912-1913*. Edited by B. K. Kiràly and Dimitrije Djordjevic. (Brooklyn College Studies on Society in Change No. 37 - War and Society in East Central Europe Vol. XVIII). 1986. (ISBN 0-88033-099-6), East European Monographs No. CCXIV. (Volume XVIII)

38. *East Central European Society in World War I*. Edited by B. K. Kiràly and Nandor F. Dreisziger, Assistant Editor Albert A. Nofi. (Brooklyn College Studies on Society in Change No. 38, - War and Society in East Central Europe Vol. XIX). 1985. (ISBN 0-88033-090-2), East European Monographs No. CXCVI. (Volume XIX)

39. *Revolutions and Interventions in Hungary and its Neighbor States*, 1918-1919. Edited by Peter Pastor (Brooklyn College Studies in Society in Change No. 39 — War and Society in East Central Europe Vol. XX). (ISBN 0-88033-100-3). (Volume XX)

46. *Germany's International Monetary Policy and the European Monetary System*. Fugo Kaufmann. (Brooklyn College Studies on Society in Change No. 46). 1985. (ISBN 0-88033-063-5), (LON 84-80972), Brooklyn College Press.

47. *Iran Since the Revolution — Internal Dynamics, Regional Conflicts and the Superpowers*. Edited by Barry N. Rosen. (Brooklyn College Studies on Society in Change No. 47). 1985. (ISBN 0-88033-975-9), Brooklyn College Press.

ATLANTIC STUDIES ON SOCIETY IN CHANGE
BOOKS IN PROGRESS

40. *East Central European Society and War*, 1750-1920. Bibliography and Historiography. Compiled and Edited by Laszlo Alfoldi. (Atlantic Studies on Society in Change No. 40 - War and Society in East Central Europe Vol. XXI).

41. *Essays on East Central European Society and War: 1740-1920's.* Edited by Béla Kiràly and Stephen Fischer-Galati. (Atlantic Studies on Society in Change No. 41 - War and Society in East Central Europe Vol. XXII).

42. *East Central European Maritime Commerce and Naval Policies*, 1789-1913. Edited by Apostolos E. Vacalopoulos, Constantinos D. Svolopoulos, and Béla K. Kiràly. (Atlantic Studies on Society in Change No. 42-War and Society in East Central Europe Vol. XXIII).

43. *Selection, Social Origins, Education and Training of East Central European Officers Corps*. Edited by Béla K. Kiràly, Walter Scott Dillard. (Atlantic Studies on Society in Change No. 43-War and Society in East Central Europe Vol. XXIV).

44. *East Central European War Leaders: Civilian and Military.* Edited by Béla K. Kiràly, Albert Nofi. (Atlantic Studies on Society in Change No. 44 - War and Society in East Central Europe Vol. XXV).

45. Pencing. (Volume XXVI)

48. *The Press During the Hungarian Revolution of 1848-1849.* Domokos Kosary. (Atlantic Studies on Society in Change No. 48 - War and Society in East Central Europe Vol. XXVII). (ISBN 0-88033-091-0), East European Monographs No. CXCVIII.

49. *The Spanish Inquisition and the Inquisitional Mind.* Edited by Angel Alcala. (Atlantic Studies on Society in Change No. 49), (ISBN 0-8-88033-952-7).

50. *Catholics, the State and the European Radical Right*, 1919-1945. Edited by Richard Wolff and Jorg K. Hoensch. (Atlantic Studies on Society in Change No. 50), (ISBN 0-88033-101-1).

51. *The Boer War and Military Reform.* Jay Stone and Erwin A. Schmidl. (Atlantic Studies on Society in Change No. 51 - War and Society in East Central Europe Vol. XXVIII).

52. *Baron Joseph Eotvos, A Literary Biography.* Steven B. Vardy. (Atlantic Studies on Society in Change No. 52).

53. *Towards the Renaissance of Puerto Rican Studies: Ethnic and Area Studies in University Education.* Maria Sanchez and Antonio M. Stevens. (Atlantic Studies on Society in Change No. 53).